HARVARD HISTORICAL MONOGRAPHS
XLI

Published under the direction of the Department of History
from the income of The Robert Louis Stroock Fund

The Urban Frontier

The Rise of Western Cities, 1790-1830

By

Richard C. Wade

HARVARD UNIVERSITY PRESS

CAMBRIDGE

1959

Library of Congress Catalogue Card Number 59–9285
Printed in the United States of America

To

My Mother and Father

Foreword

The rural West has had many historians. Its growth, influence, and importance are well known. Yet it is not always understood that from almost the very beginning there was also an urban West. In fact, Pittsburgh, St. Louis, Cincinnati, Louisville, and Lexington were laid out and settlement begun before the surrounding area had fallen to the plow. From the earliest days they became centers of economic activity for the whole region, the focuses of cultural life, and scenes of great social change. Built on the spine of the new country, the Ohio valley, the towns gave a stimulus and sophistication to a young, raw society.

This volume attempts to tell the story of the first decades of the urban West. It is written largely out of the newspapers, records, and manuscripts of contemporaries, and as often as possible in their own words. In preparing this study I have received valuable assistance from a great many people. The staffs of local historical societies and public libraries in more than a dozen cities generously gave me permission to use their rich and extensive collections. City and county clerks kindly put aside their many official duties to make available their old municipal records and papers. A Social Science Research Council fellowship in the years 1952–53 provided me with needed relief from my teaching duties. But most of all I am indebted to Professor Arthur Meier Schlesinger, who first suggested this project to me and who patiently and helpfully watched its development and completion. Only those who have worked with him know the full extent of this obligation. I should like also to thank the *American Historical Review* for permission to use portions of an article of mine which appeared in its issue of October 1958. My wife, Louise C. Wade, has rendered numberless services to this book, ranging all the way from bibliographic aid to enduring six intolerably warm summers in Ohio valley cities.

R. C. W.
Rochester, N.Y.

Contents

The Urban Frontier

Where late the savage, hid in ambush, lay,
Or roamed the uncultured valleys for his prey,
Her hardy gifts rough Industry extends,
The groves bow down, the lofty forest bends,
And see the spires of towns and cities rise,
And domes and temples swell unto the skies.

Return Jonathan Meigs, 1797

Chapter 1

The Beginnings of Western Urbanism

The towns were the spearheads of the frontier. Planted far in advance of the line of settlement, they held the West for the approaching population. Indeed, in 1763, when the British threw the Proclamation Line along the Appalachians to stop the flow of settlers, a French merchant company prepared to survey the streets of St. Louis, a thousand miles through the wilderness. Whether as part of the activity of the French and Spanish from New Orleans or of the English and Americans operating from the Atlantic seaboard, the establishment of towns preceded the breaking of soil in the transmontane west.

Ever since European nations had laid claim to the New World, the area beyond the mountains had been an arena of contention among the great powers. Though merely the haunt of Indian and animal, this region was coveted for its natural richness and strategic location. French, British, Spanish, and American interests mingled and crossed, and no matter which power had formal title to the area, the others never ceased to intrigue for its possession. While the British population filled up the coastal region, the French spun a loose web of forts and fur-trading posts in the Ohio and Mississippi valleys. However, by the treaties of Fontainebleau of 1762 and of Paris a year later, French claims were replaced by Spanish and British titles which divided the West at the Mississippi River. It was in this context of imperial rivalry that such Western cities as St. Louis and Pittsburgh had their origins.

The first towns in the central portion of the Ohio Valley are younger than those on its eastern and western flanks. Until the American Revolution this area was sealed off from settlement by

Indian hostility and British imperial policy. Colonies on the coast had claims in the Ohio and Kentucky regions, but marauding tribes made any attempt to occupy them perilous. The redmen hunted in the lands just west of the strategic gaps in the mountains and resisted the movement of whites into them. The British hoped to reduce friction by keeping the colonists east of the Proclamation Line until Indian titles could be removed. But it was hard to enforce this plan, for settlers hungered to get across the mountains and resented any efforts to stop them. The Revolution was fought in part to free the frontier from this confinement. As soon as the shooting began, Americans pushed into the "dark and bloody" grounds, opening up Kentucky and paving the way for the founding of Louisville and Lexington.

North of the Ohio, the Indians were powerful enough even after the Revolution to resist the advance of settlement. In addition, British influence, always stronger here than south of the river, lingered on, creating unrest whenever possible. The new American government made attempts to pacify the natives with treaties, but these were seldom honored, and guerilla warfare continued. Indeed, it was not until Anthony Wayne's victory at Fallen Timbers and the Treaty of Greenville that followed in 1795 that Ohio was safe for immigration. Meanwhile, the Continental Congress tried to infuse some order into the occupation process through the Ordinance of 1785 providing for a government survey previous to the sale of land. Before federal agents could complete their jobs, however, thin ribbons of population moved down the Ohio River and Cincinnati was born.

In a single generation this whole transmontane region was opened to settlement. In the process towns grew up along the waterways and in the heart of fertile farm areas. The names of many of these — such as Rising Sun, Vevay, and Town of America — were soon forgotten, but others — like Pittsburgh, St. Louis, and Cincinnati — became familiar words. This growth of urbanism was an important part of the occupation of the West, and it provided the central experience of many settlers who crossed the mountains in search of new homes. The story of Western urbanism begins, however, not where one might expect, at the foot of the Appalachians, but rather in the remoteness of the Mississippi Valley.

There were already a few French villages in the Mississippi basin in 1763 when the Governor of Louisiana granted the New Orleans firm of Maxent, Laclede and Company an eight-year monopoly of trade with the Indians of the Missouri. On the west side of the river was Ste. Genevieve, and on the east, Cahokia and Kaskaskia. As a result of the Treaty of Paris, the latter were now on British soil. Sieur D'Abbadie, the French Governor, was, however, unaware of the secret treaty of the year before by which the region west of the river was ceded to Spain. In granting trade privileges he hoped to regain for France the fur trade of Upper Louisiana which had been badly disorganized by the war. The project looked promising. Colonel Antoine Maxent, one of the richest merchants in New Orleans, supplied the company's financial strength, and Pierre Laclede Liguest became its agent in the field.

In the fall of 1763 Laclede and a large company of men went up the Mississippi to find a site for the headquarters of the new enterprise. Ste. Genevieve was discarded because it was too far from the mouth of the Missouri, and its banks were constantly endangered by flood waters. After some initial trading with the Indians, Laclede moved north seeking a permanent location. When he came to the spot where St. Louis now stands, he was delighted. He later told associates that he had found a position "which might become, hereafter, one of the finest cities in America."[1] Early the following February he sent Auguste Chouteau, then only fourteen years old, with thirty men to the site of the new settlement.

Laclede's choice for a town site was superb. St. Louis was built on a limestone bluff that juts up from the bank of the Mississippi. This was the first elevated spot south of the junction of the three great rivers, Missouri, Illinois, and Mississippi. Not only was the

[1] A. Chouteau, "Narrative of the Settlement of St. Louis," in J. F. McDermott, ed., *The Early Histories of St. Louis* (St. Louis, 1952), 48.

situation free from flood water, but the land behind it rose gently toward the west, providing a natural drainage system. Timber was plentiful, and the hinterland contained grassy tracts admirably suited for farmland. In addition to these natural advantages, St. Louis was strategically located astride the British lines to the rich fur regions of the interior.

Laclede not only chose the site for the new town, but was also its first city planner. On joining Chouteau in April 1764, he put his ideas on paper. The simple gridiron pattern with a public plaza on the waterfront derived from New Orleans, where Laclede had spent the previous decade. In the original sketch, a tract 300 feet deep along the river was reserved for public use, though this land was later sold. The town faced the stream and was only three streets deep, but it ran a considerable distance along the Mississippi. Short cross streets intersected the three "avenues" to establish a regular block system. Each block was 240 by 300 feet, except three central units which were 300 feet square.[2]

The town's growth justified early optimism. By 1780 it had become the focus of Spanish activity in the Mississippi and Missouri area. As the capital of Upper Louisiana, it was a garrison town and the residence of Spanish officialdom; as the center of the fur trade, it became a kind of rendezvous for hunters, boatmen, and agents of the fur companies. Hence, as soon as Spain sided with the rebellious Americans, the British launched a bloody but unsuccessful assault on St. Louis. Probably 100 casualties were suffered in a community which numbered less than 700. Although the invaders never returned, the town remained in a state of semi-preparedness until the end of the war.[3]

In the twenty years between the end of the American Revolution and the cession of Louisiana, St. Louis grew very slowly. At the turn of the century it had only 925 inhabitants, including 268 slaves. Indeed, the areas around the town grew more rapidly than St. Louis

[2] C. E. Peterson, *Colonial St. Louis, Building a Creole Capital* (St. Louis, 1949), 3–7 and notes.
[3] J. B. Musick, *St. Louis As a Fortified Town* (St. Louis, 1941), 11; 41; 66.

itself. A liberal Spanish policy granted land free to almost all comers, exempting them from taxation. Under these terms the farm regions behind St. Louis filled up very quickly with Americans. The town, however, remained small and intensely French. When the United States took possession in 1804, two-thirds of the people were cousins of one another.[4]

Spanish rule did little to disturb French customs. Ordinances issued from New Orleans were few, and generally dealt with relations between the town and the Spanish garrison.[5] Land grants were made verbally by the Governor, contracts were sealed by a grip of the hand, and family and religion controlled social arrangements.[6] Life was gay and relaxed, at least for the more wealthy. Dancing and parties abounded. Amos Stoddard, the first American representative in St. Louis, found this active social life a little trying. "Nothing ever restrains them from this amusement," he complained, "which usually commences early in the evening, and is seldom suspended till late the next morning."[7] As the symbol of new authority, Stoddard was entertained by St. Louis's leading families. To return this hospitality in the local fashion cost the government of the United States $622.75.[8]

Though St. Louis was small and most of its citizens were untutored, it was not unsophisticated. From the very first days this frontier town had a substantial group of well educated and highly literate men, most of whom had been schooled in Europe or Canada. They were familiar with much of the new writing of the Enlightenment and brought to the wilderness the tastes and attainments of men of culture. For example, Laclede was a graduate of the Univer-

[4] J. T. Scharf, *History of St. Louis City and County* (Philadelphia, 1883), I, 309; 308; 178.

[5] L. Houck, *The Spanish Regime in Missouri* (Chicago, 1909), I.

[6] The legal system was so informal that Amos Stoddard, the first American authority in St. Louis, complained to his superior that "it is an endless task to find out the laws and steady maxims of the last Spanish Government." A. A. Stoddard to W. C. C. Claiborne and J. Wilkinson, March 26, 1804, Stoddard MSS (Missouri Historical Society, St. Louis).

[7] Quoted in Scharf, *St. Louis*, I, 310.

[8] Stoddard to Benham, June 16, 1804, Stoddard MSS.

sity of Toulouse in France; Madam Marie Louise Chouteau, the *grande dame* of St. Louis society, was educated at the Ursuline convent in New Orleans; and Charles Gratiot, one of the most prominent merchants of the town, studied in Switzerland, London, and Montreal. They were not only educated themselves but many insisted that their children have the same opportunities. Bernard Pratte sent his sons to seminaries in Canada, most of the young Gratiots attended Catholic College in Bardstown, Kentucky, and Auguste Pierre Chouteau and Charles Gratiot, Jr., graduated from West Point in 1806.[9]

The cultural level of early St. Louis can be measured not only by the background of the men who came there, but by the libraries they brought with them. Silvestre Labbadie, who was probably the richest man in town when he died in 1794, owned over 200 volumes, which included 89 different titles. Dr. Antoine Saugrain, the town's most distinguished physician, had over 300 volumes. One of the Spanish officials, Charles De Hault Delassus, brought with him an extensive library of over 150 books, and Auguste Chouteau, though but a boy when he came to St. Louis, accumulated 170 titles before he died. At the time of the transfer of Louisiana there were between 2,000 and 3,000 volumes, not including duplicates, in this infant town of less than 700 whites.[10]

Though St. Louis's ruling group was refined, it contained few dynamic leaders. The fur trade, which was the town's most impor-

---

[9] When the inhabitants took the oath of allegiance to Spain, 40 out of the 70 adults could not sign their names. Later, in 1775, less than half the church members of St. Louis were able to sign a contract. J. F. McDermott, *Private Libraries in Creole St. Louis* (Baltimore, 1938), 12–13; 14; 15.

[10] McDermott, *Private Libraries*, 21. These books comprehended a wide range of learning. Scientific and historical subjects made up about half the titles; 12 per cent were religious; novels, poetry and literary criticism comprised another 20 per cent; and the rest were concerned with political, philosophical or commercial subjects. It is interesting to note that in a town overwhelmingly Catholic, Auguste Chouteau's library included a great many books on the Index. See McDermott, *Private Libraries*, 22; also J. F. McDermott, "Voltaire and the Freethinkers of Early St. Louis," *Revue de littérature comparée*, XVI (1936), 723.

tant business, declined in the latter days of Spanish possession. Throughout the eighties and nineties the fur lands to the northwest were overrun by British traders and trappers. This encroachment was so rapid that in 1793 the Lieutenant-Governor of Louisiana sponsored the formation of a Board of Trade in St. Louis composed of leading merchants whose object was to regulate Spanish activities and exclude the interlopers. In the next year St. Louis interests formed the Missouri Company for the purpose of penetrating the Upper Missouri, wresting the area from the British, and appropriating to themselves the trade with the Indians. The company sent some expeditions up the Missouri, but its efforts failed to halt the British or provide St. Louis with any economic stimulus.[11]

When the Americans came to take possession of the town in 1804, it had scarcely 1,000 inhabitants. Nearly a quarter were slaves; the rest were a curious mixture of gentlemen and hunters, merchants and trappers, boatmen and one-time soldiers. An early citizen summed up the first forty years' experience of this urban outpost:

. . . she was born French; but, put under the charge of a stepmother, her cradle was hung in the forest, her infancy stinted by its unavoidable privations, and her maturity retarded by the terror of the Indian yell. Her youth was more calm, but still not prosperous. . . . Abandoned subsequently by her Castillian guardians, she found herself reclaimed by her old parent, only to be once more repudiated. She had then, however, attained her majority, and had herself become a parent, whose children, born under the aegis of Liberty, opened for her a new destiny, and vowed that she would become the metropolis of a new empire.[12]

Pittsburgh was at once older and younger than St. Louis. Though it was not formally laid out as a town until 1764, its site had been coveted for more than a decade by both French and British. As early as 1753 the promise of Pittsburgh's situation was noticed by a

[11] Musick, *St. Louis,* 82–83.
[12] J. N. Nicollet, "Sketch of Early St. Louis," in McDermott, ed., *Early Histories,* 133.

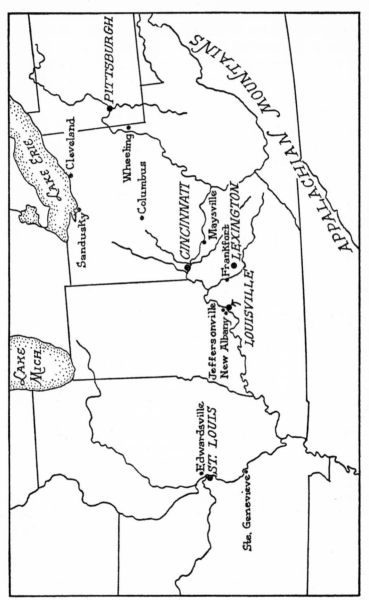

Western Towns and Cities, 1790–1830

young Virginian, George Washington, who had been sent to the upper Ohio by his governor to warn the French to get out of the area. When he arrived at the point where the Monongahela and Allegheny join to form the Ohio River, he quickly sized up its importance.

I spent some Time in viewing the Rivers, and the Land in the Fork; which I think extremely well situated for a Fort, as it has absolute command of both Rivers. The Land at the Point is 20 or 25 Feet above the common surface of the Water; and a considerable Bottom of flat, well-timbered Land all around it, [is] very convenient for Building.[13]

The French agreed on this estimate, and since they had the greater force on the scene at the moment, they prepared to build there. However, in the next year a small detachment of British soldiers hastily threw up a log fort at the union of the rivers, which they named Fort King George. In less than a month the French arrived to take over. No contest ensued, for the British were hopelessly outnumbered and readily retreated eastward. For four years afterward the French flag flew over this strategic outpost, and Fort Duquesne was raised as a physical reminder to Indians and enemies.

Ten years of intermittent warfare followed. Pittsburgh, which was the key to the whole Upper Ohio region, changed to British hands in 1758 and remained so under the terms of the Treaty of Paris. But guerilla warfare with the Indians continued. The latter saw their historic hunting grounds falling to the whites and made a supreme effort to halt this process. Under the leadership of Pontiac, the Indians rose against the British all along the frontier, and before any successful counterattack could be launched, every fortified post but Detroit and Fort Pitt had capitulated. For months even these two places were isolated. Only a concerted effort brought the uprising to an end and made western Pennsylvania safe for settlement.

In this unsettled and harassed period Pittsburgh could grow only slowly. The collection of cabins and huts that grew up outside the fort during the struggle between France and Great Britain was de-

[13] G. Washington, "Journal of George Washington," in J. W. Harpster, ed., *Pen Pictures of Early Western Pennsylvania* (Pittsburgh, 1938), 17.

stroyed during the Indian raids. Settlers to the east either found protection in Pittsburgh or hurried back across the mountains to safety. This temporary dispersal of population cleared the way for the orderly planning of the town. After the siege of Fort Pitt was lifted in 1764, Colonel John Campbell laid out four squares on the Monongahela River, bringing Pittsburgh its first and basic town plan. Though modest in scope, it determined the orientation of the town's future development.

No place in the West seemed more certain to be the site of a great city. Nature itself had made the suggestion unmistakably. At Pittsburgh two rivers join to make the Ohio, the central waterway of the trans-Appalachian West. The Allegheny River reaches 325 miles up into the heart of the fertile lake plains of New York and Pennsylvania; the Monongahela drains the incredibly rich iron and coal country of West Virginia. Where they meet was a flat triangular plain, bounded on the east by two heavily foliaged hills, and on the north and south, across the rivers, by sharp green escarpments 200 yards high. In this shaggy amphitheater Pittsburgh was placed. Here were all the classic requirements for a great city: water power, coal and iron, ready access to farm lands, and a market area of almost limitless extent.

Notwithstanding these obvious advantages, the town's development proved slow. When Washington returned to Pittsburgh in 1770, it had only two log houses and was "inhabited by Indian traders, etca." The return of troops during the Revolution increased activity in the region but brought few permanent settlers. This beginning was so feeble that it clouded the prophetic powers of a junketing Congressman, Arthur Lee, who proclaimed in 1784 that "the place, *I believe*, will never be very considerable. . . . [It] is inhabited almost entirely by Scots and Irish, who live in paltry loghouses, and are as dirty as in the north of Ireland, or even Scotland." More accurate was the appraisal of another traveler, a German doctor, in the previous year. "However little to be regarded this place is now, from its advantageous site it must be that Pittsburgh will in the future become an important depot for the inland trade." [14]

[14] "We lodgd in what is called the Town," which he estimated had about

Though Pittsburgh's early growth was not rapid, by 1784 building had already begun beyond the lines of the old Campbell survey. In that year the Penns hired George Wood and Thomas Viceroy to make a second plat. This one laid out the whole area from the old fort at the western point to Grant Street on the eastern edge of town. For fifty years this survey — with a few small additions — was the basic plan of Pittsburgh. Wood and Viceroy probably wanted to change some of the details of Campbell's work, but they consistently found that usage made innovations impossible.[15] Originally the town faced the Monongahela, which carried most of the trade and immigration. The new survey kept this orientation and used that river as a base for a plan that was shaped like a right triangle. Penn Street, which ran parallel to the Allegheny, was the hypotenuse of this figure; Grant Street on the east connected the two rivers, joining the Monongahela at right angles. This plan was not as regular as that of St. Louis. The streets varied substantially in width, and the triangular pattern created some irregular blocks. A public square, called "the Diamond," was reserved for the court house and market place. The original lots were generous, 60 feet wide and 240 feet deep, allowing space for a garden and stable in the rear.

In the eighties and nineties Pittsburgh attracted an increasing number of permanent residents. The census of 1790 listed only 376 inhabitants, but by the end of the next decade the population had increased fourfold, numbering 1,565. As important, however, as this numerical growth, was the kind of people who settled in Pittsburgh. The town was still composed largely of traders and transients who had no stake in its development. "They take this for a resting place or halfway house and think it vain to waste their labor making improvements . . . because, next year they shall go down the river." Yet among the newcomers were also men of capacity, energy and

---

twenty houses. *The Diaries of George Washington, 1748–1799,* J. C. Fitzpatrick, ed. (Boston, 1925), I (1748–1770), 410; A. Lee, "Journal of Arthur Lee," Harpster, ed., *Pen Pictures,* 157; J. D. Schoepf, "Travels of Johann David Schoefp," in Harpster, ed., *Pen Pictures,* 136.

[15] J. N. Boucher, *A Century and a Half of Pittsburgh and Her People* (Pittsburgh, 1908), I, 275.

cultivation, who came to Pittsburgh not to sojourn but to build. One of these was John Scull, a young newspaperman from the neighboring town of Washington, who established the *Pittsburgh Gazette* in 1786. Another was the West's most distinguished literary figure, Hugh Henry Brackenridge, the town's first "booster." To this element Pittsburgh represented new opportunity, "a place of great manufactory. Indeed the greatest on the continent or perhaps in the world." [16]

The flood of immigration brought not only new townsmen but also the beginnings of Pittsburgh's commercial development. Local merchants outfitted settlers as they moved into the interior. In a single year, 1794, 13,000 stopped at "the point," some for weeks.[17] Federal troops operating against the Indians and whisky rebels were stationed in town, requiring supplies and provisions in large amounts.[18] And, increasingly, Pittsburghers prospered as middlemen in a mounting trade between Philadelphia and Baltimore in the East and the new settlements in the Ohio Valley.[19]

A growing population and expanding economic activity created a demand for some measure of home rule. In 1794 the state legislature gave Pittsburgh the legal status of a borough with the same power as that granted to Reading in 1783. This charter provided for the election of a dozen officials, who were charged with promoting "rule order and good government in said town." Before this, local government had consisted of town meetings irregularly called and informally conducted. One in 1787 authorized the building of a public market and laid down the rules for its conduct. Another discussed the ratification of the Federal Constitution, and

[16] United States Census Office, 1st Census, 1790, 45; 2nd Census, 1800, 2d; *Pittsburgh Gazette*, March 17, 1787; August 22, 1786.

[17] *Pittsburgh Gazette*, February 7, 1795.

[18] "The whole of the Federal Army was now at this place, except about 1500 who were left at Washington — The number now at Pittsburgh was calculated at 12 or 13,000." J. Elliot, "The Journal of James Elliot," in Harpster, ed., *Pen Pictures*, 172; G. T. Fleming, *History of Pittsburgh and Its Environs* (New York, 1922), II, 46.

[19] C. Reiser, *Pittsburgh's Commercial Development, 1800–1850* (Harrisburg, 1951), 2.

still another drew up a petition for borough status.[20] But by 1800 local affairs in Pittsburgh were on a more regular basis, and the powers of its officers, at first inexpertly wielded, later became instruments of civic development.

Pittsburgh's first decades had been exciting ones. Though it was a mere outpost in the wilderness, great powers had contended for it. Like St. Louis, it had flown three flags, learned to live with garrisons, and narrowly escaped destruction by the Indians. None of this had been conducive to town growth. But in the last decades of the nineteenth century a measure of peace had been established in the Upper Ohio, and development was possible. Settlers came, trade and commerce expanded, and a charter gave this "headquarters of Indian traders" the dignity of a borough. A weekly newspaper, regular mail service, and a constant stream of travelers kept alive contacts with the rest of the nation across the mountains. Pittsburghers even found time for some of the lighter things of life. As one of them observed in 1786,

It must appear like enchantment to a stranger . . . to see, all at once, and almost on the verge of the inhabited globe, a town with smoking chimneys, halls lighted up with splendor, ladies and gentlemen assembled, various music, and the mazes of the dance. He may suppose it to be the effect of magic, or that he is come into a new world where there is all the refinement of the former, and more benevolence of heart.[21]

From Pittsburgh the Ohio flows almost a thousand miles to the Mississippi. In the whole course to New Orleans and the Gulf of Mexico the Falls at Louisville offers the only major obstruction. Here a limestone ridge running obliquely through the river created a violent stretch of rapids which imperiled shipping. The descent was only 25 feet in two miles, but at low water the churning could be

[20] *Pittsburgh Gazette,* May 17, 1794; *Pittsburgh Gazette,* March 10, 1787; November 17, 1781; February 15, 1794.
[21] D. McClure, "Diary of David McClure," in Harpster, ed., *Pen Pictures,* 119; H. H. Brackenridge, *Gazette Publications* (Pittsburgh, 1786), 19.

heard a half mile up the stream. Three "chutes" through the rocks permitted experienced boatmen to pass over when the river was high, but in the late summer months no one who knew the terror of the Falls would risk it.[22] Few doubted that somewhere around the rapids a city would grow up to facilitate the transshipment of men and goods around this hazard. Louisville was both the first and the most successful effort to meet this need.

There were four possible town sites at the Falls. Ultimately settlements were made on all of them — two on each side of the river, at either end of the rapids. Louisville's supremacy resulted in large degree from natural advantages over its rivals. Resting on a broad rich plain that stretched along the river, it was the center of a promising farm area.[23] In addition, Louisville had a harbor located at the mouth of Bear Grass Creek where it entered the Ohio on the east side of the town. This commodious and sheltered inlet kept barges, keels, and flatboats from being sucked into the falling waters. Portland, at the western end of the Falls on the Kentucky side, was victimized by the river itself which twisted sharply southward at the foot of the rapids, cutting off the hinterland. The Indiana sites were hemmed in by "knobs" that, rising steeply behind the river, obstructed contact with the interior. Louisville's substantial natural advantages were emphasized by the pattern of immigration. Kentucky was settled many years before Indiana, and by the time towns could grow on the northern bank of the river, Louisville had appropriated most of the trade.

The Falls of the Ohio were familiar to trappers and traders throughout the eighteenth century, yet no permanent settlement was made near them until 1778. In that year George Rogers Clark established a post at Louisville as a base for military expeditions against the British farther west. He brought with him about twenty families,

---

[22] G. Imlay, *A Topographical Description of the Western Territory of North America* (3rd edn., London, 1797), 34. A good map of the Falls can be found opposite page 33.

[23] "Perhaps no city in the universe is supported by a more fertile and productive soil than Louisville." H. McMurtrie, *Sketches of Louisville* (Louisville, 1819), 55; 11.

who spent the first year on Corn Island at the foot of the future town site. Under the protection of crude fortifications, these pioneers moved onto the mainland the next spring. The winter of 1779–80 was Louisville's "starving time," when the intense cold and lack of food almost wiped out the infant village. But in the spring 300 boats came to the Falls, bringing supplies and more families. The next year saw the influx of a large number of unmarried women, the "necessary consequence" of which was "the rapid and wonderful increase of population." [24] Clark had long viewed the Falls as the key to the Northwest, and in 1782 he built Fort Nelson at Louisville to secure his position against counterattacks from the British or raids by the Indians. With this protection the people went about the business of building the town.

The first problem was to get a clear right to the land. In 1779 the town had been surveyed and laid out under the authority of the Court of Kentucky County, trustees had been elected, improvements and building had been begun, but land titles were still vague. The inhabitants appealed to the Virginia Assembly, saying that "at great risque and expense" they had "removed to this remote part of the state [*sic*]," but that uncertainty of ownership "prevents some from settling here that are so inclined." The land on which Louisville was established had been granted in 1773 to John Conolly for his services to the colony during the French and Indian War. During the Revolution he sided with the king, however, and Virginia declared that by this act he had forfeited his right. Consequently, in 1780 the state, in response to Louisville's petition, turned the tract over to the town, investing the title in trustees appointed by the Assembly. In this manner Louisville became its own proprietor, with possession of the entire town site. The total grant was one thousand acres. Under the terms of the act the trustees were empowered to lay off the land in half-acre lots and sell them for "the best price that can be had." Each purchaser agreed to build "a dwelling house, sixteen feet by twenty, at least, with a brick or stone chimney" within two years of the date of sale. Those already

[24] B. Casseday, *The History of Louisville From its Earliest Settlement Till the Year 1852* (Louisville, 1852), 59.

on the land had the first opportunity to buy, and any disputes were to be settled by the trustees.[25]

Armed with this charter, the trustees ordered a new survey and laid out a town in half-acre lots along the lines of the 1779 map.[26] The plat was long and narrow, running twelve blocks along the river but only six away from it. A slip of ground 180 feet wide stretching the whole length of the town along Jefferson Street was reserved for a public promenade. Within the decade, however, the trustees broke up this park area and sold most of it. A little later, in 1783, there was an attempt to keep thirty feet along the river as "a common street," but soon this too passed into private hands.[27] By 1800 the town had disposed of nearly all its land, though a few scattered plots remained. This surrender of public ground has haunted Louisvillians ever since, for it left the heart of the city without parks, indeed without even land for market houses and public buildings. Mulling over this lost opportunity, the city's first historian lamented in 1819,

Had the first, or Main street, been laid off so as to have extended 90 feet from the brink of the second bank, forming an avenue in front of the town, and had no houses been permitted to exist north of that avenue . . . Louisville would have exhibited *a coup d'oeil*, surpassed, in point of beauty, by few in the world. As it is the town has turned its back on the varied and interesting prospect presented by the Ohio and its Falls.[28]

[25] J. J. Robertson, ed., *Petitions of the Early Inhabitants of Kentucky to the General Assembly of Virginia, 1769–1792* (Filson Club, Publications, No. 27, Louisville, 1914), 53–54; *Collection of the Acts of Virginia and Kentucky Relative to Louisville and Portland, with the Charters of the City of Louisville and the Amendments Thereto* (Louisville, 1839), 4.

[26] There were many surveys made of Louisville, the first by Captain William C. Bullitt in 1773. Most of the early maps have disappeared. The official plat was by Jared Brooks in 1812. Town of Louisville, Trustees Book, 1781–1827 (MSS, Filson Club Library, Louisville), January 31, 1812.

[27] H. Ford and K. Ford, *History of the Ohio Falls Cities and Their Counties* (Cleveland, 1882), I, 178; Louisville, Trustees Book, June 27, 1783.

[28] McMurtrie, *Sketches of Louisville*, 115. General George Rogers Clark had suggested such a plan in 1779. R. T. Durrett, *The Centenary of Louis-*

Louisville was situated high enough above the Ohio to escape the danger of floods. But behind the town the ground was marshy and low, containing many ponds. During the wet season that area resembled an archipelago, with islands rising out of small lakes. One pool was large enough for the owner to stock it with fish, another was used for skating in the winter, and on summer evenings the early settlers generally resorted to them. Such indeed was their attachment to the little lakes that many resisted the town's attempt to drain them. Yet the ponds were a constant source of disease, and gave Louisville the reputation of being the "Graveyard of the Ohio." From the beginning, travelers commented on the sickliness of the residents, and in 1788 an epidemic almost knocked out the entire garrison.[29]

Though it attained the dignity of a town in 1780, Louisville grew very slowly during the next two decades. The Indians, who constantly raided the settlement from their forest fastness across the river, proved the primary obstacle to expansion. In 1783 Colonel William Fleming found the place "almost deserted of Inhabitants, the few left depending chiefly on the garrison." But that same year offered signs of stability. Daniel Broadhead brought the first goods from Philadelphia, and the State of Virginia established a land office there. A decade later Louisville had over "two hundred good houses," and a traveler predicted that "there is no doubt but it will soon be a flourishing town." [30] The census listed only 359 inhabitants in 1800, yet estimates by visitors ran as high as 800. The difference probably lay in the fact that travelers based their estimates on the number of people who lived in sight of town rather than within its official boundaries.[31] The settlement not only grew, but took on some of the graces of comfortable living as well. Parties

ville (Filson Club, Publications, No. 27, Louisville, 1893), 41n. See also L. Collins, *Historical Sketches of Kentucky* (Cincinnati, 1848), 358.

[29] Casseday, *Louisville*, 49; W. Fleming, in N. D. Mereness, ed., "Journal," *Travels in the American Colonies* (New York, 1916), 621; see J. Morse, *The American Gazetteer* (2nd edn., New York, 1798), 286.

[30] Fleming, "Journal," 633; Imlay, *Western Territory*, 35.

[31] United States Census, 1800, 2P; Casseday, *Louisville*, 108.

and games were common, a Mr. Nickle opened a dancing school, and Hector St. John de Crevecoeur noted that many of the men wore silk stockings and the women sported parasols.[32] Though life was still largely unpolished, by the turn of the century broadcloth was gaining on buckskin in Louisville.

𝕒𝕖

St. Louis, Pittsburgh and Louisville were built on rivers; their ambitions of growth and prosperity rested on water-borne commerce. By contrast, Lexington was the only considerable community in the West remote from a navigable stream. The Kentucky River, which formed a crescent around the town, was at least ten miles away, and a branch of the Elkhorn which cut through Lexington was never navigable and usually dry in the summer. Set on the Blue Grass, this frontier metropolis bestrode the arteries of overland trade and migration and served as the central depot for the surrounding country, which an early traveler described as an "earthly elysium." Though many believed with Victor Collot that "as this town has no navigation, . . . its increase will not be great," Lexington was by 1800 the "Philadelphia of Kentucky" and the largest city in the West.[33]

Hunters and explorers very early crossed the ground on which the town later stood, and in 1775 a group of them, who had paused at a nearby spring, named the place Lexington, since they had just received word of the opening battle of the American Revolution. The first permanent settlement came four years later, when Robert Patterson and some twenty-five companions erected a blockhouse there. For three years the town was a wilderness fortress, "the forlorn hope of advancing civilization." Indian fighting was incessant

[32] S. S. Forman, *Narrative of a Journey down the Ohio and the Mississippi in 1789–90*, L. C. Draper, ed. (Cincinnati, 1888), 40; Durrett, *Louisville*, 96; Ford and Ford, *Falls Cities*, I, 184.

[33] *The American Museum*, XI (1792), 12; V. Collot, *A Journey in North America* (Reprints of Rare Americana, No. 4, Florence, Italy, 1924), I, 103; L. Condict, "Journal of a Trip to Kentucky in 1795," *Proceedings of the New Jersey Historical Society*, n.s. IV (1919), 120.

and bloody, and by 1782 became so serious that the few inhabitants of Lexington appealed to the Governor of Virginia:

> We can scarcely behold a spot of Earth but what reminds us of the fall of some fellow adventurer massacred by Savage bands. . . . In short, sir, our settlement, hitherto formed at the Expence of Treasure & much Blood seems to decline, & if something is not speedily done, we doubt will wholly be depopulated.[34]

Before the petition could reach the capital, however, the redmen made a supreme effort at the battle of Blue Licks to throw the whites from central Kentucky. The tribesmen were badly beaten and dispersed, which left the region reasonably secure and ensured the town's orderly growth.

Even during these hazardous days of guerilla warfare, the settlers surveyed the town and in 1781 asked Virginia's General Assembly for ownership of this "still . . . unappropriated and unclaimed land." The petitioners pointed out that "they were induced to expect a Grant of Six hundred & forty acres, in confidence of which" they had laid off a town and elected trustees.[35] The state responded by giving 640 acres and confirming the town's purchase of 70 additional acres from John Floyd. Hence, like Louisville, Lexington became its own proprietor, with title to the entire townsite.

With the application for land the trustees also submitted their original survey. This plat laid off the town in one-third-acre lots, which were to be granted to any free white male resident of Lexington over twenty-one years old. "Not less than 30 acres" were reserved for public use.[36] The regular gridiron pattern was adopted, with three streets running north of the branch of the Elkhorn and roughly parallel with it, and seven cross streets making the grid

[34] G. W. Ranck, *History of Lexington, Its Early Annals and Recent Progress* (Cincinnati, 1872), 24; quoted in B. Mayo, "Lexington, Frontier Metropolis," in E. F. Goldman, ed., *Historiography and Urbanization* (Baltimore, 1941), 25.

[35] *Petitions*, Robertson, ed. ,60; 61.

[36] Town of Lexington, Trustees Book, 1781–1830 (MSS, City Hall, Lexington), March 26, 1781.

design. The streets were narrow, most being fifty feet, though the three larger ones were eighty-two feet. The center of the town contained only eighty-seven in-lots and a two-acre public square. But stretching north and east of town were five- and ten-acre out-lots which gave ample room for expansion.

As soon as Indian depredations ceased, the town grew. By 1790 it had 835 inhabitants, and was "reckoned the capital of Kentucky." Three years later Collot estimated that there were "from three to four hundred houses," and in 1798 a local census counted 1,475 townsmen, including 360 Negro slaves. By the end of the century Lexington's population of 1,795 handily exceeded Pittsburgh's and was more than twice as large as Cincinnati's.[37] In the course of its first two decades the military outpost comprising a stockade and a few cabins had mushroomed into the most important town in the West.

Lexington throve on trade. For twenty years it was the major distributing point for men and goods heading for western Kentucky or Tennessee. Streams of overland migrants stopped here, buying everything needed for building a home and for bringing in the first crops. Later, when the land was taken up, the rising metropolis supplied most Kentuckians with merchandise from Eastern cities.[38] In addition, Lexington became the dispatching center for country produce that sought markets outside, especially in New Orleans. The latter trade began in 1787 when James Wilkinson took the first boatloads to Louisiana, opening up to Kentucky and its commercial mart an immensely lucrative exchange. Only faint beginnings of manufacturing were visible in the nineties; as yet, most Lexingtonians owed their livelihood to expanding trade opportunities.

[37] Imlay, *Western Territory*, 185; J. Morse, *The American Universal Geography* (3rd edn., London, 1797), 566; Collot, *Journey*, 103; Lexington, Trustees Book, May 9, 1798; United States Census, 1800 2P.

[38] Francois André Michaux noted in 1802 that "the majority of the inhabitants of Kentucky trade with Lexington merchants." "Travels to the West of the Alleghany Mountains, in the State of Ohio, Kentucky, Tennessea," by R. G. Thwaites, ed., *Early Western Travels, 1748–1848* (Cleveland, 1904), III, 202n.

Life in Lexington was noisy and hectic, reflecting its entrepôt origins and functions. Immigrants trekked into town, spent a night or so, bought what they could carry, and left, making room for the next wagon trains. Farmers hawked foodstuffs at the Cheapside market, purchased in the stores, and ate and drank at the Sign of the Buffalo, the Sheaf of Wheat, or the Indian Queen. For a time Lexington was Kentucky's political capital, and the legislators swarmed about the courthouse and taxed the budding city's housing facilities to the limit. The pace of this life contrasted so sharply with that of the countryside that travelers often exaggerated the size and business of the town.

Lexington was not only the mercantile center of the West but its social and cultural leader as well. By 1800 the town government had removed "the sheep and hog pens" from the streets and begun their paving, fire protection had been put on an organized basis, and a primitive police force had been established. As early as 1788 the town set aside a plot of ground for "erecting . . . a Lattin and English Schoolhouse," and in 1799 Transylvania Academy became the first university (in name, at least) in the West. Two newspapers, a public library, debating clubs, musical and drama societies, and a half-dozen churches provided Lexingtonians with a cultural fare almost as varied as that beyond the mountains. For those whose taste was less elevated, the choice was still wide — billiards and longbullets, jockey clubs and horse racing, dancing and "free Nancy's" bawdy house.[39]

In no other area in the West was the difference between town and country so marked at the turn of the century as in the Blue Grass. "ARISTEDES," writing in the *Kentucky Gazette*, observed that in Lexington the merchant lived in a fashion unknown in rural regions. "His *dwelling*, his *equipage*, his *apparent amount of his stock in trade*, the *improvements that* surround him, and his *domestic conveniences* bear the aspect of a flourishing opulence." When a young farm boy, Robert McAfee, came to the metropolis for the

---

[39] Lexington, Trustees Book, December 12, 1782; October 21, 1793; June 7, 1791; November 22, 1796; April 7, 1800; November 22, 1796; March 17, 1788; December 23, 1797.

first time in 1794, he was so awed by the luxurious carpeting in the Breckenridge mansion that he hesitated to walk on it. Indeed the contrast was observable to the traveler even before Lexington came into sight. In 1806 Fortescue Cuming wrote of the outskirts of town, "The country had insensibly assumed the appearance of an approach to a city." [40]

Nature seemed to have created the sites of Louisville and Pittsburgh as the nurseries of great cities; but her intentions were less clear in the case of Cincinnati. In fact, the "Queen City" was the second or third choice of the early settlers. Both Columbia, at the mouth of the Little Miami, and North Bend, near the Great Miami, were settled before the first houses were built at Cincinnati. The advantages of Cincinnati's situation proved more obvious after the city grew than before the location was decided upon. The "bottom" was too often flooded, and creeks entering the town at both ends created pools of stagnant water which might carry disease. The commercial prospects, however, were encouraging. Across the Ohio was the mouth of the Licking River, which reached into the rich heart of the Blue Grass, and behind the town lay the farm lands of Ohio and Indiana, whose products would have to be processed and shipped. These considerations brought the first inhabitants to Cincinnati in December, 1788.

It was not Ohio's first town. That distinction belongs to Marietta, which a company of New England veterans founded a year earlier at the mouth of the Muskingum. Cincinnati owed its origin to the political influence of a New Jersey judge, congressman, and speculator, John Cleves Symmes, who dislodged from Congress a million acres between the Miami rivers in 1788 for a relatively small sum. The first immigrants landed that same year on the eastern edge

[40] *Kentucky Gazette*, September 20, 1803; R. B. McAfee, "Life and Times of Robert B. McAfee Written by Himself," *Register of the Kentucky State Historical Society*, XXV (1927), 128; F. Cuming, "Sketches of a Tour to the Western Country," in Thwaites, ed., *Western Travels*, IV, 181.

of Symmes's purchase, erected a fort, and called the village Columbia. The leader of this little band of thirty, Benjamin Stites, laid out "the squares and streets for a great city." By 1790 there were fifty cabins, a mill, a church, and a school. But nearly every year the river, swollen with spring, covered the settlement, forcing even the garrison to vacate. Within a few years Columbia declined, many of its inhabitants moving down the river a few miles to the more promising situation of Cincinnati. Thus, ironically, the "Queen City," one of the most flood-afflicted spots in the valley, was the beneficiary of the drowning of an infant neighbor.[41]

In 1788 Symmes sold the site of Cincinnati and the land around it to Matthias Denman, who later formed a partnership with Robert Peterson and John Filson, both Kentuckians and veteran town builders. The new proprietors made a preliminary visit to their purchase in September, but no lasting settlement was made. Filson began a survey of the town, but one day he wandered off into the woods, never to be seen again. In December the partners, with Israel Ludlow replacing Filson, returned with about twenty others to reside permanently. After a few cabins had been erected, Ludlow surveyed and laid out the town, marking the course of the streets on the trees. The embryo metropolis was called Losantiville, a curious mixture of Greek, Latin and French — L-os-ante-ville — meaning "village opposite the mouth" of the Licking. This name underlines the importance of that river in the selection of the site. The founders hoped to tap the increasing prosperity of Kentucky. Indeed, Denman's interest in the whole project stemmed from his desire to run a ferry across the Ohio to the Licking's mouth. The name of Cincinnati, taken from the society of veterans, quickly replaced the original, and by the early nineties appeared on all legal documents. But the spelling was not secure, for Symmes in-

[41] Quoted in C. T. Greve, *Centennial History of Cincinnati* (Chicago, 1904), I, 179; B. W. Bond, Jr., ed., *The Symmes Correspondence* (New York, 1926), 62; for the decline of Columbia, see also D. Drake, *Natural and Statistical View of Cincinnati and the Miami Country* (Cincinnati, 1815), 37; J. Burnet, *Notes on the Northwest Territory* (Cincinnati, 1847), 46.

sisted on the ending "ta" instead of "ti," and even submitted the issue to the "literati of Jersey" for decision.[42]

Cincinnati rested on a plain of about four square miles, which was ringed about by heavily forested highlands. The townsite embraced two levels. The lower one, or the "bottom," was a narrow belt of land, two hundred feet wide at Deer Creek on the eastern edge of town, and spreading out to eight hundred feet near Mill Creek to the west. Being only seven feet above the normal high-water mark of the river, this low land was imperiled by floods almost every spring. In addition, the "bottom" tilted to the northwest, creating a pocket where water collected in idle ponds which posed a constant sanitation problem. The second level, called the "hill," rose sharply fifty feet above the first bank, forming a mile-wide table which sloped back gently to the base of the highland crescent. From the river, early Cincinnati looked like a green and open theater carved out of the hills.[43]

Ludlow laid out the town in a regular grid pattern, six blocks along the river and seven away from it. The plan used Philadelphia for a model, since its author "was well acquainted" with it. The streets were 66 feet wide, and each block was divided into eight lots, 99 by 198 feet, except those between Second and Third streets, which were smaller. Behind the town, the out-lots, which ran back to the highlands, were divided into four-acre tracts. Only a small strip was reserved for a common, and there was "not a single alley, court or diagonal." As in most frontier towns, regularity of plan was thought more important than beauty or utility. Francis Baily, who passed through Cincinnati in 1797, complained, "If they had made one of their principal streets to face the river, and the other at the brow of the second bank . . . . the whole town would

[42] Greve, *Cincinnati*, I, 155; on June 17, 1791, Symmes wrote to Jonathan Dayton in Jersey, "You have your Witherspoons and Smiths, and indeed abound in characters in whose decision I shall fully acquiesce." *Symmes Correspondence*, Bond, ed., 142.

[43] For a good topographical description of Cincinnati, see D. Drake, "Notices Concerning Cincinnati," Historical and Philosophical Society of Ohio, *Quarterly Publications*, III (1908).

have presented a noble appearance from the river." He also noticed the "inconvenience" of laying a symmetrical plan over a highly irregular terrain whose main feature, the second level, did not run parallel to the river.[44]

Cincinnati's first years were precarious. The Indians had not yet been pacified; indeed, they had turned back several army attempts to subdue them. They raided the Miami district so often that Kentuckians grimly referred to it as "the slaughter house." In 1792 Fort Washington was built at Cincinnati as the pivotal outpost in the war against the savages. During these years the "Queen City" was a garrison town, and friction between military and civilian interests dominated its life. This hostility even spilled over into violence before the commander and the settlers reached an amicable arrangement.[45] The major problem was the dissolute life of the soldiers, who went on frolics in the town, leaving great damage in their wake. William Henry Harrison, who came to Fort Washington in 1791 as an ensign, was shocked at the behavior of the troops. "I . . . saw more drunken men in forty-eight hours succeeding my arrival at Cincinnati than I had in all my previous life"; and Lewis Condict thought it "the most debauched place I ever saw." [46]

But the military brought benefits as well as trouble. In these crucial years they not only served as a shield against the Indians, but also gave a great economic stimulus to the town.[47] All major opera-

[44] D. Drake, "Dr. Drake's Memoir of the Miami Country, 1779–1794," Historical and Philosophical Society of Ohio, *Quarterly Publication*, XVIII (1923), 58; Drake, *Statistical View*, 130; Francis Baily, *Journal of a Tour in Unsettled Parts of North America, in 1796 & 1797* (London, 1856), 227ff.

[45] J. H. Perkins, *Annals of the West: Embracing a Concise Account of the Principal Events Which Have Occurred in the Western States and Territories* (Cincinnati, 1846), 306; Greve, *Cincinnati*, I, 224–25.

[46] Quoted in Rufus King, *Ohio, First Fruits of the Ordinance of 1787* (Boston, 1888), 214–5. Not all officers took such a dim view of life in Fort Washington; one confided to a friend, "We have taken quarters at Mimson's tavern, where we live in clover," 215; Condict, "Journal," 119.

[47] Cincinnati not only contained a permanent garrison but was also the rendezvous for troops moving west. For example, in December, 1793, 600 men stopped off for a week; in July of the next year 600 more stayed for ten days, and in December, 1794, 600 more "passed through this place."

tions against tribes in the north originated in Cincinnati, and the merchants throve upon supplying the troops. With Wayne's success at Fallen Timbers in 1794 the power of the Indians was broken. Gradually the army was reduced, the fort dismantled, and the land sold.

Despite the problems raised by the Indians and the armed forces, Cincinnati grew rapidly. In the fall of 1790 Symmes, whose own town of North Bend was struggling to be born, admitted that "the advantage is prodigious which this town is gaining over North Bend, upwards of forty framed and hewed-log two story houses have been and are building since last spring, one builder sets an example for another, and the place already assumes the appearance of a town of some respect." In that year it gained recognition as the most considerable settlement in the territory when the seat of government was established there. Seven years later there were "three or four hundred houses, mostly frame-built," and Francis Baily called it "the metropolis of the north-western territory." At the beginning of the new century Cincinnati had a population of "about seven hundred and fifty." [48]

Most Cincinnatians engaged in commerce either with the army or with the more than fourteen thousand inhabitants of Hamilton County. The town was the "grand depot" for produce that went down the river to New Orleans as well as for Eastern merchandise distributed throughout the Miami area. By 1802 the Mississippi trade had become so important that the newspapers published New Orleans and Natchez prices.[49] Ties with the East were maintained by a constant flow of goods and settlers coming down the Ohio. Because of Cincinnati's position at the northern bend of the river, many immigrants heading for the interior disembarked there, giving the young city the atmosphere of a large hotel.

Though life in Cincinnati in its first decade was both hard and

---

Centinel of the North-western Territory, December 14, 1793; February 15, 1794; July 12, 1794; *Western Spy*, July 30, 1800.

[48] *Symmes Correspondence*, 135; Baily, *Journal*, 228; *Cincinnati Directory for 1819* (Cincinnati, 1819), 29.

[49] *Western Spy*, May 6, 1801; Baily, *Journal*, 228.

dangerous, its people found time for cultivation and relaxation. As early as 1792 an Englishman began a school for about thirty students, and several more soon followed. *The Centinel of the Northwestern Territory*, a newspaper founded by James Maxwell in 1793, brought news of the outside world. In 1801 an amateur theater group presented "The Poor Soldier" and "Peeping Tom of Coventry," which opened with an original prologue apologizing for the unpretentious beginnings of the drama in Cincinnati:

> No practis'd actor have here your passions charms,
> Nor magic brush the vary'd scen'ry warms;
> Our house, our equipage, are all but rude,
> And little, faith, but our intentions good.[50]

Parties and balls were so common that the newspaper warned that local dancing schools had become "nurseries of dalliance, frippery and folly" to which "the most important and solemn considerations are daily sacrificed." A traveler who stopped at this urban outpost around the turn of the century remembered "hearing the harmonies of Gluck and Haydn, and the reports of champagne bottles," which "transported the guests from the wilds of the Northwestern Territory into the Lucullian feasts of the European aristocracy."[51]

Though Western cities were settled from different parts of the continent, their planning showed remarkable similarities. All were laid out in a regular checkerboard pattern with straight streets crossing at right angles. The major inspiration for this approach was Philadelphia, though St. Louis, which derived from New Orleans, adopted the same kind of design. This system had practical advantages. It simplified the problems of surveying and minimized legal disputes over lot boundaries. It also gave at least the illusion of orderliness which settlers associated with cities they had known in the East. But the significance of this rectangular format lay deeper.

[50] *Western Spy*, October 10, 1801.
[51] Quoted in Greve, *Cincinnati*, I, 364; 365.

It represented the difference between town organization and country life. "Curved lines, you know," observed Daniel Drake, "symbolize the country, straight lines the city." [52] Early planners connected regularity in design with cities, and refused to make any deviation, even when the configuration of the terrain suggested it.

The shortcomings of this grid pattern were evident to contemporaries. Francis Baily noticed that "oftentimes it is a sacrifice of beauty to prejudice." No allowance was made for irregular contours of the townsite, or of the face of the surrounding country. "It not unfrequently happens that a hill opposes itself in the middle of a street, or that a rivulet crosses it three or four times, thereby rendering its appearance very disgusting, and its passage very inconvenient." It would have been better if the plan accommodated itself to the terrain. "If they would fix upon all the eminences upon the site as so many central spots from which the streets were to proceed like rays from a centre, and make all other minor streets subservient to these, . . . they might preserve an uniformity, a cleanliness, and agreeable prospect." Thus a town could "preserve the straight line, and yet avoid that disgusting appearance which many of the new towns in America make." Baily was greatly impressed by the planning of Washington and thought that it presented a better model than Philadelphia.[53]

Robert Stubbs maintained the same view. Speaking of Cincinnati, he complained of the "want of spacious alleys, open courts and squares, diagonal streets, public walks and reserves for public buildings," and protested against "the dull monotony inseparable from designs devoid of variety." Henry Marie Brackenridge was so disturbed by St. Louis's plat that he wished "that as happened to Detroit, a conflagration would seize it and burn it to the ground" so that a new design could be adopted.[54]

[52] Quoted in Greve, *Cincinnati*, I, 349.

[53] Baily, *Journal*, 226–27.

[54] R. Stubbs, *The Ohio Almanac, 1810* (Cincinnati, 1810), unfolioed; *Missouri Gazette*, October 11, 1810. On June 11, 1805, the whole town of Detroit was destroyed by fire. When it was rebuilt it was patterned after Washington. F. C. Bald, *Detroit's First American Decade, 1796–1805* (Ann Arbor, 1948), 240–43.

Part of the legacy of early town plans was the paucity of public space. Original reserves were skimpy, and even those were quickly broken into. The initial mistakes were not irrevocable, but the policy of most of these places in their first years aggravated the inadequacy. Hoping to attract inhabitants, the young cities were inattentive to future need and often sacrificed civic elbow-room by the sale of public ground. Lexington was successful in protecting its lots, but the others soon found themselves buying back land for public buildings, markets, wharves, and later for parks. There was some protest against this tendency to alienate town lots, but it did not become organized or effective until the late 1820's, after most of the damage had been done.

Another striking conformity in early city plans was the relationship of town and river. All these settlements, except Lexington, were on waterways, deriving their importance and prosperity from water connections. Early planners, for that reason, made the river the central street, so to speak, in their design. Plats tended to be long rather than wide, allowing maximum access to the water. The names of the main streets reflected this orientation: nearly every city had its Water or Front street. But soon the waterfront became commercialized. Wharving, warehousing, and shipping interests bought up the landings and the ground behind them, while residential building retreated inland. Soon travelers coming down the river spoke of the business of a city, not its beauty.

Since early plans did not reserve much land along the waterfront, its despoilment was almost inevitable. When Brackenridge reached St. Louis in 1810 this process had already begun. "But surely," he complained, "for the sake of business, of health, of promenade, there should have been no encroachment on the margin of the noble stream. This defect is much to be lamented, more especially as it is beyond the power of correction." McMurtrie said that the failure of early surveys to protect the waterfront meant that Louisville "has turned its back . . . on the varied and interesting prospect" of the Ohio. Even more caustic was Moses Austin's judgment: "Louis Ville by nature is beautiful but the handy work of Man has insted of improving destroy'd the works of Nature and made it a detestable place." [55] Western townsites were chosen for their commercial promise, not beauty, and it is not surprising that early plans mirrored that predilection.

◄ℓ

Not all the towns founded in the trans-Allegheny West in the late eighteenth and early nineteenth centuries became large cities. Many never developed much beyond a survey and an advertisement. Others, after promising beginnings, slackened, and settled down to slow and unspectacular development. Still others rode a cycle of boom and decline, leaving behind a grim story of deserted mills, dilapidated buildings, and aging people — the West's first harvest of ghost towns. Most of these enterprises were mere eddies in the westward flow of urban culture, but at flood tide it was often hard to distinguish the eddies from the main stream. All seemed promising to at least some people, and their hopes were an important part of the atmosphere in which immigration took place.

From the time the West was first opened to settlement, it was the scene of not only land speculation, but intense city speculation as well. Men in the East with surplus capital scanned maps looking for likely spots to establish a town, usually at the junction of two rivers, or sometimes at the center of fertile farm districts. Their information often came from a traveler's account, or from personal contact with someone who had been across the mountains. They bought up land, laid it out into lots, gave the place a name, and waited for the development of the region to appreciate its value. Looking back over this period, one observer spoke of the *"city-making mania"* that caused everyone to go about "anticipating flourishing cities in vision, at the mouth of every creek and Bayou." Though many people engaged in this speculation, few profited from it. Even those who were fortunate in their choice of sites realized little gain in the long run. James Hall believed that "town making has

[55] *Missouri Gazette*, October 11, 1810; McMurtrie, *Sketches of Louisville*, 115; M. Austin, "A Memorandum of M. Austin's Journey . . . 1796–1797," *American Historical Review*, V (1899–1900), 527.

not generally proved profitable. Of the vast number of towns which have been founded, but a small minority have prospered, nor do we think that, as a general rule, the founders of these have been greatly enriched by their prosperity." [56]

For three decades urban speculation raged throughout the new country from Western Pennsylvania to Missouri. To proprietors, the prospects seemed boundless. As early as 1787 New Athens was "established at the confluence of those majestic rivers, the Mississippi and Missouri, . . . on perhaps the most desirable spot in the known world." It offered settlers not only a "perfect situation" but complete freedom of religion as well. To sketch adequately so bright a future, the founders turned to verse:

> Again shall Athens bid her columns rise,
> Again her lofty turrets reach the skies,
> Science again shall find a safe retreat,
> And commerce here as in a centre meet. [57]

In the same manner, New Lisbon confidently asserted that its location at the middle fork of the Beaver River in Ohio "is exceeded by none in the Western Country." On Swan Creek at Lake Erie, Port Lawrence claimed that its "natural advantages . . . seem to have been designed for the great *depot* of the north-west." Palermo, Kentucky, looked forward not only to a commercial future as an Ohio River town, but its "inexhaustible coal mine" assured that it would "become one of the greatest places on the whole river for steam works." The classic example of city speculation, however, was the Town of America, located at the junction of the Ohio and Mississippi. "The mind is . . . free to expatiate upon the advantages of this situation," the proprietors wrote, "and the undersigned can leave it to any man of sense and candor to say whether any point upon our continent has ever presented a fairer prospect of a greater inland commercial city." A rich back country and unimpeded ac-

---

[56] *Missouri Republican*, August 29, 1825; J. Hall, *The West: Its Commerce and Navigation* (Cincinnati, 1848), 227.

[57] *American Museum*, V (1789), 284.

cess to New Orleans made it "difficult to assign a reason why this town should not in a few years rank with the first in America." [58]

By the second decade of the nineteenth century the propaganda of the speculators had become formalized. Newspapers throughout the country ran notices proclaiming the matchless situation of the proposed city. A detailed and sympathetic description of the surrounding country and rivers followed; then settlers were urged to buy quickly before the price of town lots began to skyrocket. The "town-making mania" became so prevalent that many grew cynical. The *Augusta Chronicle* ran an advertisement, widely copied throughout the West, satirizing the whole process. The editor observed that "notwithstanding nearly all the lands on the banks of the several watercourses have been laid off and offered for sale as town lots," still there are people "who may be prevailed on to become rich, provided it can be done without much trouble." The "City of Skunksburgh" seemed to offer every opportunity for both settler and speculator.

This charming place, better known as Log-Hall, heretofore the residence of *Fiddler Billy*, is situated in Wilks county, not far from the junction of Pickett's main spring branch, and a Western fork, called the Slough, which runs in the rainy season, and washes the confines of Farnsworth's lower hog pens. This noble stream, by the use of *proper* and *sufficient* means, may be made navigable to the sea. It abounds in delicate minnows, a variety of terrapins, and its frogs, which, in size, voice, and movement, are inferior to none. . . . A noble bluff of 18 inches commands the harbor, and affords a most advantageous situation for defensive military works. This bluff slopes off into nearly a level, diversified only by the gentle undulations of surface, as will give a sufficient elevation for the princial public edifices. Commodious and picturesque positions will be therefore reserved for the Exchange and City Hall, a church, one Gymnastic and one Polytechnic foundation, one Olympic and two Dramatic theatres, an Equestrian circus, an observatory, two marine and two Foundling Hospitals, and in the most com-

---

[58] *Pittsburgh Gazette*, August 26, 1803; *Mercury* (Pittsburgh), September 12, 1817; *Pittsburgh Gazette*, October 15, 1809; *Pittsburgh Gazette*, October 15, 1809.

mercial part of the city will be a reservation for seventeen banks, to each of which may be attached a lunatic Hospital. . . .

The future advantages of this situation is now impossible to calculate; but already it is the emporium of all the water mellons, ground pease, and suck collars, and all the brooms, chickens, and baskets, that are bought and sold among the before mentioned places, in the course of commerce. To mercantile men, however, a mere statement of its geographical position is deemed sufficient, without comment. It stands on about the middle ground betwen Baltimore and Orleans, Charleston and Nickajak, Savannah and Coweta, Knoxville and St. Mary's, Salisbury and Cusseta, and between Little Heil on the Altamaha, and Telfico block house. A line of Velocipede stages will be immediately established from Skunksburgh straight through the O-ke-fin-o-cau Swamp, to the southernmost point of the Florida peninsula; and, as soon as a canal shall be cut through the rocky mountains, there will be direct communication with the Columbia river, and thence to the Pacific Ocean. Then opens a theatre of trade bounded only by the Universe!

.   .   .

> ANDREW AIRCASTLE
> THEORY M'VISION
> L. MOONLIGHT, Jr., & Co.
> *Proprietors* [59]

By the twenties the West was littered with ambitious towns that never grew. Much of this speculation was fanciful. "The Gentlemen who had fixed on a spot in the wilderness, and marked out the boundaries of a city, disdained, of course, the idea of building a *'castle in the air'* — he was looking forward to something more *solid* — he could not doubt his own taste or his own judgment — the wilderness was to blossom, and his city to be peopled — before payday would come." [60]

In retrospect it would be easy to account for the failure of each. Some were too easily inundated at high water, others too remote from a navigable stream, and still others were too close to already successful towns. James Hall, however, penetrated to the heart of the matter: "It requires the united influence of many individuals and

---

[59] *Liberty Hall* (Cincinnati), October 1, 1819.
[60] *Louisville Public Advertiser*, August 20, 1823.

various interests and the concurrence of a diversity of circumstances, to give impulse to the healthy growth of a town; so that while, on the one hand, it is almost impossible to foresee such a combination of events," on the other, their occurrence is essential.

We have in our eye a notable instance of this kind. At the junction of two noble rivers, upon a spot which, as presented upon the map, seems to combine every advantage, a city of noble dimensions has been laid out. An engineer of high reputation has been induced to give the sanction of his name to the scheme; plats beautifully executed have been circulated industriously, and immense sums of money are supposed to have been collected abroad, for shares of this magnificent city, which, after being owned by several successive companies, and puffed for many years, is the residence only of frogs and musquitoes, while hundreds of towns have grown up within the same period without effort.[61]

Most of this town planting was abortive; but the failures were nevertheless important. They not only illustrate the extensive city speculation of the period, but also help to reveal the nature of much of the immigration moving westward. Many settlers came across the mountains in search of promising towns as well as good land. Their inducements were not so much fertile soil as opportunities in infant cities. It was to these people that hopeful enterprisers addressed their propaganda. Daniel Drake, who was among the earliest urbanites of the frontier, later observed,

It is worthy of remark, that those who made these beginnings of settlement, projected towns, which they anticipated would grow into cities . . . and we may see in this origin, one of the elements of the prevalent tendency to rear up towns in advance of the country which has ever since characterized Ohio. The followers of the first pioneers, like themselves had a taste for commerce and the mechanic arts, which cannot be gratified without the construction of cities.

Proprietors competed for these urban migrants who came from "those portions of the Union which cherish and build up cities." [62] The preference of some settlers for towns was so great that in 1787

[61] Hall, *The West*, 227–28.
[62] Drake, "Memoir," 58.

Lexington petitioned the Virginia legislature for incorporation, to "be an inducement to well disposed persons, artizans and mechanics who from motives of convenience do prefer a Town life." [63]

By 1800 the urban pattern of the West had been established. Environment and circumstances had chosen some cities and discarded others. Many new towns would rise later, but every major metropolis in the transmontane region, with the exception of Chicago, Milwaukee, and Indianapolis, had its beginnings in the eighteenth century. Even many of the lake towns, whose dynamic growth belongs to a later period, were established by the turn of the century. Of course, all these cities were still young and small, but a wedge of urbanism had been driven into the backwoods. Where only two decades earlier Indians had ranged through hunting grounds, now could be found newspapers, schools, libraries, theaters, churches, local governments, and police. Merchandise from Europe and luxuries from the Orient landed at town wharves where they met the produce of nearby farmers waiting shipment down the rivers to New Orleans. Travelers were awed by this sudden transformation of the Western wilderness. Yet even these promising beginnings did not presage the remarkable development of the next fifteen years.

[63] *Petitions*, Robertson, ed., 106.

PART ONE
1790–1815

Chapter 2

The Economic Base

A city is many things: it is a cultural focus, a social resort, a political center, but before all — though not above all — it is a place where people earn a living. This priority is especially striking in young cities where a vigorous social and cultural life must await the establishment of a stable economic structure. A literary editor in Pittsburgh early resigned himself to this fact. "The first exertions of the colonist will be directed toward the attainment of the necessaries of life and the struggle against wild nature," which must "for a long time retard the progress of the human mind, and the liberal culture of science and literature." [1] For this reason during the first fifteen years of the nineteenth century the pulse of Western cities was their trade and manufacturing. Development along these lines was rapid, so much so that by the end of the war with Great Britain each town had erected an economy whose general outlines would not change substantially until the coming of the railroad.

The key to this economic growth was transportation. It determined the pattern of settlement, the direction and volume of commerce, and the ease and speed of the occupation of the West. Until the advent of the railroad the most important highways were rivers. Roads in the trans-Allegheny area were poor, and travel over them slow and expensive. Though land routes were usually passable in summer, they turned to quagmires in fall and spring. Mountainous regions yielded only reluctantly to traffic, and great effort was required to keep passes open from year to year. Hence, the clumsiness of land traffic put the major transport burden on the rivers. Until the adoption of the steamboat this was largely a southward move-

[1] *Pittsburgh Mercury*, November 25, 1813.

ment, because the difficulty of ascending the Mississippi and Ohio made the cost almost prohibitive. It is hard to convey the arduousness of this upstream navigation. Timothy Flint's description, however, reveals something of the problem.

Those tugs and unwieldly boats . . . required twenty or thirty hands to work them. I have seen them day after day, on the lower portions of the Mississippi; where there was no other way of working them up, than carrying out a cable a half mile in length, in advance of the barge, and fastening it to a tree. The hands on board then drew it to a tree.[2]

Under these conditions the trip proved not only physically harsh, but slow as well. The two-way passage between Cincinnati and New Orleans took about a hundred days, and for those going on to Pittsburgh another month was added.

The expense of this travel led to a search for speedier methods. Pittsburgh, Marietta and Wheeling tried to meet the problem with sailing schooners, only to find that most of the vessels that reached the Gulf preferred to take their chances on the high seas rather than return up the tortuous inland rivers. In 1805 two Cincinnati firms rigged barges with sails, inaugurating a round-trip trade with New Orleans which enjoyed some success for almost a decade. These expedients did little to disturb the downward commercial flow of the river, and in 1807 over 1,800 boats arrived in the Louisiana port, while only 11 went upstream.[3] The war, however, accomplished what ingenuity could not. New Orleans' customary Atlantic routes broke under British pressure, and its merchants turned to the expensive interior waterways. By 1815 keelboats were reaching Pittsburgh daily from the South. *Niles' Register* reported that this trade was "assuming immense importance," and some Westerners urged the exclusive use of New Orleans for both exporting and importing.[4] The new pattern, begun under war conditions, was later solidified

---

[2] Timothy Flint, *Recollections of the Last Ten Years*, (Boston, 1826), 106–7.

[3] W. F. Switzler, "Report on the Internal Commerce of the United States," *House Executive Documents*, 50th Congress, 1st Session, XX, no. 6, part 2, 185.

[4] *Niles' Register*, July 31, 1813; *Kentucky Gazette*, February 7, 1804.

by the steamboat, which for the first time permitted easy and regular upriver traffic.

Despite the attempts to equalize the flow of commerce on Western rivers, the great bulk of it moved toward New Orleans. On barges, keelboats, and flatboats the growing surplus of the new country floated to market in the South. In 1801 the Gulf port's inland trade was valued at $3,649,000, six years later it had grown to $5,370,000, and in 1816 the West poured goods worth $8,062,000 into New Orleans. During the six months ending in May 1811, *Niles' Register* calculated, nearly 1,200 boats passed over the Falls at Louisville. The most important item in this down-river commerce was flour, though the variety was great, including $355,624 in Western merchandise.[5]

Since the lines of commerce moved in one direction, the boats used were built at points well up the major rivers and tributaries, and constituted an important item in the economies of Western towns. These vessels, constructed for a single trip, were usually dismantled in New Orleans and sold for lumber. The constant turnover led to experimentation in design, and Western yards spawned all kinds of ships. Timothy Flint recalled that what struck him most at the Pittsburgh landing was "the singular, whimsical, and amusing spectacle, of the varieties of water craft, of all shapes and structures . . . . You can scarcely imagine an abstract form in which a boat can be built, that in some part of the Ohio and Mississippi you will not see, actually in motion." Ultimately three types proved most satisfactory — barge, flatboat, and keelboat. Nearly every town made some of them, though the biggest producers were Brownsville, Cincinnati, Marietta and Pittsburgh. Indeed, at the last place, Christian Schultz thought that "boat building, boat buying and boat selling, seem to be part of the business of at least half of the town." These craft were generally small, keels and barges averaging around 40 tons; but in the first decade of the century, ocean-going vessels, some upwards of 300 tons, were also launched from inland yards, over sixty of them entering the Caribbean or Atlantic trade.[6]

[5] E. W. Gould, *Fifty Years on the Mississippi; or, Gould's History of River Navigation* (St. Louis, 1889), 190, 191, 202; *Niles' Register*, July 31, 1813.

[6] Flint, *Recollections*, 14; Christian Schultz, *Travels on an Inland Voyage*

With a river system oriented to the South and with awkward land contacts with the East, little bilateral exchange was possible. Instead, an extensive system of triangular trade arose. The new country imported Eastern goods across the mountains on credit extended by Philadelphia, Baltimore, or New York firms. Western merchants then found a market for their produce in New Orleans, where, as a traveler described it, "their brokers . . . sell, as much as they can, for ready money; or rather take in exchange cottons, indigo, raw sugar, the produce of Low Louisiana, which they send off by sea to the houses at Philadelphia or Baltimore, and thus cover their first advances." [7] This pattern was the best that the transmontane region could wring from an unfavorable situation, but soon cries of "extortion" and "colonialism" were raised. Payments to the East kept specie scarce, and prices in the West, absorbing the high transportation costs, tended to move upward. This constant imbalance induced some cities to manufacture at home, and others to seek more favorable conditions in the New Orleans market. Thus arose the two most dynamic movements in the Western economy; and the towns, as the commercial nerve centers of the frontier, took the lead in the adjustment.

It was in the context of this relationship with the outside world that Western towns developed their basic economic structures. Though they shared a common dilemma, their responses to it varied. Peculiar locations, resources, and historic origins precluded uniformity and produced important differences. Some cities, such as Pittsburgh and Lexington, turned enthusiastically to industry; others, like St. Louis, maintained their reliance on commerce; while Cincinnati and Louisville experimented with both. By 1815, however, the direction of growth of each frontier city had been pretty well fixed, though the question of speed of development still held perils.

ℰ

. . . *in the Years 1807 and 1808* (New York, 1810), 126; L. D. Baldwin, *The Keelboat Age on Western Waters* (Pittsburgh, 1941), 52–53, 173ff.

[7] Michaux, "Travels," in Thwaites, ed., *Western Travels*, III, 159.

Pittsburgh, like other Western towns, was cradled in commerce; but while still very young it showed remarkable manufacturing promise. Indeed, this new interest spread so rapidly that by 1810 a native likened the town to "a large workshop," and John Melish recorded that "in the course of my walks through the streets I heard everywhere the sound of the hammer and anvil." In the first decades of the new century mills, shops, and factories sprang up, their engines and furnaces laying a cloud of coal smoke and dust over the city, almost hiding it from the approaching traveler.

> Here PITT, compassed by hills and streams around,
> Compactly built within its narrow bound,
> Stands gloomily magnificent in mantling smoke,
> The western workshop, where useful arts convoke;
> Here chiming hammer and loud puffing steam,
> The rattling dray and the thundering team;
> A bustling crowd with hurried pace,
> And oft brown industry's sooty face,
> Are seen and heard throughout the busy place.[8]

Pittsburgh had already become the Birmingham of America.

Its rise as a manufacturing center was accompanied by a population growth which made Pittsburgh by 1815 the largest city in the West. In that decade and a half the town increased more than five-fold, from 1,565 inhabitants in 1800 to an estimated 8,000 in 1815.[9] The greatest influx occurred during the later years, when over 3,000 new residents came in a half decade. Much of this astonishing expansion was artificial, reflecting the prosperity occasioned by international complications and war, but few doubted the permanence of the boom, and pessimists were scarce. "Pittsburgh appears to be in

---

[8] Z. Cramer, *Pittsburgh Almanack for the Year of Our Lord 1810* (Pittsburgh, 1810), 52; J. Melish, *Travels in the United States of America in the Years 1806 & 1807, and 1809, 1810, & 1811* (Philadelphia, 1812), II, 60; *Pittsburgh Gazette*, February 19, 1819.

[9] Population of Pittsburgh:

1800	1,565	U. S. Census, 1800, 2D.
1810	4,768	U. S. Census, 1810, 44.
1815	8,000	*Pittsburgh Directory for 1819*, 17.

full tide of successful experiment," wrote one visitor, "and promises fair, within thirty years more to be the largest inland city in the United States." Nor did the coming of peace dampen this enthusiasm. Henry Marie Brackenridge, for example, confidently asserted that "its progress will be more rapid than before the war." [10]

One of the sources of this optimism was the constant flow of immigrants across the mountains towards the interior. As the most publicized Western town, and situated on the best route to the new areas, Pittsburgh became the focus of the avenues of migration, "the Thermopylae of the west," as one observer put it.[11] Travel over the Appalachians was so difficult and costly that most people converted their goods into cash before moving. When they arrived at the head of the Ohio, they needed nearly everything — food, furniture, and even clothing. Farm implements and building tools, too heavy to carry, would be indispensable in the next months. Hence migrants sold their horses and wagons in Pittsburgh, used up their cash, and moved down the river. The numbers involved were large, but before the days of the toll road no one kept count. An official estimate for 1794 put the figure at 13,000. Two years later, the *Pittsburgh Gazette* claimed that 1,200 persons crossed over the Allegheny River in a single month. In the first decades of the nineteenth century the volume grew, and sixty three shops, including twenty three general stores, serviced the great human stream.[12] This transient immigration, along with Pittsburgh's own increase, made up a home market for local merchants and manufacturers that was of central importance to the town's economy.

The merchant could rely on a much broader demand, however, than that of the townsmen and migrants: the entire transmontane region offered opportunity. At first he was a middleman handling

[10] Melish, *Travels*, II, 55; Schultz, *Travels*, 125; "HMB" in Z. Cramer, *Cramer's Almanack for 1816* (Pittsburgh, 1816), 39.

[11] T. Nuttall, *Journal of Travels into the Arkansas Territory, During the Year 1819* (Philadelphia, 1821), 18.

[12] *Pittsburgh Gazette*, February 7, 1795; March 5, 1796; H. C. Douds, "Merchants and Merchandising in Pittsburgh, 1759–1800," *Western Pennsylvania Historical Magazine*, XX (1937), 128.

Eastern goods; indeed, initially he was usually a partner or factor of a Philadelphia or Baltimore firm.[13] Wagons brought merchandise over the mountains to Pittsburgh,[14] where it was either sold locally or sent by boat to the interior, often as far south as New Orleans. But this triangular trade was clumsy and sometimes inefficient. If Pittsburgh could manufacture some of these items itself, the expensive overland transit could be eliminated. This situation very early created an inducement to manufacture in the young city. The mountains formed a protective wall, or tariff, around new industries, allowing them to flourish even when their cost structure was relatively high. Hence for a time Pittsburgh got the best of both worlds; it remained an important link in the mercantile chain that bound Eastern cities to the frontier, and yet became a manufacturing center of increasing importance to the West.

The activities of Pittsburgh's merchants reflected this dualism. Money accumulated in commerce was invested in new industrial enterprises. Joseph McClurg, for example, who established the first foundry in the city, also owned a store where he sold Philadelphia and Baltimore goods "wholesale or retail." Anthony Beelen, too, led this double life, being both a commission merchant and proprietor of the Eagle Foundry.[15] More illustrative perhaps was the career of Colonel James O'Hara, probably the most successful Pittsburgher of his day. He built his fortune supplying the armies in the West during the eighties and nineties, but in the next decade he opened a glass factory, a brewery, and a shipyard, while at the same time carrying on extensive trade with St. Louis, New Orleans, and London.[16] In 1809, when a public meeting created a committee to explore the possibility of organizing a society for the encouragement of manufacturing, almost all its members were merchants.[17]

[13] Michaux, "Travels," in Thwaites, ed., *Western Travels*, III, 161.

[14] Between January 1, 1813, and January 1, 1814, 4,055 wagons came from Philadelphia on the "great road" alone. *Pittsburgh Gazette*, November 22, 1814.

[15] *Pittsburgh Gazette*, December 7, 1810.

[16] See the Denny-O'Hara MSS (Historical Society of Western Pennsylvania, Pittsburgh).

[17] *Pittsburgh Gazette*, March 29, 1809.

Most of the money invested in Pittsburgh manufacturing came from the town itself, very little being supplied from the East until the railroad era.[18] This reliance on local capital makes the rapid growth of the city's industry even more remarkable. In 1803 the value of manufactured products was more than $350,000. Seven years later it had jumped to over $1,000,000, and by 1815, it exceeded $2,600,000. The progress was so startling that *Niles' Register* exclaimed, "Pittsburgh, sometimes emphatically called the 'Birmingham of America,' will probably become *the greatest manufacturing town in the world*." [19]

The principal factor in this development was iron, which by 1815 accounted for more than a quarter of the value of all goods manufactured in Pittsburgh. Though originally a rural industry, it very early became important in the town's economy. The Juniata region shipped metal bars to local blacksmiths who fashioned them into household utensils and tools for the immigrant or resident. The first Pittsburgh factories made nails, one being established in 1799 and five more before 1812.[20] Iron activity greatly expanded in 1804 when Joseph McClurg established the first air foundry, which turned out not only the customary articles but also cast parts for machinery. Within five years the latter items replaced household and farm equipment as the firm's major interest.[21] When in 1808 Mahlon Rogers opened a factory to make steam engines, Pittsburgh became

[18] For capital formation in Pittsburgh's iron industry, see L. C. Hunter, "A Study of the Iron Industry of Pittsburgh before 1860" (unpublished doctoral dissertation, Harvard University, 1928), 338ff. For glass, the city's second industry, see W. Bining, "The Glass Industry of Western Pennsylvania, 1797–1857," *Western Pennsylvania Historical Magazine*, XIX (1936), 258. For many smaller interests, see Douds, "Merchants and Merchandising," 129–130.

[19] Reiser, *Pittsburgh*, 203; *Niles' Register*, May 28, 1814.

[20] Francis Baily noticed the importance of this industry as early as 1797: "Ironmongery forms another considerable article of commerce in this town, but it is chiefly of the coarser sort, such as is used for . . . ploughs, and the various articles of husbandry" (*Journal*, 147); *Pittsburgh Gazette*, February 23, 1799; Hunter, "Iron Industry," 6.

[21] This change can be seen in McClurg's advertisements. *Commonwealth* (Pittsburgh), June 11, 1806, and February 1, 1809.

the machine provider for the West. But whether the blacksmith pounded metal bars into implements or factories poured castings, they both used refined iron which had been processed in rural furnaces.

The establishment of the town's first rolling mill in 1811 was the next step in bringing ironmaking to the city.[22] Now Pittsburgh imported large slabs of iron, called blooms, which could be much more easily reduced to bars by steam rolling than by water-driven hammers on country streams. In 1819 another rural function became urbanized when the Union Rolling Mill introduced the puddling process, which refined the metal in the factory. The mines then furnished Pittsburgh with pigs — irregular masses of crude iron — rather than blooms. By 1830 the entire iron industry had moved to the city, divesting the countryside of all but the extractive role, and transforming a commercial town into America's "Iron City."

The growth of the industry reflected the advantages of this centralization. In 1815 Pittsburgh turned out over $750,000 in iron products, a fourteenfold increase in a dozen years. More important, however, than the statistics of expansion were the implications of the technological shift they denoted. Steam power quickly replaced water power, not only in Pittsburgh but in other Western cities as well. As it did so, settlement patterns were altered and the drive toward urbanization intensified. Water power had meant dispersion, the location of machines on many rivers and streams, and an emphasis on local markets. Steam power required concentration, location near reservoirs of raw materials and human skills, and large-scale production for extensive markets. Pittsburgh's iron industry set off this quiet revolution by making machinery available at reasonable prices and leading in the adoption of new methods.[23]

[22] *Commonwealth* (Pittsburgh), March 11, 1811. This was not the first rolling mill in the Western country, at least four others having been established in the Pittsburgh region before it. J. M. Swank, *History of the Manufacture of Iron in All Ages* (2nd edn., Philadelphia, 1892), 216.

[23] Reiser, *Pittsburgh*, 203. Even flour milling early turned to steam; see *Commonwealth* (Pittsburgh), December 6, 1809; February 9, 1810; June 1, 1810.

While Pittsburgh's iron manufacture grew because metal goods were too heavy and costly to carry across the mountains, its glass industry flourished because that material was too fragile for rough overland conveyance. Colonel James O'Hara began making glass in 1795 in the first such factory in the United States to use coal for fuel. In 1803 the town's two houses produced $13,000 in white and green glass. By 1810 this figure had jumped to $63,000, and five years later a half-dozen firms valued their product at $235,000. Though commercial capital established the first factories, others were owned by men who had earlier worked in local plants.[24] Benjamin Bakewell opened the most famous one in 1807. It was his work more than any other which made "Pittsburgh Glass" a label of quality and beauty throughout the nation.[25] By the time peace with Great Britain came, glass was firmly entrenched in the city's economy, ranking next to iron in value and employment.

Success in manufacturing did not cause Pittsburgh to neglect commerce. Indeed, industrial expansion lent new urgency to the young city's economic connections with the outside world. Located at the head of water navigation in the West, the town turned down river where it found outlets either in settlements along the Ohio or in New Orleans. Though promising, this kind of trade involved many risks. Markets were unpredictable and payments were often delayed. Most of all, merchants could not foresee conditions in New Orleans and were unable to calculate the best time to send their merchandise there. In 1814, Zadock Cramer estimated that "nine out of ten lose rather than gain by the trip."[26] Yet, despite many handicaps, the commerce of the "Iron City" continued to expand.

By 1815 Pittsburgh surpassed Lexington as the largest town in the

[24] D. Daniel, "The First Glasshouse West of the Alleghenies," *Western Pennsylvania Historical Magazine*, XXXIII (1949), 97; Reiser, *Pittsburgh*, 203; W. Bining, "The Glass Industry," 256.

[25] Ease of water transit allowed Bakewell's glass to circulate widely both in the West and East. See, for example, *Missouri Gazette*, December 6, 1809; *Western Spy* (Cincinnati), May 24, 1809; *Pittsburgh Gazette*, December 6, 1809. The last tells of the acceptance of Pittsburgh glass in Philadelphia.

[26] Z. Cramer, *Cramer's Almanack*, 1814 (Pittsburgh, 1814), 63.

West, and was unchallenged in importance. Travelers had early recognized it as "the key to the Western territory," but now it was more than a gateway. Pittsburgh merchants traded on the Mississippi as well as on the Atlantic seaboard, while ships built on its wharves frequented the West Indies and Europe. "Iron City" manufacturing was already as famous as its smoke was notorious. The war stimulated almost breath-taking expansion in all commercial and industrial enterprise, and only pessimists thought that this handsome edifice might shake under the impact of peace. Henry Marie Brackenridge answered the timid in 1816 by reminding them "that *before the war*, the western country, so far from being at a stand, was flourishing in the most surprising degree: and certainly nothing has occurred since the war" to produce an unfavorable change.[27]

Lexington, like Pittsburgh, owed its early importance to commerce, but in the first decades of the century it turned increasingly to manufacturing. Though landlocked, in a country where the main highways of travel were rivers, the city grew so rapidly that in 1815 *Niles' Register* predicted it would be "the greatest inland city in the western world." Situated on an "extensive plain of the *richest land*," it had been Kentucky's central mart since its savage days. The road from Limestone connected Lexington with the Ohio by a trip of only two and a half days, and the Wilderness Road tapped Virginia and the Carolinas by a land passage which, though long and difficult, was much traveled. The town's merchants, using Eastern goods brought over the water route, supplied "not only their own state, but that of Tenasse [*sic*] . . . and part of the Indiana territory." [28] As the hemp industry grew, however, traders turned to manufacturing

[27] T. M. Harris, "Journal of a Tour . . . Northwest of the Alleghany Mountains," in Thwaites, ed., *Western Travels*, III, 342; "HMB" in *Cramer's Almanack for 1816*, 39.

[28] *Niles' Register*, January 28, 1815; T. Ashe, *Travels in America, Performed in 1806, for the Purpose of Exploring the Rivers Allegheny, Monongahela, Ohio, and Mississippi, etc.* (London, 1808), 193.

cordage, bagging, and sail, and, later, under the impact of embargoes and war, expanded into other industrial areas as well.

During the resulting prosperity, Lexington's population speedily increased. It expanded from 1,795 to 4,326 in the ten years following 1800, and by 1815 travelers estimated it at from 6,000 to 7,000. A large number of the townspeople were Negroes, mostly slaves, though a few were free. Indeed, the colored population in this period grew more rapidly than the white, rising from 461 in 1800 to 1,594 in 1810, when it comprised over thirty-five per cent of the whole. This growth bred a general optimism about the future that most visitors and natives shared. John Melish commented that "as it is progressing in manufactures and wealth, and the adjoining country is rapidly settling up, there is every probability that it will increase in the [same] ratio for a considerable time to come." [29] Swelling numbers, then, created a widening home market that was one of the important props of the young city's economy.

Though an increasing number of Lexingtonians sought employment in industrial enterprises, and the newspapers constantly encouraged the immigration of skilled tradesmen, the town's basic business was commerce. Like Pittsburgh in the Ohio Valley, it became the pivotal dispatching point for Eastern goods needed on Kentucky and Tennessee farms, and, in turn, the merchandiser of the hemp, grain, and tobacco that increasingly flowed from Western soil to outside markets.

Initially mercantile profits were great. Manufactured goods were scarce and traders few, and the demand was constantly expanding. Samuel and George Trotter, for example, came to Lexington in 1797, and "for a series of years," a contemporary asserted, "nothing equalled" their wholesale business where "sales amounted to Sixty thousand dollars per month for some length of time." Some others grossed $100,000 monthly during the busiest season, though their sustained earnings were less. These handsome profits attracted an increasing number of people into the mercantile field. John Melish estimated that in 1810 there were thirty retailers, and wartime inflation brought many newcomers. "Men were tempted to engage in

[29] United States Census, 1800, 1P; 1810, 71a; Melish, *Travels*, II, 187.

business with slender capital and fake and chimerical hopes," one observer later recalled, and even "Farmers and Mechanics essayed to become Merchants." [30] Many of these enterprises ultimately came to grief, but in 1815 few doubted the soundness of the town's commercial position.

Consistent profits from mercantile ventures enabled some Lexingtonians to accumulate sizable capital reserves. Though most of these earnings went into land speculation and opulent living, many merchants invested heavily in manufacturing. The continued unfavorable trade balance with the East combined with huge hemp surpluses on the Blue Grass to promote large-scale production of cordage and bagging. Merchant-manufacturers like Thomas Hart and the January brothers, foreseeing the increasing demand for cloth and rope in the West, opened factories in the 1790's. The beginnings were modest until the commercialization of cotton in the South created a new market for both rough cloth and twine. By 1809 there were "13 extensive rope-walks, five bagging manufactories, and one of duck," with a total output of over $500,000. In 1814 *Niles' Register* asserted that the number of ropewalks had doubled since 1810, some of them being *"very* extensive establishments." [31]

While processing hemp was Lexington's principal industry, it comprised only a part of the general movement toward manufacturing. As early as 1801 "Cato," writing in the *Kentucky Gazette*, argued that the whole area might be turned over to it, and predicted that in textiles the town "might overtake the English in one year." Nine years later "eight cotton factories, three woolen manufactories

---

[30] W. Leavy, "A Memoir of Lexington and Its Vicinity," *The Register of the Kentucky State Historical Society*, XL (1942), 118; T. G. Gronert, "Early Trade in the Blue Grass," *Mississippi Valley Historical Review*, V (1918–1919), 317; Leavy, "Memoir," *Kentucky Hist. Soc. Register*, XLI (1943), 317.

[31] Michaux, "Travels," in Thwaites, ed., *Western Travels*, III, 200. Melish, *Travels*, II, 187. The *Kentucky Gazette* claimed that all nineteen were profitable, September 18, 1810. In 1811 D. B. Warden estimated hemp production in the city at $900,000: *A Statistical, Political, and Historical Account of the United States of North America from the Period of Their First Colonization to the Present Day* (Edinburgh, 1819), II, 341. *Niles' Register*, June 11, 1814.

an oil cloth factory" had begun operations. War shortages brought further diversification. A group of merchants formed the Lexington White Lead Company, and Thomas Copeland opened a factory for making steam engines. By the end of the hostilities the town boasted no fewer than six steam mills engaged in grinding grain, making paper, or spinning and weaving textiles. In one section of the city, along the fork of the Elkhorn, new industry grew so fast that townsmen referred to the district as "Manchester." Though one authority undoubtedly exaggerated in estimating industrial investment in Lexington at $2,500,000 in 1815, it is clear that the young metropolis had achieved in its own state a supremacy in manufacturing no less certain than its primacy in commerce.[32]

Lexington's industrialization was stimulated not only by an unfavorable trade balance and the proximity of such raw materials as hemp and wool, but also by a chronic shortage of labor. "The want of hands excites the industry of the inhabitants of this country," observed a traveler. "This scarcity proceeds from the inhabitants giving so decided a preference to agriculture, that there are very few of them who put their children to any trade, wanting their services in the field." The deficiency led to the widespread adoption of slave labor in the new factories, especially in hemp operations where the work was uncomplicated and special skills readily acquired. Though some operators owned enough Negroes to man their ropewalks, most of them were "hired out" by other slave-owners on a monthly or yearly basis. Many factories were extensive, a cotton and a woolen one each employing over 150 hands.[33]

In 1815 Lexington's optimism about its economic future exceeded even that of Pittsburgh. The contagious enthusiasm infected townsman, traveler, and speculator alike. "It is the seat of a great commerce, and has many flourishing manufactures," said one visitor,

---

[32] In *Kentucky Gazette*, August 3, 1801. Melish, *Travels*, II, 187; Leavy, "Memoir," *Kentucky Hist. Soc. Register*, XL (1942), 118; *Kentucky Reporter*, April 20, 1813; April 26, 1815; Leavy, "Memoir," *Kentucky Hist. Soc. Register*, XLI (1943), 317. Gronert, "Trade in the Blue Grass," 318.

[33] Michaux, "Travels," in Thwaites, ed., *Western Travels*, III, 200, 201; Warden, *Account*, II, 341.

who called it "the future metropolis of the west." Land values sky-rocketed, and "*town lots* sell nearly as high as in Boston, New York, Philadelphia or Baltimore, which shows that this is not a place in the wilderness, as some people suppose it to be." [34] The end of the war was certain to bring adjustments, but Lexington could meet them as well as the next city.

Yet a cloud drifted lazily toward the town. The steamboat *Enterprise*, docking at Louisville in 1815 after a successful run against the Mississippi and Ohio Rivers, demonstrated a new dimension of trade. Kentucky newspapers hailed this as a new and exciting era in the West's unfolding history. Few realized then that the next chapter of this story contained the economic ruin of Lexington, and that the steamboat, which liberated the new country from an unfavorable trade predicament, would be the agent of the disaster.

Increasingly diversified economies accompanied the growth of Pittsburgh and Lexington, but their most ambitious rival, Cincinnati, remained essentially commercial. Some thought this emphasis on trade excessive and even dangerous, and many merchants anxiously encouraged manufacturing. Yet in 1813 a native described the town as "a seaport," and three years later a local bard called it "THE GREAT EMPORIUM OF THE WEST." Cincinnati's strategic position in the Ohio Valley set it astride the great highways of travel and exchange, and around it lay the fertile farm lands of a considerable part of Ohio, Kentucky, and Indiana. "Thus it is the permanent mart and trading capital of a tract whose area equals the cultivable portion of New Hampshire, New Jersey or Maryland, surpasses the state of Connecticut and doubles the states of Rhode Island and Delaware taken together." As the mercantile heart of this vast hinterland, Cincinnati grew in two decades from a "remarkable sprightly, thriving town" to the West's most dynamic city.[35]

[34] *Niles' Register*, January 28, 1815; *ibid.*

[35] Quoted in C. E. Cabot, "The Carters in Early Ohio," *New England Magazine*, XX (1899), 352; *Liberty Hall* (Cincinnati), January 3, 1816;

Though the whole Miami region attracted large numbers of settlers after the crushing of the Indians in 1794, the proportional increase was greater in Cincinnati than in the surrounding country. With about 500 in 1795, the town doubled its residents during the next decade. This was merely a prelude, however, to the striking expansion of the next ten years. By 1810 there were 2,540 inhabitants, and four years later the population had reached 4,000. In the next 24 months more than 2,000 additional people crowded into the budding city to make their homes. This great influx caught Cincinnati unprepared, creating a serious housing shortage and pushing prices skyward in the local market.[36]

These population figures lost some of their meaning during the navigable season of the river, when immigrants streamed into town on their way to the interior, swelling the city and straining its already overloaded facilities. An early settler later recalled the "bustle and hurry" created by the sojourners who "thronged the streets as they took their departure for rich valleys on the banks of the Miamis."[37] The immigrant constituted an important element in Cincinnati's prosperity, for he not only purchased heavily while passing through but was utterly dependent for a year or two on the town's merchants for nearly every kind of supply.

Cincinnati, however, did not grow because immigrants stopped there; rather, settlers disembarked at the "Queen City" because it was the most important trading center between Pittsburgh and the Falls of the Ohio. Merchandise from Philadelphia, Baltimore and New York was sold there, and the older inhabitants of the region bought European and Indies imports in Cincinnati stores. In addition, an increasing number of artisans fashioned household and farm

Drake, *Statistical View*, 232; Josiah Espy, "Memorandums of a Tour in Ohio and Kentucky in 1805," *Ohio Valley Historical Series Miscellanies*, No. 1 (Cincinnati, 1870), 7.

[36] Drake, *Statistical View*, 142; United States Census, 1810, 62; *Western Spy* (Cincinnati), February 15, 1814; February 19, 1816; *Cabot*, "The Carters," 350.

[37] E. D. Mansfield, *Memoirs of the Life and Services of Daniel Drake, Etc.* (Cincinnati, 1855), 48.

implements for their fellow townsmen and the rapidly filling hinterland. Farmers on both sides of the Ohio took advantage of the
port's wharves and shipping facilities, or found a market for their
surplus grains in its mills and breweries. Lines of barges carried on
a lively trade with New Orleans, taking Western produce to the
Gulf and bringing back sugar, cotton, and molasses. These trade
patterns, established early, remained essentially unaltered until the
coming of the steamboat.

The city's commercial growth in the early nineteenth century
was not so much the result of opening new markets as of exploiting
established ones. The number of merchants rapidly increased. In
1805 there were twenty-four merchants and grocers, and four years
later John Melish estimated the number of merchants alone at
thirty and their annual importations at from $200,000 to $250,000.
In 1815 Daniel Drake counted over seventy mercantile establishments handling imported items. Shipments from Eastern cities,
especially Philadelphia and Baltimore, were still "much greater than
New Orleans," and many merchants "engaged in a wholesale business with . . . the adjoining country in Kentucky, Indiana and
Ohio." [38] Hence by the end of the war Cincinnati had carved a
commercial shed out of the surrounding country, and established
fruitful connections with both East and South.

Large companies were exceptional, most of this trade being carried
on by individuals, partners or "partial associations." Indeed, some
of this enterprise was "rugged individualism" in the literal sense.
One trader, for instance, made fourteen trips to New Orleans with
Miami flour, and walked home on at least eight occasions. But
successful entrepreneurs reaped handsome profits. "One New England man who came here six years ago with $300 traded to New
Orleans and is now worth ten thousand dollars in cash," testified
a merchant who himself was "making money very fast." The principal shippers, however, were small companies like Baum and Perry

---

[38] F. P. Goodwin, "Building a Commercial System," *Ohio Archeological
and Historical Quarterly*, XVI (1907), 322; Melish, *Travels*, II, 126; Drake,
Statistical View, 150; quoted in M. Neufeld, "Economic Life of Cincinnati,
1815–1840," *Ohio Archaeological and Historical Quarterly*, XLIV (1935), 67.

or Riddle, Bechtle & Co., which ran lines of barges rigged with sails between Cincinnati and the Gulf for more than a decade. In 1815 ten prominent business leaders — "Our first citizens for Integrity and wealth" — undertook a more elaborate scheme, involving direct trade with England and "making the Mississippi the channel of our imports as well as exports." One agent went to Liverpool and another to New Orleans to handle the trade. This operation was on a large scale, one shipment being valued at over $200,000.[39]

Cincinnati's major commercial problem stemmed from its remoteness from the manufacturing East and the great expense of transporting merchandise across the mountains. Prices in the West reflected this added cost, all of the increase being passed on to the consumer. The war years, 1812–1815, aggravated conditions by creating constant shortages of Eastern goods and raising prices still further. Two movements arose to cope with this situation. One hoped to make New Orleans not only the receiver of Western goods but the import center for Eastern products as well. "We must learn to ascend our natural current," urged a local editor.[40] The other sought to relieve the dependence on Atlantic cities by encouraging local manufacturing. Both of these drives enjoyed limited success, though neither disturbed Cincinnati's basic commercial matrix.

Upriver trade with New Orleans developed only slowly until the introduction of the steamboat, though rigged barges reduced freight charges from eight and nine dollars a ton to five and six. Hunt, Riddle & Co., the prime movers in trying to reverse the commercial flow of the Mississippi River, made some progress and believed that this upriver system was "everyday becoming more important."[41]

[39] *Western Spy* (Cincinnati), November 10, 1802. Goodwin, "Commercial System," 327. Quoted in Cabot, "The Carters," 348, 352. Goodwin, "Commercial System," 327. Hunt, Riddle & Co. to T. Sloo, Jr., November 7, 1815, MS, Aaron Torrence Papers (Historical and Philosophical Society of Ohio, Cincinnati). *Liberty Hall*, December 30, 1816.

[40] *Liberty Hall* (Cincinnati), August 21, 1815.

[41] Goodwin, "Commercial System," 327; Hunt, Riddle & Co., to T. Sloo, Jr., November 7, 1815, MS, Torrence Collection. The name of this company often included other members of the firm such as Baum, Burnet, Yeatman,

More spectacular and articulate was the campaign to encourage manufacturing in the city. Though travelers often predicted industrial expansion, and an increasing number of wood and iron objects were made in Cincinnati's shops, little manufacturing on a substantial scale developed in the first decade of the nineteenth century. Occasionally a successful merchant like Martin Baum invested in an iron foundry or a brewery, but this scarcely altered the commercial orientation of the town. Wartime scarcities, however, caused many to consider the advantages of local manufacturing. "It is well known," asserted a letter in *Liberty Hall*, "that a great city can be raised and an immense population supported, by extensive manufacturing establishments," so long as a home demand existed.[42] Another writer, worried about the continuous flight of hard money from the city, proposed a remedy: "to promote, by all means . . . the establishment of manufactures in every possible branch [the lack of] which drains us of our specie and operates against the accumulation of permanent wealth in Cincinnati." And when in 1815 Daniel Drake published his *Statistical View, or Picture of Cincinnati*, designed to attract immigration to the region, he emphasized its industrial opportunities rather than commerce.[43]

This manufacturing drive represented the major economic current in Cincinnati during and immediately following the war with Great Britain. Behind the campaign were the town's most important people, many of whom invested in some industrial project. Though much of the talk was merely speculative, the achievements were substantial. In 1815 Drake pointed to a steam sawmill, driven by a twenty-horsepower engine, capable of cutting two hundred feet of board an hour. The Cincinnati Manufacturing Company, owning

Anderson, Longworth, Platt, Spencer, and Findlay. This group represented the very top of Cincinnati's mercantile community.

[42] *Liberty Hall* (Cincinnati), August 28, 1815. The writer argued from the examples of Manchester, Birmingham, Philadelphia, Pittsburgh, and, less cogently, from Chinese cities, which he claimed "present a magnificent spectacle of manufacturing industry and enterprise."

[43] *Liberty Hall* (Cincinnati), August 14, 1815; Drake, *Statistical View*, 137–147. He devoted ten pages to manufacturing and less than half that to commerce.

a similar machine, used it in "an extensive woolen manufactory" which hoped to produce sixty yards of broadcloth daily. The same firm also planned to open a red and white lead factory capable of processing six or seven tons a week. The breweries had always been the city's great pride, and in 1815 they consumed 40,000 to 50,000 bushels of barley from the countryside. In that same year Anthony, Hough & Rees began glassmaking, and a few months later the Cincinnati Foundry advertised that it was ready to make copper, brass, and iron castings up to 700 pounds if "given a short time." By mid-1816 the movement had developed so well that one of its spokesmen, the editor of *Liberty Hall*, announced, "we are gratified in noticing the growing prosperity of the manufactures in this town." [44]

The symbol of the crusade, however, was the mammoth steam mill built on the river's edge and rising nine stories and 110 feet above the water — a monument alike to the "enterprising genius of the west" and the bumptious optimism of its entrepôt. This "stupendous pile" of brick and stone, which took three years to build, weighed over 15,000 tons and cost nearly $120,000. Half of the structure housed a seventy-horsepower engine, designed by Oliver Evans, which could grind 700 barrels of flour a week, while the other half was reserved for a woolen factory. Its massive blue limestone walls frowned over the water approach to the town, startling the traveler and awing the countryfolk. "It was much the largest building I had ever seen," Sheldon Kellogg remembered, "and I used often to count the number of stories it was in height." [45] For over a decade, until it was consumed in a spectacular fire in 1823, this mill was the showpiece of Cincinnati.

These manufacturing schemes, however, overextended local financial resources, causing many new firms to collapse in the postwar depression. As a result, this campaign probably retarded the city's

[44] Drake, *Statistical View*, 145–146; *Liberty Hall* (Cincinnati), August 28, 1815; September 25, 1815; January 1, 1815, June 17, 1816.

[45] Samuel R. Brown, *The Western Gazetteer; or Emigrant's Directory* (Auburn, New York, 1810), 277; S. I. Kellogg, Autobiography (typewritten MS, Ohio Archeological and Historical Society, Columbus).

industrial development, for throughout the twenties capital hesitated to invest in fields which had so recently proved fruitless. Cincinnati's economy turned again to commerce, though many citizens continued to preach diversification. Looking back over the abortive experiment, a contemporary observer caught its importance.

There was a class of men in Cincinnati, who would long since have given a different turn to the business of this country. Their experience and acquaintance with the *capacity* and *wants* of the west, gave them full power to appreciate the importance of manufacturing institutions, and they had made important preparation to embark in this interesting operation, when the storm broke that involved them in one general ruin, and made room for a new race of men, equally enterprising, equally valuable, but who were not sufficiently acquainted with facts, to induce them to enter upon an untried theatre of operations. The new population was composed of men of commercial habits, and, flattered by the immediate prospects of realizing immense profits in their business, which required no preparation, and involved no loss of time, they devoted themselves at once to mercantile pursuits.[46]

Unlike other Western towns, St. Louis in the first decades of the nineteenth century still had an Indian problem which reduced immigration and retarded its economic development. Even after the transfer of the Louisiana Territory to the United States, the red men kept the area around the town lively. Though most of the trouble occurred in the hinterland, the city itself acquired a reputation for wildness. The stigma was partially self-imposed, for the *Missouri Gazette* constantly overstated the danger, hoping to panic federal troops into "exterminating . . . those vicious bands." [47] Farther east, where Indian warfare was now a memory, St. Louis was regarded as a savage place. Frederick Bates, the Secretary of the Louisiana Territory, tried to calm the fears of a Kentucky friend who

[46] B. Drake and E. D. Mansfield, *Cincinnati in 1826* (Cincinnati, 1827), 59–60.

[47] *Missouri Gazette*, December 7, 1808; see also issues of July 26, 1808; August 2, 1808; May 30, 1811; June 27, 1811; March 21, 1812.

contemplated moving west. "No thank God! we are not yet scalped, and indeed it is only the extreme frontier which appears to be in any danger. Our villages are as safe as Lexington." [48]

The fear, though greatly exaggerated, kept many immigrants away from St. Louis. Indeed, a petition to Congress in 1812 complained that some people were moving back across the river for safety. In the first decade of the nineteenth century only about five hundred residents were added to the town's population. Ironically, however, the outbreak of war with Great Britain in 1812 created the security needed to attract the hesitant by bringing troops into the area, and in 1815 St. Louis had around two thousand inhabitants. This "astonishing emigration" found the young city unprepared to handle the influx. Housing shortages developed, rents leaped upwards, and pressure on town lots for building forced constant division. [49] The somnolent capital of Spanish Upper Louisiana suddenly became a boom town in the center of a rapidly expanding region.

Under the American flag as well as under Spanish or French authority, St. Louis's most important economic activity remained the fur trade. As early as 1769 an official Spanish report stated that "the sole and universal trade consists in furs." The town was the child of a fur company, and that business remained for three-quarters of a century its most important interest. Not only was this trade the core of St. Louis's economy, but the river metropolis was the commercial heart of America's fur empire. Almost all expeditions organized and outfitted there; all the principal companies centered in St. Louis, or had important branches there; most of the skins seeking markets in the East and Europe passed through there. It was the focus of activities that stretched north to the Canadian border and west almost to the Pacific. "It is doubtful if history affords the example of another city," wrote the industry's most dis-

---

[48] Quoted in T. M. Marshall, *Life and Letters of Frederick Bates* (St. Louis, 1926), II, 229, 232.

[49] *Missouri Gazette*, November 21, 1812; J. A. Paxton, *St. Louis Directory and Register* (St. Louis, 1821), unfolioed; United States Census, 1810, 84; *Missouri Gazette*, December 9, 1815; May 18, 1816.

tinguished historian, "which has been the exclusive mart for so vast an extent of country as that which was tributary to St. Louis." [50]

The great stimulus to St. Louis's fur industry was not the coming of the Americans in 1804 but, rather, the Lewis and Clark expedition. This brought new information about the resources of the Northern Rockies, and presented an opportunity to the town to regain the supremacy lost to the British twenty-five years before. Manuel Lisa organized this movement in 1808 by bringing the principal traders of the town together in the Missouri Fur Company. St. Louisans carefully kept power in their own hands by providing in the constitution that new members could be admitted only by unanimous consent. Directed in part against John Jacob Astor, this restrictive policy excluded Eastern investors who might have alleviated the chronic financial shortages which hampered the company's operations.[51]

The firm never fulfilled its own hopes, yet the entire fur industry of St. Louis took on new life. In 1811 more than three hundred American trappers and traders were in the Columbia River area, and the *Missouri Gazette* estimated that the trade above the mouth of the Missouri alone exceeded $100,000 a year. But war with Great Britain halted this promising expansion. Hostility with the Indians sharpened, trade was disorganized, and the European market was shut off.[52] When the fighting was over, however, the young city was ready and anxious to renew its effort to commandeer for itself the rich trade of the interior.

Though fur was the town's main economic prop, lead continually gained in importance.[53] The most productive mines were in Wis-

[50] Quoted in Houck, *Missouri*, II, 243; H. M. Chittenden, *The American Fur Trade of the Far West* (New York, 1902), I, 99.

[51] I. Lippincott, "A Century and a Half of Fur Trade at St. Louis," *Washington University Studies*, XIV (1916), 226; Chittenden, *Fur Trade*, I, 140, 156; K. W. Porter, *John Jacob Astor, Business Man* (Cambridge, Mass., 1931), I, 61, 62, 273–5.

[52] *Missouri Gazette*, April 11, 1811; *Missouri Gazette*, April 25, 1812; *Missouri Gazette*, June 5, 1813; Chittenden, *Fur Trade*, I, 146.

[53] This interest was older than the city, and one of its historians contended

consin and Missouri, and initially Ste. Genevieve became the chief shipping port because of its proximity to those mines. However, the same considerations which made St. Louis the center of the fur trade ultimately combined to establish it as the central mart for lead. It was the only town on the river which could assure a constant stream of supplies into the digging areas, and which could provide the capital needed for equipment and land.

It is hard to estimate the exact value of the lead industry in St. Louis's economy, but contemporaries thought it extremely important. In 1811 the *Missouri Gazette* observed that "the peltry and fur trade is diminishing, and that it is necessary to give up in part the old staple, and turn . . . attention to the more important one of lead." The glass factories of Pittsburgh and the shot industry of Philadelphia comprised the major market, though large quantities also went down the Mississippi to New Orleans.[54] The Eastern demand increased as American-British relations disintegrated, and by 1813 trade was considerable, not only in crude metal but in its red and white processed forms as well.

Commerce in both lead and furs depended less on the size of St. Louis than on its advantageous location. The emergence of the town as a mercantile center, however, was connected with its growth in numbers and wealth. While nearly all merchants engaged in fur and lead trading to some extent, many turned increasing attention to the local market. A dozen general stores lined Main Street in the heart of the business district, serving the mounting population of the young city and the surrounding area. Most of their merchandise came from Philadelphia and Baltimore, though some came up the Mississippi from New Orleans. A few merchants dealt on a grander

that "it may be almost said that St. Louis owes its existence to lead." Scharf, *St. Louis*, II, 1249.

[54] *Missouri Gazette*, June 20, 1811; Philadelphia manufacturers like Wetherill, Baker, Gratz, and Strong were large importers, making shot of all sizes. Gratz received 4,000 pigs in one consignment. Bakewell's glass works in Pittsburgh was a heavy consumer; in 1814 Christian Wilt, the leading lead manufacturer in St. Louis, sold his entire stock to that firm. Sister M. Jennings, *A Pioneer Merchant of St. Louis, 1810–1820, the Business Career of Christian Wilt* (New York, 1939), 83.

scale, like Charles Gratiot, who was "better known in Paris, London and Geneva than on this continent."[55]

Regional trade developed rapidly. As Brackenridge noticed in 1811, the "settlements in the *vicinity* on both sides of the Mississippi, resort to this place as the best market for their produce, and to supply themselves with such articles as they may need." This demand put greater emphasis on local specification and taste. One merchant, noticing this, urged his Eastern agent to send a greater variety of shoes because "some of the 'aime fairs' have monstrous feet and some of the Creoles *mighty* small ones. . . . Pointed and old fashioned kid and morocco shoes will never sell," and "the fur bonnets won't sell because they are not the proper form." Newspaper advertising constantly catered to St. Louisans with Philadelphia and Baltimore stylings.[56] As the city grew, many merchants came to recognize the townsmen as their most regular customers.

But they did not have to discover the army as a good customer, for ever since the early days of Indian hostilities, trade with the troops, either in the neighborhood or up the rivers, was an important source of income for the town. With the coming of war and the spectacular rise in prices this trade flourished. Though fighting in the St. Louis area was negligible, the garrisons and volunteer corps needed provisions, and St. Louis merchants were quick to respond. Bernard Pratte, Sr., for example, who supplied the Illinois Mounted Rangers, made $10,000 a year on this single operation.[57] When the conflict was over, this trade declined but did not disappear. Troops remained on the frontier, and government "factories" were established among the Indians, both creating a regular and lucrative market for St. Louis.

By 1815 the outlines of St. Louis's economy had been established. Though manufacturing existed on a limited scale, commerce was the fundamental activity. The town was both the distributing center

[55] Quoted in Scharf, *St. Louis*, II, 287.

[56] *Missouri Gazette*, March 21, 1811; quoted in Jennings, *Pioneer Merchant*, 176–177; *Missouri Gazette*, September 1, 1808; September 14, 1808; November 9, 1808; August 2, 1809; March 1, 1810.

[57] Jennings, *Pioneer Merchant*, 174.

for Eastern goods on the Mississippi frontier and the dispatching point for Western produce to the outside world. Though but a new community of two thousand people, its trade stretched across much of the continent. Trappers from St. Louis gathered fur in the Rockies, while its traders haggled over prices in New Orleans, New York, and London. Lead dug in Wisconsin and processed on the town's edge was sold in Pittsburgh and Philadelphia. Farmers from both sides of the Mississippi brought their surplus to the rising metropolis, whence it was forwarded to New Orleans. Watching the almost imperial extent of this trade, Henry Marie Brackenridge prophesied in 1811 that "St. Louis will become the Memphis of the American Nile." [58]

Louisville, like St. Louis, grew with river trade. Its strategic location "at the head of ascending and the foot of descending navigation," a contemporary observed, meant that "all the wealth of the western country must pass through her hands." Its major business was the transshipment of goods around the Falls when the water was low and the rapids treacherous. Wagons carried merchandise two miles south to Shippingport, or brought them to Louisville from there, while passengers dined and purchased in the town's taverns and stores. Though the introduction of the steamboat made "the prosperity of Louisville . . . a fixed fact," its wharves already reflected the increased river trade of the West. In the three months ending July 18, 1814, twelve barges totaling 524 tons and seven keelboats amounting to 132 tons docked at the port with cargoes valued at $266,015. Steam navigation, however, soon transformed this halfway house on the Ohio into a commercial center whose expansion a native called "perhaps unparalleled in the history of nations." [59]

This mercantile prosperity and promise attracted a growing number of people to Louisville. Gilbert Imlay had found "upwards of

[58] *Missouri Gazette*, March 21, 1811.

[59] Casseday, *Louisville*, 121; 138–39; McMurtrie, *Sketches of Louisville*, 193.

two hundred houses" at the Falls in the 1790's, though the official census listed only 359 inhabitants at the end of the century. By 1810 that figure jumped to 1,357, and it doubled again in the next five years. The Negro population increased with the white, remaining at about a quarter of the total throughout the period. No doubt this population growth would have been even greater had it not been for the widespread belief that the town was "sickly." [60]

The new residents prospered with the older ones. The city's tax lists provide a convenient index of economic expansion. In 1803 officials assessed the townspeople's property at $90,550. A decade later the value had risen to $189,797, and just two years later the figure was $326,705. In addition, McMurtrie noticed the rapid appreciation of real estate during the same period. "For a length of time after the settlement of this place, lots on the principal streets were sold at from $700 to $1,400," he recalled. But by 1815 the same land went for $4,000 and $5,000. Moreover, local financial circles expressed their confidence in Louisville's future by opening there a branch of the State Bank of Kentucky in 1815.[61]

These generally favorable prospects brought forth a lively manufacturing interest. As early as 1810 Richard Steele proposed to build an iron factory at the Falls, where he would have "the advantage" of "working with slaves." Two years later Paul Skidmore's iron foundry turned out steam engines on a modest scale. In 1815 the Tarascon brothers began work on the Merchant Manufacturing Mill, one of the most ambitious industrial projects of the time, which was six stories high and ultimately cost $150,000. At the same time a New England company erected an immense distillery to carry on its business "in a much more extensive mode than any hitherto established in the United States." Louisville's first historian could later say of the early period that "nothing particularly interesting is known beyond the hair-breadth escapes, and daring expeditions

[60] Imlay, *Western Territory*, 35; United States Census, 1800, 359; United States Census, 1810, 72a; Cuming, "Sketches of a Tour," in Thwaites, ed., *Western Travels*, IV, 260.

[61] Louisville, Trustees Book, July 9, 1803; December 10, 1813; March 10, 1815; McMurtrie, *Sketches of Louisville*, 116.

of Indian warfare until we come to the establishment of steamboat navigation," but in fact the years were marked by enterprise and economic growth.[62]

Though each town evolved an economy peculiar to its own location and resources, some elements were shared by all. The central nexus of the urbanization of the West was commerce. All towns sprang from it, and their growth in the early years of the nineteenth century stemmed from its expansion. The Ohio River was the chief agent of this development, and the towns on its banks were the initial beneficiaries. Remoter places did not participate in this prosperity, and even Lexington found its landlocked situation an increasing handicap. But other factors too played an important part in laying the economic foundations of frontier urbanism, notably the influence of the army, the tide of immigration, the emergence of manufacturing, the development of banking, and, most spectacular of all, the coming of the steamboat.

Though the army was never popular in Western towns except in time of danger, its influence on the economies of these communities was immense. Not only did the troops protect infant settlements against Indian raids and foreign incursions, but, more important, their purchases provided a constant stimulus to urban expansion. "The increase of Pittsburgh was not rapid until 1793," a contemporary observed, but in the next year the Whisky Rebellion brought 15,000 soldiers into the region, "throwing into circulation a good deal of public money," and giving the town "a new and reviving impulse, it having since that time progressed very rapidly." [63] Throughout the nineties Pittsburgh served as a supply headquarters

[62] R. Steele to W. Lytle, December 15, 1810, MS, William Lytle Collection (Historical and Philosophical Society of Ohio, Cincinnati); Casseday, *Louisville*, 134. McMurtrie, *Sketches of Louisville*, 163–64; 127; 109.

[63] S. Jones, *Pittsburgh in the Year Eighteen Hundred and Twenty Six* (Pittsburgh, 1826), 26. For example, see *Liberty Hall* (Cincinnati), May 6, 1812; September 25, 1812; October 27, 1812; March 25, 1813.

for troops in the Northwest, and when war came in 1812 the young manufacturing city provided Western forces with ordnance and shot. For better than two decades the army was the town's best customer, and many local fortunes were built on this trade.

Cincinnati, too, from its very first days, profited from federal military spending. Since it served as an outfitting depot for operations against the Indians and later the British, the army leaned heavily on the town's merchants. During the war this dependence deepened. Troops rendezvoused in the Queen City before heading to the front, and left behind hard money badly needed in the town. Indeed, government buying became so great in 1813 and 1814 that local prices suddenly rose, contributing to the general optimism that launched the overly ambitious manufacturing drive in the war years.[64] Though no estimate can be accurate, the total amount of this spending was immense, and its abrupt cessation undoubtedly contributed to the sharpness of the postwar decline.[65]

The role of the military in the economic development of other Western towns is a similar story. An exposed settlement such as St. Louis still looked to federal troops for protection, and in time of war became a garrison site. In addition, it benefited in peacetime from supplying the line of forts that the army strung along the Western rivers to pacify the Indians and control fur trading. Curiously enough, during the War of 1812, the navy rather than the army patronized Lexington, whose hemp manufacturers replaced foreign providers of marine and sail cloth for oceangoing vessels. One factory alone filled a $12,000 order for sails, and in the last two years of the conflict Kentucky manufacturers provided over 180 tons of yarn and rope.[66] In some cases this military purchasing was smaller and irregular, but the government was always the most sought-after customer, because its payments were prompt and in

[64] W. S. Merrill, Diary, Oct. 16, 1820, MS, Merrill Collection (Historical and Philosophical Society of Ohio, Cincinnati).

[65] In November, 1812, the War Department sent $200,000 for the purchase of supplies in Cincinnati. J. Findlay to Office of Discount and Deposit, Pittsburgh, November 16, 1812, MS, Torrence Papers (H.P.S.O., Cincinnati).

[66] J. F. Hopkins, *A History of the Hemp Industry in Kentucky* (Lexington, Kentucky, 1951), 153–54; *Niles' Register*, June 11, 1814.

specie. In immature economies this priming stimulated commerce and often provided the surplus needed for modest beginnings in manufacturing.

In 1815 most adults in Western cities were immigrants. They came largely from the older sections of the country, but an increasing number arrived directly from Europe without loitering in the East. The population growth of these urban centers reflected the magnitude of the human stream that moved across the mountains into the West. The immigrant impact on their youthful economies, however, is not encompassed merely in numerical increase. These people did more than create an expanding local market; they also brought with them skills to perform new jobs and capital to invest in new enterprises. Choosing cities as carefully as farmers selected land, mechanics and entrepreneurs sought the place of maximum opportunity and brightest future. And Western towns competed for these urban migrants, advertising openings for profitable enterprise and specific types of employment.

As the cities grew, some turned to industry. By 1815 manufacturing had transformed the economic structure of Pittsburgh, made great strides in Lexington, and found advocates in Cincinnati and Louisville. Other towns, more modest in their hopes, embarked only on limited projects, usually for local purposes. Travelers, however, were astonished to see this remarkable development in an area so recently rescued from the wilderness. Some of this industrial growth proved artificial, having been stimulated by embargoes and war which kept foreign goods off the American market. In the depression that rocked the West at the close of hostilities many business firms failed, factories closed down, and widespread distress resulted. Yet even after this fat had been pared away, an impressive achievement remained. And the increasing adoption of steam power in Western factories strengthened the established urban pattern by concentrating manufacturing in the larger towns where labor and capital could be readily secured.

This development, remarkable as it was, might have been even more extensive if so much urban capital had not been drained off into land speculation. Most of the towns were older than the surrounding country, and capitalists tended to invest in nearby tracts, low in price, whose value was "certain to rise." Only in Pittsburgh, where much of the hinterland was either already appropriated or of poor quality, did commercial profits readily seek industrial channels. In other places the most successful merchants, finding land "a powerful inducement," tended to avoid manufacturing because of the high costs and uncertain returns. Daniel Drake, an influential spokesman for industrialization in Cincinnati, noticed this in his own city. "The conditions which . . . constitute the basis of manufacturing establishments, have not . . . existed in the same degree as if the town had been *younger* than the adjoining country." [67]

The towns were not only the commercial and industrial centers of the West, but its financial leaders as well. Though capital constantly streamed across the mountains into land or commercial enterprises, the new areas continually complained of a kind of colonial status, in which money always seemed to be moving eastward. Soon commercial interests began to demand some kind of banking facilities to increase the volume of money. But banks were unpopular, and new states hesitated to grant charters for issuing notes. Hence banking came to the West through the back door as part of the operations of insurance or trading companies. In 1802 the Kentucky Insurance Company at Lexington was given certain privileges of note issue in connection with its marine insurance, and subsequently put out a large circulation. Similarly, the Miami Exporting Company in Cincinnati, capitalized at $150,000 in 1803 as a trading company, turned four years later exclusively to banking. Pittsburgh's Ohio Company, organized in 1802 for Mississippi commerce, became a branch of the Bank of Pennsylvania within two years and dropped completely its earlier objectives. All these companies were composed of leading merchants, an indication of the intimate relationship between commerce and early financial institutions.

Soon Western states chartered banks directly. By 1815 Cincinnati had three, one without a charter, and all seemed thriving. The Miami Exporting Company had a "reputation and notoriety . . . equal to that of any bank in the western country," its dividends

[67] Drake, *Statistical View*, 142.

fluctuating between 10 and 15 per cent. The Farmers' and Mechanics' Bank with $200,000 of capital paid between 8 and 14 per cent, and even the unauthorized Bank of Cincinnati issued notes of "excellent credit." [68] These returns were so handsome that merchants began to circulate their own notes, usually without state sanction. In the same period Pittsburgh supported four banks. Indeed, during the war the whole West outgrew its antagonism to banks and developed a policy of easy incorporation. The issues of these institutions broke the log jam of scarcity and soon flooded the Western country with paper, most of whose value was questionable.

Nothing, however, accelerated the rise of the Western cities so much as the introduction of the steamboat. Expanding commerce offered attractive opportunities in new towns, and manufacturing created an increasing demand for skilled labor, but steam navigation, by quickening transportation and cutting distances, telescoped a half-century's development into a single generation. It was an enchanter's wand transforming an almost raw countryside of scattered farms and towns into a settled region of cultivated landscapes and burgeoning cities. The steamboat, observed James Hall, "has contributed more than any other event or cause, to the rapid growth of our population, and an almost miraculous development of our resources." The French Minister of Marine in 1824 also noted its impact on the urbanization of the Western country. "In the brief interval of fifteen years, many cities were formed . . . where before there were hardly the dwellings of a small town. . . . A simple mechanical device has made life both possible and comfortable in regions which heretofore have been a wilderness." Another contemporary, Morgan Neville, added his enthusiastic testimony. "The steam engine in five years has enabled us to anticipate a state of things, which in the ordinary course of events, it would have required a century to produce. The art of printing scarcely surpassed it in beneficial consequences." [69]

[68] Drake, *Statistical View*, 150.
[69] Hall, *The West*, 10; M. Marestier, *Mémoires sur les bateaux à vapeur des Etats-Unis d'Amerique* (Paris, 1824), 9–10; M. Neville, "The Last of the

Though developed in the East, the steamboat had a peculiar importance for the West. "The invention of the steamboat was intended for us," observed the editor of the *Cincinnati Gazette*. "The puny rivers of the East are only as creeks, or convenient waters on which experiments may be made for our advantage." The successful run in 1815 of the *Enterprise* up the Mississippi and Ohio from New Orleans to Pittsburgh established the practicability of steam navigation on inland waters, though the trip of the *Washington*, a larger ship, two years later, seemed more conclusive to contemporaries.[70]

The flow of commerce downriver was now supplemented by a northward and eastward movement, giving trade and manufacturing new opportunity for expansion and growth. "To feel what an invention this is for these regions," wrote Timothy Flint, "one must have seen and felt . . . the difficulty and danger of forcing a boat against the current of these mighty rivers, on which progress of ten miles a day, is a good one." The shift was not only one of direction, but of speed. "You are invited to a breakfast, at seventy miles' distance. You get on board the passing steam-boat and awake in the morning in season for your appointment." [71]

The coming of the steamer in 1815 wrought such basic changes that it might be said to have ended the first era in the urban history of the west. The watershed might be fixed a little earlier or later, but this technological innovation altered all the conditions of transmontane development. That year, moreover, saw the end of wartime prosperity and the beginning of the painful adjustment to a new economic situation. The date also has significance in the internal history of Western cities, for in 1815 Daniel Drake published his *Natural and Statistical View, Or, Picture of Cincinnati*, a book which represented a new awareness of the urban problems arising out of a generation of town-living on the frontier.

Boatmen," in J. Hall, ed., *The Western Souvenir, A Christmas and New Year's Gift for 1829* (Cincinnati, 1828), 108.

[70] Quoted in L. C. Hunter, *Steamboats on the Western Rivers: An Economic and Technological History* (Cambridge, Massachusetts, 1949), 4; 19.

[71] Flint, *Recollections*, 106; 108.

Chapter 3

The Emergence of Urban Problems

Legally cities are the children of states, but in the West many off-spring antedated their parents. With the exception of Pittsburgh, the major frontier towns were established before the creation of their states. Indeed, St. Louis saw a half century pass before Missouri entered the Union, while Louisville and Lexington were more than a decade old by the time Kentucky gained its independence from Virginia. Even the youngster, Cincinnati, had passed its tenth birthday when Ohio split off from the Northwest Territory. Though these places existed prior to their states, they possessed little local authority. Living under territorial law, they developed no governing power of their own. Hence, when the states turned to organizing the new settlements, they had no experience to draw upon, and had to lean on precedents developed in older parts of the Union.[1]

Eastern urban life was over a century old when the Revolution brought national independence to the colonies. The new state constitutions generally reaffirmed or regularized established practices or confirmed ancient privileges of local self-rule.[2] Town traditions were strong, and in Boston the claim was even made that that city constituted "an incorporated Republic."[3] Indeed, the strength of

[1] Laws in the Northwest Territory derived from Eastern state codes. In the compilation of 1795 nearly all statutes began with a clause acknowledging their source. Connecticut, Massachusetts, and Pennsylvania, as well as Kentucky, contributed part of the code. *Laws of the Territory of the United States North-west of the River Ohio* (Cincinnati, 1796), 7, 9, 11, 12, 23, 25, 28.

[2] O. and M. Handlin, *Commonwealth, A Study of the Role of Government in the American Economy: Massachusetts* (New York, 1947), 100, and M. Hoffman, *A Treatise upon the Estate and Rights of the Corporation of the City of New York as Proprietors* (New York, 1853), 32.

[3] Quoted in Handlin, *Massachusetts*, 100.

local bodies was so great that in some states towns received separate representation in constitutional conventions, and in Massachusetts the Commonwealth had to extend its authority quickly over the cities to head off possible arrogations of power.[4] Hence their charters recognized a long accumulation of prerogative and competence and bestowed broad governing rights.

In the West, on the other hand, town organization either did not exist or was very new before the adoption of state constitutions. Young communities had no experience with self-government, urban problems were still undefined, and rural interests clearly predominated. This situation tended to exalt state power. When local authorities petitioned for incorporation, legislatures responded with specific grants of narrow privileges. Indeed, Louisville's and Lexington's first rights extended merely over land, with no other authority.[5] The most striking feature of early city-state relations was this reluctance of parent bodies to yield power. Charters conceded small jurisdiction, and failed to allow for urban expansion. As towns grew, they created problems which could be met only with further legislation. Louisville's basic document was amended twenty-two times before 1815, and Cincinnati's underwent five major changes between 1815 and 1827, when a new charter replaced the patched one. Others, though altered less often, were constantly adjusted and remade until finally scrapped.

These charters varied greatly. This was partly because of their diversity of origin, Pittsburgh's authority deriving from Pennsylvania, St. Louis's from the Louisiana Territorial Government, Louisville's and Lexington's from Virginia and Kentucky, and Cincinnati's from the legislature of the Northwest Territory. But differences also existed between cities in the same state, such as Chillicothe and Cincinnati, which Ohio incorporated in the same year. Much of the variation stemmed from the nature of the problem it-

---

[4] C. C. Hall, *Baltimore, Its History and Its People* (New York, 1912), I, 3; Handlin, *Massachusetts*, 100.

[5] *Collection of Acts of Virginia and Kentucky,* 4ff; W. Littell, *The Statute Law of Kentucky: with Notes, Praelections, and Observations on the Public Acts* (Frankfort, 1809, 1810, 1811, 1814, 1819), I, 110ff.

self. Most of the states were new, and the towns quite small. No formula seemed to embrace the needs of all localities; power appropriate for a community of 2,000 became hopelessly inadequate for one of 6,000. "On fair experiment," Pittsburghers wrote to the Pennsylvania legislature in 1804, "[we] have found the existing law insufficient to promote conveniency, good order and public utility." [6] Yet experience was not a perfect guide, for even older states and much larger cities encountered constant difficulty. Indeed, so long as cities remained creatures of the state, urban governments would feel confined and claim that outside control needlessly complicated their situation.

Within their diversity, the charters had much in common, notably in the formal arangement of town government and the power it exercised. All provided for a single ruling council or board of about a half-dozen members, though the number tended to enlarge. Terms were short, never more than three years and ordinarily less. In every case, qualifications restricted election to city office, though these later became nominal. Usually officials had to be householders or freeholders having lived a year in town and paid a local tax. Cincinnati further required property equal to $36 annual rent, and Lexingtonians needed £25 in real or personal assets to serve. [7]

Qualifications for voting paralleled those for holding office, involving property and residence requirements. The disenfranchised, however, increasingly gained recognition, and some later charters extended the suffrage to all free adult males who had resided in the city for a year or perhaps two. But tax payment generally held on through the war period as a test for participation in municipal affairs. Pittsburgh erected no special bar against Negro voters in local elections, though the South from the beginning and Cincinnati by the 1820's denied both free colored people and slaves this right. Thus urban democracy in the West remained incomplete down to 1830, but in no case did it lag behind state practices of that date. And

[6] *The Statutes-at-Large of Pennsylvania* (Harrisburg, 1911), XVII (1802–1805), 648.

[7] *Laws of the North-west Territory*, III, 195; Littell, *Statute Law of Kentucky*, I, 110.

generally barriers came down more rapidly in the new country than in Eastern cities, where traditional privileges were deeply rooted and often difficult to alter.[8]

The charters also established the limits of town authority. Though states differed in the amount of power delegated or the nature of its exercise, they agreed that certain problems fell properly to local jurisdiction. The regulation of markets, the cleaning, repairing, and paving of streets, the removal of nuisances, providing water and lighting, and fire and police protection quickly devolved on the corporations. This legislation was permissive, allowing communities to proceed in their own ways and in their own time. Peculiar circumstances often induced additional grants, such as the restraining of slaves in Kentucky towns and St. Louis, or the licensing of pilots for Falls traffic at Louisville. Though many other items ultimately came under local control, basic urban problems very early became the responsibility of the cities.

Sometimes states surrendered jurisdiction only with reluctance. For example, county courts were slow to relinquish the right to try cases arising out of local ordinances, and the regulation of wharves and ferries, so important to river towns, remained uncertain for many years, entailing constant legislation. Often state law was so specific that it almost implied a denial of general authority. The accumulation of such special regulations became so clumsy, however, that broader provisions sometimes resulted. The Kentucky legislature, admitting in 1808 that "the several laws heretofore passed relative to the town of Louisville, are inadequate to the purposes intended," enacted an omnibus measure which amounted to a new charter. St. Louis, on the other hand, received in that same year a model charter which conveyed wide powers to meet specific problems and avoided later intervention in particular instances. In addition, it permitted the council "to pass such by-laws for the regulation of the place and common . . . as they shall deem necessary, if not

[8] See, for example, S. I. Pomerantz, *New York, An American City, 1783–1803* (New York, 1938), 133ff, for the struggle to extend popular control in New York.

contradictory to the laws of the land" — which represented a sweeping mandate.[9]

Though sometimes reluctantly, the states ultimately turned over to the cities the responsibility for managing their own affairs. But they withheld from local authorities the most important tool of self-government — the right to tax freely. All charters, with the exception of early Ohio grants, included stringent limitations on taxation. Sometimes expressed in a total sum, though more often in a percentage of property valuation, these boundaries were narrow. In the 1780's Lexington's levy could not exceed £100, while Louisville's maximum assessment was placed at a quarter of that amount. Restrictions on other towns varied, but the rate never surpassed one per cent of real and personal property, and in one instance Ohio set a limit at a fifth that figure.

When originally devised, these systems probably provided adequate income, but growing cities soon bumped their heads on such low ceilings. Louisville's case was typical. Almost a yearly supplicant in Frankfort, the town continually pleaded for greater taxing authority. The legislature responded by increasing its allowance, but never leaving much room for new needs. In 1803 $200 replaced the original £25, and for fifteen years repeated adjustments pushed the figure upward. Within two years it reached $800, and in 1812 the amount jumped to $2,000, only to be tripled with the next half decade. Lexington faced the same difficulty, and in 1810 a local editor uttered a familiar complaint. "Are we to be constantly running down to Frankfort — pray give us 1000 dollars, this year — 500 more the year after — and 100 more the next?"[10]

The cities, finding their revenue from taxation restricted, turned to other sources. Rent from market stalls, tavern licenses, wharfage, wagon, cart, and dray fees, and court fines all augmented receipts, but usually accounted for no more than a quarter of the whole income. Together with property levies, this money covered normal

[9] *Collection of Acts of Virginia and Kentucky*, 22; *Laws of the State of Missouri, Revised and Digested* (St. Louis, 1825), II, 766.

[10] Littell, *Statute Law of Kentucky*, I, 110; *Collection of Acts of Virginia and Kentucky*, 11, 21, 27, 32; *Kentucky Reporter*, December 15, 1810.

expenditures, but could not begin to meet any extraordinary demands on the treasury. Any large project, such as Louisville's drainage program, Pittsburgh's street-lighting scheme, or waterfront construction in Cincinnati, demonstrated the hopeless inadequacy of this budget situation. "The proceeds of seven years taxes," complained the trustees of Lexington in 1796, "will be insufficient to build stone bridges, and to make sewers for carrying off water, to sink wells and erect pumps . . . and to make such other repairs, as are necessary for the health, safety and convenience of their fellow citizens." [11] Inevitably local governments turned to financing improvements by borrowing, either from private banks or by issuing their own notes. When many overextended themselves in the war years and after, the states stepped in with debt-limitation legislation. This fiscal problem constituted the basic conflict between the two governing bodies. Many other issues developed, but the decisive struggle usually centered on this point.

Essentially, legislatures assumed a certain irresponsibility in town authorities, fearing that if left unrestrained they would jack up tax rates and impair the solvency of both city and state. Ironically, however, the class of men who dominated municipal affairs for better than four decades tended to share this anxiety. The merchants, who commanded the frontier's economy, also controlled its local government. From the very beginning, leadership gravitated toward them as representing at once the most wealthy and the most articulate segment of commercial settlements. An analysis of almost any elected body demonstrates this. For example, St. Louis's five-man

---

[11] In 1817 Cincinnati's total income was $12,857.96, of which $8,033.86 came from taxation and the remainder from these other sources. In the same year its expenditures reached $39,802. Street paving and repair amounted to $16,417, but this was raised by a special levy. The rest represented regular expenses plus more than $10,000 for a new wharf and waterfront repair. *Liberty Hall*, March 26, 1819; *Kentucky Gazette*, May 21, 1796.

board of trustees never contained fewer than three prominent traders, and ordinarily more.

To be sure, other influences were present. John Bradford, a newspaper editor, spent most of his adult life as a Lexington trustee, being chairman of the board numberless times. The same was true in St. Louis, where Joseph Charless of the *Missouri Gazette*, a familiar figure in public life, served frequently on the council. Cincinnati's physician, Daniel Drake, though never elected to office, filled many important appointive posts. Occasionally, too, artisans and tradesmen won places on municipal boards, but since the city paid no salaries, few could afford the time. Even when non-commercial elements were represented, however, they seldom conflicted with the mercantile viewpoint and certainly never challenged its supremacy.

Urban affairs were managed not merely by merchants, but usually by the most successful ones. In 1819, to cite but one instance, Cincinnati's thirteen-member governing body held property within the corporation valued at over $225,000, an average of more than $10,000 each, which placed most of them in a category with only thirty-eight other well-to-do Cincinnatians. In southern cities, traders were also large slave-owners, adding another ingredient represented in town government. In 1813 the eleven Lexington trustees, for example, owned a total of 146 Negroes within the corporation. These men were wealthy not only in slaves but in property as well. Assessment books reveal that the members paid taxes on over $90,000.[12] Throughout the West the pattern was everywhere the same, with city-council lists reading like the local business directory.

Despite its dominance of municipal affairs, the mercantile community constituted no rich man's cabal. Its official spokesmen were honest and well known, having been active in many areas of town life before being raised to public office, and if they ruled with a commercial outlook, their government reflected the attitude of most people. Since trade was the major pursuit of these towns, no other interest clamored for a hearing. Even manufacturing with its conquest of Pittsburgh and remarkable inroads in Lexington proposed

[12] Cincinnati Tax List, 1818, MS, Torrence Collection; Tax Assessment Book of the Town of Lexington, 1807–1809 (MSS, Lexington City Hall).

no urban program in conflict with that of the merchants. Indeed, industrial development grew out of commercial capital, and its owners combined both functions. Merchant-manufacturers like Lewis Sanders, James O'Hara, or Martin Baum served as council-men without any fracture of interest. So long as the economies of the cities remained young and undiversified, no basic differences complicated local administration, and elections for municipal offices revolved around personalities rather than matters of policy.

Mercantile control in city government had an important though subtle influence on the growth of town facilities in the West. This was not particularly visible in the techniques used to meet urban problems, for they would probably have been similar no matter what group or groups predominated. When faced with a variety of urgent questions, however, the merchants selected their issues in a way that reflected their commercial outlook. By 1815 needs had developed along many fronts, but since funds were limited, no city could embark on improvements all along the line. Authorities had to select programs carefully, realizing that some things would have to wait. If, for example, wharves were built, pond drainage might have to be deferred; a new market house would eat up money which could have been used for a night watch. In the establishing of these priorities the influence of the mercantile outlook was apparent. Henry Mc-Murtrie despaired as he watched Louisville spend on projects which had commercial importance while police protection ran downhill. "As long as the trustees or other officers are chosen from among mercantile men . . . so long will the town have to take care of it-self." [13] Merchant supremacy in local affairs, then, provides a frame-work for understanding the substantial urban development of frontier settlements in the first years of the nineteenth century.

Control of local trade was one of the oldest functions of cities, in both the Old World and the New. Hence it is not surprising that

[13] McMurtrie, *Sketches of Louisville,* 144.

authorizations of public money for market houses and detailed regulations for their operation were among the earliest ordinances. The community's obligation involved both laying down general rules and erecting and maintaining buildings. Occasionally private funds assisted in construction or buying land, and in some cases unofficial groups did both, but this did not mean escape from city law. When the Scotch Hill subscribers in Pittsburgh finished work on their market, they appealed to the town's burgesses "to be put under such Borough regulations as your Honourable Body may think proper." [14] Public control in this field constituted one of the greatest responsibilities of early municipal government.

Every town had at least one public market, and some boasted of more. Twice a week throughout the year farmers flocked to these exchanges to sell and barter, to deal with merchants and mix with the townspeople. Though initially only a few articles were involved in this trading, by 1806 Fortesque Cuming was "astonished at the profusion and variety of most of the necessaries and many of the luxuries of life" in Lexington. A decade later its "prices current" listed over 51 items, including a large group of manufactured products. [15] As cities grew, markets multiplied, Pittsburgh having three by 1811, and Lexington and Cincinnati two each a few years later. This expansion was premature, and many marts had to be abandoned in the postwar collapse. Nevertheless the market place remained for better than a half century the central economic institution of Western towns, and local officials showed a keen interest in its proper conduct.

They promptly adopted measures to protect the public against adulterated food, false measurements, and rigged prices. Their charters allowed legislation in the first two fields, and custom sanctioned the latter. Market ordinances in Western cities were strikingly similar. They alerted clerks to prevent the sale of "any

[14] Borough of Pittsburgh, Borough Papers, June 1, 1811 (MSS, Carnegie Free Library, Pittsburgh).

[15] Cuming, "Sketches of a Tour," in Thwaites, ed., *Western Travels*, IV, 182; *Kentucky Reporter*, January 8, 1817.

unsound, unwholesome . . . Meat or other provisions," and bread made of "injured flour or otherwise corrupted and rendered . . . unpallatable." St. Louis's 1819 ordinance was more graphic in this prohibition, stating that "no person shall sell or expose to sale any blown stuffed unsound unwholesome tainted or putrid meat or other articles or provisions or measly pork." The attending official was instructed to "seize upon all such as proves . . . defective" and bring the vendor before local magistrates, who levied fines up to $20 for the first offense and double that amount for the second.[16]

False weights and measures proved even more troublesome to townsmen than spoiled goods. Each town issued a series of ordinances to prevent fraud. The precautions included checking scales in the market house and inspecting coal, butter, lumber, and the like to make certain that the bushels, pounds, and cords were honest ones. As cities expanded, this policing became so complex that a clerk and his assistants could no longer handle the job alone, and new officials were appointed to measure separate items such as hay, salt, flour, or whisky. Certain products crucial to the local economy received more detailed treatment. In St. Louis, for example, firewood became so difficult to get in the twenties that a fuel crisis developed and regulations were tightened. The increasing amount of legislation covering more and more products bore testimony to the urgency of the problem and to the difficulty of enforcement.

The authority of local government went beyond merely establishing standards of marketing honesty. Its responsibilty involved nothing less than "seeing justice is done between buyer and seller." In search of this objective, towns fixed prices on some goods, sealed off the market from monopolists, and tried to equalize opportunities for small purchasers. Some charters included the assize of bread, and nearly all councils established some control over this key commodity. "A Mechanick of Pittsburgh" complained in 1813 that the price of bread was too high, adding that "the redress, it is believed, is

[16] Louisville, Trustees Book, May 25, 1819; Town of St. Louis, Ordinances, 1811–1823 (MSS, City Hall, St. Louis), April 6, 1816; September 18, 1819; *Missouri Gazette*, September 5, 1819.

within your power." Three years later St. Louis issued lists adjusting the price of flour and the weight of the loaf.[17]

When inflation swept the West following the war, Lexington legislated to hold down charges to the consumer. The Board of Trustees asserted that "it is the practice of Bakers in this town to vend Bread which bears no proportion to the price of flour as in other large Towns & Cities, in the United States and the civilized world generally." A loaf sold for six and a quarter cents, which gave the processer "a clear profit of at least 60 per cent; which is an imposition not suffered in any other part of the world." [18] No question was raised of the competence of the community to act, although the depression made the bakers honest before a law could be passed. Other items, such as tavern charges for room and board in Louisville and Lexington, were also fixed. But direct intervention represented only one segment of municipal activity in the market place.

A more important governmental function was the attempt to maintain equal opportunity for consumers in buying goods. The towns constantly strove to prevent "forestalling" and "huckstering," which raised prices. Under this system large merchants cornered the supply of some product on its way to market, procuring "whole wagonloads of certain articles, thereby thining [sic] the market at once." Cities tried to halt this practice by prohibiting the sale of goods outside the market in the hours it was open, or outlawing the interception of goods before they reached the exchange center. Ordinances also struck at the same evil inside the mart by forbidding sales to "hucksters" of "any kind of provision to sell again." Stopping these "grivous [sic] monopolizing practises" was difficult. Yet merchants on local councils had a great stake in preventing any-

---

[17] *Pittsburgh Gazette*, March 9, 1810; *Statutes-at-Large of Pennsylvania*, XV, 164; *Pittsburgh Gazette*, April 23, 1813; St. Louis, Ordinances, April 6, 1816.

[18] Lexington, Trustees Book, June 4, 1818. See also City of Pittsburgh, Minutes of the Pittsburgh City Council, 1816–1830 (MSS, City-County Building, Pittsburgh), November 4, 1820. In Pittsburgh the profit was estimated at 75 per cent. *Pittsburgh Gazette*, April 23, 1813.

one from rigging the market, and the body of legislation on this topic indicates their deep concern.[19]

If the market was the city's heart, its streets and highway approaches were its vital arteries. The passage of men and goods into town and through it represented the major business of trading centers, and the betterment of roads both in and around the corporation early earned the attention of local government. Hoping to facilitate movement, the towns paved central thoroughfares and regulated traffic. The aim was not simply the comfort and convenience of the residents, but to meet the important commercial need for rapid transit. It is significant that the first efforts and greatest funds went into paving avenues leading to wharves; only later did other surfacing get under way. The demand for these improvements was so great in the first decades of the nineteenth century that most municipal energy went into them, causing official council minutes to read more like street commissioners' meetings than the proceedings of a general legislature.

The first problem was the redemption of town land that had been originally reserved as a right of way. Lax supervision had permitted haphazard building, much of which spilled onto public property. In 1785, for instance, Lexington trustees warned "all persons having cabbins [*sic*], cow pens, hog pens or other inclosires [*sic*] whatever within the main streets of Lexington" to get them out within sixty days. The situation became so serious that cities instituted many recovery suits, indeed, sometimes against their most prominent citizens. Nor was the question ever completely settled. Municipalities had to keep on the alert for cellar entrances sticking into the street, trees obstructing traffic, and, later, wooden shop awnings hanging over sidewalks. But the towns pushed ahead energetically, for, as St. Louis's board chairman Clement Biddle Penrose predicted, "the

[19] Cincinnati City Council, Ordinances of the City of Cincinnati, 1801–1830 (MSS, City Hall, Cincinnati), December 3, 1812; St. Louis, Ordinances, May 20, 1823; Lexington, Trustees Book, October 21, 1800 — see also November 3, 1806, March 5, 1810, February 3, 1814; City of Pittsburgh, Council Papers (MSS, City-County Building, Pittsburgh), February 9, 1818.

more such encroach are prolonged the more difficult the recovery of property." [20]

The earliest streets were dusty in good weather and muddy in bad, and their uncleaned state evoked constant complaint from both visitors and residents. In 1806 Fortesque Cuming found only Market paved in Pittsburgh, while all other streets were so "extremely miry, that it is impossible to walk them without wading over the ankle." Nor were natives any more charitable. "Smug" later asked Pittsburgh's burgesses if it were true that "the mud, at the corner of 4th and Wood Street . . . has been reduced to the moderate depth of two feet." And there were other hazards. "Baptiste" contended that a person in St. Louis could not walk more than a few paces without having his "nerves assailed by the putrid carcasses of Hogs, Dogs, etc." that cluttered the pathways. Some of the obstructions were large enough to inconvenience even the most hardy. In Lexington, for example, the trustees hired "Davy," a free negro, to take "four dead cows out of the street." [21] As traffic increased, these bad conditions worsened, until some governments faced a near-crisis in transportation. In the years leading up to 1815, cleaning, repairing, and paving constituted the most extensive activity of Western municipalities.

In many ways the cleaning program proved more important than paving, for it involved all streets rather than merely the central ones, and even the surfaced areas needed constant attention. Initially the responsibility for sweeping and removing nuisances rested on the residents of the neighborhood, and town officials merely made periodic inspections to enforce relevant regulations. In some cities, however, a more systematic approach replaced this simple arrangement. In 1813 the trustees divided Lexington into ten wards or

[20] Lexington, Trustees Book, August 9, 1785; Cincinnati, Ordinances, January 8, 1803; City of Louisville, City Journal, 1827–1830 (MSS, City Hall, Louisville), July 25, 1829; Town of St. Louis, Minutes of the Board of Trustees, 1808–1823 (MSS, City Hall, St. Louis), December 13, 1813.

[21] Cuming, "Sketches of a Tour," in Thwaites, ed., *Western Travels*, IV, 76; *Commonwealth* (Pittsburgh), March 23, 1814; *Missouri Gazette*, April 12, 1809; Lexington, Trustees Book, August 5, 1805.

sanitary districts for "the purpose of employing scavengers to clean the streets of mud, dirt, fiilth &c." Three years earlier Pittsburgh had ordered that the job be done once a week "at the expense of the Borough," with a committee to supervise the work. But generally the streets remained ill-kept, cluttered with an assortment of "fire wood . . . Hog and pig fecus, dead animals, stable manure, shaving and litter from buildings," while authorities piled ordinance on ordinance in a vain attempt to improve matters.[22]

Very early the towns embarked on ambitious paving programs which aimed at surfacing at least central thoroughfares. Drawing on Eastern experience, they soon developed methods that were strikingly similar. Pittsburgh's 1807 ordinance, which embodied most of the features of such legislation, can be conveniently taken as a sample.[23] Decision to pave rested with the property owners of each block, two-thirds of whom could set the machinery in motion by petitioning the local authorities. Street commissioners or overseers then prepared the ground, put in the bed, and surfaced the area.

In some cities the owners paid for this improvement while the government provided only direction. In others the city performed the entire job and assessed the proprietors later. In still others the taxpayer wound up with the bill, when funds came directly from the treasury to undertake the task or when property holders received tax relief to the extent of their costs. Curbing and sidewalks, however, remained the obligation of those possessing land fronting on streets. Bridges across creeks within the corporation and roads leading to the city were financed from public funds. Activity along all these lines developed so rapidly that soon local governments established departments presided over by commissioners or overseers to attend to these matters. This work was also the most expensive municipal service, often claiming close to half the total budget.[24]

[22] Lexington, Trustees Book, February 11, 1813; *Pittsburgh Gazette*, March 9, 1810; Louisville, Trustees Book, May 18, 1805.

[23] Printed in *Pittsburgh Gazette*, June 16, 1807.

[24] In Lexington's 1811 budget street improvement and repair took $1,790 out

The rapid expansion of Western cities placed new burdens on primitive traffic systems. The problem was twofold: to keep vehicles moving and at the same time reduce accidents. These questions confronted the biggest towns first, and as early as the nineties Lexington and Pittsburgh legislated to slow down speeders. St. Louis prohibited carriages from traveling "quicker or beyond a moderate trot or pace, unless in case of urgent necessity," while Louisville laid fines for galloping horses within the corporation limits. More difficult to handle than reckless riders, however, was the clogging of passage by loitering carts and wagons. Ordinances forbade blacksmiths from shoeing in the streets, builders from blocking traffic with equipment, and vans from standing more than six hours while loading, while others were designed to prevent double parking and to keep all conveyances off public ways at night.[25]

By 1815, however, none of the cities had come close to resolving the problem of building adequate all-weather streets and keeping them clear and in good repair for the smooth flow of passengers and goods. Only a few streets in each town had adequate covering, and Cincinnati had none at all, though the council had been generous in granting power and funds for the purpose.[26] All kinds of obstructions littered even the best roads, slowing traffic and endangering health. A crisis developed which could be solved by nothing short of concentrated effort. By itself this situation would not have been dangerous, but it came at just the time that other urban questions demanded resolution.

Like markets and streets, the town's landing and wharves were of special interest to the mercantile community, and commercially minded councils spent time and money expanding and repairing

---

of a total income of $4,300. Lexington, Trustees Book, May 2, 1811. As late as 1828 Cincinnati paid out $14,221 from a budget of $38,800. Cincinnati City Council, Minutes of the Proceedings of the Council, 1813–1830 (MSS, City Hall, Cincinnati), March 24, 1828. Pittsburgh's 1814 expenditure on streets was $5,306 out of a total budget of a little over $10,000. *Mercury* (Pittsburgh), extra, March 28, 1815.

[25] St. Louis, Ordinances, February 9, 1811; Louisville, Trustees Book, May 6, 1811; *Pittsburgh Gazette*, August 31, 1804; May 21, 1813.

[26] See "Aristides" in *Liberty Hall* (Cincinnati), April 2, 1819.

them. Paving and cleaning the river bank and regulating traffic in boats constituted the government's chief function. It was difficult to keep water approaches free for incoming vessels, particularly at high water. Ordinances limited the stay of visiting craft, usually allowing only a few days for loading. Louisville's problem, however, was especially acute. Nearly every boat on the Ohio used its installations at one time or another, jamming its limited facilities. Hence its trustees limited the stay of any craft to forty-eight hours, and instructed the harbor master to sell the offending vessel if it parked overtime.[27]

Though the funds for keeping the landing in good repair came initially from general receipts, the cost soon became so large that most towns sought to meet expenses by wharfage. At first these charges were small. St. Louis's 1811 ordinance levied a tax of two dollars on all "Boats, Barges, & Pirogues" of over five tons which came from outside the territory, and fifty cents for every additional ton. Early nineteenth-century commerce on inland waters grew so rapidly that the facilities of these port cities became inadequate, and many searched around for room for expansion. Some bought up private docks, while others extended the public landings, and Pittsburgh joined with Bakewell's glass firm in a cooperative project of building new docks.[28] The coming of the steamboat in 1815 put a new strain on these limited installations, but until that time the handling of river traffic represented a conspicuous civic success in Western settlements.

๙౽

The development of police and fire protection had long been a subject of official attention, and as the cities expanded both rapidly reached a critical phase. Like cleaning and paving programs, they caused a heavy drain on small budgets; hence many towns initially tried various expedients to avoid large expenditures. But the prob-

---

[27] Louisville, Trustees Book, June 7, 1797.

[28] St. Louis, Ordinances, February 25, 1811; Pittsburgh, Borough Papers, August 1, 1812.

lems went beyond haphazard solutions. Increased population and wealth created greater inducements for criminals, while crowding and jerry-building enhanced fire risks. Though most towns had made important strides in securing life and property by 1815, all found the evils accumulated faster than the remedies.

All towns legislated very early to set up some police arrangement, but only those with large slave populations maintained men on the streets with any degree of regularity. In 1804 a wave of burglaries in Pittsburgh led to a temporary patrol, and a year later Cincinnati created a night watch in which all voters were forced to serve.[29] But both of these experiments lived only a short while, and protection and law enforcement reverted to county sheriffs and local constables. On the other hand, Lexington and Louisville organized systems supported largely or wholly by public funds. These were the most advanced in the West. Their purpose, however, was less the security of the inhabitants and their property than the control of slaves, and instructions to captains and men on the beat continually emphasized that function. Indeed, it was this fear of Negroes that provided Kentucky communities with the incentive, lacking north of the Ohio, to establish effective police.

As early as 1796 Lexington formed a modest watch, and four years later expanded it to cover nights and Sundays when citizens complained that "large assemblages of Negroes" had "become troublesome to the Citizens." The trustees appointed two men to "parade at least three nights in the week from nine Oclock until six Oclock in the morning." A decade later an ordinance laid off the town into five districts, doubled the personnel and provided each policeman with a "Rattle." In 1813 two additional men joined the force, and the watch was put on a 24-hour basis.[30] Louisville's progress, while less impressive, followed a similar pattern, though a part of the support came from private subscription.

Other Western towns acted only sporadically, marshalling civic

[29] *Pittsburgh Gazette*, November 25, 1803, August 31, 1804; *Liberty Hall* (Cincinnati), November 19, 1805.

[30] Lexington, Trustees Book, July 7, 1800; September 25, 1801; January 4, 1812, February 13, 1812; June 17, 1813, January 20, 1814.

forces when crime rates rose, but generally leaving the problem to irregular constabularies. St. Louis institutionalized this partial system in an 1811 ordinance which declared that "whenever circumstances shall require," the chairman of the Board of Trustees or any two justices of the peace could call out a patrol in which all males over 18 had to serve. Though St. Louis's Negro population was small, the law gave the same instructions for the restraint of slaves as in Louisville and Lexington. Three years later Pittsburgh organized its first paid watch, raising nearly $3,000 on a special levy for its maintenance.[31] Yet, as late as 1815, Cincinnati, the fastest growing transmontane city, had no night patrol, and indeed was not to get one for over a decade.

Establishing a force was only the first step in assuring adequate protection and law enforcement.[32] Departments had to draw up their rules and procedures, contrive methods of operation, and build morale. This was not easy, since salaries were low, facilities poor, and, evidently, temptations many, for often trustees had to shield the public from the police. Lexington authorities, for instance, received constant complaints about the "improprieties," "delinquency," and "sundry misdemeanors and neglect of duty" of their men.[33] Teen-agers and rowdies loved to "bait the watch," and even adults obstructed their work. In no town in 1815 were the police strong enough to quell riots or major disorders, or even to stop waves of vandalism.

Initially, municipalities used county jails, most of which contained only a few poorly kept and unhealthy cells where criminals and debtors, men, women, and children were indiscriminately mixed. Even "the calls of nature," charged the *Western Spy*, "are compelled

[31] St. Louis, Ordinances, February 9, 1811; *Mercury* (Pittsburgh), March 28, 1815.

[32] Poor enforcement was a familiar lament in every city. "We have had Hog Laws, Dog Laws, Theatre Laws, and Laws about Hay Scales . . . Kitchen Slops, Soap Suds, and Filth of every kind, and in no single instance have they been executed." *Kentucky Reporter*, August 26, 1809.

[33] For these examples, see Lexington, Trustees Book, May 2, 1808, April 14, 1814, September 15, 1814. For charges against Pittsburgh's constable, see *Commonwealth* (Pittsburgh), September 24, 1813.

to be answered . . . in the very apartment in which they are confined." [34] Discipline was impossible, and a Pittsburgh editor asserted that, "instead of being places for correction and amendment,
[they have] become scenes of debauchery, and means of corruption." Henry McMurtrie laconically described Louisville's jail as
"a most miserable edifice, in a most filthy and ruinous condition,
a first cousin to the black hole of Calcutta." [35] Their only redeeming
feature lay in the fact that escape was possible, and every town had
its spectacular breaks. Occasionally conditions became so bad that
civic indignation demanded improvement, but in the fight that
followed, advocates of economy prevented any real reform. Later,
cities constructed their own prisons, which somewhat alleviated
the crowding and promoted better sanitary facilities.

Police activity might have been greatly improved if street lighting
in Western towns had been better. But until 1815 only Lexington
provided its citizens with a public system. In 1812 the trustees authorized the erection of twenty lamps throughout the corporation, five
of them along Main Street. Samuel Trotter traveled to Philadelphia
at the treasury's expense "to examine the lamps in that City and
have one made for this place." By the end of the year the Blue
Grass metropolis became the first frontier city with night lighting.
A year later municipal officials added to this service by offering free
oil to those who put their own lamps on the street.[36]

In other communities taverns and homes provided the only illumination, but since lamp breaking was a popular outdoor sport of
Western teen-agers, only a few householders risked it. McMurtrie
observed that in Louisville "not a single lamp lends its cheering light
to the nocturnal passenger, who frequently stands a good chance
of breaking his neck." In Cincinnati, however, private lighting

---

[34] *Western Spy* (Cincinnati), March 31, 1817. A Pittsburgh grand jury in
1815 found the county jail "insecure" and objected to mingling debtors and
criminals. *Pittsburgh Gazette*, December 2, 1815. A sheriff's investigation in
St. Louis nine years earlier revealed similar conditions. Town of St. Louis,
Court House Papers (MSS, Missouri Historical Society), VIII, 45.

[35] *Pittsburgh Gazette*, June 8, 1793; McMurtrie, *Sketches of Louisville*, 122.

[36] Lexington, Trustees Book, January 18, 1812; Lexington, Trustees Book,
May 7, 1812; January 16, 1813.

spread rapidly after 1810, developing so haphazardly that it created a fire risk, and the council moved in 1815 to establish some control. A fine of $50 — one of the steepest penalties in local law — awaited any person erecting a lamp without official authorization.[37] But in general the new settlements lived in darkness after sundown, while criminals plied their trade under a black mantle which shielded them from both their victims and the police.

An ineffective police force not only left life and property insecure but weakened the defense of cities against fire. The evening watch was designed in part to be an alarm system, since the hazard greatly increased at nightfall when blazes could begin unnoticed and quickly get out of hand. Early urban history abounds with serious conflagrations. "We seldom pass a week," lamented an editor, "without reading some melancholy account of the disasters occasioned by the most destructive of all elements — fire." [38] From the first days of settlement this danger haunted Western communities. Builders continued to use wood exclusively, though the number of brick and stone houses multiplied every year. As the towns grew, crowding increased, and it was difficult to confine the flames to a single shop or dwelling. Though it is impossible to estimate the total fire damage in these frontier communities, it must have been considerable, and was certainly greater than losses incurred in all other ways.

No city escaped its ravages. Small fires were so common that they received only passing notice in the newspapers, but each community had its spectacular blazes. In 1806 flames swept through Hart and Dodge's rope factory in Lexington, leaving an $8,000 establishment in ashes. Six years later a whole block in Pittsburgh was wiped out, with losses which would have been even greater if the evening had not been "remarkably calm." David Embree lost his brewery in Cincinnati in 1815, just a year after the court house burned down. Outbreaks became so frequent that many thought incendiaries were at work. The *Western Spy* charged in 1799 that "an association of wicked men" ignited four buildings in a week,

---

[37] McMurtrie, *Sketches of Louisville*, 143; Cincinnati, Ordinances, February 23, 1815.

[38] *Liberty Hall* (Cincinnati), August 4, 1807.

plundering homes while the citizens turned out for the emergency. More than a decade later, when a "whole range of fine brick houses" on Pittsburgh's Wood Street caught fire, causing $35,000 loss, the authorities also suspected arson.[39]

Though large-scale destruction continued throughout this period, protection remained weak. A wave of excitement and agitation followed each big blaze, and constructive steps often resulted. But each new outbreak found the town somewhat unprepared. The engines worked badly or not at all, volunteers arrived too late, or bystanders preferred to watch the flames rather than fight them. Efforts to improve equipment and techniques could not be sustained after public interest lagged and money ran low. An old hand at fire reform finally became convinced that people enjoyed the spectacle and did not want improvement. Retreating into satire, he proposed two schemes to indulge their appetites. The first, called "*plan dilatory*," required the government to burn all its apparatus so that no one need fear that the show might be stopped. His alternative, "*plan Immediate*," stipulated that the city should buy twelve houses annually from a "conflagration fund," and light one every month as a kind of civic celebration.[40]

Though communities attacked the question along many fronts, the remedies never caught up with the problem. Municipal efforts were both public and private, involving the formation of largely self-governing companies using city funds and equipment and bolstered by ordinances designed to reduce risks. The charters of Louisville and Lexington forbade wooden chimneys within the corporation, and in the following years the trustees widened the prohibition to include shavings, more than twenty-eight pounds of gun powder, and frame and log houses that might be dangerous. In Pittsburgh, local authorities issued detailed regulations for stove pipes, the "Altitude of Chimneys," and bonfires.[41] Though some

[39] *Kentucky Gazette*, June 24, 1806; *Pittsburgh Gazette*, July 31, 1812; *Liberty Hall* (Cincinnati), March 8, 1814, February 11, 1815; *Western Spy* (Cincinnati), December 17, 1799; *Pittsburgh Gazette*, October 23, 1815.

[40] See "Admirer of a Fire," in *Pittsburgh Gazette*, January 18, 1809.

[41] *Collection of the Acts of Virginia and Kentucky*, 3; Lexington, Trustees

localities naturally emphasized their own peculiar dangers, by 1815 the codes of Western cities looked very much alike and contained similar restrictions.

Fires were considered a city emergency, and the whole community was expected to respond. Pittsburgh required all men living in the district to serve when called "unless a good and sufficient cause be offered." Failure to turn out led to a fine. A Lexington ordinance obligated those between sixteen and sixty to appear at every blaze and take orders from the Union Fire Company.[42] This system admirably suited the needs of small villages, but as settlements grew, it proved clumsy and outmoded, and the burden of firefighting fell more and more to volunteer companies. Though these associations had existed almost as long as the towns themselves, their activity did not take on great importance until the communities became too big to expect everyone to respond to an alarm. Then municipal authorities handed increased power to these quasi-official bodies. The relationship between the companies and the city was ambiguous. Local governments granted them charters and usually funds and equipment, but the organizations made their own rules and determined admission requirements. No question of jurisdiction or independence arose in this period because the same people who sat on official boards and councils were also prominent in the fire societies.

The public provided the volunteer organizations with equipment, either through subscriptions or from governmental funds. Communities further aided by providing hoses, hooks and ladders, and building stations to house the apparatus, and assuming the cost of repairs. Since engines were few and seldom really effective, great responsibility rested on the bucket brigades which brought water from wells or rivers to the fire by a human chain. Each city required householders and shopkeepers to have available at least two leather

---

Book, November 22, 1796; February 17, 1808; April 8, 1815; Pittsburgh, Borough Papers, January 15, 1805; February 10, 1803. *Pittsburgh Gazette*, August 31, 1804.

[42] Pittsburgh, Borough Papers, February 28, 1811; Lexington, Trustees Book, February 17, 1818.

pails for immediate use, in addition to those furnished by local authorities. All these services constantly claimed about ten per cent of municipal budgets, and sometimes more when new equipment was purchased.[43]

Though some communities displayed more energy than others in tackling the fire problem, all lived under the fear that a windy night might reduce the town to ashes. The detailed accounts in the press of great conflagrations in other cities reflected the general anxiety of Western urbanites, while the rates of the Kentucky Mutual Assurance Fire Company, ranging from one to six per cent annually, testified to the local risks. By 1815 every municipality owned at least one engine, and Lexington and Pittsburgh had three. Legislation tended to outrun enforcement, and local inventories of equipment were never reassuring. In 1809 a Pittsburgh committee reported only 59 buckets in good repair in homes and shops, one engine "of which we can make no report," and some hooks and ladders "nearly compleated." [44] As residential building moved away from the river, hazards increased, and townspeople realized that future fire control would require a much greater supply of water.

ಆಲ

Since all these cities except Lexington overlooked major rivers, the volume of water for town use was never a serious question. During the early days of settlement all buildings stood near the bank of a stream, and in case of fire plenty of water was available if it could be brought to the scene quickly enough. Later the population moved inland — which usually also meant upland — and new sources had to be found elsewhere, at least for emergency purposes. Public and private wells provided some, but this supply was uncertain, and soon discussion turned to the establishment of city-wide systems using steam power. As early as 1810 Calvin Adams peti-

---

[43] See Lexington, Trustees Book, May 2, 1811, and *Liberty Hall* (Cincinnati), March 26, 1819.

[44] *Kentucky Reporter*, April 9, 1814; Pittsburgh, Borough Papers, January 11, March 28, 1808.

tioned the trustees of St. Louis for "exclusive privileges" for "bringing fresh water into the Town by Mean [*sic*] of Pipes." Though no community actually embarked on such an ambitious project, Pittsburgh and Lexington had similar suggestions under consideration before 1815.[45]

At the same time that adequate fire protection demanded more water, increasing populations required larger supplies for drinking. For this purpose Western townsfolk used springs, rivers or wells, depending on which was most accessible. Uninformed about germ theories, they chose by taste and appearance rather than purity. St. Louisans drank from the Mississippi, though they were careful to let the water stand in jars until the dirt settled. Henry McMurtrie thought the Ohio an "extremely pure" stream, but the people of Louisville preferred well water, which he claimed was "extremely bad, containing, besides a considerable quantity of lime, a large portion of decomposed vegetable matter." [46] Except for Lexington, which drew from the spring which had attracted the first settlers, the urban centers relied on both rivers and wells.

River water was free, but many wells were not. Some private owners, having incurred expenses in digging, sold water to users by the week or year, while vendors peddled it from door to door in carts. But, generally, cities undertook to provide their citizens with water, and very early erected public wells. In 1802 Pittsburgh adopted an ordinance instructing the burgesses to build pumps "wherever they think most advisable," beginning with two on Market Street. It further provided for buying private wells "in useful and necessary parts of the Borough." As towns expanded, municipalities entered into this activity on a considerable scale, and in 1813 Cincinnati contracted to drill "possibly 30" in a single season.[47] Public control of the water supply, then, was firmly established in Western cities before 1815.

[45] St. Louis, Minutes, August 16, 1810; *Pittsburgh Gazette*, November 26, 1813, and Lexington, Trustees Book, November 4, 1813.

[46] McMurtrie, *Sketches of Louisville*, 139.

[47] *Western Spy* (Cincinnati), May 28, 1799, July 1, 1801; printed in *Pittsburgh Gazette*, August 9, 1802; *Western Spy* (Cincinnati), July 30, 1813.

At the same time, local governments continually expanded their activity in protecting the health of their citizens. Epidemics, like fire, were among the hazards of urban living, and the image of Philadelphia's yellow-fever scourge in 1793 haunted Western townspeople. Fortunately, early charters granted municipal authorities broad powers to deal with problems of disease and sanitation. Nor was it long before conditions in the new settlements demanded their exercise. In 1802 a writer in the *Pittsburgh Gazette* charged that "the increase of diseases in this place, has of late been greater in proportion, than the increase of population," a fact he attributed to the "vitiated state of the air." "Narrow streets and alleys . . . filthy gutters, putrid vegetable and matter, the stench from the foul slaughter houses, the exhalations from ponds of stagnant water," all combined to threaten residents.[48]

No town was immune from these nuisances. Slaughtering inside the corporation limits led quickly to protests and municipal regulations. Initially, local authorities established sanitary standards requiring butchers to keep their blocks and floors clean. But complaints continued, and soon most towns turned to licensing for control, restricting the number within the city, or at least within its center. Cincinnati's council went further, insisting that all meat be prepared at "a regular slaughter house" designated by the city.[49]

A more persistent and dangerous health hazard was stagnant water. All the river towns suffered from it, though only in Louisville and Cincinnati did it reach threatening proportions. In the former, large ponds covered the outskirts of the city, while overflow from the river deposited a "creamy mantling surface" on the banks of the Ohio. In the summer these "depots of universal mischief" brought extraordinary sickness, giving Louisville the reputation of being the West's graveyard. The trustees constantly encouraged individuals to drain ponds on their property whenever possible, and in 1811 began a series of public projects to take water

---

[48] *Pittsburgh Gazette*, July 23, 1802.

[49] Louisville, Trustees Book, July 13, 1812; *Liberty Hall* (Cincinnati), March 16, 1803.

off Main and Jefferson Streets with brick sewers.[50] No other question bothered municipal officials quite so much, and Louisville
records reveal constant concern with them. But the problem was
too large for piecemeal solutions. It took an epidemic in 1817 to
convince people that the situation had become intolerable.

Swamps and marshes imperiled Cincinnati in much the same
way. The Ohio drowned the mouth of Mill Creek on the town's
west end, and the low river bank along the city collected water
which bred mosquitoes throughout the summer and accumulated
filth the year round. In addition, the building industry complicated
this drainage question by establishing brickyards, "every one of
which," according to Daniel Drake, who counted nine in 1815, "is
surrounded by several pools, which litterly consist of washings,
of nearly the whole town." Rains cleaned the streets and alleys and
then gravitated towards these pits, which became "hotbeds of corruption, the laboratories of poison, and the sinks of human life."
In the even more grisly expression of "Sydeham" in *Liberty Hall*,
they were a "rich solution of dead cats and pigs." In 1815 Cincinnati embarked on an extensive clean-up campaign — "the great
purification," as Drake described it — but until that time progress
had been "neither creditable to the energy of the corporation, honorable to the proprietors of those lots, nor beneficial to the public
health." [51]

Sewage disposal also proved troublesome in the first years of urban
living. Private vaults took care of family waste, while surface gutters
carried away public and industrial garbage. Throughout this period
towns contented themselves with the regulation of privies, requiring
pits to be deep enough to prevent offensive odors, and outhouses to
be cleaned regularly. Rapid building, however, led to carelessness in
furnishing basic toilet facilities. The *Pittsburgh Gazette* charged in
1802 that "in all parts of the Borough there are tenements unprovided
with Vaults — three or four families occupying buildings erected on

---

[50] McMurtrie, *Sketches of Louisville*, 142; Louisville, Trustees Book, July
29, 1811, May 21, 1813, September 10, 1813.
[51] Drake, *Statistical View*, 191; *Liberty Hall* (Cincinnati), January 31,
1810; July 28, 1812.

a single lot of ground, are known to be without this necessary convenience . . . the dangerous consequences of which must be evident." In Lexington, the water table lay so close to the surface that cesspools threatened "to communicate with these wells . . . to jeopardise the health of our citizens," and soon the town limited their depth.[52] In no city did sewer improvement keep pace with increased population and building, and in each the situation by 1815 moved rapidly toward a crisis.

Inadequate sanitation generated a constant fear of disease, especially in summer months when the danger was greatest and when almost every death engendered anxiety. Though no town except Cincinnati tried to keep vital statistics, it is clear that smallpox, malaria, and influenza took many lives annually and occasionally reached epidemic proportions. Frequent newspaper accounts of sickness in the valley, though usually exaggerated, increased Western apprehensiveness, and the red flag of quarantine on housetops grimly reminded residents each year that the dreaded visitor was back in town. Against smallpox, the worst killer, local authorities encouraged vaccination, though initially there was some distrust. In 1804 a town meeting in Cincinnati forbade the new system, condemning any doctor using it as "an enemy to the health and prosperity of the town," [53] but later the practice became an accepted medical weapon.

Quarantine laws, a much broader use of municipal power, enabled cities to remove the infected from the corporation, paying all expenses if necessary. Sometimes emergencies drove localities to more direct attacks on contagions. In 1809 the St. Louis council, hearing that a boat coming from Natchez carried a smallpox case and "being desirous to prevent the danger," authorized its chairman "to Call out Such Members of Male Inhabitants . . . as he may deem necessary . . . to prevent the landing of said boat." [54] But not even task forces prevailed against influenza and malaria or the "fever and

[52] Pittsburgh, Borough Papers, September ?, 1803; Lexington, Trustees Book, May 5, 1814.

[53] *Western Spy* (Cincinnati), December 13, 1804.

[54] Lexington, Trustees Book, December 30, 1801; St. Louis, Minutes, December 16, 1809.

ague," which did their annual damage without fear of government intervention.

☙

By 1815 Western towns had witnessed the appearance of all the urban problems which confronted Eastern cities, and already these questions exerted a growing pressure on local governments. In nearly every field of municipal authority — police, fire, streets, water, and health — conditions deteriorated so rapidly that a series of emergencies appeared, requiring decisive action. Any one of these was grave enough to tax the ingenuity of local authorities, yet the crises came on many fronts. Indeed, the multiplicity of issues was the real danger. Communities could handle some of the challenges, but not all. Yet their interrelatedness made success in any single one difficult.

This was an ironic situation, for in the first years of the nineteenth century the expansion of municipal power to cope with these problems constituted the central tendency of local government in the West. Having begun with extremely limited jurisdiction, towns managed to broaden their authority continually until it covered wide areas of town life. Some of this increased control was embodied in amendments to early charters, and the rest resulted from the cities' inching into the twilight zone which separated state and local power, pleading "necessity and immemorial usage as their authority." [55] By the end of the first generation of city life on the frontier, communities were largely self-governing, having appropriated either by grant or arrogation nearly all the necessary weapons to deal with problems arising from urban conditions.

One crucial weapon, however, was still lacking — the right to raise adequate revenues by taxation, which states continued to limit rigidly. The critical position of the cities demanded wide-scale improvements, all of which required funds greatly in excess of their annual income. In a desperate search for funds, municipalities resorted to borrowing, first modestly and later extravagantly. In addi-

[55] St. Louis, Minutes, May 3, 1824. See the speech by Mayor Carr Lane.

tion, some, like Pittsburgh and Cincinnati, sought to increase their corporate status from that of a borough or town to a city, hoping in this way to enhance their powers. By 1815 all these communities had become concerned about the problems mounting around them, and the minutes of local councils and boards breathed a new urgency that grew out of the impending crises. "It has become evident," the trustees of Lexington admitted, "that the present municipal regulations are insufficient in governing the place." [56] It was not that previous action had been fruitless, but rather that growth and expansion brought pain and sometimes peril. The burgeoning cities of the West had begun to feel both.

[56] Lexington, Trustees Book, September 12, 1815.

Chapter 4

Urban Society

In the quarter century following the American Revolution the curtain of wilderness was lifted from the Ohio Valley. The outposts of settlement passed beyond Louisville and moved toward the Mississippi, where St. Louis held the frontier for the surging population. The transformation was startling both in extent and speed. In 1810 Henry Marie Brackenridge described Cincinnati as "a beautiful little city in the midst of a highly cultivated country," though but thirteen years before it "was covered with the native forest, excepting the space occupied by a rude encampment." Joseph Charless, the editor of the *Missouri Gazette*, remembered that on his first trip to the West in 1795 the banks of the Ohio were "a dreary wilderness, the haunt of ruthless savages," yet two decades later he found them "sprinkled with towns" boasting of "spinning and weaving establishments, steam mills, manufactures in various metals, leather, wool, cotton and flax," and "seminaries of learning conducted by excellent teachers." This great conversion moved a Cincinnati bard to lofty couplets:

> Here where so late the appalling sound
> Of savage yells, the woods resound
> Now smiling Ceres waves her sheaf
> And cities rise in bold relief.

Travel on Western waters, once a hazardous undertaking, became routine, and scheduled runs connected the major river ports. Nothing emphasized the vast changes as much as the development of transportation facilities. In 1793 a Pittsburgh company began regular service to Cincinnati with boats specially constructed for the trade.

Each carried six artillery pieces, while high walls enclosed the entire vessel, leaving slits for rifle fire against attacking Indians.[1] By 1815 the danger had passed. New steamboats, open on all sides, advertised the scenic attractions of the journey and provided almost luxurious accommodations for passengers. These craft were, in Timothy Flint's phrase, "moving cities," and the guns, once so important in the defense of travelers, now saluted settlements along the way, though larger communities soon outlawed the practice as "disturbing to the peace." [2]

Changing townscapes dramatized the growth of the West. Within a generation forts and trading posts became the commercial centers of the frontier country and the focuses of an increasingly rich social and cultural life. Samuel Brown, whose *Western Gazetteer* was the immigrant's bible, witnessed this transformation in his adult lifetime. In 1797, when he visited Lexington, he had found fifty houses, "partly frame, and hewn logs, with chimnies on the *outside*," and town lots selling for $30 each. Returning less than 20 years later, he exclaimed, "How changed the scene! Everything had assumed a new appearance." The log cabins were gone, and "in their place stood costly brick mansions, well painted and enclosed by the fine yards, bespeaking . . . taste and wealth." [3]

The development was the same elsewhere. Timothy Flint, viewing Cincinnati from Kentucky in 1816, remembered it as "a large and compact town" with "fine buildings rising on the slope of the opposite shore" and "steam manufactories, darting their columns of smoke aloft." "All this moving picture of wealth, populousness, and activity," he reflected, "has been won from the wilderness within forty years." And Henry Marie Brackenridge, who moved in and out of Pittsburgh for almost a half century, observed that "such has been the extraordinary growth of this city, that every ten years pro-

[1] H. M. Brackenridge, *Recollections of Persons and Places in the West* (2nd edn., Philadelphia, 1868), 185; *Missouri Gazette*, July 13, 1816; *Liberty Hall* (Cincinnati), June 11, 1815.

[2] Cincinnati, Ordinances, March 9, 1825.

[3] Brown, *Western Gazetteer*, 91.

duce such a change as to render the person, who has been absent during that period, almost a stranger." [4]

This urban flowering particularly struck travelers, since the activity and movement of the towns contrasted sharply with the more static life of the countryside. Indeed, visitors' accounts increasingly gauged the West by its cities, describing them in detail and organizing their narrative around urban sojourns. In time the comforts and refinements of these frontier centers were as well known in the East and Europe as the hardships of rural living. By the second decade of the nineteenth century their repute created images which observers brought as preconceptions to the new country. "I was pretty well prepared, by previous information, for the view of Lexington," wrote John Melish, "but it did exceed my expectation." Not all were so pleased, and some, like Gorham Worth, did not find the settlements "equal [to] the picture my imagination had drawn." [5] But by 1815 travelers no longer "discovered" cities in the wilderness; instead they planned their itineraries to include every town of respectable size.

The accounts of visitors not only underlined the strategic importance of urban communities, but displayed an increasing interest in the social and intellectual life of the towns. This new emphasis is significant because earlier descriptions generally concentrated on population growth and commercial and manufacturing expansion. Thus Flint noted that "Lexington has taken on the tone of a literary place," claiming to be the "Athens of the West," while Cincinnati was "struggling to become its Corinth." "Our advances in learning as in every other kind of improvement, are altogether astonishing," exulted a Pittsburgh editor in 1813, speaking for the whole West. "We see everyday new schools established for the education of youth; our towns teem with newspapers . . . ; the number of our bookstores and presses is incessantly increasing; public libraries are

[4] Flint, *Recollections*, 37–8; Brackenridge, *Recollections*, 61.

[5] Melish, *Travels*, II, 184; G. Worth, "Recollections of Cincinnati," Historical and Philosophical Society of Ohio, *Quarterly Publications*, XI (1916), 27.

instituted, and societies are rising, . . . and the Muses even have their worthy and successful Votaries." [6]

This social and cultural advance is surprising partly because it appeared so soon, and partly because it occurred in the face of discouraging conditions. The cities were not only young, but their people came from many different backgrounds, and commercial values everywhere predominated. Even Western boosters lacked confidence. Daniel Drake, for example, cautioned in 1810 that "a population derived from such distant sources, and so recently brought together, must necessarily exhibit much . . . moral diversity," which would retard the full growth of society until "customs, manners and laws" created "the necessary cohesion." [7]

Furthermore, the incessant flow of migration kept infusing additional elements into new and unformed societies, complicating the process of community growth. Since the newcomers constituted the life-blood of the youthful towns, no one wanted to discourage immigration, but the continual introduction of people with different backgrounds, attitudes, and cultures hampered assimilation. Pittsburgh, wrote a literary editor in 1813, "exhibits . . . a motely group, whose component parts, far from melting into one common mass, are yet in many instances separated by the unfriendly barriers of almost invincible prejudice." [8] Most local observers, while believing that the new residents would ultimately enrich the life of the cities, expected a period of disorganization before the ground could be prepared for social advance.

In addition, the dominant mercantile temper of frontier centers seemed to militate against rapid cultural development. Merchants, though not necessarily averse to the better things, tended to consider them less important than other matters. In Louisville they had "one single object in view, that of acquiring money," wrote Henry McMurtrie. "Absorbed in the great business of adding dollar to dollar," traders devoted "no time to literature, or the acquirement of those graceful nothings, which, of no value in themselves,

[6] Flint, *Recollections*, 63, 48; *Mercury* (Pittsburgh), November 25, 1813.
[7] Drake, "Notices," 30.
[8] *Mercury* (Pittsburgh), November 25, 1813.

still constitute the one great charm of polished society." Nor was Louisville unique in this respect. "This eternal hunger and thirst after money, to the exclusion of almost every other pursuit, is not . . . peculiar to this place," he observed, "but [is] rather a general trait in the character of all newly formed commercial cities." Cincinnati's "Curtius" was no more favorable when he spoke of the "entire contempt among our money making gentry, for everything like the cultivation of Literature and the Arts." [9] These indictments were probably too strong, but undoubtedly the mercantile atmosphere of Western communities retarded the growth of a rounded society.

Despite these handicaps the cities produced a surprisingly rich and diversified life for their citizens, offering opportunities, in many fields, similar to those in Eastern urban centers. In a single generation people drawn from all over the Union and many parts of Europe came together, built homes, contrived a livelihood, erected churches, schools and theaters, organized social clubs and learned societies, even laid the groundwork for universities. "Society is polished and polite," *Niles' Register* said with some astonishment of Lexington, "and their balls and assemblies are conducted with as much grace and ease as they are anywhere else, and the dresses at the parties are as tasty and elegant. Strange things these in the 'backwoods!' " [10]

ஃௐ

The societies which produced this culture were in many ways sophisticated. Local boosters talked a great deal about egalitarianism in the West, but urban practice belied the theory. Social lines developed very quickly, and although never drawn as tightly as in Eastern cities, they denoted meaningful distinctions. The groupings were basically economic, though professional classes were set apart

[9] McMurtrie, *Sketches of Louisville*, 119, 125; *Liberty Hall* (Cincinnati), February 26, 1816.

[10] *Niles' Register*, June 11, 1814.

by their interest and training, and Negroes by their color. No rigid boundaries divided these classes, and movement across them was constant. Yet differences did exist, people felt them, and contemporaries thought them significant. It is suggestive in this regard that the first great literary product of the West, *Modern Chivalry*, satirized the notion of equality, and its author was one of Pittsburgh's leading citizens.

In fact, social cleavages developed so rapidly in the first decades of the nineteenth century that some groups formalized their position in society. A variety of associations grew up to express the exclusiveness of their members. The St. Cecilia Society, for instance, became a kind of Junior League for Cincinnati's best young ladies, who gathered monthly to gossip and hear piano recitals. Pittsburgh's well-to-do bachelors formed the Quintilian Society in 1815 for the ostensible purpose of promoting literature and science, but letters of its members speak more of the marriage of "Brother Alexander" which "made some noise in P'G" than problems of learning.[11] In addition, by 1815 the wives of leading merchants and professional men had established female benevolent associations in every city to aid the poor through relief and religion, using a vocabulary that smacked of *noblesse oblige*.[12] Nor was this process confined to the upper strata, for each urban center had its Mechanical Society, which enabled wage earners to club together and give dignity to their calling. The drive for status, so strong in older communities, appeared very early in the new ones.

The merchants headed this rapidly stratifying social structure. Next in influence stood the lawyers, ministers, doctors, teachers, and journalists, who, if they had less income than commercial leaders, often had as much prestige. Beneath them lived most of the people — skilled and unskilled laborers, clerks and shopkeepers — "the

[11] *Liberty Hall* (Cincinnati), April 29, 1816; A. B. Bolles to S. Bolles, October 12, 1820, Samuel Bolles Letters, Wilson Collection (University of Kentucky Library, Lexington).

[12] *Liberty Hall* (Cincinnati), October 16, 1815. The first report of the Female Society of Cincinnati for Charitable Purposes is signed by seven women, all wives of prominent merchants or ministers.

respectable workingmen." Lower still in the hierarchy were the transients and rootless — wagoners, rivermen, hangers-on, and ne'er-do-wells — who had no stable connections with the community but whose activities formed an important part of its life. The Negroes, slave and free, occupied the bottom rung of the ladder, performing the most menial tasks and excluded from white society by both custom and law.

The primacy of the merchants reflected their economic prowess. Since most towns sprang originally from exchange posts, their leadership was established early. When Thomas Wilson and his wife went to Pittsburgh in 1804 to establish a branch of the Bank of Pennsylvania, they took no letters of introduction "because they very justly considered that the very committal to their care of perhaps one-half million of money was of itself proof of their high standing in Philadelphia." The directors' wives, however, refused to visit the newcomers who "came here in such a strange way." Tarleton Bates, an older resident, sarcastically watching this jockeying, commented "our ladies are of too *high origin*, they have too pure blood in their veins, to mix with any but patricians." Fortescue Cuming noticed the same haughtiness a few years later, and explained that "wealth acquired suddenly generally operates on the ignorant, to make them wish to seem as if they had always been in the same situation . . . this accounts for [their] forgetting that some among them could not tell who had been their ancestors in the second generation." [13]

More renowned than Pittsburgh's was Lexington's upper class, whose charm, hospitality, and "conscious superiority" captivated visitors. Thomas Ashe, who deplored the egalitarianism of the older sections of the country, was enthusiastic about this "small party of rich citizens" who tried "to withdraw themselves from the multitude, or to draw a line of distinction between themselves as *gens comme il faut* and the *canaille*." An "Early Adventurer," who

---

[13] E. M. Davis, "The Letters of Tarleton Bates 1795–1805," *Western Pennsylvania Historical Magazine*, XII (1929), 48; Cuming, "Sketches of a Tour," in Thwaites, ed., *Western Travels*, IV, 86.

had come West before many of Lexington's first families, condemned the pretentiousness of these people who claimed "the upper seats," demanding to know "who established their privileged societies and companies, their privileged balls and assemblies from which the mechanick, however respectable by virtue or industry, is excluded?" He then traced the rise of this aristocracy, drearily chronicling the end of Arcadia, and summoning farmer and laborer alike to re-capture the people's "liberties." [14]

Even in the smaller towns this division appeared. In Louisville "there is a circle, small 'tis true," wrote McMurtrie, "but within whose magic round abounds every pleasure, that wealth, regulated by taste, can produce, or urbanity bestow. There, the 'red heel' of Versailles may imagine himself in the emporium of fashion, and whilst leading a beauty through the maze of the dance, forget that he is in the wilds of America." Gorham Worth's testimony in Cin-cinnati was similar. "Talk of the *back woods*! said I to myself, after dining with Mr. Kilgour . . . I have never seen anything east of the mountains to be compared to the luxuries of that table! the costly dinner service, — the splendid cut glass, — the rich wines. . . ." Thomas Ashe had a like experience in the Queen City, admitting that its leading group "would be respected in the first circles of Europe." In St. Louis successful American traders joined the old French ruling families to maintain the "proud, aristocratic spirit" and the "propensity to ostentation" of colonial times.[15]

These merchants were firmly entrenched in their communities. Most of them came West with little capital and grew with their cities. While the settlements were young, land was cheap and suc-cessful businessmen acquired property rapidly. Others, coming later, gambled on the town's expansion by buying on the outskirts or in the surrounding country. By the beginning of the nineteenth cen-

---

[14] J. McBride, "Journey to Lexington, Kentucky, 1810," Historical and Philosophical Society of Ohio, *Quarterly Publications*, V (1910), 25; Ashe, *Travels*, 193; *Kentucky Reporter*, July 29, 1809.

[15] McMurtrie, *Sketches of Louisville*, 119; Worth, "Recollections," 38; Ashe, *Travels*, 203; Marshall, *Bates*, I, 239, 241.

tury the best lots had passed into the hands of a select few. This centralizing process took place in every community except St. Louis. Even there merchants like Gratiot, Sarpy, the Chouteaus, Lucas, Mullamphy, and O'Fallon accumulated large holdings adjoining the town, but inside a considerable diffusion existed.

The social leadership of the merchants rested on a visible economic pre-eminence, as measured by either property or living standards. City assessment records, whenever available, emphasize the wealth of the business community. In Lexington in 1808 over a third of the total valuation of more than a million dollars belonged to sixteen men, all of them merchants or manufacturers. Furthermore, the incomplete returns of the next year show that the traders had substantially increased their position. William Leavy's assessment, for example, rose from $25,817 to $46,710, while George Trotter's $61,564 jumped to $100,300. Henry Clay's fortune took a good turn in the same twelve months, growing from $6,000 to $32,180, the latter figure including four houses, three lots, an office, and at least a large share of two hotels.[16]

Cincinnati's records indicate the same trend. In 1805 only 198 people paid a corporation tax in a population of nearly 2,000, and 14 of these — nearly all merchants — accounted for over a third of the total. Thirteen years later, of over 8,000 residents, 39 had assessments of over $10,000, one of which was more than $130,000. A large portion of this property comprised town lots and improvements, and revealed the commercial interests as rentiers as well as traders. John Piatt, with thirty-one houses in 1818, was the city's most important landlord, while Nicholas Longworth owned fourteen and many others collected rent from better than a half dozen dwellings.[17]

St. Louis's records are equally conclusive. In 1811 the town's total assessments stood at $134,516, $82,774 of which was held by six men. William Clark headed the list with $19,930 and William Christy followed with $16,000, while the next four, Auguste Chouteau, John O'Fallon, J. B. C. Lucas, and Henry Von Phul, held property valued

[16] Town of Lexington, Tax Assessment Book, 1808, 1809.

[17] Town of Cincinnati, Duplicate of Corporation Tax for the Year 1805, MS, Torrence Collection.

at $15,664, $12,450, $10,555, and $8,175, respectively. In short, six business leaders and landowners accounted for more than half of the city's assessed valuation.[18]

Living standards demonstrated mercantile primacy even more graphically. Stoddard found the French traders in St. Louis in 1804 living "in a style equal to those in the large port towns," and Christian Schultz estimated the cost of "two or three BIG houses" at "twenty to sixty thousand dollars." Even in Louisville, the roughest frontier city, McMurtrie thought the best houses "would suffer little by being compared with any of the most elegant private edifices of Philadelphia and New York." When Flint visited Cincinnati, he, too, was struck by the affluence and comfort of the well-to-do. "The elegance of the houses, the parade of servants, the display of furniture, and more than all, the luxury of their overloaded tables, would compare with the better houses in the Atlantic cities." [19]

Nowhere in the West, however, did the wealthy live in more opulence than in Lexington, where prosperous merchants and members of the bar signalized their success by acquiring country seats. In 1816 Samuel Brown counted "between fifty and sixty villas" in the vicinity. The most famous was Colonel David Meade's Chaumiere du Prarie where "no less than thirty hands" were engaged in "laying out, planting, sowing, harrowing and mowing his lawns and walks." The Colonel always *"dressed for dinner"* and nearly every evening entertained fifteen or twenty people. Most proprietors supported these estates out of urban income; indeed, William Leavy, who knew nearly all of them, said that John Hunt was the "only farmer I have known that made his farm investment produce him a good interest." But rural retreats were not the only evidence of affluence in Lexington. In 1806 Cuming noted thirty-nine two-wheel carriages valued at over $5,000 and over twenty four-wheel ones worth almost $9,000. "This may convey some idea

[18] I. Lionberger, "Glimpses of the Past: St. Louis Real Estate — In Review," *Missouri Historical Review*, IV (1937), 125.

[19] A. Stoddard to Mrs. Benham, June 16, 1804, MS, Stoddard Papers (Missouri Historical Society, St. Louis); Schultz, *Travels*, II, 40; McMurtrie, *Sketches of Louisville*, 117; Flint, *Recollections*, 52.

of the taste for shew and expense which pervades this country." [20]

Thus set apart from the rest of the townspeople, merchant families were the center of a lively social whirl. The "season" was studded with balls, parties and "assemblies." Dancing teachers, who met with "more encouragement than professors . . . of literary science," brought the "City Cotillion . . . of New York, Philadelphia and Baltimore" to frontier towns. Keen competition among the men kept things humming, but if the pace slackened, the traditional observance of leap year authorized feminine aggression. Though most entertainment took place in homes, the better taverns vied for preference. In Lexington, for instance, Postlethwait's was the fashionable hotel, but its rival, Bradley's, was "perpetually crowded," and in the spring it had parties "each day for several days . . . where upwards of 60 gentlemen attended and more than 40 ladies." [21]

Wives and daughters of wealthy merchants composed the West's only leisure class. Leading a sheltered life, they ordinarily escaped work outside the home before marriage and often afterwards as well. John Wrenshall, a successful merchant and preacher, raised some eyebrows in Pittsburgh society at the beginning of the century by allowing his daughter to clerk in his store. "Many of our wealthy neighbours would throw out indirect hints" about their assisting behind the counter, "as if such employment was unfit for Young Ladies." In the summer months the well-to-do retired to the "uninterrupted harmony and refined social intercourse" of resorts such as Kentucky's Olympian Springs, Ohio's Yellow Springs, or Indiana's Jeffersonville. Though originally established for health purposes, these retreats soon existed "to amuse those who seek relaxation from the ordinary pursuits of life." [22]

[20] Leavy, "Memoir," *Kentucky Hist. Soc. Register*, XLI (1943), 251; 260; Cuming, "Sketches of a Tour," Thwaites, ed., *Western Travels*, IV, 187–88.

[21] Cuming, "Sketches of a Tour," *ibid.*, 189; *Western Spy* (Cincinnati), November 19, 1799; December 19, 1804; R. Bradley to W. Lytle, May 17, 1804, MS, William Lytle Collection (H.P.S.O., Cincinnati).

[22] John Wrenshall (1761–1821), MS Journal (Pittsburgh Conference Methodist Historical Collection, Western Pennsylvania Historical Society Library, Pittsburgh), IV, 114, V, 2; *Kentucky Gazette*, April 2, September 10, September 17, 1805; August 25, 1806.

The masculine side of mercantile life displayed more vigor and less frivolity. The merchants took their business very seriously, rising early, working late, and often traveling extensively. Though willing to join the ladies in the dining room or dance hall, they preferred the political arguments of the coffee house or tavern and the unrestrained language of card games, billiards, and horse-racing. As the town's most wealthy and articulate group, they took the lead in establishing libraries and schools and erecting churches and public buildings. With one eye always cocked on possible profit, traders also invested in local improvements such as turnpikes, bridges, or schemes to cut a canal around the Falls in the Ohio. Though many of the businessmen became familiar figures in New Orleans and Eastern commercial circles, they never lost their close connections with their own communities and could be counted on to preside at town meetings, serve on official committees, or fill a place on the Board of Trustees.

This commanding social and economic position paved the way for political leadership. The merchants very early emerged as the spokesmen for Federalism in the West.[23] Even after the virtual disappearance of the party on the national level, its adherents remained powerful in frontier cities. Indeed, in Pittsburgh it was not until 1810 that the Democratic Republicans won a borough election. Yet two years later John Woods, running for Congress as a "Friend of Peace" in protest against the war with Great Britain, carried both the city and county by almost two to one. Farther West, where the Federalist party never gained a firm foothold, the commercial interests enlisted under different banners, though preaching the same ideas. Later, when the Whigs refashioned Hamiltonian notions, they recruited about 75 per cent of the Western merchants.[24] Until that time, however, the mercantile community influenced

[23] "At this period, with very few exceptions," Henry Marie Brackenridge recalled, "the professional men, persons of wealth and education, and those in public offices, were on the Federal side." *Recollections*, 70.

[24] *Pittsburgh Gazette*, March 23, 1810; October 23, 1812; L. Atherton, *Pioneer Merchants in Mid-America* (Columbia, Missouri, 1929), 24.

nearly all parties and factions, suffering no real challenge to its urban supremacy.

❧

Closely connected with the merchants, but separated from them by background and training, was the professional class — doctors, lawyers, ministers, teachers, and journalists. These people had no easily identifiable community of interest and seldom acted in concert, yet all held preferred positions in young urban societies. Their status rested on service, and was unconnected with income. Indeed, for most this social importance compensated for poor financial returns, the lawyers alone enjoying an economic situation commensurate with their public standing. Many were college graduates, some had taken advanced work in Eastern universities, and nearly all exhibited a learning and refinement that distinguished them from the rest of the townspeople.

Lawyers found merchants their most lucrative clients, and in the days before publicly financed education, teachers discovered that the well-to-do paid most of the tuition that kept school doors open. Even ministers, often presiding over small congregations, depended upon businessmen for substantial donations with which to build churches and pay salaries. Many doctors operated apothecary shops to supplement their income, and thus were merchants themselves. As a group these men shared the social outlook of the commercial interests, though there were always outstanding exceptions. Dr. William Goforth in Cincinnati, for example, became such an enthusiastic Republican that many well-to-do patients deserted him.[25]

The professional men, however, from the earliest days exercised a social influence far greater than their numbers warranted. Strategically located astride the avenues of opinion — the press, the pulpit, and the podium — they had direct and continuous contact with the bulk of the people. In addition, they sat on local governing boards,

[25] D. D. Shira, "Sidelights on Two Famous Pioneer Physicians," *Ohio State Medical Journal*, XXIV (1938), 911.

founded religious and cultural associations, encouraged schools and colleges, and generally embodied the civic conscience of urban centers. Educated, articulate, and energetic, possessing the confidence of the business community as well as the townspeople, they rubbed off the roughest edges of frontier society. Each place had its men of learning, refinement, and taste, whom travelers increasingly sought out, and who softened their harshest judgments on the West.

Of these cultural leaders none was more renowned than Cincinnati's Dr. Daniel Drake, whose talents and versatility entitled him to be called the "Franklin of the West." Though his scientific reputation rested on several treatises on disease in the Mississippi and Ohio valleys and on his *Picture of Cincinnati*, Drake was better known to his contemporaries as a civic figure. To visitors and townspeople alike, his tall, commanding frame, his springy, almost elastic walk, and his infectious amiability seemed as much a part of the town as its hills and court house. He was instrumental in founding the Lyceum, a circulating library, the School of Literature and the Arts, the Lancastrian Seminary, the Western Museum, and numerous clubs for debate and learned discussion. As a trustee of the town he lobbied for better public health and increased precautions against epidemics. His drugstore not only carried the best line of medicines, but also introduced soda water to the city. As a successful merchandiser he shared the viewpoint of the commercial interests and joined them in bringing to Cincinnati a branch of the United States Bank, of which he was later made a director. This listing includes only a small part of his work, for no segment of urban life seemed untouched by his guiding hand.

In Lexington, John Bradford, the editor of the *Kentucky Gazette*, fondly called "Old Wisdom," played a comparable role. Having come to the Blue Grass in 1786 with the second press west of the mountains, he exercised a molding influence on town life for four decades. Not only did he serve longer than any other man on the city's Board of Trustees, but there were few committees which did not think his participation essential for success. Town meetings invariably called him to the chair, and the state legislature recognized him as a spokesman for the metropolis. His reputation as a booster made him secretary of Lexington's Emmigration Society, and his intense interest in education led him more than once to the chairmanship of Transylvania University's trustees. Though essentially conservative, he planted some youthful wild oats in the Democratic Society of Kentucky in the nineties and remained an ardent Jeffersonian. His closest friends were merchants, manufacturers, and lawyers, whom he joined in promoting many enterprises, including the Kentucky Insurance Company and an Episcopalian society known as "the gentleman's church." Bradford was Lexington's candidate for the title of "The Benjamin Franklin of the West," and his credentials at least rivaled those of his neighbor and friend, Dr. Drake.[26]

Though members of all professions participated extensively in town life, none were more active than the lawyers, whose success in their calling depended not only on their achievements in the courtroom but on the cultivating of prospective clients. This requirement led them to serve in many capacities in civic affairs. Fortescue Cuming, no friend of the legal fraternity, noted that "throughout the whole country" they "fill all the respectable offices in the government as well as the legislature." Indeed, nearly all the leading spokesmen of the West on the national scene — like Clay or Benton — were urban lawyers who started as prominent city figures. Though most attorneys shared the prevailing commercial values of their towns, some could always be found on every side of each issue. Unlike members of other professions, they were never in short supply, and their prominence often bred hostility. Critics charged that they wore "a certain air of superiority" and arrogated "to themselves the title or epithet of esquire, which the uninformed mass of people allow them."[27] No matter how accurate the com-

[26] Bernard Mayo, *Henry Clay, Spokesman of the New West* (Boston, 1937), 121. This term was applied to many leading civic figures in new cities and generally denoted a versatility in public affairs that was unconnected with any specific accomplishments of Franklin.

[27] Cuming, "Sketches of a Tour," in Thwaites, ed., *Western Travels*, IV, 87.

plaints, most lawyers brought to the cities education and tastes considerably more developed than those of their fellow townspeople.

If the West seemed to teem with legal talent, no one complained of an excess of doctors. Actually, however, from the very earliest days of settlement the ratio of practitioners to population in the towns was relatively high. For instance, in 1810 Cincinnati, with just over 2,500 people, boasted eight doctors, while a few years earlier Cuming found four in Pittsburgh — "all of considerable practice, experience and reputation" — and five in Lexington. In St. Louis eight physicians advertised in the *Missouri Gazette* between 1809 and 1815, and most of them stayed permanently in that place, while McMurtrie counted twenty-two in Louisville in 1819, when the population barely exceeded 4,000.[28] Their training varied greatly, both in extent and quality. Though the University of Pennsylvania's medical school in Philadelphia supplied the new country with most of its leading doctors, many of the earlier ones learned their trade in the office of local practitioners or with the army. As their numbers increased, they banded together in associations to discuss scientific problems and establish professional standards.[29] Like other men of this class, physicians preferred a life of broad social contacts to narrow technical interests, and most participated in many phases of urban development.

Probably the most influential segment of the professional group were the ministers. Being preachers of the gospel and among the best educated citizens, they enjoyed a unique status. Most were earnest and dedicated men, highly respected by the community, who

[28] Stubbs, *Ohio Almanac, 1810*, unfolioed; Cuming, "Sketches of a Tour," in Thwaites, ed., *Western Travels*, IV, 87, 187; *Missouri Gazette*, January 11, October 19, December 21, 1809, April 26, 1810, December 28, 1811, July 25, 1812, October 21, 1814; McMurtrie, *Sketches of Louisville*, 133.

[29] Lexington, Cincinnati, and Pittsburgh all had associations before 1815, usually as part of a state system. In 1803 Kentucky adopted the practice of such older states as Maryland, New York, New Jersey, and Delaware in forming the Kentucky Medical Society. *Kentucky Gazette*, August 16, 1803. Ohio's arrangement was the most detailed and effective; see J. Forman, "The Beginnings of the Licensing of Physicians in Ohio," *Ohio State Medical Journal*, XXXII (1936), 5–6.

gave immense time and energy to civic improvement. They not only served on public boards and committees but also guided their congregations along useful paths. Since salaries were low, many supplemented their income by other employment. A few became merchants but most opened schools, taught in academies, or, later, occupied chairs in the colleges. Though their contacts were wide and church membership was socially mixed, the ministers' most natural and intimate connections were with the articulate sections of society and the prominent people who were lay leaders of their religious organizations.

Wage earners — craftsmen, mechanics, clerks, and small shop-keepers — constituted the bulk of urban society in the West as well as in the East. Differences existed among these elements, especially between skilled and unskilled labor, yet they shared similar economic conditions and social status. Until the postwar depression, the demand for workers far exceeded the supply; hence this group generally enjoyed good pay and full employment. Even the unskilled commanded consideration — at least north of the Ohio where slaves could not compete for jobs. Shortages often became so acute that employers recruited men in the East, promising increased wages and better opportunities in the new country. Early marriages kept women off the labor market and made even domestics a scarce and prized item. Thomas Carter's enthusiastic letter from Cincinnati in 1813 to his brother in New England summed up the prospects held out by young cities. "This town . . . is a fine place for mechanics; carpenters and masons can . . . make five to ten dollars per day; bricklaying is $3.50 a thousand. . . . Mechanics here can make their fortune in four or five years." [30]

Though jobs abounded in frontier communities, good housing did not. Nowhere did building keep pace with the expanding population, and congested living quarters characterized almost every city. Drake estimated that on the average ten people lived in each

[30] Cabot, "The Carters in Early Ohio," 350.

dwelling in Cincinnati in 1815, a number which "greatly transcends the limits which health and comfort would prescribe." In St. Louis Brackenridge reported that "every house is crowded, rents are high and it is exceedingly difficult to procure a tenement on any terms." [31] In addition, the immigrants constantly increased the pressure on these limited facilities, keeping rents and building costs up.

Urgent need for new housing led to jerry-construction, many dwellings never being painted and some even lacking decent toilet facilities. Yet in time the permanent residents found adequate shelter, and many wage earners moved into brick homes. However, it was not until bad times that any mobility developed. Probably most workers ultimately owned their own homes, though a large number continued to rent. The little gardens and "large spaces" between the buildings, which characterized most towns in the early days of the century, disappeared at an alarming rate, though this tendency was especially resisted in St. Louis.[32] Housing for working people was generally better in Western cities than in the East, but by 1815 flimsy construction and inadequate maintainence had created dangerous areas.

Wage earners could have afforded better homes if some had been available, for they shared generously in the prosperity of the period. Few observers failed to comment on their success. In 1810 Zadock Cramer watched Pittsburgh's "ingenious and active workmen" go home "of a morning, loaded with turkies, fowls, fat beef, fresh butter, &c. &c.," which was "clear" evidence that "they not only live, but live *well*." A few years later Thomas Hulme noticed the "decency and affluence of the trades-people and mechanics at Lexington, many of whom drive about in their own carriages." [33] These

---

[31] Drake, *Statistical View*, 170; *Missouri Gazette*, March 21, 1811.

[32] Pittsburgh, Borough Papers, September ?, 1803; Drake, *Statistical View*, 134; Melish, *Travels*, II, 128; Michaux, "Travels," in Thwaites, ed., *Western Travels*, III, 156.

[33] Cramer, *Cramer's Almanack*, 1810, 52; T. Hulme, "A Journal Made During a Tour in the Western Countries of America," in Thwaites, ed., *Western Travels*, X, 66.

generally high standards obscured some important fluctuations in employment, but until the end of the war these cities provided as much opportunity for workers as any place in the country.

High compensation and good working conditions stemmed fundamentally from a chronic labor shortage, but some wage-earners, refusing to rely upon this, established unions to maintain their position. Only a few crafts were affected, but these proved strong enough to set pay rates and occasionally to call effective strikes. Each town saw some activity, the shoemakers, weavers, tailors, cord-wainers, and carpenters being the most successful. These associations carried on a two-front war: against employers and against unskilled workers. It is significant that the first walkout came after the "hiring gentlemen" attempted to better the situation of the apprentices. Organization gave these trades control over the admission of new men, and created the unity required to fight employers. However, unionized labor represented only a small portion of even the skilled workers. Out of 97 classes of master craftsmen in Pittsburgh in 1807, only a handful were organized.[34]

Though the largest element in Western towns, wage earners were not a static class. Immigration constantly swelled their numbers, while some workingmen rose to a higher status and others dropped to a lower one. In a loosely structured society, boundaries between groups were never rigid, and many crossed them easily. Anthony Doyle, who came to St. Louis from Ireland, noticed this two-way traffic among his compatriots. "Some Irish men . . . are 20 years here in rags and not worth a dollar," but, he added "on the other hand them that are men of conduct . . . are rich and respectable." Movement upward is always easier to trace than failure and broken hope, but success was common in these cities and clearly constituted the dominant tendency. Doyle himself came to St. Louis without means; in a few years he asserted that "I have ½ of a grocery store. . . . I have $700 more sunk in a limestone quarry," and he hoped to make $1,000 that year on the sale of furs in New York, if it

[34] *Pittsburgh Gazette*, December 21, 1804; Zadok Cramer, *The Navigator, Containing Directions for Navigating the Monongahela, Allegheny, Ohio and Mississippi Rivers* ([Pittsburgh], 1808).

"please God." "Industrious journeymen," observed John Melish, "very soon became masters," and most of the successful glassmen in Pittsburgh began as craftsmen in the shop.[35]

Most working people managed to feed, clothe and shelter their families, but some did not. By 1815 the number of charitable societies and complaints about the rising poor tax afforded clear evidence of the growing relief problem in Western communities.[36] "In all manufacturing towns," "H" wrote philosophically to the *Pittsburgh Gazette*, "there are a great proportion of persons who can barely support their families in health" and who in sickness become "a burden to the city." But considering the local situation intolerable, he asked the corporation to aid "these unfortunate persons . . . scattered about the dirty alleys . . . compelled to breathe unwholesome air, badly lodged, [and] coarsely dieted." In Cincinnati in 1815 the Benevolent Society admitted that it was overwhelmed, and urged the erection of a poor house. As early as 1806 the Kentucky Musical Society sponsored concerts to raise additional money for the care of the destitute "good people" of Lexington. Hence, even before the coming of hard times in 1819, all frontier cities had to struggle with the question of the increasing number of the needy.[37]

The wage earners, being permanent residents, eagerly drove roots into their communities, joining churches, sometimes sending children to school, and taking an increasing part in city life. By contrast, the group of transients — wagoners, boatmen, adventurers, and ne'er-do-wells — who lived at least part of the time in the towns, developed few stable contacts. Rough, boisterous, often drunk, usually fighting and swearing, without families or relations, sometimes preying on strangers, they seemed to have been barbarized by the wilderness

[35] A[nthony] Doyle to A[ndrew] Doyle, May 31, 1819, Missouri History Papers, (Missouri Historical Society, St. Louis); Melish, *Travels*, II, 188.

[36] As early as 1800 "Philanthropy" in Cincinnati complained of high poor taxes, *Western Spy* (Cincinnati), October 23, 1800. For a similar argument see *Commonwealth* (Pittsburgh), December 16, 1811; *Pittsburgh Gazette*, May 14, 1813.

[37] *Pittsburgh Gazette*, December 8, 1818; *Liberty Hall* (Cincinnati), November 21, 1815; *Kentucky Gazette*, July 8, 1806.

of the new country. When in town they patronized cheap hotels and flop houses along the water front, gambled and caroused in grog shops, tippling houses, and brothels, and ran up the crime rate. Ironically, these men were the first contacts most travelers made with the West, a fact which sustained the dark reputation of the frontier.

Folklore, legend, and Morgan Neville's short tale about Mike Fink have been kind to the boatmen, throwing a charitable veil over their life and transforming a collection of questionable toughs into amphibious Robin Hoods.[38] But the boatmen more accurately described themselves as half-alligator, half-horse, and tipped with snapping turtle. Though extremely skillful on the water and absolutely essential to the West's economy, they comprised a disturbing element in urban society. They hit town with distressing regularity, spending all their earnings in a few days, carousing about, often engaging the residents in pitched battle, and then shipping out again. In 1820 the Western Navigation and Bible Tract Society estimated that there were 20,000 rivermen on the Ohio, most of whom were "thoughtless, profligate, and degenerate, whose influence, wherever they go, and wherever they stop, has a most deleterious effect on all with whom they associate." The association's analysis was more realistic than its remedy, which involved distributing the Bible and religious tracts such as "The Happy Waterman" and "The Drunkard's Looking Glass" among the boat hands.[39]

Though wagoners were an unstable component of urban societies in the West, they were never as numerous or explosive as the river crews. Travel by land brought them nightly to taverns and hotels, sparing them the long periods of isolation which characterized the life of keelmen and bargers. Yet they too were drifters, with no settled contacts and few attachments. Occasionally some tired of the road and, capitalizing on their mercantile experience, opened shops and disappeared into the routine of community living.[40] But

---

[38] M. Neville, "The Last of the Boatmen," 107–122.

[39] For a good treatment of the boatmen, see Baldwin, *The Keelboat Age,* 85–116; *Liberty Hall* (Cincinnati), May 17, 1820.

[40] Cramer noticed that sometimes a boatman, too, left the water. "He

more often they continued to exist chaotically, drinking their earnings, harassing innkeepers, widening the vocabularies of respectable travelers, and enlivening the night life of the towns.

No matter what their impact on the settled life of the West, the wagoners and boatmen played a critical role in the trade of the new area. Not this much could be said, however, for another transient class, which the mayor of St. Louis described as composed of "the adventurous, reckless and disolute [*sic*]." They came "in pursuit of pleasure and . . . almost everything but what is lawful and honorable." Each town had this kind of floating population. At first it was fed from the outside, but the early development of gangs — some teen-aged — suggests that cities bred as well as attracted the rootless. "In so new a spot," a Cincinnati editor wisely observed, "whose citizens are made up of all nations, and colors, and tongues, it can scarcely be supposed that the very cream of human nature should be accumulated, — or at best, that some unseemly dregs should not have come in to defile the mixture." [41]

This low life centered in the grog shops, tippling houses, and brothels located on streets and alleys near the waterfront. Here criminals and other transients mingled with local riffraff and some respectable people, enjoying heavy drinking, lots of gambling, and a little time with scarlet women. Much of this was just straightforward dissipation where falling men received a good nudge; but increasingly these districts became reservoirs of vice and lawlessness which flowed over onto the rest of the town, producing night revels, brutal assaults, burglary, and property destruction. More ominously, however, these amusement areas became the centers of partially organized crime which operated throughout the city, often making contact with the better classes.

No community escaped. In 1805, for example, Cincinnati authori-

---

sets himself down in some town or village as a wholesale merchant, druggist, or apothecary, practicing physician, or lawyer, or something else that renders him respectable in the eyes of his neighbors" and assiduously conceals his origins. Cramer, *Navigator*, 1814, 33.

[41] St. Louis, Minutes, January 14, 1829; *Liberty Hall* (Cincinnati), April 1, 1816.

ties uncovered a ring of horse thieves which included "many persons who have always been esteemed as worthy," and three months later they broke up a band of counterfeiters operating through the central-valley region. In 1814 arson racketeers terrorized Pittsburghers with letters demanding protection money to avoid having their property burned. A wave of burglaries baffled St. Louis police for some months in 1812 until they found "many light fingered gentlemen" were working together in various parts of the city.[42] More significant still was the celebrated case of Cincinnati's Charles Vattier, whose associate, the mulatto Charles Britton, became a house servant of the Receiver of Public Monies in order to steal $47,000. Their trial disclosed that Vattier owned a gambling empire, including grog shops, bawdy houses, and taverns. His social and financial prestige was so great that he had no trouble in raising $20,000 bail and retaining the legal services of Nicholas Longworth. After his conviction, more than a dozen leading citizens successfully petitioned the Governor to suspend part of the sentence, and while in jail he received very genteel treatment.[43]

These instances reveal but a small part of the ugly layer of vice, crime, and lawlessness which existed in early urban society. No class had a monopoly on delinquency, but the great bulk of it sprang from the aimless and uncertain life of floaters. Many localities increased police forces to restrain them, while moral and religious associations sought more fundamental reform. Churches, Sunday schools, and charitable organizations tried to reach them and failed. In some places concern verged on panic. At the end of the war, leading Pittsburghers felt that "irregularity and vice" had developed so rapidly as to threaten the very foundations of society. Calling on the citizens to act to preserve order, they asked for support of their Moral Society, declaring, "We make no innovations — we embark on no novel experiment — we set up no new

[42] *Western Spy* (Cincinnati), January 30, 1805; April 17, 1805; *Pittsburgh Gazette*, April 15, 1814; *Missouri Gazette*, February 22, 1812.

[43] For a discussion of this fascinating case, see "Two Gentlemen of Law Knowledge," *The Trial of Charles Vattier* (Cincinnati, 1807). See also *Liberty Hall* (Cincinnati), March 24, April 28, July 14, August 3, November 3, 1807.

standards of morals — we encroach on no man's liberty — we lord it over no man's conscience — we stand on the defensive merely." [44] But neither public nor private measures could get to the heart of the problem, and as towns grew and prospered, so did their dangerous classes.

✍

Lowest in the social hierarchy of the urban West were the Negroes, slave and free, who constituted a menial class. In Southern cities they performed nearly all the unskilled labor, and in Northern towns like Pittsburgh and Cincinnati they fared hardly better. Though excluded from any real participation in town life, they nevertheless exercised an immense but subtle influence on these societies. Since blacks did so much of the heavy toil, many whites shied away from manual labor; this gave a special status to employment requiring skill or, better still, no physical effort at all. In Southern cities the existence of slavery tended to sharpen distinctions throughout the whole social structure. To a lesser degree this was true in the North as well. "The evils of slave-holding are not confined to the parts of the country where involuntary labour exists," observed Timothy Flint, "but the neighborhood is infected. Certain kinds of labour are despised as being the work of slaves." [45] In Southern towns slaveowning became a convenient symbol of status, and retirement to a country estate surrounded by blacks was the crowning achievement.

Until the 1820's the Negro urban population in the West lived south of the Ohio, Northern cities having few colored residents. The 1810 census counted only 185 free blacks in Pittsburgh and less than 100 in Cincinnati. Though the number grew in both places, it never constituted more than two per cent of all townspeople. [46] On the other hand, Negroes in Lexington and Louisville comprised

⁴⁴ This was the program of the Pittsburgh Moral Society, which had been organized as early as 1799. *Pittsburgh Gazette*, August 20, 1816.

⁴⁵ James Flint, *Letters from America* (Edinburgh, 1822), 218.

⁴⁶ United States Census, 1810, 44, 62.

nearly a third of the entire population, and their numerical growth in the first decades of the century matched that of the whites. In Louisville the number of blacks jumped from 77 in 1800 to almost 500 in 1810; in Lexington, from 462 to 1,594.[47] No official figures are available for St. Louis before 1810, but in that year Brackenridge estimated "four hundred people of color" in a city of about 1,400.[48] In these localities the overwhelming majority of blacks were slaves, less than one per cent being free except in St. Louis, where it was somewhat higher.

Though some urban whites held more than a dozen Negroes, slave ownership was more widely diffused in the cities than on the countryside. In 1810 about half the heads of families in Fayette County possessed slaves, whereas in Lexington the figure was nearly 75 per cent. Some townsmen had extensive holdings. John Bard, for example, owned 71 blacks, Richard Higgins listed 55, and the Barr brothers accounted for 62 between them, while thirty-one others held more than 10. But generally the urban colored population was split up into small units, with a few Negroes living behind the master's house in a cabin facing an alley lined with the shacks of other slaves.[49] The plantation system had no counterpart in town, and even large owners did not have the space to isolate their blacks from the rest of the neighborhood.

Most slaves in urban Kentucky worked as domestics and general handymen. "Almost all the labor is performed by slaves," James McBride noted in Lexington; "they are the only waiters, and very few of the white people can wait upon themselves in the smallest matter." In the Falls City they served as porters in the transshipment business and toiled on the dock and landings, loading and unloading river cargoes. In both towns, too, they built most of the streets, bridges, and canals, and put them in repair in the spring. As these

[47] United States Census, 1800, 29, ap; United States Census, 1810, 71a, 72a. In 1816 a local census in Lexington numbered 1,845 slaves in a total population of 5,448. Lexington, Trustees Book, June 6, 1816.

[48] H. M. Brackenridge, *Views of Louisiana* (Pittsburgh, 1814), 222.

[49] United States Census, 1810; MS, Lexington Public Library, Lexington; Leavy, "Memoir," *Kentucky Hist. Soc. Register*, XLI (1943), 323.

places turned increasingly to manufacturing, factories utilized Negroes in unskilled chores or in jobs where simple techniques were easily learned. Melish found "a number of black fellows busily employed" in "several ropewalks," and McBride visited one concern which "employed forty or fifty negro boys." Success in using Negroes in hemp works led to a general confidence that they could be adapted to many industrial lines. In 1810, when Richard Steele and his brother planned to build an iron mill, they chose Louisville as the site because of "the advantage we will have in working with slaves." [50]

Except for a few factories and large hotels, there was no way to utilize great numbers of Negroes in the city. Hence, large slaveholders hired out their blacks to people who needed additional labor. Most of these contracts ran for a year, though some covered a specific job or continued for an irregular length of time. Soon this system became formalized and the wages and terms were standardized.[51] In fact, many large owners on the countryside found the practice so profitable that they sent their Negroes to town for work in the ropewalks, mills and factories.

Urban conditions and the hiring-out custom put severe strains on the structure of slavery, whose basic institutions were formed in a rural setting. Control of the Negroes, never easy even on isolated plantations, proved more difficult in the city, where blacks lived as neighbors and often worked together far from the owner's view. In many cases the hired-out slave became virtually free, bringing home his monthly pay but developing the habits of a wage earner. Sometimes this independence increased to such an extent that blacks hired themselves out, making their own bargains with employers and paying the master on a monthly basis. In such instances bondage was nominal, and the relationship was much like that of a landlord and tenant. Contemporaries themselves recognized that the

[50] McBride, "Journey to Lexington," 25; Melish, *Travels*, II, 186; McBride, 24; R. Steele to W. Lytle, December 15, 1810, MS, William Lytle Collection (Historical and Philosophical Society of Ohio, Cincinnati).

[51] *Kentucky Gazette*, November 20, 1804; January 3, 1809, January 8, 1811, November 22, 1813.

city environment weakened the structure of slavery and threatened to dissolve the web of restraints on which the institution rested.[52]

As a result townspeople showed continual concern. From the first days of local government citizens urged their officials to tighten the controls over slaves. In 1800 the Lexington watch, which had been on a part-time schedule, was extended to cover Saturday night and Sunday to disperse the "large assemblages of negroes" which had "become troublesome." In that same year "numerous complaints" reached the city's trustees about slaves "being permitted to hire themselves, and keep houses that disturb the peace and quiet of society." Two years later, a petition noticed that the blacks in the South "are strongly bent on insurrection" and demanded rigid enforcement of the town codes.[53] Though Kentucky laws forbade slaves to hire themselves out, the problem became so serious that both Louisville and Lexington passed ordinances toughening the state provisions and requiring the police to enforce them "with the utmost vigor."[54] Clearly urban conditions disturbed the historic relationship of slaves to the master and the community, and town records reveal the frantic effort of local governments to find appropriate means to sustain the system.

South of the Ohio, white society both shunned and feared the few free Negroes who many thought would create unrest among the slaves. The Northern attitude toward colored people was still untested, but in cities like Pittsburgh and Cincinnati the response was a mixture of sympathy and reserve. This ambivalence was no where better illustrated than in the constitution adopted by Ohio

[52] There is abundant evidence that slavery in cities produced a different kind of Negro from that of the country plantation. As early as the 18th century a visitor to South Carolina described country slaves as "contented, sober, modest, humble, civil and obliging," contrasting them to the Charleston slave who was "rude, unmannerly, insolent, and shameless." Quoted in C. Bridenbaugh, *Myths and Realities: Societies of the Colonial South* (Baton Rouge, 1953), 63.

[53] Lexington, Trustees Book, July 7, 1800; July 25, 1800; June 22, 1802.

[54] Louisville, Trustees Book, March 9, 1809. Lexington's new ordinance included 10 lashes for slaves "loitering in the streets, corners . . . off the owner or hirers premises" or for "strolling about the Town."

in 1803. Here the Negro was given his freedom both from slavery and indenture, but he was also consigned to a clearly inferior status. He could not vote, hold office, or serve in the militia. In the convention the Cincinnati delegates, taking a liberal view on these matters, supported nine to one a motion to extend suffrage to colored citizens, and heavily opposed a move to strip them of all their civil rights. Generally, however, free blacks occupied the lowest rung of the social ladder. "Disciplined to laborious occupations," they were increasingly cut off from other citizens, living apart and finding each year more barriers to their participation in religious, educational, and civic affairs.[55]

Within a generation Western cities developed stratified societies, whose lines, though never as well defined as in the older sections of the country, represented distinctions which contemporaries thought important. Since urban communities were still young and their social structures still loose, movement up and down the hierarchy took place constantly. But this mobility did not diminish the strong drive for status that characterized townspeople. Having come from places where differences mattered, city dwellers early tried to recreate as much as possible the familiar social landscape they had known. To visitors this seemed quite extraordinary. Fortescue Cuming commented that it was a "matter of ridicule and amusement to a person of the least philosophy."[56] Yet to Western urbanites, anxious to establish roots in fresh soil, these distinctions were meaningful, and as the towns grew, the boundaries sharpened.

[55] Drake, *Statistical View*, 172; R. C. Wade, "The Negro in Cincinnati, 1800–1830," *The Journal of Negro History*, XXXIX (1954), 43–57.
[56] Cuming, "Sketches of a Tour," in Thwaites, ed., *Western Travels*, IV, 87.

Chapter 5

The Seeds of Culture

Though the process of settlement and growth produced social cleavages, there were many elements in urban culture which tended to draw people together and blur artificial distinctions. All classes mingled in churches, schools, and a large variety of civic organizations. In addition, the men, at least, shared the same amusements — horse racing, billiards, drinking, and even the theater being great levelers. These cohesive factors proved especially effective while the towns were still small. Though they could not prevent stratification, they at least fostered a certain intimacy among groups, blunting differences and increasing mobility. This kind of fraternization, while important, was also deceptive, for some travelers mistook it for the genuine egalitarianism which had in fact disappeared from frontier cities in their first decades.

The smallness of the towns was in itself a cementing force in the early stages. None was yet large enough to create the impersonality of the modern metropolis, though the appearance of city directories in Lexington in 1806 and Pittsburgh in 1815 hinted that things were beginning to change. Still, in the first decade of the century, most people knew everyone else, and why not? They saw their fellow citizens on the street during the day, joined them at the races or the fair, haggled with them in the market, drilled with them in the militia, and perhaps played a hand of whist or drank a tankard of ale with them at the tavern. This tendency was doubtless stronger among the men than the women. Thrown together in their work and relaxation, they mingled more freely than the ladies, who chose their acquaintances with more deliberation.

These contacts often became formalized in associations which brought together people from many walks to indulge a certain interest or perform a given service. The largest of these organizations were military companies and Masonic lodges. In the days of Indian fighting, the work of the local militia was a grim and serious business, but by the beginning of the century their meetings featured dinners, drinking, and sociability. Masonry, of course, was fraternal from the outset. Its yearly meetings in June to celebrate the festival of St. John the Baptist let loose the carnival spirit of the people. Though the officers' lists demonstrate that leadership in these groups was drawn largely from the merchant and professional classes, membership was open to almost all. Volunteer fire companies also had their social side, and the nature of their work prevented them from becoming overly exclusive.

The most important unifying element of urban culture, however, was the newspaper. Read by nearly everyone, it was a plumb line which touched all levels of society. Mrs. Trollope noticed that, although "all ranks of society, from the successful merchant, which is the highest, to the domestic serving man, which is the lowest," were too busy for much reading, they always found time for "a peep at a newspaper." Along with makeshift schools and churches, a paper was the first outward sign of civilization in frontier settlements. Pittsburgh, Lexington, and Cincinnati had at least one before 1800, and Louisville and St. Louis got theirs in the following decade. Though never very profitable financially, the newspapers were well received both in the towns and the surrounding country. Cincinnati's *Liberty Hall*, founded in 1804 with 150 subscribers, within five years twice doubled that number, and by 1813 it printed 2,000 issues weekly. The *Mercury* in Pittsburgh, established in 1811, enjoyed an even more flattering reception, reaching 1,400 customers by the end of its first year.[1] Competition was stiff. In both these instances, the new papers had to vie with older journals in the cities, as well as with many coming by mail from the East.[2]

[1] Frances Trollope, *Domestic Manners of the Americans*, Donald Smalley, ed. (New York, 1949), 92f; *Liberty Hall* (Cincinnati), November 16, 1813; *Mercury* (Pittsburgh), January 7, 1813.

[2] So many people took Philadelphia papers that Hugh Henry Brackenridge thought they endangered local enterprises. *Pittsburgh Gazette*, April 12, 1797.

Being weeklies, these sheets performed more the function of news-magazines than of newspapers. Local information spread faster by mouth than by print, causing editors to devote town coverage to commentary rather than to straight reporting. Greatest space was given to clippings from Eastern papers or journals, with particular emphasis on national and international affairs. Joseph Charless, in preparing a prospectus for his *Missouri Gazette* in 1808, summed up both the ideals and practice of the early journalists. Its columns would include "foreign intelligence" and pay "particular attention" to the "details of domestic occurrence with extracts from the proceedings of state and national legislatures." Nor was that all. "To diversify the scene we shall glean whatever may be most instructive and amusing in the Belles Lettres with historical and Poetical extracts." Most of this material would be reprints, but Charless called upon St. Louis's "men of genius" to send their work to him, though he counseled them to write about important matters, since the *Gazette* "will disdain to direct its flights at smaller game." [3] Though much in these journals was trivial and ephemeral, they did connect readers with the outside. And for many they formed a link to places and things they had known before, giving continuity to disrupted lives.

The papers grew with the towns. By 1815 their number had greatly increased, more local authors contributed, and town news and commentary were no longer slighted. John Scull, Jr., who took over the *Pittsburgh Gazette* in 1816 after his father's thirty-year editorship, noticed this striking development. Very early, he observed, the paper was one of many "village appendages, too much in the light of an alehouse, or blacksmith's shop." Most issues concentrated on "announcing to the world, the important intelligence of stray cattle, runaway apprentices, and cheap stores." But now "a new era is commencing," when people have "enough of that spare time, which is classically called 'elegant leisure,'" and editors can "offer the world a Journal of correct taste as regards literature and the soundest principles as relates to politics." The focus and function of the paper had changed. Now with a "phalanx" of "talents and

[3] *Missouri Gazette*, broadside, 1808.

achievements," the *Gazette* would send Pittsburgh's genius abroad as well as bringing the outside world to the Iron City.[4]

Like the newspaper, religion was a unifying force. Denominational infighting and theological controversy often obscured this function, but in many churches people from different classes came together, organized congregations, erected buildings, and later engaged in charitable and educational work. This helped to soften, though it did not erase, social lines. John Bradford and his wealthy Episcopalian friends still established "a gentleman's church" in Lexington, and in Western cities generally the well-to-do gravitated toward Presbyterianism. The Great Revival later accelerated this division, causing the upper strata to look upon the lower classes as "fanatics and zealots" and leading the underlings to interpret the reserve of the "well informed and wealthy" as "infidelity."[5] But most individual churches were not exclusive — at least so far as whites were concerned — and their ministers recruited wherever they anticipated success.

The men who founded frontier cities had economic rather than religious motives; hence there were no churches at first, and itinerant preachers stopped only occasionally. Composed of merchants, soldiers, immigrants, and boatmen, these posts did not seem receptive even to missionary activity. "I feel the power of Satan in those little wicked western trading towns," Francis Asbury remarked in 1803.[6] But as soon as more stable elements appeared, they formed congregations and prepared to build houses of worship. Beginnings were necessarily modest, since the numbers of church members were small.

Out of this unpromising ground, religious life in urban centers

[4] *Pittsburgh Gazette*, August 9, 1816.

[5] See N. H. Sonne, *Liberal Kentucky, 1780–1828* (New York, 1939), 16; E. P. Anderson, *The Intellectual Life of Pittsburgh*, 1786–1836 (n.p., n.d.), 21; Drake, *Statistical View*, 162; Espy, "Memorandums of a Tour," 24.

[6] F. Asbury, *Journal* (n.p., 1821), III, 127.

presently began to flower. John Wrenshall, who planted Methodism in Pittsburgh, found the town in 1796 "a Sodom in Miniature," but within a decade eight churches had been established and five of them owned permanent meeting houses. Among the new ministers were men of education and refinement. Most churches in that city were fundamentally Calvinist, a fact which greatly reduced sectarian animosity, though it did not avert schisms. Roman Catholicism remained weak there until the manufacturing boom brought a large influx of immigrants. They built a church in 1808, and the 100 to 150 Catholics in the area — "mostly poor" — intermittently supported a priest through this formative period. As early as 1803 visitors noted spiritual improvement. "A Sojourner" asserted that "the current report" across the mountains was that Pittsburgh was "a young hell, a second Sodom," but after visting four churches "expecting to see a disorderly croud [*sic*] of people," he admitted that all were filled with "well dressed decent people paying greatest attention to divine service." [7]

Religious development in other transmontane cities paralleled the Pittsburgh story. By 1815 six denominations were organized in Cincinnati, and the Methodist Episcopal Church alone had over 400 members. Cuming found five churches in Lexington, while Louisville, a much smaller place, had three. The bulk of Western urbanites were Protestant, though each town had its priest and parish. St. Louis was the exception, being not only overwhelmingly Catholic, but also the center of that faith's activity in the entire Mississippi Valley region. After 1817 it became the site of a cathedral and the seat of the Bishop of Upper Louisiana. Before that time, however, St. Louis had been badly neglected. Father de Andres, arriving in 1818, summed up the situation. "The chief part of the population is French (Creole as it is called), and consequently Catholic, but without any religious culture, on account of the long

[7] Wrenshall, Journal (see above, p. 111, n. 22), III, 39; Cuming, "Sketches of a Tour," in Thwaites, ed., *Western Travels*, IV, 84–85; F. Filner, ed., "Trials and Triumphs of Catholic Pioneers in Western Pennsylvania (As Recorded by Their Correspondence)," *Records of the American Catholic Historical Society*, XXXIV (1923), 334; *Pittsburgh Gazette*, September 23, 1803.

period during which the place has been destitute of clergymen and every means of instruction." [8]

Religious progress in the cities during this period was steadier and more substantial — though less spectacular — than in the surrounding areas. Its growth owed little to the Great Revival, which burned across the Western countryside at the beginning of the century. That godly upheaval was essentially rural, having its roots in the isolation of agricultural living and the spiritual starvation of people unattended by regular services. Urban life, with its constant human contacts and its settled church organization, involved neither of these elements. Indeed, in the cities religion often served as a refuge from the bustle of crowded living as well as an avenue to increased fellowship.

The flames of the Great Revival licked very close to the towns, but could not find inflammable material in them. This imperviousness brought complaints from religious enthusiasts, who felt that urban indifference sprang from wickedness. In a letter to a Washington friend, a devout "Gentleman" from Lexington wrote in 1801 that the revival was having great success "near this place . . . at Bryant's Station, Boone's Creek, Marble Creek, Shawne Run, etc.," but "alas, poor L[exington], yet in measure stands out, though I trust even in this Sodom there are a few brought to the saving knowledge of Christ." [9] Western newspapers — all published in the towns — ignored the rural excitement, and though Kentucky was the center of the movement, its four weeklies never once mentioned the meetings.[10] Pittsburgh was so unreceptive that

[8] Drake, *Statistical View*, 162–65; Cuming, "Sketches of a Tour," in Thwaites, ed., *Western Travels*, IV, 183; McMurtrie, *Sketches of Louisville*, 126; J. Rothensteiner, *History of the Archdiocese of St. Louis in its Various Stages of Development from A. D. 1673–A. D. 1928* (St. Louis, 1928), I, 271.

[9] W. W. Sweet, *Religion on the American Frontier: The Baptists, 1783–1830* (New York, 1931), 609–10.

[10] See W. B. Posey, *The Development of Methodism in the Old Southwest* (Tuscaloosa, Alabama, 1933), 15n. A study was made of four Kentucky newspapers between 1788 and 1804, and in over 500 issues not a single mention of the revival was discovered. Sonne interprets this to mean that the editors were largely Presbyterian and hence enemies of revivalism. However,

Wrenshall charged that preachers "only pretended to visit," though some of them claimed modest success.[11] Many of the great gatherings took place within thirty miles of the cities, yet no evidence exists of any activity or even concern in urban records.

The failure of the towns to respond to the Great Revival reflected special social conditions, not infidelity, for in the first years of the century urban religious life matured rapidly. Progress could be measured in increased membership, additional churches, new ministers, or the initial appearance of substantial and in some cases elaborate buildings. But equally significant were the new functions assumed by congregations, demonstrating that the ordeal of organizing had passed and that the churches could turn outward. Cincinnati's experience was typical. In 1814 the First Presbyterian women formed the Cincinnati Female Society for Charitable Purposes to give relief to indigents of their own sect, distribute Bibles, and send money to the theological seminary at Princeton. The First Baptists in the same year formed two societies for the support of foreign missions, while other groups established Sunday schools, and all denominations joined the Cincinnati Miami Bible Society to get the scriptures to the poor.[12] Far from being sinks of depravity, Western cities by 1815 had become religious centers which felt secure enough at home to worry about the spiritual state of frontiersmen and foreign heathens and the financial straits of Eastern students of theology.

Education, like religion and the newspaper, constituted another plumb line in frontier society touching all classes. From the first days of settlement Western townspeople showed a deep interest in providing their young with some formal training. In 1761 a

---

my own investigation of Pittsburgh and Cincinnati papers of the same period, where most editors were not Presbyterian, shows the same indifference.

[11] Wrenshall, Journal (see above, p. 111, n. 22), IV, 110.

[12] Drake, *Statistical View*, 162–65. Regional Meetings of the Methodist Episcopal Church were generally held in Cincinnati.

handful of traders, "the soberer sort of people," around Fort Pitt subscribed sixty pounds to hire a teacher for twenty students.[13] But for many years schooling was sporadic, depending on transient teachers of uncertain quality and reliability. A durable educational base needed a more stable community, and some towns did not get permanent facilities for many decades. In Lexington, however, Transylvania Seminary was founded as early as 1785, and the Pittsburgh Academy opened its doors in that city four years later. Other localities had to rely on less public and more informal instruction.

Though the need for schools increased rapidly, many obstacles stood in the way. Tuition fees kept many children of wage earners from attending any institution. Their youngsters played in the streets while small, and then picked up jobs as they became old enough to make their own way. As the towns expanded, this situation disturbed many who saw a generation "growing up like weeds, without benefit of cultivation." Even as late as 1816 one observer estimated that less than a quarter of the school-age youth of Pittsburgh were getting any formal education, and many were frightened by "the great number of children with which our town abounds, running daily through out streets, in an almost savage state." Most who could afford tuition stayed only long enough to acquire basic skills and then moved into the mercantile world. "As soon as a boy can read, write, and cast up a bill," McMurtrie remarked, "he is withdrawn from school and placed at a desk, there to be initiated into the mysteries of buying and selling." [14]

The first response to this growing educational problem was additional private schools. They were easily established since they required only a teacher, a rented room, and some students. Their curriculum included everything from classical languages to surveying and bookkeeping for the boys, and courses ranging from

[13] J. Kenny, "Diary of James Kenny," *Historical Magazine*, II (1858), 273–74.

[14] *Western Spy* (Cincinnati), September 24, 1800; *Commonwealth* (Pittsburgh), October 29, 1813; *Pittsburgh Gazette*, October 29, 1813; McMurtrie, *Sketches of Louisville*, 125. Thomas Ashe made the same observation a decade earlier, saying that men "enter into business so early, that they are obliged to abandon their studies before they are half completed." *Travels*, 27.

English literature to needlework and knitting for the girls. Most of these schools were short-lived, but usually a city had a half dozen of them in any given year,[15] and some, like Brevost's in Pittsburgh or Stubbs's in Cincinnati, achieved local distinction. Teachers found the competition for paying scholars pretty stiff, and many employed huckstering techniques to attract patronage. Timothy Flint, both disturbed and amused by the advertisements he saw in the Western press, gave this advice to the aspiring instructor: "Call your school by some new way of instructing children, by which they can learn twice as much in half the time, as by the old ways. Throw off all modesty. Move the water, and get in while it is moving."[16]

This haphazard arrangement satisfied few, and as the population increased, its inadequacy became everywhere apparent. However, to embark on a new system would cost money, and towns gave priority to other calls on their limited finances. At this critical juncture the Lancastrian system, already tested in the East, was introduced into Western cities. By this scheme advanced pupils acted as monitors for the newer ones, allowing the instructor to spend most of his time supervising student teachers. Thus a single instructor could reach five hundred children. "This mode of teaching is particularly adapted to Towns of extensive population," one Pittsburgher observed, while another noticed that "with the trifling expense of the price of a slate only, a child can be taught to spell, read and write with considerable facility."[17] Though these were not free schools, they substantially reduced tuition and stretched teachers over a large number of children. The enthusiasm with which Western communities received the new system was a measure

[15] Pittsburgh had at least 43 different schools between 1800 and 1825 and Lexington had 42 between 1789 and 1820. Anderson, *Pittsburgh*, 12; R. L. Rusk, *The Literature of the Middle Western Frontier* (New York, 1925), 51n.

[16] Flint, *Recollections*, 186–87. Christopher Frederick Sheve's advertisement in St. Louis in 1809 typifies the technique. He claimed that he taught English and French "with a particular method of teaching" which succeeded in one-sixth the time. "Pupils have found the method more amusing and agreeable, none have complained about being overloaded with rules, and fatigued with the dryness of theory." *Missouri Gazette*, January 11, 1809.

[17] *Pittsburgh Gazette*, October 29, 1813; October 14, 1815.

of the urgency of their need. By 1815 most had embarked on the experiment.

These cities, not satisfied with merely providing opportunities for elementary education, also strove to plant the seeds of higher learning. Names of secondary institutions were usually misleading, for "academies" and "seminaries" were hardly more than glorified grammar schools. Until the 1820's most young men went East for college degrees, though many towns had established their own "universities." This drive for community colleges was in part economic, for the cost of sending students to the East was generally prohibitive. Kentucky led the way in bringing higher education to the frontier by creating Transylvania University in 1799, and Cincinnati followed within a decade. Yet the experiments were not wholly successful. Transylvania became immediately embroiled in denominational squabbles, and Cincinnati lost its building in a high wind in 1809.[18] Other towns also felt the urge. In 1819 the Pittsburgh Academy became a university, and at about the same time Bishop Dubourg opened the doors of St. Louis University.

Within a few years after the second war with Great Britain nearly every city in the West could offer its young people educational opportunities ranging from elementary schools to college training. Though the quality was irregular, especially on the upper levels, and economic barriers excluded many, the first steps showed promise. The Lancastrian plan not only absorbed a substantial part of a greatly increased child population, but also popularized the idea of mass instruction, thus paving the way for the free public-school system two decades later. The establishment of academies and colleges made the towns educational centers attracting students from the surrounding areas and providing teachers for new rural schools.[19]

Not all education was formal and for young people. Adults

[18] Drake, *Statistical View*, 157. For an excellent treatment of Transylvania University, see Sonne, *Liberal Kentucky*, 46–77.

[19] Small communities advertised in urban papers for school teachers throughout this period. For Cincinnati's role in this process in the first decade of the century, see Western Spy (Cincinnati), May 27, 1801, August 31, 1803, *Liberty Hall* (Cincinnati), April 16, 1805, January 14, 1807.

formed societies and clubs to promote knowledge and discussion. Some, like the Coffee Room and Exchange in Pittsburgh, were dedicated to reading contemporary literature; others, such as the Pittsburgh Franklin Society, met for debate on current topics, while still others devoted their efforts to learned papers. The Transylvania Philosophical Society attracted many prominent Lexingtonians after its foundation in 1802, sponsoring monthly meetings which featured lectures on medicine, law, philosophy, and national and international affairs. Specialists also organized for intellectual exercise and self-improvement. The Chemical and Physiological Society of Pittsburgh, for example, not only held fortnightly meetings, but acquired a library, a cabinet of curiosities, and chemical apparatus.[20] Neither Louisville nor St. Louis matched the other cities in offering their older citizens such opportunities, but in larger communities the variety was surprisingly rich.

Since books form another integral part of the apparatus of learning and civilized living, their number, quality, and availability evidence the cultural stature of these new communities. By 1815 the achievement was substantial. Subscription libraries had been established in almost every urban center; schools and academies accumulated working collections; and many individuals acquired private holdings that bore comparison with Eastern ones. As impressive as the number of books was their variety. In Lexington, for instance, the library offered over 2,000 different titles, embracing nearly all fields of knowledge. Moreover, private listings, booksellers' advertisements, and college records clearly demonstrate that neither the classics nor the best of contemporary writing was unknown, and that access to them was not limited to a few.[21]

[20] *Pittsburgh Gazette*, March 2, 1810; October 29, 1813; *Kentucky Gazette*, March 26, April 30, 1802; *Pittsburgh Gazette*, November 18, 1813; Anderson, *Pittsburgh*, 63–64.

[21] Lexington Library, *A Catalogue of the Books Belonging to the Lexington Library Company* (Lexington, 1821).

Prior to the establishment of subscription libraries, bookstores were the primary distributors of reading material. Editors kept a few volumes on hand for sale, and merchants usually carried a small number of Bibles, almanacs, and primers. Shops dealing largely in books appeared quite early. John Mullanphy started one in Lexington in 1793, and seven years later Zadock Cramer opened the most famous book mart in the West, advertising over eight hundred titles. In every town these men played a crucial role in bringing culture to frontier regions. William Leavy, a Lexington merchant, recognized this contribution to the development of his city. "Perhaps nothing," he asserted, "illustrates more the rise and progress of Lexington and its vicinity in its society and wealth than the rise of the Book Business here." After noting the arrival of each new proprietor, he observed that due to them "Lexington had become a reading population." [22]

Another center for the distribution of books was the local newspaper office, which not only imported works from the East for sale, but increasingly printed its own.[23] John Scull of the *Pittsburgh Gazette* issued the third volume of Hugh Henry Brackenridge's *Modern Chivalry* in 1793, and many editors turned out bound copies of state laws and large numbers of pamphlets and almanacs and even slim collections of native poetry. The print shop was a kind of clearing house where interested citizens found magazines, books, and journals from all parts of the country, and a lush file of the nation's leading newspapers. Editors and booksellers throughout the West kept in close touch with each other and in 1805 formed a trade association "similar to the Literary Fair in the Atlantic States to facilitate the publication and exchange of works of merit." [24]

Out of local bookshops and Eastern stores grew many substantial

---

[22] *Pittsburgh Gazette*, June 28, 1800; Leavy, "Memoir," *Kentucky Hist. Soc. Register*, XLI (1943), 319.

[23] Some editors handled books on a reasonably large scale. In 1811 *Liberty Hall's* editor in Cincinnati offered 179 different titles for sale, and the next year his competitor, John W. Browne, advertised over 200 new books. *Liberty Hall* (Cincinnati), July 31, 1811, January 2, 1812.

[24] *Liberty Hall* (Cincinnati), August 20, 1805. John Bradford was the association's first president.

private libraries. Even before the founding of some towns in the Ohio Valley, many St. Louisans had collections of over one hundred volumes, including the works of leading European contemporaries. Fortesque Cuming, who fell ill in Pittsburgh in 1808, was surprised to find that two chance acquaintances could offer him "judiciously selected libraries" to help pass the time, and Henry Marie Brackenridge found his father's assortment too large even for his voracious appetite. Every town contained a few very extensive personal libraries and many good ones. William Leavy, who considered his own holdings quite modest, acquired, among other items, twenty-nine volumes of the "British Classical Essayists" and Brewster's *Edinburgh Encyclopedia* in twenty volumes, and he subscribed yearly to the *North American Review*, the *American Quarterly Review* and the *Edinburgh Review*. Even more interesting is the testimony of Robert McAfee, a farm lad who went to school in Lexington between 1795 and 1797, where he collected over fifty volumes, including many of the latest novels.[25]

Private libraries often took on a public flavor since some owners encouraged borrowing, and many young men first whetted their appetite at a neighbor's bookshelf. Academies, coffee houses, and reading rooms supplemented these personal collections. Cuming found a coffee house in Lexington in 1808 which subscribed to forty-two different newspapers purchased out of the dues of more than sixty members, and Melish visited a similar place in Pittsburgh two years later. The better-established schools built small libraries for students and supporters. In fact, Lexington's subscription library grew from a core of books initially gathered at Transylvania University.[26]

These various sources satisfied the needs of fledgling settlements, but as the towns grew, a demand arose for circulating libraries, which, though not free, were open to anyone who paid a member-

[25] McDermott, *Private Libraries*, 65ff; Cuming, "Sketches of a Tour," in Thwaites, ed., *Western Travels*, IV, 79; Brackenridge, *Recollections*, 91ff; Leavy, "Memoir," 131; McAfee, "Life and Times of Robert McAfee," 140.

[26] Cuming, "Sketches of a Tour," in Thwaites, ed., *Western Travels*, IV, 188; Melish, *Travels*, II, 58; *Pittsburgh Gazette*, March 2, 1810; Lexington, *Catalogue*, 111.

ship fee. As in most other cultural matters, Lexington led the way. In 1796 Transylvania University, finding that it could not support its student library, appealed to the public for help. A group of citizens "of the best standing in the community for integrity and means" responded by forming an association of dues-paying members which took over the library, changed its location, and began buying on a considerable scale.[27]

Other cities, feeling the same need, also witnessed efforts to establish subscription libraries. Zadock Cramer, who pioneered in almanacs and navigating guides, became the driving force behind Pittsburgh's first experiment in 1800. Its success induced others to follow, and in 1814 all joined in the Pittsburgh Permanent Library, which within a few years owned nearly two thousand volumes. Louisville's record was less impressive, but by 1815 its library association had been formed, though rocky days lay ahead. St. Louis, which boasted some of the best private collections, was slow in getting organized on a broader basis, and a failure in 1811 hurt subsequent endeavors. Cincinnati spent the first decade of the century in at least four futile attempts to open a library. In despair, "Curtius" asked his fellow townsmen "why . . . must we be destitute of literary advantages equal to that flourishing town [Lexington] when our commercial ones are so much superior?" The 1814 launching proved successful, however, and within two years the library boasted better than a thousand volumes.[28] None of these was free to users, but the circulating library, like the Lancastrian system in education, paved the way for later democratic expansion.

[27] Leavy, "Memoir," 56.

[28] *Pittsburgh Gazette*, June 28, 1800, June 12, December 4, 1801, May 7, 1802, February 8, 1811, October 29, 1813, December 17, 1813, December 20, 1814, January 3, 1815, January 7, 1817; *Louisville Public Advertiser*, February 24, 1821, February 4, 1826; *Missouri Gazette*, January 16, 1811; *Western Spy* (Cincinnati), February 13, 1802, February 17, 1806, December 29, 1808, January 5, 1809; *Liberty Hall* (Cincinnati), August 21, 1815; *Liberty Hall* (Cincinnati), April 1, 1816.

While frontier urbanites built schools and organized libraries, they also enjoyed amateur theatricals, and by 1815 were welcoming professional players. The drama moved West under trying circumstances. Stages had to be improvised in barns and old buildings, and the actors pretended to no artistry. These pioneer thespians, however, sensed the importance of their efforts, and in 1801 a Cincinnati bard summed up their mission in a prologue:

> When wealthy cities shall extensive rise,
> And lofty spires salute our western skies;
> When costly theatres shall loud resound
> With music, mirth, & every joyous sound;
> T'will be remember'd that in days of yore,
> Between a ragged roof and sorry floor,
> The laughing muse here for the first time sate,
> And kindly deign'd to cheer our infant state.[29]

The theater not only encountered the usual difficulties confronting cultural enterprises in young communities, but also faced additional obstacles. Many people, especially powerful religious leaders, considered the drama too worldly and charged it with corrupting the morals of the people. In addition, local governments classified stage performances along with circuses, magic shows, and traveling zoos and hence required licenses for each appearance. But playhouses prospered in spite of these attitudes, finding support in almost every class and establishing themselves in popular favor.

Amateurs dominated the drama until about 1810, when traveling companies began to swing West on their way to New Orleans. As early as 1799 the students at Transylvania University treated Lexingtonians to "The Busy Body" and a farce, "Love à la Mode," on a stage in the court house. In the next decade the second story of a brewery was transformed into the "New Theatre," where many organizations like the Military Society and the Roscian Society frequently put on plays. Though a city ordinance required a $5 license for each performance, the enforcement against local citizens was lax. However, with the coming of the strolling performers a kind

[29] *Western Spy* (Cincinnati), October 10, 1801.

of guerilla warfare broke out between town officials and the visitors, who claimed that the tax was discriminatory. Despite this harassment, the drama was widely accepted in Lexington, which became one of the anchors for troupers playing Western cities.[30]

Pittsburgh, though often charged with being hostile to culture, was in many ways the best theater town in the new country. Its first amateur efforts followed Lexington's by only a year, and within a decade it had two organizations — one of lawyers and one of mechanics — who performed once a month during the winter. Because of a shortage of musicians, they imported a group from Philadelphia at the expense of several hundred dollars. "The theatre is in the great room of the upperstory of the court house," Fortesque Cuming reported, "which from its size, and having several other contiguous apartments which serve for green rooms, dressing rooms, &c is very well adapted to that purpose." This arrangement soon proved inadequate, and in 1812 the Pittsburgh Theatre was erected. A building forty by sixty feet, its auditorium accommodated over four hundred people, and until the postwar economic collapse it presented local actors, professional companies, and artists of "first rate talent" from New York, Philadelphia, Boston, and Charleston. In 1815 Pittsburgh's local players went on the road, appearing in Cincinnati, Lexington, and smaller towns.[31]

A similar development took place in other towns, though more slowly. Probably because St. Louis and Louisville were smaller than the cities farther east, the amateur theatricals were less active. However, their river locations made them easily accessible to traveling companies, which included them in their earliest itineraries. The growth of Cincinnati's stage came only after a running battle with stubborn religious forces which equated the stage with immorality. This conflict existed to some degree in every city, but only in Cin-

[30] *Kentucky Gazette*, February 28, 1799; July 4, 1809, June 2, 1810, September 15, 1810; Lexington, Trustees Book, May 6, 1805, May 2, 1811.

[31] Anderson, *Pittsburgh*, 46; Cuming, "Sketches of a Tour," in Thwaites, ed., *Western Travels*, IV, 82–83; *Mercury* (Pittsburgh), February 22, 1815; N. M. Ludlow, *Dramatic Life as I found It* (St. Louis, 1880), 65; *Pittsburgh Gazette*, June 6, 1817; *Liberty Hall* (Cincinnati), May 8, 1815.

cinnati did the opposition gain strength enough to contest seriously the progress of the drama.

Though a local group put on O'Keefe's comic opera "The Poor Soldier" in 1801 and repeated it several times during the next year, amateurs were less ambitious in Cincinnati than in Pittsburgh or Lexington. The Turners, a professional company, stopped in 1811, but still performances were few. Three years later a move to build a theater converted the smoldering hostility of some religious people into open attack. Spearheading the assault was Joshua L. Wilson, a Presbyterian minister and one of the town's most influential citizens. Writing in the *Western Spy*, and probably with its support, he asserted that the stage corrupted both actors and audience, and that the accompanying orchestra was blasphemous because all music ought to be reserved for the church.[32]

In his fight to crush the drama in Cincinnati, Wilson found allies in many places. The town's ne'er-do-wells often arrived at the theater in a frolicsome mood and in the course of the performance would whoop it up a bit, insulting the good people and cat-calling the actors. Soon it was argued that the public peace was endangered and that the police should close the playhouse. The city council added to the trouble by setting the license fee at ten dollars a night, which the editor of *Liberty Hall* considered so high as to discourage traveling troupes. When all else failed to halt the increasing enthusiasm for the stage, "Non Interpretandum" turned to more direct action, stealing the green curtain of the Thespian Corps, which forced them to "retire . . . from the *Boards* to their Dormitories." "I did it for a moral purpose," he later admitted, "i.e., to destroy the prolific source of mountebanks (who are the bane of morality) and by that means promote the interest of philosophy; and this I have accomplished." [33]

Through 1815 its adversaries had Cincinnati's theater backed against the wall. Defenders of the stage retaliated by asserting that

[32] *Liberty Hall* (Cincinnati), January 14, 1815, January 23, 1815, March 4, 1815.

[33] *Liberty Hall* (Cincinnati), April 8, 1815; May 22, 1815; April 1, 1816, December 8, 1816; December 16, 1816.

the drama — at least as performed in the Queen City — strengthened rather than corrupted moral values, and that all the proceeds went to the relief of the poor and other worthy causes. "Whatever may be thought of the deleterious influence of our Eastern playhouse upon the morals of the multitude," wrote "A Dramatic Amateur," "the same danger need not be apprehended on a Western stage, and least of all, where, as in the present instance, the *citizens themselves,* are the performers." But the basic position was best stated by the players themselves in an advertisement for *John Bull,* "the well known comedy":

> To bring relief to meagre want and pain,
> Unawed by bigotry — unbribed by gain, —
> To touch the heart, with sentiments refin'd
> Amuse, instruct and dignify the mind.[34]

Though many Westerners remained unreconciled, the theater by 1815 had clearly won the right to live. Though the quality of the performances was poor, public support was widespread. Constant complaints about disturbances in the pit demonstrated that the underlings often attended, if not always respectfully. The better classes came too, sitting in the boxes, hoping for amusement and edification. The editor of the *Pittsburgh Gazette* expressed the outlook of many thoughtful people when he observed, "Whatever . . has a tendency to mingle us harmoniously together, to soften manners, to relax the brow of care, and to wear off those sharp points of character which seem to grow out of an exclusive devotion to business, deserves attention." "Nothing," he added, "is better calculated for the purpose than a well regulated stage." [35]

Music and painting fared less well than the theater. Requiring some training and usually instruments or equipment not readily available, these skills demanded a greater specialization than young

[34] *Liberty Hall* (Cincinnati), January 8, 1816; March 18, 1815.
[35] *Pittsburgh Gazette,* November 13, 1818.

communities were able to support. Yet very early there were signs of awakening. Lexington's Kentucky Musical Society presented a concert of "vocal and instrumental music" in 1805, though they carefully protected their amateur standing by disclaiming "all mercenary views" and promising that the proceeds would go to charity. Throughout the next year they continued to play before "very respectable audiences," even in bad weather. The Apollonian Society in Pittsburgh was probably the foremost musical organization. In 1807 Fortesque Cuming heard them perform Haydn, Pleyel, Bach, and Mozart "with a degree of taste and execution, which I could not have expected in so remote a place." The Harmonical Society served the same function in Cincinnati, offering concerts to the public and an opportunity for those with some talent and training to use them.[36]

Music students also gave concerts. These were less ambitious than the programs of adult societies. In 1801, Declary, who called himself Pittsburgh's "music master," presented his pupils, and thirteen years later Miss Demilliere's students played selections from Mozart, Martini, Nicoli, and others. By 1815 each city had at least one teacher, if not a class, which offered a wide variety of musical instruction. An increasing number of Western urbanites owned some instrument, pianos being especially popular. Joseph Green began the manufacture of "Patent Piano Fortes" in 1805, and within a decade they could be counted "by the dozens" in Cincinnati.[37] Musical taste rose perceptibly as the cities grew, with an increasing number of concerts meeting the more elevated interests of the few, while church singing and military bands fulfilled a more popular demand.

Painting as an art found fewer practitioners and patrons than music. Eastern portraitists traveled through the West, passing a week here and a week there, doing likenesses of prominent people and

---

[36] *Kentucky Gazette*, November 21, 1805; December 4, 1806; Cuming, "Sketches of a Tour," in Thwaites, ed., *Western Travels*, IV, 81; *Liberty Hall* (Cincinnati), April 18, 1810.

[37] *Pittsburgh Gazette*, October 30, 1801; *Liberty Hall* (Cincinnati), April 29, 1816. The ladies of Cincinnati organized the St. Cecilia Society for piano playing, mixing a taste for music with a greater taste for socializing.

occasionally teaching a little. But before 1815 only John James Audubon in Louisville showed more than pedestrian talent. No city seems to have had a resident artist, though one transient miniaturist stayed in Pittsburgh for many years after announcing his visit as a "few days." He was so poorly supported, however, that he made a living from other pursuits and is better remembered as the founder of the Apollonian Society.[38]

One of these transient artists brought unique powers to the West. This was the naturalist, Audubon, who came across the mountains in 1808 at the age of twenty-three to set up storekeeping in Louisville. Finding patrons in a few physicians and among the well-to-do French, like the Berthods and Tarascons, he began to do his first serious painting. For a while his business and art mingled comfortably, because he used his many trips to the East and South and into the backlands to collect new specimens for his work. But Audubon did not take easily to mercantile life, and his leisurely habits allowed his competitors at Louisville to cut into his trade, forcing him to move farther down the Ohio to Henderson, Kentucky. No other important talent appeared in the West until Lexington's Matthew Jouett rose to break the new country's dependence on the East. In fact, a new era opened in 1815 when this confident youth, accused by his father of being nothing but a "damned sign painter," rode off to Boston to study with Gilbert Stuart.[39]

This varied social and intellectual life prepared the soil for the appearance of a few cultural figures of some distinction. To be sure, these men were not giants, nor could they compare with leading contemporaries across the mountains, but they were men whose work was substantial enough to have lasting interest. All of them were urban products who spent most of their time in cities and found

[38] *Pittsburgh Gazette*, June 23, 1804; Cuming, "Sketches of a Tour," in Thwaites, ed., *Western Travels*, IV, 82.

[39] C. Rourke, *Audubon* (New York, 1936), 45–68; S. W. Price, *The Old Masters of the Bluegrass* (Louisville, 1922), 21.

there the stimulation, leisure, and support needed for their work. Some, like Hugh Henry Brackenridge, Daniel Drake, and Joseph Buchanan, identified themselves closely with the entire civic progress of their communities as well as making their own cultural contributions. Though many professional men distinguished themselves in special fields, about a half-dozen authors deserve special attention not only for what they wrote, but also because their lives throw some light on the intellectual texture of early Western cities.

The most important literary figure at the beginning of the century was Hugh Henry Brackenridge, who was among the first permanent settlers in Pittsburgh and for twenty-five years its most prominent and controversial citizen. His early days were spent at Princeton and Philadelphia, where during the Revolution he wrote intensely patriotic poems. When he came to the new country in 1781 a good part of his work was behind him. He quickly became a Pittsburgh booster, writing a series of articles in the local newspaper designed to lure people to "The Point." In a fit of enthusiasm he not only prophesied that the city would be the "greatest manufacturing center in the continent or perhaps in the world," but also asserted that in 1786 it already had 1,500 people, an estimate he knew to be about three times too high. "As I pass along," he added hastily, "I may remark that this country is in general highly prolific." A year later when he ran for the state assembly he did not hide his local chauvinism. "I conceive it to be a public good to this country," he wrote in his platform, "that the town of Pittsburgh be encouraged, that it be made a borough, that it have a seat of justice, that it have a school endowed in it." [40]

Brackenridge's sally into public affairs did not prove wholly satisfactory, for his support of the new Federal Constitution made him a target for western Pennsylvania's antifederalist majority, whose leaders chopped him down in the next election.[41] "My

[40] Brackenridge, *Gazette Publications*, 7–19; *Pittsburgh Gazette*, August 26, 1786; September 9, 1786.
[41] Pittsburgh itself was Federalist in temper and generally supported the Constitution, but the back country, part of which was included in Brackenridge's election district, heavily opposed the new document.

character was wholly gone with the populace," he remembered with disappointment, adding, however, that "pride and good policy would not permit me to leave the country, until I conquered the prejudice." [42] Brooding over his defeat, he became convinced that the mass of people did not recognize or respect quality and that when confronted with two men, they invariably chose the lesser. *Modern Chivalry*, Brackenridge's substantial claim to literary fame, spins out this thesis in detail.

Brackenridge was only secondarily a product of Pittsburgh and the West. He had completed his formal education and finished the bulk of his writing before he came to the new country, and *Modern Chivalry*, though its setting and situation pertain to the back country, traces its literary genealogy to the Old World. His son, Henry Marie, on the other hand, was born in Pittsburgh and grew up in the West, and his life illustrates the accomplishments that were possible — though not normal — in the young city. By the age of ten, young Brackenridge had traveled over 3,000 miles, learned two languages besides English, and read such classics as *Don Quixote*, *Tom Jones*, and *Robinson Crusoe*, to say nothing of his father's writings. In the next decade he picked up Latin, Greek, Italian, and Spanish and charged through the ancients as well as Bacon, Locke, Newton, and other moderns. He later wrote five books, contributed to local publications, and became, like his father before him, a kind of cultural leader. His *Views of Louisiana* was the first serious inventory of the vast area purchased from France, and his *Recollections of Persons and Places in the West* remains one of the most valuable memoirs of the period.

Neither of the Brackenridges had the intellectual audacity or versatility of a contemporary Lexingtonian, Dr. Joseph Buchanan, whose book, *The Philosophy of Human Nature*, was a pioneer study in the history of American materialism and whose life touched nearly all the nerve centers of Western cultural life. Born in Virginia, Buchanan spent his early days in Tennessee and entered Transylvania University in 1804. There his independence kept him in

[42] H. H. Brackenridge, *Incidents of the Western Insurrection in the Western Parts of Pennsylvania in the Year 1794* (Philadelphia, 1795), III, 13–14.

trouble with the faculty because he insisted on criticizing the texts, and when he discovered an error in Ferguson's *Optics,* he clashed with the most powerful man at the college. Without then taking a degree he studied medicine with Dr. Samuel Brown, who steered him toward the writings of Erasmus Darwin, Hume, Locke, and Hartley. After two years' study he went to Port Gibson, Mississippi, where he prepared a paper on fever, while in general practice. In 1809 he returned to Transylvania in order to be a professor in the medical department. Actually, its doors did not open until later, but Buchanan prepared his lectures, which he published as *The Philosophy of Human Nature.*[43]

This is in many ways a remarkable volume. Not only is it a witness to the intellectual possibilities in the new country, but it also holds an interesting position in the central philosophic controversy between spiritualists and materialists raging in England and America at that time. Buchanan, after reading Darwin and Hartley, became impatient with the cautiousness of their approach toward a physical interpretation of psychic events. His analysis is sober and provoking, many of his experiments are "ingenious," and in general his own assertion that some of the material is original is borne out. Buchanan has received increasing attention in the last half century, with Woodbridge Riley calling him our "earliest native physiological psychologist," and another philosopher asserting that the work was "one of the earliest systematic and consistent presentations of materialism to be published in America."[44]

Contemporaries were not so enthusiastic. Jefferson sent a copy to John Adams, who received it with some reserve, saying, "I am not sorry that the Philosophy has been published, because it has been a maxim with me for sixty years at least, never to be afraid of a book." But he felt that the controversy itself was arid. "Why should time be wasted in disputing about two substances, when both parties

[43] J. Buchanan, *The Philosophy of Human Nature* (Richmond, Kentucky, 1812). The best treatments of Buchanan are to be found in Sonne, *Liberal Kentucky,* 78–107, and I. W. Riley, *American Philosophy: The Early Schools* (New York, 1907), 178–95.

[44] Riley, *American Philosophy,* 375; Sonne, *Liberal Kentucky,* 86.

agree that neither knows anything about either." In Lexington, Buchanan stirred up the Presbyterians, who looked upon his book as the entering wedge of infidelity. Before the Kentucky Synod, the Reverend John P. Campbell equated him with the "atheist Hobbes, and the vermine of the ancient Epicurean style," adding sarcastically that "when the lights of the *Philosophy of Human Nature* shall be reflected in an appropriate system of education by the author . . . our western region must surely be thrown into a blaze of philosophic effulgence." The Reverend James Fishback also assailed Buchanan on the same score. Though *The Philosophy of Human Nature* never became popular reading, most townspeople assumed that Buchanan's views were "sceptical and anti-Christian." A few years later, perhaps as a result of orthodox pressure, or, more likely, from further brooding, he qualified his position, trying to accommodate both idealism and materialism.[45]

Philosophy was merely a single facet of one of the most versatile personalities in the West. Within the next two decades he was a doctor, lawyer, scientist, educator, historian, and journalist, and lived in Louisville, Cincinnati, and Harrodsburgh as well as in Lexington. As a Pestalozzian he experimented with teaching methods in several schools, writing constantly on the problem and later publishing a text. As an editor he printed an extraordinary amount of new information on science and literature and strove to better the intellectual level of the new country. He so revised Robert B. McAfee's *History of the Late War in the Western Country* that it became a new book and a standard source on the conflict. Retiring in manner, cultivating only a few close friends, plagued by financial failure, and constantly moving from city to city, he received little recognition and his work has been constantly underestimated.[46]

Less influential but not less interesting than the Brackenridges and

---

[45] A. E. Bergh, ed., *The Writings of Thomas Jefferson* (Washington, 1907), XV, 121; Sonne, *Liberal Kentucky*, 102; Leavy, "Memoir," 117; Sonne, *Liberal Kentucky*, 103–6.

[46] This neglect is in large part due to the fact that no Western city has adopted him, hence no local historians have done much with his life. For his retiring manners, see *Kentucky Reporter*, September 9, 1829.

Buchanan was John Robert Shaw, whose autobiographical *The Life and Travels of John Robert Shaw* appeared in 1807. He claimed to be "almost totally illiterate" and earned a livelihood "blowing rocks and digging wells." He came to America from England during the Revolution, and after changing sides in the middle of the conflict he decided to stay in the new republic. He dug his way West, perfecting his trade, submitting constantly to the "bottle fever," and tomcatting among barmaids and acquiescent women. Settling in Lexington in 1791, he later married and became tame. The new Shaw was hard working and generally sober, traits he emphasized in his rhymed advertisements.

> In all the branches of my trade
>   So punctual will I be
> It never shall be said,
>   John Shaw has cheated me.[47]

Despite his low station and lack of training, Shaw must have had a literary reputation, because nearly 1,000 people from Kentucky, Pennsylvania, and Ohio subscribed to his book to help meet the costs of publication. Many of his fellow-townsmen were no doubt surprised to read in the *Kentucky Gazette* his announcement of the publication of "a narrative of thirty years of my life and travels — 5 different times a soldier — 3 times shipwrecked — 12 months a prisoner of war — 4 times blown up, and my recovery — with a number of little anecdotes which will cause the reader occasionally to laugh and cry." Even with this unusual and attractive plot the book did not sell well, and he later complained that the effort cost him $800, and that "the neglect of my subscribers is like to be my ruin." Shaw had considerable talent and might have done much more, but in 1813 he mixed too much liquor with his work and blew himself up decisively.[48]

---

[47] J. R. Shaw, *A Narrative of the Life and Travels of John Robert Shaw, the Well-Digger, Now Resident in Lexington, Kentucky* (2nd edn., Lexington, Kentucky, 1930), 16; *Kentucky Gazette*, February 15, 1806.

[48] *Kentucky Gazette*, December 11, 1806; January 17, 1809; *Kentucky Reporter*, September 4, 1813.

Shaw, in presenting his work to the public, humbly admitted that he wanted to "have thrown the materials in better order, retrenched some redundancies, and made some improvements in the diction." But his subscribers were so "impatient" that he felt compelled to publish it in an unfinished state. *The Life and Travels of John Robert Shaw* is a picaresque tale; the author concedes that "the greater part of my life (with regret I speak it) has been little else than a series of errors and follies, and consequent misfortunes." Told in the manner of Swift and Defoe, the book amusingly chronicles young Shaw's unhappy tilts with armies, whiskey, "the lassies," sharpers, and employers. Every revel is followed by deep remorse and repentance, which in turn provides the background for the next debauch. "But alas! transient was my resolve, for falling in company with some of my old associates I relapsed again and pursued as usual the broad road to destruction." In the end, however, after near-death and a series of visions, he turns to religion and "the comfortable doctrines and promises of the received Revelation." [49]

Shaw's writing has a flavor hard to convey, but the author's description of an evening frolic catches some of the charm of the narrative:

For my part I went to captain Hollowback's still-house one day, with two of my fellow soldiers and having called for a quart of whiskey, we drank it before the fire. But upon attempting to rise, with an intention to return to the barracks, I fell down motionless, and to all appearance dead; so that the alarm went to the barracks that *Shaw was dead.* A company then collected to my wake, and having procured a good cag of whiskey, were determined to have a merry frolick: but they were sadly disappointed; for, as soon as the operation of the liquor began to abate, I rolled off the board upon which they had laid me, and uttered a heavy groan, accompanied by a loud explosion of *flatus* from beneath, which so startled the company, that they all run out swearing that the dead was come to life. However, they soon returned, and conveyed me to the barracks, where I was seized with a fit on insanity, and behaved in such an outrageous manner, that they were obliged to confine me with chains and take off my clothes. By some means, I got loose, and ran through the fort like a Bedlamite, climbed to the top of the roof of the barracks, and walking to the farther end of the ridge, jumped down,

[49] Shaw, *Life and Travels*, 16–17; 201; 207.

without any injury, and ran out of the garrison, until I came to the cliffs by the side of the river, from whence I leaped down, (the distance not being less than 30 or 40 feet) to the bottom, seated myself, naked as I was, on a cake of ice, and floated for a considerable distance down the river, before my fellow soldiers could get me off. I was then taken care of and doctored up with a little more of the usquebaugh, which in the condition I then was, produced no bad effects, but seemed rather to contribute to the restoration of my health, and the recovery of my senses.[50]

The *Life and Travels of John Robert Shaw* has more than a literary interest, for it is also the only good firsthand account of wage-earning life in frontier towns. When the bizarre incidents of the welldigger's life are stripped away, there remains a unique social document. Shaw arrived in Lexington with no money or property but with a skill that was scarce. By 1807 he owned five acres adjoining the city, containing an excellent quarry valued at $2,000. In addition, "I have made considerable improvements, such as a dwelling house, spring house, smoke house, work house, a stable and waggon house, all of which I estimate at two thousand dollars." His social contacts in Lexington were confined to people of his own station, and his relaxation consisted in a round at the local tavern "with a gallon of mulled beer, qualified with a quart of good spirits," often topped off with a friendly brawl.[51] When he found religion, it was Methodism, and he warned his readers to beware of the intellectualized belief prevalent among the town's prominent people. The book thus contains the common experience of Western workingmen — hard labor, reasonable success, marriage and family, hearty relaxation, and emotional religion — and it becomes an historical document of considerable importance.

If *The Life and Travels of John Robert Shaw* was the work of an obscure welldigger, *The Natural and Statistical View or Picture of Cincinnati* was written by Cincinnati's best-known citizen. Its author, Daniel Drake, had been in the Queen City less than a decade when the book appeared in 1815, but already his civic zeal had won

[50] Shaw, *Life and Travels*, 106–7.
[51] Shaw, *Life and Travels*, 197; 149.

him reputation and respect as a leader of the community as well as its most distinguished doctor. The *Picture of Cincinnati* grew out of two impulses. The first was to give wider circulation to a small scientific treatise prepared five years earlier, called *Notices Concerning Cincinnati*, which dealt with the topography, meteorology, botany, and medical conditions of the town. The other purpose was propagandistic: to publicize the promise of the new city and attract an increasing share of the immigrant stream.[52] His model was Edward Mease's *Picture of Philadelphia*, which appeared in 1809 and gave an historical and statistical survey of the place Drake considered to be the first seat of learning and culture in America.

The importance of the *Picture of Cincinnati* is not literary. The author freely concedes that his style is open to criticism. Its interest is primarily historical, for it represents the first systematic attempt to present the development of a Western city in its many dimensions. The book not only includes a sketch of the growth of the town in its economic, social, and intellectual aspects but frames it in the experience of the entire region. "The *relations* of a town with the surrounding country, are an essential part of its history," he asserted "and cannot be understood without studying both."[53] Drake's approach is both statistical and analytical, and his assemblage of facts is studded with keen observations on early Cincinnati life. The medical section is the most exhaustive, containing the results of many years' work as a physician, and including the first description of a local malady called "trembles" or "milk sickness."[54]

Most of Drake's work was still ahead of him in 1815, but the *Picture of Cincinnati* established his fame. More important, however, it announced Cincinnati to the outside world, and in so doing underlined urban growth in the West. In this regard, it was the culmination of a process that had commenced two decades earlier when travelers began to discover the new towns in the wilderness, and had continued as numberless gazetteers and guides gave increasing at-

[52] Drake, *Statistical View*, v, vi.

[53] Drake, *Statistical View*, vii.

[54] E. F. Horine, "Daniel Drake and His Medical Classic," *The Journal of the Kentucky State Medical Association*, L (1952), 69.

tention to cities. The uniqueness of Drake's account was its authoritativeness, its rich detail, and the serene confidence of the author. Substituting a mature and sober discussion of the Queen City's future for the absurdities of the boosters and real-estate hucksters, he spoke candidly of its shortcomings and need for improvement along many fronts. But on the record he could predict that transmontane towns were "destined, before the termination of the present century, to attain the rank of populous and magnificent cities." [55]

Drake's confidence in frontier towns seemed well-founded. Their spectacular economic development, easily reduced to statistics, overshadowed a rapidly maturing cultural and intellectual life. Trading and manufacturing were still the heart of the young city, and the predominance of their values caused thoughtful people to lament that the arts had grown up as "the appendages to commerce" rather than as a "part of the very body of society." Yet travelers were continually astonished at the cultivation and polish of the townspeople and the many opportunities for better living that Western cities offered. By 1815 these amenities had already lost their novelty to the residents, and some even thought the civilizing process had got out of hand. "Twenty sermons a week —" a Cincinnatian wearily counted, "Sunday evening Discourses on Theology — Private assemblies — State Cotillion Parties — Saturday Night Clubs, and chemical lectures . . . like the ague, return every day with distressing regularity." [56]

[55] Drake, *Statistical View*, 226.
[56] E. D. Mansfield, *Memoirs of the Life and Services of Daniel Drake*, 56; *Liberty Hall* (Cincinnati), December 9, 1816.

PART TWO
1815–1830

PART TWO

Chapter 6

Depression, Recovery, and Expansion

In 1812 the West insisted on war with Great Britain, and at the conclusion of the war that section seemed its primary beneficiary. Though the fighting netted no new land on the frontier, it removed the Indian menace, parried British ambition, and, just as important, gave an immense stimulus to the economic growth of the area. Embargoes, blockades, and the demands of war quickened the pace of development, leading to an extraordinary expansion along all fronts — agricultural, commercial, and industrial. Though town and country participated in this prosperity, urban centers recorded the most startling gains. Pittsburgh and Lexington emerged from the conflict as manufacturing cities, while river communities generally fattened on the increasing flow of trade. Most Westerners welcomed the Treaty of Ghent, feeling that peace would carry them to an even higher plane of abundance.

Nearly every index seemed to support this optimism. Prices, wages, employment, and the value of industrial and agricultural products all soared to new heights. Pittsburgh's situation looked so secure that Zadock Cramer contended that its manufacturing "has almost rendered us independent of the eastern states." The postwar boom in Cincinnati astonished travelers, James Flint admitting that "such an active scene I never expected to see amongst the backwoods of America." Louisville announced its expansion by petitioning for a branch of the new Bank of the United States. Niles thought its case good. "The capital accumulation there is very respectable, and it is rising to importance with a rapidity never excelled, even in the western country." St. Louis's prosperity appeared boundless. Thomas Hart Benton, who settled there in 1815 with $400, was "comfortably established" four years later. His only lament was that if he had brought $20,000 he might be worth a quarter million. *Niles' Register* reflected the general buoyancy of Lexington, asserting in 1815 that "the manufacturing establishments of this town, have reached an eminence which ensures their permanent prosperity and usefulness."[1]

Many realized that the war created a large portion of this prosperity and that peace was certain to bring some contraction. Yet certain factors suggested that good times in the West had a more secure foundation than the artificial demands of national emergency. The flow of immigrants, slowed but not stopped during the conflict, picked up, bringing the largest numbers the area had yet known. Though most of the new settlers moved onto farm lands, the cities got more than their proportional share. Coming with capital, needs, skills, and energy, the newcomers represented a permanent contribution to economic resources of young communities.

The coming of the steamboat constituted another justifiable source of optimism. The potentialities were apparent from the first trial runs before the war. "The Mississippi . . . is conquered," Robert Fulton wrote to a friend in the spring of 1812, "the steamboat which I have sent to trade between New Orleans and Natchez carried 1500 barrels = 150 tons . . . against the current 313 miles in 7 days, working in that time 84 hours. These are conquests perhaps as valuable as those at Jena." By 1819 33 were operating on Western waters, and Daniel Drake laconically observed that "the people on this river anticipate many substantial advantages."[2]

But the conflict left economic dislocations that went too deep to be waved away, even by the magic of immigration and innovation. British manufacturers, no longer producing for armies and governments, and faced with declining prices throughout the world, sought to recapture markets cut off during the fighting. This policy had the support of the British government. "It was well worthwhile," Henry Brougham candidly told the House of Commons in 1816,

---

[1] Cramer, *Pittsburgh Almanac*, 1817, 36; J. Flint, "Letters from America," in Thwaites, ed., *Western Travels*, IX, 150; *Niles' Register*, July 20, 1816; T. H. Benton to [?] Preston, November 14, 1819, Benton Papers (Missouri Historical Society, St. Louis); *Niles' Register*, June 15, 1815.

[2] Hunter, *Steamboats*, 16n; Drake, *Picture of Cincinnati*, 148.

"to incur a loss upon the first exportation in order by the glut to stifle in the cradle those rising manufactures in the United States which the war has forced into existence contrary to the usual course of nature." [3] These decisions in London's counting rooms and Parliament set off a chain of events which soon smashed Lexington's industrial beginnings and seriously crippled Pittsburgh for nearly a decade.

Though manufacturing centers suffered the worst shocks of the postwar crash, declining agricultural prices very early began to undermine the prosperity of Western farmers and consequently the well-being of the cities which handled their produce. European fields rebounded once the armies stopped marching, and in a few years their wheat contended with American grain in the world's markets. A shortage of specie, stemming from the disorganization of Mexican and Peruvian mines during the Latin American revolutions, combined with increased production to depress commodity prices further. The West was caught up in a global disturbance, and frontier cities, which had known only a generation of growth and expansion, were suddenly whipped by economic winds whose force threatened their very foundations.

Warning signals appeared as early as 1816, and in the East gloomy prophets predicted the worst. Even Niles unrolled the crepe. "If only half of the evil that is anticipated by intelligent gentlemen be felt, we shall have 'such times' as the present generation has never seen." For most people, however, and for Westerners particularly, an extraordinary currency inflation and a speculative boom in land values concealed the danger until 1818. Credit buying and paper money hoisted the bubble aloft, and for three years it grew. These giddy times defied declining prices, the decay of manufactures, and commercial disintegration. "An expansion so sturdily maintained," one Cincinnatian remembered, "that it yielded to no contraction, but that of unqualified explosion." [4]

[3] Quoted in Dangerfield, *The Era of Good Feelings* (New York, 1952), 177.
[4] *Niles' Register*, April 13, 1816; T. S. Berry, *Western Prices Before 1861* (Cambridge, Mass., 1943), 388.

Abandon and optimism raced through every branch of economic activity. "The private citizen drew forth his earnings of former days to vest it in manufactures," one Pittsburgher remembered, "the merchant dived deep into the business of his calling, and the farmer . . . took land jobbing speculations, with an uncommon avidity." Though gambling in public land in the West was the most spectacular aspect of this development, urbanites concentrated on city real estate. McMurtrie shuddered as he watched the price of "lots on the principal streets" of Louisville soar from $700 each in 1812 to $300 per foot five years later, an inflation he attributed to "banks, rag money, speculators, shavers, *et id omne genus.*" "Property in Louisville and its vicinity," wrote a land agent, "is I think all out of rational bounds, it is higher than it is in Baltimore." [5]

The story was the same elsewhere. In St. Louis the frenzy continued into 1819. In that year Benton described the rise of real-estate prices since 1815. "Ground around St. Louis, then selling for thirty dollars an acre, sell at this day for two thousand"; and "daily" he saw "fortunes passing in review before me, and falling into the hands of those who look a few days ahead." "Scaevola," writing in Lexington's *Kentucky Reporter*, asserted that "everywhere within the state has property of this description [town lots] at some time or another within the last few years been pushed up to the most enormous prices justified by no present uses to which it would be applied nor profits which it could yield." [6]

Land speculation both fed and fed upon the extraordinary currency expansion of the war and postwar years. Early in the century, banks, attacked as monopolies, had been unpopular in the West, though merchants and manufacturers found them indispensable. At first trading companies issued notes in limited amounts, but even before the war states began granting charters to banks. Then, in the following years, legislatures incorporated them with complete abandon. Pennsylvania led the way in 1814 by authorizing

<hr>

[5] S. Jones, *Pittsburgh in 1826*, 49–50; McMurtrie, *Sketches of Louisville*, 116; D. McClellan to W. Lytle, September 23, 1818, William Lytle Collection.

[6] T. H. Benton to [?] Preston, November 14, 1819, Benton Papers (Missouri Historical Society, St. Louis); *Kentucky Reporter*, August 11, 1819.

forty-one. Ohio had twenty-six by 1818, and Kentucky set a record by establishing thirty-three in a single session. "A new idea seems to have sprung up," wrote the editor of *Liberty Hall*, "that the only way to destroy the monopoly of banking, is to make it universal." [7]

The demand for a looser currency, then, came from the most conservative urban circles, the merchants and manufacturers, who wanted and needed a moderate inflation. As members of local bank boards, which controlled the issue of notes and the extension of credit, these men encouraged a general expansion of the paper money supply. For a few years this policy proved successful. Under its stimulus new factories, shops, and mercantile houses sprang up, contributing importantly to the rapid development of the cities.

This inflationary policy, however, soon got out of hand. Banks multiplied recklessly, every city having at least two and Cincinnati boasting five.[8] Each issued its own notes, with slight concern for adequate specie backing. A splendid chaos resulted. The West found itself swimming in paper money, all of it of uncertain value and much of it almost worthless. "If the months of May, June, July and August of 1815, were the 'golden age of Philadelphia,'" wrote William Gouge, "the first months of the year 1818 were the golden age of the western country. Silver could hardly have been more plentiful at Jerusalem in the days of Solomon, than paper was in Ohio, Kentucky and the adjoining regions." [9]

The initial inflationary impulse came in 1811 when Congress, in destroying the first Bank of the United States, removed its restraining hand on the volume of currency. Many thought that the second Bank would bring some order into the increasing confusion. The new institution, opening its doors in January 1817, established

---

[7] *Liberty Hall* (Cincinnati), January 26, 1818. See also P. W. Huntington, "A History of Banking in Ohio," Ohio Archaeological and Historical Society, *Publications*, XXIII (1914), 320ff.

[8] Cincinnati was the focus of banking activity in Ohio. "It was a peculiar fungus of that locality, and was doubtless produced by the unnatural and hot-bed expansion of Cincinnati." *Cincinnati Daily Gazette*, September 21, 1833, quoted in Berry, *Western Prices*, 288–89.

[9] W. C. Gouge, *A Short History of Paper Money and Banking in the United States* (Philadelphia, 1833), part ii, 129.

branches throughout the country, including such Western cities as Pittsburgh, Cincinnati, Chillicothe, Lexington, and Louisville. It immediately ordered the resumption of specie payments, which many local banks had suspended in 1814 when the British captured Washington. This policy proved only partially effective, being more successful in the East than the West.[10]

Meanwhile, the offices in the new country, swayed by local interests and generally mismanaged, added to inflationary pressures by extensive discounting, renewing notes over and over again, loaning on mortgages, inventing "race horse" bills, and issuing notes and drafts without furnishing means for redemption. Far from curtailing paper in circulation, they increased it. The Cincinnati branch discounted over $1,800,000 in June 1818, and Lexington almost matched it the same month with $1,619,000, while Louisville's figure for November was $1,229,520.[11] In short the United States Bank found the nation's currency suffering from too much sail and not enough ballast, and its remedy was to roll up another jib. By the middle of 1818 the situation had become so precarious that the bank's president ordered a general contraction and specifically demanded that Cincinnati call in its loans to local and state banks. This restrictive policy did not stop the expansion in all places, but, combined with other factors, it punctured the boom, and by 1819 the economy suffered a drastic deflation.

Even before the crash, however, it was clear in some quarters that the postwar prosperity was hollow, and that speculation and inflation merely obscured basic weaknesses in the economy. Pittsburgh, in fact, never shared the good times. In 1816 the influx of cheap British goods challenged its manufacturing and within two years had pushed it to the wall. The industrial decline was so abrupt that in December

[10] This account follows the admirable analysis of W. B. Smith, *Economic Aspects of the Second Bank of the United States* (Cambridge, Mass., 1953), 99–117.

[11] R. C. Catterall, *The Second Bank of the United States* (Chicago, 1903), 34, 34n; 35–36.

of 1816 a town meeting appointed a committee to find the extent of the damage. In February the group reported that after hearing from 259 establishments it "found that the manufacture of Cottons, Woollens, Flint Glass and the finer articles of Iron, has lately suffered the most alarming depression." The value of iron products decreased from $764,200 to $525,616 between 1815 and 1817; textiles fell from $115,500 to $82,080 in the same period, while brass and tin items dropped from $249,633 to $200,000. Across the board the report estimated a loss of 14 per cent, and only two categories, leather and glass, showed strength.[12]

But the worst was yet to come. Early in 1819 the editor of the *Gazette* candidly admitted that "the general pressure seems to encrease [*sic*]; the gloom which overhangs us becomes darker and darker; the mechanical and manufacturing community is languishing into annihilation." Later in the year another committee examined the situation. Industrial employment had dropped from 1,960 in 1815 to 672, and the value of all manufactured goods fell from $2,617,833 to $832,000. Some key items revealed the extent of the stagnation even more graphically than composite figures. Steam-engine factories, for example, which Pittsburgh pioneered and which were its showcases, almost disappeared. Glass works, which had carried the name of the city to all parts of the Union, suffered in the same way; employment slumped from 169 to 40 and company income slid from $235,000 annually to $35,000.[13] The bird was not only starving, but seemed to be losing its brightest plumage as well.

No segment of Pittsburgh's economy escaped the dreadful contraction; indeed, the city seemed dying. "Caleb Cowhyde," who described himself as "a ruined manufacturer," tried to capture the changing scene in rough verse:

> That humming, and buzzing, and quick-stirring din,
>   So wont to effect one with dizziness, —
> The rolling of iron and the pounding of tin,
>   Steam engines and all noisy business

[12] *Niles' Register*, February 22, 1817.

[13] *Pittsburgh Gazette*, February 5, 1819; *Pittsburgh Gazette*, January 11, 1820.

Are silent as Sunday! — I listen in vain,
  For the clash of a dray or a wagon,
The wheels are all still; and the late restless train
  Seemed crush'd by the paw of a dragon! [14]

More telling still was the testimony of another townsman who made
a tour of the town's industrial heart in 1821. "I went down Diamond-
Alley," wrote "A Pittsburgher," "passed the old woolen factory;
it was shut up — there used to be a great deal of noise there; it is
very quiet now." He turned into Liberty Street: "it was very still."
Heading for the river, he walked through Marbury Street and
"passed the iron factory — one or two ragged children came to the
door — . . . the shop was like the woolen factory, shut up." All
about this nerve center, he remarked, "there used to be a terrible
racket, and clattering of hammers in the two steam engine factories; now it is all over — you might rock a child to sleep in an
unfinished cylinder." [15]

As the depression persisted, human suffering deepened. Once the
props of the economy caved in, few people escaped injury. The
debtors' cell swallowed rich and poor alike. "For the most part,"
wrote "Caleb Cowhyde," "the men who inhabit our jails, were
lately among our best livers." But the "pressure of the times" bore
hardest on the wage-earning population. In six weeks during the
summer of 1819, 115 people were imprisoned for debt, only three
of whom owed more than $100, two-thirds having obligations of
less than $10. One judge sent to jail a man who could not pay
back a loan of 18¾ cents. Distress hit everywhere. The town's
poor tax exceeded its operating budget, and the Female Benevolent
Society set up soup kitchens, appealing to bakers to save "such stale
bread as may remain on hand unfit for sale." [16] Only a few months
separated full employment in this young city from the relief rolls
and the hand-out.

[14] *Statesman* (Pittsburgh), September 14, 1819.

[15] *Mercury* (Pittsburgh), May 23, 1821.

[16] *Statesman* (Pittsburgh), August 28, 1819; *Statesman* (Pittsburgh),
July 17, 1819; *Pittsburgh Gazette*, February 8, 1820; February 18, 1820.

The depression in Pittsburgh was no mere panic. Beginning in 1816, it was under way for three years before the crisis hit the rest of the country. Hope for an early recovery melted away as every index continued to fall. A city which for a generation had more than doubled in population each decade began to lose people. The exodus made the industrial area look like a ghost town. " 'To let — To Let — For Sale' — window shutters closed, upper windows broken and empty, no tenants," wrote "A Pittsburgher." "There are now more buildings than families; in old times there were two families to a house, now there seem two houses to a family." [17] As the decade of the twenties began, the economic crisis deepened, and thoughtful people feared that the city could not survive the intolerable pressure.

Since manufacturing towns felt the first impact of British post-war trade policies, Lexington, like Pittsburgh, ran into rough weather very soon. The full gravity of the situation was concealed not only by speculation in land and currency but also by a mild prosperity enjoyed by merchants handling English goods. By 1819, however, the depression gripped every part of Lexington society, exposing the malady that had existed since 1816. Hemp manufacturing, the core of the city's economy, suffered almost from the day of the declaration of peace. Unable to compete with imported products, some of the biggest firms went under. Morrison, Boswell and Sutton closed its doors on December 31, 1817, and Warfield followed by only a few months. Thomas January's factory, which had operated successfully for a quarter of a century, threw in the towel in 1819. A year later only one of eight bagging works remained open.[18] Moreover, the industry recovered very slowly. It was a full decade before it got back on its feet.

The damage to hemp manufacturers could be repaired, even if it took ten years, but the steamboat's injury to Lexington's commerce was fatal. As river transportation expanded, the inland position of the Blue Grass metropolis — the "city of the plains" as

[17] *Mercury* (Pittsburgh), May 23, 1821.
[18] All the material on the hemp industry is from Hopkins, *Hemp Industry of Kentucky*, 126ff.

William Faux called it — jeopardized its mercantile supremacy in Kentucky. Though some concerns enjoyed a brief prosperity following the war, many gave up in 1818 and 1819, and throughout the twenties established firms continued to fail.[19] The tremendous expansion of Transylvania University after 1818 gave a temporary stimulus to local business, but the university faltered a decade later, removing even this slight compensation. The decline did not come suddenly, but rather after more than a decade of attrition which slowly undermined the town's merchants. Lexington's trade died with a whimper not a bang.

Throughout these years there was abundant evidence of the town's economic agony. The curve of property valuations sketched the story in cold statistics. Rising from $1,696,249 in 1809, the figure soared to $2,745,300 in 1815 and to $3,136,455 the next year. After this crest, the descent was precipitous, and recovery was so slow that property values had barely returned to $2,000,000 by 1830. Population tables tell the same story. Between 1800 and 1810 the number of residents increased from 1,795 to 4,326, but the postwar collapse cut the pace considerably, and in 1820 the new census counted only 5,279 people. In the next ten years less than 400 were added to the total, and most of these were Negroes.[20] The depth of human suffering caused by hard times in Lexington is hard to estimate, because the bulk of the unemployed were slaves whose well-being was the responsibility of their masters, and whose distress therefore cannot be traced in enlarged charity costs and swelling debtors' prisons.

After prostrating both Lexington and Pittsburgh, the storm headed for Cincinnati. Though the Queen City continued to enjoy

[19] W. Faux, "Memorable Days in America," in Thwaites, ed., *Western Travels*, XI, 194; William Leavy's memoirs contain sketches of the town's leading merchants, and it is extraordinary how many failed in the years after the war. See "Memoir," *Kentucky Hist. Register*, XL (1942), 107ff, 253ff, 353ff.

[20] See Lexington, Trustees Book, June 3, 1813, June 6, 1816; *Kentucky Gazette*, May 2, 1809; *Kentucky Reporter*, May 12, 1830; United States Census, 1800, 2P; United States Census, 1810, 71a; *Kentucky Reporter*, October 31, 1820, May 12, 1830.

prosperity even into 1819, its leading merchants were uneasy, expecting the worst. "As yet we have felt little of it here," wrote one editor. "Our city is improving almost beyond example — we have no bankruptcies — no imprisonment for debt; but we need not expect to escape the general shock." When the wind hit, it left the familiar wreckage. "The town does not now present anything like the stir that animated it about a year and a half ago," James Flint remarked. "Building is in a great measure suspended, and the city which was lately overcrowded with people, has now a considerable number of empty houses. . . . Many mechanics and labourers find it impossible to procure employment." [21]

The sudden contractions of business crippled the city's commerce, which was its bread and butter. Flagging imports suggest the extent of the decline. In the three years following the war, Cincinnati's trade with the East and South expanded spectacularly. In 1815 it absorbed merchandise valued at $534,680. In the next two years this figure jumped to $1,442,266 and $1,619,030. In 1819, however, imports fell off to $500,000 and they did not rally until the early years of the next decade. The town's manufacturing was smaller and more diversified than either Pittsburgh's or Lexington's, and many concerns kept going until the commercial collapse, but by 1819 industrial failures caused widespread unemployment.[22]

The depression afflicted all levels of society. Martin Baum, one of Cincinnati's richest men, lost a fortune almost overnight, liquidating assets of more than $200,000 to meet his debts to the Bank of the United States. Likewise, Jacob Burnet, who held stock in a sugar refinery, an iron foundry, and a host of other projects, incurred a loss of better than $80,000. More symbolic still was the failure of Daniel Drake, who, more than anyone else, embodied the optimism and growth of the West. Though never affluent, he engaged in the speculation of the day, and during the crash was forced to move into a log cabin above Liberty Street which he grimly dubbed

[21] *Liberty Hall* (Cincinnati), July 23, 1819; Flint, "Letters from America," in Thwaites, ed., *Western Travels*, IX, 238.
[22] *Cincinnati Directory*, 1819, 52–53; *Liberty Hall* (Cincinnati), June 29, 1819.

"Mount Poverty." [23] "A Friend of the Poor" winced as he watched the pauperization of a whole class of people "who have hitherto been considered in easy circumstances." In urging his fellow townsmen to establish soup kitchens in each ward, he asserted that "many, very many" are "actually suffering for the common comforts of life, particularly the articles of food and fuel." Need was so extensive that the township reported in 1823 that all its funds had been spent on relief and none remained for the repair of roads and bridges. "God save the people!" wrote Gorham Worth in 1821. "This year and part of last, I should not like to live over again. I think I would rather throw up the commission of life than bear it with its present pains." [24]

Like Cincinnati, Louisville was essentially a commercial town. Because of its strategic location at the Falls of the Ohio, it might have been expected to be particularly sensitive to the ebb and flow of Western business, registering the slightest changes and suffering most from a general stagnation. Yet Louisville felt the postwar contraction less than other frontier cities. In fact its growth after 1815 exceeded all rivals west of the mountains. The steamboat set off this upsurge and sustained it through the worst days of the depression. Though some manufacturing concerns folded and many mercantile leaders ceased operations, Louisville went through the wringer more quickly and easily than other communities.

But few expected that St. Louis could avoid the general collapse. "The signs of the time are alarming," wrote the *Missouri Gazette*, "a dark and dreadful cloud hangs over our country, which may break to the ruin of many." By 1821 the same forces that had paralyzed other frontier communities gripped the Mississippi metropolis. "The evil beginnings in the Atlantic cities has gradually extended itself to this state," a St. Louisan admitted, "and produced

[23] W. Lytle to M. Baum, August 23, 1820, William Lytle Collection (Historical and Philosophical Society of Ohio, Cincinnati); E. D. Mansfield, *Personal Memories, Social, Political and Literary, with Sketches of Many Noted People, 1801–1843* (Cincinnati, 1879), 158; 171f.

[24] *Liberty Hall* (Cincinnati), January 7, 1820; March 25, 1823; G. Worth to T. Sloo, August 2, 1820, Torrence Collection (H.P.S.O., Cincinnati).

pecuniary embarrassment and distress, both public and private, heretofore unknown among us." [25]

Once the economy began to fail, a rout developed. "Rents were falling, men breaking and running away, banks failing, money disappearing, and on all sides, anxiety and despondency," a prominent citizen later recalled. "It was indeed a period of doleful looks, and fearful presages." As elsewhere, when land values caved in, the large speculators suffered the most spectacular losses. But the real distress was at the lower income levels, especially among "that worthy and useful class of our citizens, the laboring and industrious poor." Debtors could no longer meet their obligations, and newspapers abounded with notices of bankruptcy. "We have seen men of integrity and sensibility destroyed by the sense of degradation consequent on commitment to jail," an editor complained.[26]

Though many people felt the lash of bad times, the depression was generally less severe in St. Louis than in most Western cities. As in the case of Louisville, the Mississippi depot enjoyed some compensating expansion even during the lean years following 1819. To be sure, the fur trade, disorganized during the fighting, did not recover until the mid-twenties,[27] but the lead industry prospered, suffering only a light decline during the contraction.[28] In addition, commerce with the Indians, long centered in Mackinaw, gravitated quickly to St. Louis, once English influence was lessened by the peace settlement. These two factors, along with the influence of the steamboat, lessened the effect of the deflation and prepared the way for the startling growth of the town in the next decade.

[25] *Missouri Gazette*, July 14, 1819; June 6, 1821.

[26] *Missouri Republican*, July 4, 1825; for speculators' difficulties see J. O'Fallon to D. Fitzhugh, September 9, 1821, John O'Fallon Collection (Missouri Historical Society, St. Louis); *Missouri Gazette*, July 25, 1821.

[27] In 1819 Chittenden listed only four companies operating out of St. Louis, and their business was less than $50,000. Recovery did not come until the next decade. *Fur Trade*, I, 157.

[28] Lippincott, "Lead Industry," 707ff.

The crash came so suddenly and the collapse appeared so complete that Westerners were at first too shocked to think about what had happened. "All things are changed," wrote a Cincinnatian, "the rich have become poor, the poor distrust, one universal state of embarrassment exists; tis want, and fear and prosecution and suspense and terror and dismay and bankruptcy and pauperism on all sides and on all hands." [29] The impact was traumatic. Until now these young communities had known only good times, and their residents had come to think that prosperity was the normal condition of life in the new country, if not in the rest of the world. Hence when the storm broke, few were prepared either psychologically or economically for its consequences. As the initial paralysis wore off, however, people began to look through the ruins hoping to find some clues which explained the origins of the disaster. Though some analyses centered on local conditions, the general nature of the depression made thinking along broader lines more appropriate.

The first reaction was to blame the banks. Since nearly everyone held some of their notes, most of which were now almost worthless, their role seemed obvious. Indeed, the whole cycle of good times and bad appeared bound up with currency inflation and deflation, and when the banks refused to redeem their own paper, evil intent was added to the whole process. "Damn the Banks, and the Witch that begot them," wrote Gorham Worth, a cashier himself, to a close friend. "I have a great mind to . . . curse them as bad as Obadiah was cursed for tying the Knots." In almost every city civic leaders called town meetings to condemn the bankers and fix a united policy toward their notes.[30]

More vulnerable than local and state institutions was the Bank of the United States, whose restrictive policy set in motion the deflationary pressures which brought down the speculative balloon. Hostility became especially sharp when it was discovered that the contraction policy netted the "monster" large amounts of urban

---

[29] G. Worth to T. Sloo, August 2, 1820, Torrence Collection.

[30] G. Worth to T. Sloo, August 2, 1820, Torrence Collection; *Liberty Hall* (Cincinnati), November 17, 1818; *Kentucky Reporter*, December 2, 1818; *Mercury* (Pittsburgh), March 27, 1822.

property. Branches had lent money to local residents, accepting property as security, and when people could not pay, the Bank picked up homes, lots, and even business establishments. Everywhere it became a large landowner, and in Cincinnati its holdings included some of the most valuable buildings and locations. Thomas Hart Benton did not exaggerate when he later charged that "I know towns, yea, cities . . . in which the bank already appears as a dominant and engrossing proprietor." Less accurate, but characteristic of the Western view, was his assertion that "all the flourishing cities of the West are mortgaged to this money power. They may be devoured at any moment. They are in the jaws of the monster!" [31] Urban antipathy to the Bank stemmed not only from its role in bringing on the depression, but also from the tenant's traditional hatred of the landlord.

The analysis which held banks responsible for the depression was the most popular, but others focused on the British and the policy which flooded the American market with cheap goods. Though this explanation found advocates in every city, it appealed most to manufacturing centers. A Pittsburgh grand jury, for example, put an official stamp on this interpretation, declaring that the "most prominent evil" afflicting the country was the sale of British goods. A meeting of Cincinnati's business leaders fixed the blame in the same place and pleaded with fellow townsmen to patronize domestic producers and shun imports.[32]

Both of these theses sought the origins of the depression outside the West and in events over which people in the new country had no control. Others thought these explanations too facile. "Nothing is more absurd, and yet hardly anything more common," wrote "A Citizen of Pittsburgh," "than for men when things go wrong . . . to get in a fit and abuse others for their own bad management. Instead of coming home to seek and correct the evil in themselves, where nine times out of ten it is to be found, they endeavor to find it in others." This argument connected the spending and speculation

[31] Quoted in Catterall, *Second Bank*, 67.

[32] *Pittsburgh Gazette*, December 7, 1821; *Liberty Hall* (Cincinnati), April 20, 1819.

of the postwar spree with the collapse that followed. "It is the result of universal extravagance and desire of wealth," wrote the
editor of Cincinnati's *Liberty Hall*. A St. Louis "Citizen" spelled
out this idea more explicitly, blaming the "Hats — the dandies —
the gigs — the grog shops."[33] In the grey light of the morning
after, these people admitted that they had been hitting the bottle too
hard.

In seeking the causes of hard times, Westerners were engaged in
no merely academic pursuit. They hoped their diagnosis would
suggest a remedy which could arrest the disintegration. Though a
few expected initially that "things will correct themselves," most
believed that public policies of some kind would hasten recovery.
City leaders, generally, rejected "rugged individualism" as inadequate during the crisis, preferring concrete programs to stimulate urban economies. Some proposals called for action by the federal
government, others looked to the state for aid, while still others
urged less formal solutions involving private organization and citizen cooperation. " 'Hard Times' is on the mouth of every man,"
observed a writer to the *St. Louis Enquirer*, "how to remedy the
evil, has employed the time and talents of our legislators. . . . On
this subject the opinions of politicians are almost as variant as their
faces or watches."[34]

Theses which centered on currency inflation generally sought
relief in a change in the banking system, especially in the repeal
of the charter of the United States Bank or the heavy taxation of
its local branches. Those who blamed the British for the collapse
found their cure in a protective tariff. People who thought the depression stemmed from extravagance and reckless spending placed
less reliance on government aid, preaching that salvation lay in a
return to thrift and toil. "Go to work," counseled the editor of the
Missouri Gazette, "all of us have something to do . . . live within
your income — borrow less — banquet less — visit less — but labor

[33] *Pittsburgh Gazette*, August 31, 1821; *Liberty Hall* (Cincinnati), August
24, 1819; *Missouri Gazette*, February 16, 1820.
[34] *Pittsburgh Gazette*, February 5, 1819; *St. Louis Enquirer*, April 13, 1822.

more." [35] This Spartan response to bad times was not as dramatic as seeking government aid, but it seemed attractive to people tinged with guilt engendered by years of prodigality.

* e*

These reactions, both in analysis and remedy, were not peculiarly urban ones, since they found acceptance in the countryside as well as in cities. As bad times persisted, however, and the banking and tariff arguments brought more controversy than relief, townspeople increasingly relied upon themselves for measures which might bring recovery, at least on the local level. A rigid self-examination followed. Each city surveyed itself, appraised its own economic organization, theorized about what makes a healthy community, pondered the delicate relationship between town and farm, and tried to discover how to use government — local, state, and national — to help people in trouble. Before the crisis had passed, harsh words flew between old friends, political lines blurred, mercantile supremacy was challenged, and the distribution of urban economic power in the West was radically altered.

The scenes of the most intense introspection and most vigorous antidepression activity were the manufacturing centers of Pittsburgh and Lexington, where the suffering was greatest. In both cities hard times continued for nearly a decade — ten agonizing years during which frustrated citizens struggled to revive prostrate industry and stagnating trade. By 1826 Pittsburgh's economy reached the early postwar level, though the effects were still clearly visible for many years afterward. Lexington, however, never really recovered, and by 1830 it had lost its important manufacturing and commercial position in the West and even its primacy in Kentucky. In both places the depression hit so hard that it not only shattered self-confidence, but among thoughtful people raised the question of survival.

Pittsburgh's position seemed especially precarious. For just when

[35] *Liberty Hall* (Cincinnati), May 4, 1819; *Missouri Gazette*, December 15, 1819.

hard times bore down most heavily on its economy and spirit, an even greater challenge confronted the crippled city. The federal government built the toll-free National Road from Baltimore to Wheeling on the Ohio, threatening to divert a large amount of freight and immigrant traffic from Pittsburgh. In addition, to the north the Erie Canal sought to link the West with New York, further jeopardizing the Iron City's preferred position as the head of river navigation. To make matters worse, Ohio planned to participate in the latter scheme by building a water network which would tilt its commerce toward the Great Lakes. To Pittsburgh, already staggered by the postwar collapse, this looked like the *coup de grâce*.

The new problem was connected with the depression only in point of time, but the economic stagnation of the city made urgent the need for a solution. The return of prosperity seemed impossible if the lines of trade and travel were turned into other channels. Pittsburgh's response to the National Road and the Erie Canal was the improvement of the road from Philadelphia to the Point. This project, while not expensive, required cooperation from many places, and most of all Philadelphia. That city, like Pittsburgh, was menaced by the energy and imagination of its great rivals, Baltimore and New York, which boldly reached out to gather in Western trade. "We consider that the crisis has arrived," wrote the *Gazette*, "when the question of all others the most important to Philadelphia and Pittsburgh, is to be determined. New York is straining every nerve for the consummation of her great canal scheme . . . Every act, no matter how unconnected in appearance with the real object, is made . . . to aid the grand design." [36] Only an effort of similar magnitude could save the Pennsylvania cities from strangulation.

Though this issue was a matter of life and death to Pittsburgh, Philadelphia's perspective was quite different. It had many interests. As one of the world's major seaports, its commerce stretched across the globe, and Western trade, while increasing in volume, was not yet critical. Iron City editors tried to rouse the Eastern metropolis by pointing out the impending danger. "What can Philadelphia and

[36] *Pittsburgh Gazette*, June 30, 1818.

Pittsburgh become but deserted villages?" one newspaper asked after describing the progress of the Erie Canal and the National Road.[37]

When the Eastern giant finally stirred, it chose a course of action suited to its own long-range requirements rather than the pressing needs of Pittsburgh. It replied to Baltimore and New York with an elaborate canal-and-rail project to carry goods across the mountains. It was an enormous undertaking, involving nothing less than hauling boats over the Appalachians.[38] Of course, Pittsburghers were delighted to see such interest in Western trade, but they thought this overdid it. Pittsburgh could not wait for such a large venture; it wanted a decent road quickly, not "the Wall of China." Though almost everyone liked the idea of a canal, it did not meet the immediate problem of improving the highway to the East. If this limited objective were achieved, one editor wryly agreed, "we might . . . proceed to the business of connecting the Schuykill with the north Pacific ocean." [39]

Improving connections with the East was only one phase of Pittsburgh's effort to keep open the avenues of traffic to the city. The National Road raised its Western terminus, Wheeling, to a point where some feared it threatened the Iron City's upriver trade. "Where now are the thousands of wagons which formerly gave life to our streets and employment to our draymen?" asked "A Real Friend to Pennsylvania" in 1821. "They are gone to Wheeling. Where now is the enlivening hum of the boatmen, and the numerous fleets of boats that formerly covered our rivers? They have stopped at Wheeling." [40] Pittsburgh sought to minimize its losses on the Ohio by removing the obstacles in the river which prevented boats from ascending to the Monongahela during low water.

Like the turnpike to Philadelphia, the improvement of the Ohio became one of Pittsburgh's obsessions. Though unconnected with

[37] *Statesman* (Pittsburgh), November 26, 1818.

[38] Philadelphia's thinking on Western trade is embodied in S. Breack, *Sketch of the Internal Improvements Already Made by Pennsylvania, etc.* (Philadelphia, 1818).

[39] *Pittsburgh Gazette*, July 31, 1818; December 15, 1818.

[40] *Pittsburgh Gazette*, February 5, 1821.

the causes of the town's economic collapse, it now seemed essential
to its recovery. The river did not yield easily to treatment, however,
and throughout the twenties Pittsburgh carried on a running fight
with snags, bars, and rocks. But the citizens, determined to "remove
even the *shadow* of a reason, for driving *one solitary* wagon to
Wheeling," kept doggedly after it, and by 1830 steamboats moved
easily to and from the city's docks.[41]

The maintenance of trade supremacy met only one half of the
problem which the depression brought to Pittsburgh. Industrial
recovery was the other side of the coin, for manufacturing comprised the town's major economic activity, claiming most of its capital and employing two-thirds of its residents. The glass works alone
hired more labor than all retailers combined. To Pittsburghers, the
future of the city was wrapped up in industrial revival. "The history of all nations," a committee asserted, "demonstrates that manufactures have been inseparable allies of wealth and power. Their
prosperity or declinsion [*sic*] constitutes an epoch in the rise and
fall of cities and nations." [42]

Pittsburgh's remedy for its flagging industry was a higher tariff.
Protection quickly became the town's central aim, and soon its
citizens and spokesmen petitioned state and national governments,
lobbied in Harrisburg and Washington, and even pleaded with
travelers for support. As in the case of the road to Philadelphia, a
high tariff became the official policy of the city, supported by a
resolution of the council.[43] No politician could survive who took
another view, or, indeed, who thought any issue more important.

As the economic crisis deepened, the tariff campaign intensified.
In 1820 an extraordinary public meeting of over 600 voters proposed
a protectionist slate cutting across party lines, nominating Federalist
Henry Baldwin for Congress and Republican William Wilkins for

[41] *Pittsburgh Gazette*, September 7, 1819.

[42] *Commonwealth* (Pittsburgh), February 4, 1817; *Mercury* (Pittsburgh),
July 18, 1817; *Commonwealth* (Pittsburgh), February 4, 1817.

[43] Pittsburgh, Minutes, December 28, 1816. William Wilkins sponsored the
resolution, which also sent two delegates to Harrisburg and Washington at
the city's expense.

the state assembly. The latter had his party's designation for the House but withdrew because "the general pressure so loudly calls for a union of sentiment and of action." What few manufacturers had Republican leanings dropped them to enlist in the coalition. One admitted in 1822 that "for the five or six years passed" he had voted for Baldwin "with a single eye to this important subject, in the hope that something might be done in our favour." [44]

Political activity comprised an important part of Pittsburgh's industrial recovery program, but business leaders also put great emphasis on more immediate measures. With factories closing down all through the city and local purchasing power rapidly diminishing, every effort was made to keep open concerns that had withstood the first shocks and to encourage others to begin work again. In 1819 some merchants and industrialists organized the Pittsburgh Manufacturing Company and bought a warehouse where local producers could display their wares and where people could pay with goods rather than cash. It met with marked success, and after a year the directors announced that it had "answered the expectations of its founders, in affording facilities for the interchange of commodities — supplying raw materials to the mechanic, and manufactured articles to the farmer and country merchant, in exchange for produce." [45] Within a few years the enterprise paid good dividends to its stockholders, and most agreed that it deserved great credit for keeping many people busy during the worst days.

Though Pittsburgh did not fully recover until 1825 or 1826, signs of better times appeared a few years earlier. In 1821 the *Gazette* found many factories "slowly and timidly rising, from the prostrate state in which the late revolution, like the 'dread Samuel' had left them." Two years later "F.A." wrote that factories had been closed for so long that many people had forgotten what a smoke problem they caused, but he was happy to announce that the situation was once again "intolerable." Though prosperity returned, few could forget the agonizing years through which the city had passed. Speak-

[44] *Mercury* (Pittsburgh), August 1, 1820. *Statesman* (Pittsburgh), November 5, 1822.

[45] *Mercury* (Pittsburgh), April 25, 1820.

ing for a chastened citizenry, "Mutius Scaevola" philosophized that it was perhaps all for the good. Pittsburgh "has gained experience, which will be of more worth than fine gold, if it prevents her from dreaming of outlots at a thousand dollars an acre, and of fortunes to be realized by a lively speculation, or at worst a few years application, if it teach her that slow and patient industry is the condition of . . . prosperity among men." [46]

෧ඵ

Lexington, like Pittsburgh, suffered greatly at the hands of the depression, but, unlike the Iron City, its prosperity did not return. The steamboat rendered its inland position commercially untenable, while the postwar collapse accelerated the pace of its inevitable decline. The Blue Grass metropolis, however, did not tamely submit to this grim fate, and before admitting the jig was up, its leaders tried to recoup losses through a variety of expedients. The city sponsored roads, canals, and railroads in a frantic effort to get a lifeline to the expanding trade of the Ohio River. At the same time, it sought to compensate for the damage to its commerce and manufacturing by developing cultural activities which would attract people to the city from all over the West.

Even before Lexington felt the full impact of the depression, many of its most thoughtful citizens foresaw the problem created by the steamboat. But without minimizing the danger, they believed the town had the strength to meet the challenge. "The commercial wealth and connexions of Lexington, her . . . facilities in banking institutions, her great resources in manufacturing establishments, in her enterprising and industrious population, and in the rich, productive and populous country around her," one editor wrote with assurance, "must continue to give her a commanding pre-eminence in commerce and manufactures. It would be vain for any other town in this quarter of the country to attempt to rival

[46] *Pittsburgh Gazette*, February 26, 1821; November 7, 1823; *Pittsburgh Gazette*, August 16, 1822.

her in these respects." [47] Yet to maintain this primacy in the age
of steam travel, Lexington would have to forge new links with the
Ohio. To accomplish this the town fashioned a program comprising
turnpikes to Maysville and Louisville, the improvement of the navigation of the Kentucky River up to Frankfort, and ultimately a
railroad to the Falls.

Though residents eagerly supported all these schemes, the city no
longer had the resources to prosecute all of them. In 1829 the town's
leaders lowered their sights and urged that everyone concentrate
on a single objective. A town meeting chose the turnpike to Louisville, declaring that it was "of paramount consequence, and that section of it from this place to the seat of government, claims the first
and strenuous efforts of the people of Lexington." To underline
the gravity of the city's plight, Henry Clay, its most famous citizen,
personally took the program to the state legislature, looking for
financial support. The situation was critical, and "Clinton" warned
of the consequences of defeat. "So much exertion has already been
made that a present failure would be a permanent misfortune —
The scheme hereafter will be regarded as desperate, and hopeless-
ness of success will deter public-spirited men." Delay, he added,
would be fatal. "If Lexington is to be brought out of the disadvantages of her inland condition *now* is the time to attempt it." [48]

Hence the city decided to make its stand on the turnpike to
Louisville, but many people still had interest and money involved
in the road to Maysville. That project had developed very slowly,
and the directors could show little after fifteen years of promotion
and work. In 1830, however, the company's fortunes changed rapidly.
The state subscribed $25,000 for the road's completion, and an addi-
tional windfall came when Congress authorized the purchase of
$150,000 of the company's stock. The gloom which had hung over
Lexington since the early days of the crash suddenly lifted. A pike
to the Ohio would remove "the one single circumstance which
chains her to poverty and a secondary rank amongst western cities,"

[47] *Kentucky Reporter*, December 25, 1816.
[48] *Kentucky Reporter*, November 4, 1829; *Louisville Public Advertiser*,
December 8, 1830; *Kentucky Reporter*, November 11, 1829.

an editor exulted.[49] It was in this context of hope against a background of despair that Lexingtonians heard of Jackson's veto of the Maysville Road appropriation. This action stunned the city; the blow seemed cruel and deliberate. Town meetings excoriated the President; leaders threatened political retaliation; the newspapers fumed; but many people accepted the sentence resignedly, convinced that history had loaded the dice against Lexington.[50]

After this project failed, the Blue Grass metropolis turned excitedly to a railroad to break through its land confines to the river. Incorporated in January 1830, the Lexington and Ohio Railroad Company purposefully left its northern terminus undecided, waiting to see what kind of welcome the project received in other parts of the valley. When the subscription books were opened, Lexingtonians took up $204,000 the first afternoon and nearly $800,000 in the next ten days. The town's wealthiest men, such as John W. Hunt, John Brand, Elisha Warfield, and Robert Wickliffe, pledged especially large sums, while nearly all businessmen invested generously.[51] Indeed, the city embraced the railroad with the frantic intensity of a drowning man.[52] Louisville was the obvious river connection, but the Falls City hesitated to accept the proposal since it could not gauge the impact on its own position. Lexington, however, could not afford delay, and immediately began to flirt with Cincinnati, believing any marriage preferable to continued isolation.

While everyone on the Blue Grass hoped that the city could find an outlet on the Ohio, some came to believe that the steamboat made Lexington's position hopeless. These people argued that only

[49] *Kentucky Reporter*, May 12, 1830; November 11, 1829.

[50] For typical reactions to Jackson's veto, see *Kentucky Reporter*, June 9, 16, 23, 1830.

[51] *Kentucky Reporter*, February 10, 17, 1830. Hunt and Brand subscribed $25,000, Warfield and Wickliffe pledged $20,000, and eight others invested over $10,000.

[52] For the publicity campaign surrounding the launching of the railroad, see *Kentucky Reporter*, February 3, 10, 17, 24, June 23, September 1, November 10, 17, 24, December 15, 22, 1830. The *Reporter* virtually dropped its enthusiasm for roads and began to look upon pikes as feeders to the railroad's main line. See especially February 24, 1830.

a radical shift in the town's economy could save it from ruin. If Lexington could not get to distant markets, then let the markets come to it. Their program called for transforming this manufacturing community into a cultural center with Transylvania University as the central attraction. "It will fill her empty streets, it will people her tenantless houses, it will afford a market to her manufactures and produce of that charming and fertile country with which she is surrounded." It was a pleasant as well as prosperous prospect. "She will be filled and surrounded with rich men who will patronize the arts, encourage genius and afford a society equal in refinement and intelligence to any of which the world can boast." [53]

The use of education to shore up a sagging economy became the conscious policy of the city. "Her ablest and best citizens have endeavoured to give an impetus to the business of the place," a Louisville paper observed, "by the encouragement of her literary . . . establishments." The great expansion of Transylvania University was a response to the depression, and, symbolically, in the same week that Lexington banks suspended specie payments in 1818, Horace Holley arrived from Boston to preside over the development of the institution. Within four years its enrollment rose to 350 students, and colleges of medicine and law were added. "Franklin" recognized the economic importance of Transylvania, declaring after the 1826 commencement that "these young gentlemen are eloquent witnesses of what that Institution has done for our country; the fact that you cannot find an empty house in Lexington, where in 1818 you may have found many, tells loudly what it has done for the town." [54] In addition, a number of academies and girls' schools grew up around the University, attracting younger students from many parts of Kentucky and neighboring states.

Though the college charged tuition, its major financial backing came from the state.[55] But the city, aware of the institution's eco-

---

[53] Quoted in the *Kentucky Reporter*, October 4, 1820.

[54] *Louisville Public Advertiser*, March 6, 1826; *Kentucky Reporter*, March 6, 1826.

[55] Support for the university of the state level also had depression overtones. "One of the best measures of RELIEF for the state is to endow the

nomic usefulness, also supported it in a variety of ways. In 1820 it lent the medical division $6,000 for a "Library and Anatomical Museum," and at the same time gave $500 for a grammar school to be attached to the university. In 1827 the town council insured Transylvania's buildings for $10,000 and endowed a "Lexington Professorship" with $800. Two years later the city offered over $1,300 in scholarships to young men throughout the state. Nor was encouragement confined to the governmental level. In 1826 private citizens subscribed money for a chair in modern languages, admitting that they had "reapt [*sic*] and will reap great advantages from the College, and it is but fair that they should reciprocate." [56] This cultural pump priming, involving municipal, state, and private funds, was no substitute for genuine recovery, but at least it sustained many local merchants and landlords who would otherwise have been ruined.

None of these measures, however, could arrest the economic decay. No big factories or large business concerns opened in the town during the twenties. Even Transylvania fell on evil times, and after President Holley's resignation in 1828, internal dissension seriously undermined its prestige. Lexington's sickness could no longer be concealed. Even visitors sensed it, and those who had known the city in its golden age looked mournfully at its decline. A Baltimore traveler was shocked on returning to it in 1829. "I am sorry to say it has degenerated beyond measure." The disintegration was both material and human. "The homes and tenants seemed to me to have suffered an equal or similar dilapidation. Where was once the dwelling of gaiety and friendship, with every good and noble

---

University, and thus to introduce double the present number of students from abroad. . . . *True economy does not consist in reducing the expenses of a government to the smallest sum, but in making the sum, whether large or small, produce the most and the best fruit." The Western Review and Miscellaneous Magazine,* IV (1821), 93.

[56] Lexington, Trustees Book, March 27, 1820: Lexington, Trustees Book, April 5, 14, November 1, December 6, 1827; Lexington, Papers of the Board of Trustees (MSS, Lexington City Hall, Lexington); *Kentucky Reporter,* June 5, 1826.

sentiment, was now a rusty and moss-grown mansion of ill nature and repulsive indifference." [57]

✑

Commercial cities in the West recovered much more rapidly than manufacturing ones; the depression came later and left sooner. But in the midst of hard times no one could foresee this resilience, and Cincinnati, Louisville, and St. Louis all devised measures to meet the new situation. As mercantile towns, they put greatest emphasis on reviving trade, though local manufactures also received a sympathetic hearing. Uninhibited as yet by any theoretical objections to government intervention, they sought aid, like Pittsburgh and Lexington, wherever they could find it, assuming that all public bodies — city, state, and federal — should lend whatever help seemed appropriate. Part of their program involved projects which were not new, and, indeed, had been stated objectives for many years, but the postwar collapse made many things look necessary which hitherto had been thought merely desirable.

Cincinnati's prosperity lasted well into 1819, and its leading merchants, anxious to secure its growing primacy in the West, looked around for methods to stave off the impending collapse. "Great plans on foot," a Pittsburgher noted enviously; "whenever two or three meet at a corner nothing is heard but schemes." Most of these projects were canals or roads aimed at increasing the flow of goods to and from the Queen City. Interest centered on cutting a channel around the Falls in the Ohio to loosen up the shipping to New Orleans which got tied up at Louisville during low water. Support of this undertaking dated back to the beginning of the century, but the introduction of the steamboat increased its utility. Better roads to the interior and canals to the Great Lakes also found advocates. When the depression struck, the need for these improvements seemed greater, and their spokesmen intensified their efforts. In 1819 a large public meeting endorsed them all, urging the federal

[57] *Louisville Public Advertiser*, November 28, 1829.

government to subsidize them as public works.[58] Nothing was accomplished, however, and when prosperity returned, the campaign lost its edge.

Louisville, like Cincinnati, endured a few uncomfortable years, but the distress never created the panic and desperation which gripped Pittsburgh and Lexington. The crisis was largely monetary, and business leaders opposed any formal attempt to remedy the situation, feeling that the safer course was to let it work itself out. "We never did place the least reliance in that kind of legislative interference which has taken place in this state," explained the *Public Advertiser*, speaking for the mercantile community. However, the merchants did try to coordinate policy toward out-of-state bank notes, at one time refusing to accept any Indiana paper.[59] Since a canal around the Falls had been official policy for better than a decade, the depression's only influence was to increase support for it and strengthen those who believed that federal funds should be used on the project. Louisville's reply to hard times was patience, since it expected the beneficial effects of the steamboat to offset any extraordinary losses.

St. Louis had less confidence that natural forces would bring back prosperity, but the storm did not last long enough for the city to establish a formal anti-depression program. Despite a great many personal bankruptcies, the town's business never came to a standstill. The pinch of the times brought the usual attack on banks, led to schemes for a metallic-money system for the state, encouraged assaults on imprisonment for debts, and fostered a number of suggestions for the increase of trade. One plan involved building a canal to the Great Lakes, while "Proponent" urged the city to send an expedition to the Pacific Northwest to open trade with the Orient. "Then New Orleans would no longer be mistress of the West" and people could go to China by way of St. Louis.[60]

---

[58] *Pittsburgh Gazette*, February 5, 1819; *Liberty Hall* (Cincinnati), September 7, 1819.

[59] *Louisville Public Advertiser*, June 21, 1820.

[60] *Missouri Gazette*, December 22, 1819; June 20, April 4, 1821; *St. Louis Enquirer*, February 5, 1820.

Less fanciful was St. Louis's drive to break up the factory system in the fur country by which the government controlled the Indian trade. The chain of federal stations along the rivers prevented unrestrained commerce with the natives, and for more than two decades the peltry interests had pressed for its removal. The pressure of the depression and the skillful leadership of Thomas Hart Benton in the Senate combined to get these restrictions lifted in March 1822. The stimulus was immediate. Within six months one thousand men shipped up the Missouri and five hundred more operated on the Mississippi.[61] Aside from this campaign and relief work among the poor, town leaders were content to wait for better days, confident that their economy could absorb the shock and quickly resume its expansion.

By the mid-twenties the worst was over, and, except in Lexington, the signs of recovery abounded in every Western city. "Three years ago, our population did not exceed eight thousand — it is now near eleven thousand," exulted the Pittsburgh *Statesman* in 1824. "Many of our manufacturing establishments were then idle and vacant — they all now exhibit the pleasing bustle and busy hum of employment." Cincinnati boosters were back in business, again filling the air with statistics demonstrating the progress of the Queen City. Congressman Anderson, though himself still suffering "some uneasiness about my pecuniary situation," happily recorded as early as 1822 that "there has been great activity" in Louisville, and the prospects were even brighter. In St. Louis "the arrival and departure of steamboats" was "almost incessant," and the demand for its key products clearly outstripped the supply.[62]

[61] Chittenden, *Fur Trade*, I, 13–17.
[62] *Statesman* (Pittsburgh), December 25, 1824; *Liberty Hall* (Cincinnati), January 21, 1823. R. C. Anderson, Diary, 1788–1826 (microfilm, Filson Club Library, Louisville), June 30, 1822; *St. Louis Enquirer*, June 16, 1823.

Throughout the West, urbanites turned with relief from the diagnosis of sick economies to the care and feeding of prosperous ones.

By the end of the decade Western cities had resumed their interrupted expansion. Cincinnati, with a population of twenty-five thousand, wrested economic leadership from Pittsburgh, while Louisville and St. Louis had more than doubled in size. The latter emerged as the "capital of the far west," presiding over the fur trade of the mountains, the lead industry of Illinois and Wisconsin, and the increasing commerce of the Southwest.[63] The Falls City became the center of steamboat operations, welcoming over a thousand of the new craft annually and handling the bulk of the immense tonnage that moved over the Ohio. Pittsburgh, though replaced as the first city of the transmontane region, maintained its industrial supremacy, and as the decade closed its residents heard the happy clanging of its foundries.

The key to this remarkable growth was the improvement of transportation facilities. In the twenties the steamboat became the large carrier of goods and people; new canals tied together the avenues of commerce; and an extended and improved road system eased local travel to nearby cities. Of all these, the most dramatic and important was steam navigation. By 1830 it had established a monopoly of passenger traffic, and, except at low water, handled most upstream freight. Its operations covered all the main rivers, while smaller steam craft plied many of the bigger tributaries.

The first successful runs were between Louisville and New Orleans, there being little activity on the upper Ohio until after 1820. Following the *Velocipede*'s first regular trips between Pittsburgh and Louisville in that year, however, steamboats multiplied rapidly. Both in number and tonnage the increase was remarkable. In 1817 there were 17 steam craft on Western waters with an aggregate tonnage of 3,290. Within the next five years over 60 more were added, and by 1830 187 steamboats totaling 29,481 tons plied the lakes and rivers of the new country. This represented about half

[63] F. J. Turner, *The Rise of the New West, 1819–1829* (*The American Nation: A History*, XIV [New York, 1906]), 98. For a good appreciation of the economic importance of Western cities, see 96–98.

of all American steam tonnage and roughly equaled the volume of merchant steam shipping in the entire British Empire.[64]

The arrival of one of the new vessels at a city wharf, which had once signaled a mild civic celebration, now became a routine occurrence. In the mid-twenties Pittsburgh docked at least one every week, while Cincinnatians saw steamers stop daily, and during the brisk season the average was one every twelve hours. Louisville, standing at the break in navigation, benefited most by these new developments and became the focus of movement on the Ohio. In 1829 over 1,000 steamboats touched Louisville, which was almost 300 more than the arrivals at New Orleans and ten times those at Pittsburgh. In the next year St. Louis welcomed 278 vessels, many of which operated out of the Ohio Valley or traded with the upper reaches of the Missouri and Mississippi.[65]

Western cities not only fattened on this increased commerce, but further profited by becoming shipbuilding centers. Three-fourths of the steamboats and four-fifths of the tonnage constructed in the West came from the yards of Pittsburgh, Cincinnati, and Louisville. Even during hard times the Iron City kept producing, turning out 48 vessels at a total cost of about $500,000 between 1812 and 1826. In the next four years, however, it equaled the output of the previous fourteen, and by 1830 boasted that nearly 20,000 tons had been launched from its docks. Local citizens took great pride in this accomplishment, Samuel Jones confiding that "to speak *modestly* . . . our steamboats are . . . the best on western waters." Cincinnati challenged this claim, and, indeed, at the end of the twenties had floated more tonnage than its upriver competitor. Louisville's contribution was much smaller, and St. Louis did little of her own construction until later.[66] Yet generally, the steamboat had not only added a new dimension to trade, but created one of the West's major industries.

Despite the rapidity and low cost of steam travel, older modes of transportation persisted on Western waters. In fact, keelboats, flat-

[64] Hunter, *Steamboats*, 32ff.
[65] Hunter, *Steamboats*, 34–37, 644–45.
[66] Hunter, *Steamboats*, 105–107; Jones, *Pittsburgh in 1826*, 90–91.

boats, and rafts increased markedly during the two decades following the trip of the *Enterprise*. Though they quickly yielded to upstream carriers, they maintained a monopoly on the smaller tributaries. Pittsburgh still depended heavily for its raw materials on flats coming down the Allegheny and Monongahela, while a large portion of Cincinnati's Ohio Valley trade used these vessels. As they were especially valuable in handling bulky farm products and crude and semifinished goods, their usefulness expanded throughout the twenties. It was not until 1830 that the steamboat equaled their volume of freight, and for many years after they continued as important participants in the commerce of the West.[67]

Of less immediate importance but immense long-range influence was the spread of the canal fever into the transmontane region. Throughout the post-depression years, Westerners dug a series of key water routes which by-passed the Falls in the Ohio and connected the entire Ohio Valley with the Great Lakes on the north and New York and Philadelphia on the east. Since these projects were not completed until about 1830, they did not alter trade patterns until later, but every city throughout the decade of construction jockeyed and maneuvered in anticipation of the changes the new arteries might bring. Though some work was done on many routes, three had particular significance for Western commerce: the Pennsylvania Canal, connecting Pittsburgh with Philadelphia; the Ohio Canal, which linked the Muskingum with Lake Erie at Cleveland; and the Louisville and Portland Canal, which skirted the Falls, smoothing the flow of traffic to the Mississippi.

Western cities enjoyed quicker benefits from the improvement and extension of their roads than from the excitement of canal speculation. Less dramatic in its impact on trade than steamboats, this development continually pushed freight rates down and stepped up the pace of overland travel. The National Road, completed to Wheeling on the Ohio in 1818, was the major project of the period, but its chronic bad condition prevented it from realizing the extravagant dreams of its promoters. Probably more important to the West, and unquestionably so to Pittsburgh, was the Pennsylvania

[67] Hunter, *Steamboats*, 52–59.

turnpike between Philadelphia and the Iron City. By 1820 most of it was in good repair, and even during bad times it carried over 4,000 tons annually. Its usefulness increased with prosperity, and in 1825 one Philadelphia house alone sent more than 200 wagons over it to Pittsburgh.[68] However, even at its best the Pennsylvania pike was no match for water transportation, and its limited success did not lessen the demand for a canal to the East.

Improvements in transportation laid the groundwork for a great expansion in the economies of Western cities. All except Lexington enjoyed a general prosperity in the last half of the twenties. Population mounted, manufacturing increased, commerce burgeoned—every index climbed rapidly as if anxious to regain the ground lost during the depression. In these years, too, the center of urban power moved westward, settling in Cincinnati, which emerged from the postwar crash with the leadership formerly held by Lexington and Pittsburgh. Louisville and St. Louis, however, also recorded great gains, being transformed from trading towns to booming commercial capitals openly ambitious for still greater conquests.

Pittsburgh recovered very slowly, but the renewal of its population growth reflected the appearance of better times. Though the largest transmontane community at the end of the war, it lost nearly 1,000 of its 8,000 residents during the depression.[69] The next decade saw this trend reversed as the city received an increasing number of immigrants. So many newcomers arrived in the late twenties that the *Gazette* estimated that the 1830 count would find over 25,000 Pittsburghers. This guess was too optimistic, the census figure being 12,450. The error was not as large as it might seem, however, since the newspaper's calculation included the people living in the small

[68] C. B. Smith, "The Terminus of the Cumberland Road on the Ohio River," M. A. Thesis, University of Pittsburgh, 1951, 86–93; Reiser, *Pittsburgh*, 77; *Pittsburgh Gazette*, March 11, 1825.

[69] The *Directory of 1815* listed the population as "upwards of 9,000," 3; United States Census, 1820, 15.

industrial towns which contained the city's overflow. Allegheny, Bayardstown, Birmingham, Lawrenceville, Hayti, and East Liberty had a combined total of 9,803 inhabitants, which brought "Pittsburgh and its environs" to 22,433.[70] But even without these additions the expansion for ten years was 73 per cent, which was demonstration enough that the "Gateway to the West" was back in business.

Manufacturing returned to the 1815 level in 1826, when the value of all industrial products reached $2,553,549, which was just $64,284 below the previous high.[71] Iron goods, always the heart of the city's economy, climbed back first and in 1826 accounted for nearly half of the total output. Steam engine factories reopened and once again became the town's pride. "Pittsburgh, in this branch of business, has already acquired great celebrity," Jones boasted. "It may be said, without an exception, that there is no place in the world, that can surpass Pittsburgh, as to the means and materials, which it affords for the manufacture of these powerful machines." Glass joined metals as showpieces of the West's Birmingham. The same author noted that it was "known and sold from Maine to New Orleans. — Even in Mexico they quaff their beverage from the beautiful white-flint of Messrs. Bakewell, Page and Bakewell of our city." Furthermore, he added, "at a recent exhibition of American manufactures, by the Franklin Institute of Philadelphia, where specimens of the first glass in the United States were brought forward," the prizes went to that firm. Though glass lost ground in Pittsburgh's economy, dropping from third to fourth place, it remained one of the largest employers.[72]

Commercial recovery went hand in hand with industrial revival and the renewal of immigration. "The vast increase of population and the consequent demand for the various necessities of life," the directory of 1826 noted, "the extensive range of country that is

---

[70] *Pittsburgh Gazette*, August 17, 1830; United States Census, 1830, 68–69; *Pittsburgh Gazette*, November 16, 1830.

[71] Jones, *Pittsburgh in 1826*, 49; Reiser, *Pittsburgh*, 24–25. Niles estimated in 1828 that "about 2,600 persons with two millions of capital" were engaged in Pittsburgh's factories. *Niles' Register*, February 23, 1828.

[72] Jones, *Pittsburgh in 1826*, 60–61; 69; Reiser, *Pittsburgh*, 25, 203.

supplied from our city, and the facilities which are afforded for transportation by our numerous streams and turnpike roads, combined with the spirit and enterprize of our merchants, are the great causes of our prosperity." The Monongahela docks alone handled 22,400 tons of freight in 1825 while better than 6,000 more came over the Eastern turnpikes.[73] Within six years the river trade more than doubled and land exchange continued brisk. By 1830 Pittsburgh's commerce, both in extent and vitality, had surpassed all previous levels, and gave every indication of continued expansion.

🙞

Though the Iron City recovered rapidly after 1825, it could not regain its Western primacy lost during the depression. Cincinnati forged ahead confidently and by 1830 easily outdistanced its older neighbor up the river. It now became the symbol of the rising new cities of the West. Immigrants — at least "those classes which seek large towns" — found it "the largest, the most increasing, and the most convenient." It had, moreover, "acquired a name across the mountains, men looked to it as the chosen city. . . . Manufactures . . . had been established; steamboats were building in great numbers, . . . and from 1820 to 1830, 15,000 persons became inhabitants of Cincinnati." [74] Optimism grew with the community. "It needs not the gift of prophecy," the editor of *Liberty Hall* declared, "to foretell that the future destiny of Cincinnati cannot be less than the LONDON of the western country." [75]

An expanding population provided the Queen City with a good basis for economic growth. The 6,493 inhabitants of 1816 became 9,642 four years later, and in 1826 Drake and Mansfield estimated the city's residents at 16,230. As the 1830 census approached, many Cincinnatians expected its findings to exceed 28,000, but the official number was 24, 831. As in Pittsburgh, however, this calculation did

[73] Jones, *Pittsburgh in 1826*, 85, 88.

[74] *Illinois Monthly Magazine*, II (1832), 2. James Hall, the editor of the magazine, was probably the author of this analysis.

[75] *Liberty Hall* (Cincinnati), March 23, 1830.

not include the 2,000 people living just outside the municipal limits in the Eastern and Northern Liberties. Nevertheless, the decade witnessed a growth of 152 per cent, which the *Advertiser* asserted had no historical equal. "If you know a man with ten grandchildren have him send them all out to Cincinnati," wrote a settler to his friend in Boston. "But make him do it soon, for if he doesn't ten thousand will take up their place." [76]

This immense immigration did not alter the basic mercantile posture of the town. "The commerce of Cincinnati," Drake and Mansfield observed in 1826, "is co-extensive with steamboat navigation on the western waters." The Queen City was "the point of importation and distribution for most of the goods" which supplied the area west of the Muskingum in Ohio, "nearly all" of Indiana, and "large portions" of Kentucky, Illinois, and Missouri. Timothy Flint estimated that it was the central market for over 1,000,000 people. Nor were exports confined to the United States, "the principal part" being carried to the West Indies and South America. Some enterprising merchants set their sights even higher, and formed a company to go whale and seal fishing in the Pacific and Indian Oceans. [77]

The volume of this commerce was as impressive as its extent. In 1826 Drake and Mansfield estimated the city's imports at $2,528,590 and its exports at $1,063,560. Three years later these totals jumped to $3,800,000 and $3,100,000 respectively. [78] The apparent unfavorable balance involved in this trade bothered some contemporaries, but the statistics obscured the fact that many incoming items were sold again on the countryside, representing a net gain for Cincinnati's merchants though never listed as exports. Dry goods brought over-

[76] *Liberty Hall* (Cincinnati), February 19, 1816; United States Census, 1820, 35; Drake and Mansfield, *Cincinnati in 1826*, 58; United States Census, 1830, 126–27; *Cincinnati Advertiser*, August 18, 1830. *Liberty Hall* (Cincinnati), November 12, 1830.

[77] Drake and Mansfield, *Cincinnati in 1826*, 71, 76; T. Flint, "Thoughts Respecting the Establishment of a Porcelain Manufactory at Cincinnati," *Western Monthly Review*, III (1830), 512; *Niles' Register*, March 1, 1823.

[78] Drake and Mansfield, *Cincinnati in 1826*, 77; *Cincinnati Directory*, 1829, 167–68.

land from the East to the head of the Ohio comprised about half of all imports, while iron and hardware from Pittsburgh, timber from the Allegheny region, and Queensware, sugar, coffee, and tea from New Orleans made up the rest.

Meat packing became the town's central export item in the twenties, over 40,000 hogs being shipped out in 1826 alone. "The pork business of this city," wrote Drake and Mansfield, "is equal, if not of greater magnitude than that of Baltimore; and is, perhaps not exceeded by that of any place in the world." Visitors dubbed the place "Porkopolis," for the animals seemed to be everywhere. Mrs. Trollope contended that if she tried to cross Main Street "the chances were five hundred to one against my reaching the shady side without brushing by a snout fresh dripping." [79] Three-quarters of the slaughtering took place inside the corporation limits, setting up a stench that did not let residents or travelers forget the town's connection with the pig.

Manufactured goods constituted only a small part of the town's shipments to the outside. In fact, industry was so weak that many businessmen feared that Cincinnati's economy was dangerously unbalanced, and in the late twenties civic leaders embarked on a second campaign for industrial expansion. Ironically, they used Pittsburgh as a model, where "there is no complaint about dull times — money is plenty, and the cheerful sound of industry is heard from every quarter." "We must imitate Pittsburgh," Timothy Flint counseled.[80]

The Ohio metropolis had no sooner raised itself above Pittsburgh and Lexington than a challenge to its supremacy came from another quarter. Down the river at the Falls, Louisville, though still

[79] Drake and Mansfield, *Cincinnati in 1826*, 78. The introduction of rock salt greatly improved the quality of Cincinnati's meat and increased its marketability. *Cincinnati Directory*, 1829, 169; F. Trollope, *Domestic Manners of the Americans*, 88–89.

[80] Drake and Mansfield, *Cincinnati in 1826*, 70; Flint, "Thoughts Respecting a Porcelain Manufactory," 513.

half the size of Cincinnati, grew so rapidly and displayed such
energy that some thought it might soon rival the Queen City.
"The population of this place has increased near a hundred fold
in the last eight years," crowed the *Public Advertiser*; "the number
of mechanics is daily increasing; manufactures are taking root in
our soil; and each succeeding year brings important accessions to
the mercantile class of our city." Commerce was the mainspring
of Louisville's economy, and its merchants constantly enlarged their
trading area. "The advantages necessarily growing out of our location are daily developing themselves," the paper continued. "The
people of the greater part of Indiana, all Kentucky, and portions
of Tennessee, Alabama, Illinois, Missouri, &c. now resort to this
place for dry goods, groceries, hardware and queensware." [81]

The most striking aspect of Louisville's development was its
population increase. In 1810 the town barely exceeded 1,000, yet
ten years later it numbered 4,012, not including Preston's and Campbell's "enlargements" or Shippingport and Portland, which were
economic appendages to the Falls City. The depression did not
halt this expansion, and in 1827 a local count found 6,563 inhabitants, while the contiguous places brought the total to 9,063. By
1830 the city had cleared the 10,000 mark, with its suburbs adding
another 3,000.[82] This was a great achievement by any standards,
but the growth might have been even larger if Louisville had not
earned a general reputation for sickliness and suffered a terrible
epidemic in 1822.

The basic stimulus for this expansion was the coming of the
steamboat. "From this event," wrote a contemporary, "we may
date the prosperity of Louisville." Arrivals of the new craft mounted
through the twenties. In 1823, 196 steam vessels docked at the Falls
City; the next year the figure jumped to 300, and by 1829 over
1,000 stopped annually. The warehouse had now become the town's
symbol. "The store rooms of the principal wholesale merchants are

---

[81] *Louisville Public Advertiser*, October 17, 1829.

[82] United States Census 1810, 72a; United States Census, 1820, 33; *Louisville Public Advertiser*, January 3, 1821; January 13, 1827; United States Census, 1830, 114–15.

larger and better adapted to business purposes than any to be found in the commercial cities of the East," asserted a traveler. Some were four stories high and contained fireproof vaults for books and papers. Though estimates of Louisville's commerce are at best approximate, one historian has calculated from the "books of leading houses" that the total for 1829 was $13,000,000.[83]

The steamboat not only created prosperity at the Falls City, but it also increased the Western demand for a canal around the rapids. Louisville publicly favored the project, but the residents were divided on its desirability. Many groups had a vested interest in the transshipment activity required by the break in the river. "The storage and forwarding business would probably be diminished — and there might be less use for hacks and drays," the *Advertiser* candidly admitted. Many people also feared that a canal might wipe out the economic foundations of the city because it would eliminate the need for stopping at the Falls. But the advocates of the improvement argued that there would be compensations. "We should acquire the necessary power for manufacturing and the requisite increase of population for prosecuting . . . domestic industry." In addition, steamboat building and extensive dry docks would more than offset any losses.[84] The most powerful contention of the proponents, however, was that the alternative of a route on the Indiana side would be fatal to every segment of the Kentucky community.

By the mid-twenties the pressure throughout the new country became so strong that postponement and debate were no longer possible. In 1825 Kentucky incorporated the Louisville and Portland Canal Company for opening navigation around the Falls "with suitable locks, docks and basins." The charter authorized the directors to issue stock up to $600,000. Seventy capitalists from both East and West invested generously, and the federal government ultimately put more than $200,000 into the project. Over 30 contractors bidded for the job, and work began in March 1826. Within

---

[83] Casseday, *Louisville*, 121; Hunter, *Steamboats*, 644; quoted in Ford and Ford, *Falls Cities*, I, 260; 261.

[84] *Louisville Public Advertiser*, February 7, 1824.

a few months, between 700 and 1,000 men were at work and the townspeople, basking in the prosperity of the company's heavy spending, put aside their worries. After many delays, and a total cost of $750,000, the first ships went through the installations on December 5, 1830.[85] Louisville's gloomy prophets proved mistaken, for in the next decade the city blossomed commercially and industrially as never before.[86]

St. Louis, like Louisville, passed through the economic crisis quickly. As early as 1822 the *Missouri Republican* noticed that "the cry of *hard times,* which formerly almost deafened us from every quarter has relapsed into low murmurs of complaint from only a few directions." The crash had been a sobering experience, however, and when rebuilding, the city carefully worked on sounder foundations. "The citizens have, in a great measure," wrote Lewis Beck, "abandoned their wild and visionary schemes of money-making." By 1830 St. Louis enjoyed unprecedented prosperity. "Many good homes are building. . . . The arts and useful manufactures are multiplying and improving. Mills, breweries, mechanical establishments, all seem to be advancing," an editor observed. "The trade and navigation of this port are becoming immense. Steamboats are daily arriving and departing, for east, west, north and south. . . . A bright prospect is before us." [87]

[85] *Louisville Public Advertiser,* January 19, 1825; *Niles' Register,* September 30, 1826; *Louisville Public Advertiser,* May 16, 1827; December 21, 1825; Hunter, *Steamboats,* 182–4.

[86] Some thought that Louisville had an industrial as well as commercial future. Caleb Atwater became almost lyrical when he thought of them. "Such are the manufacturing advantages of Louisville, far preferable in my mind to anything presented by the silvery heights of Potosi, or the far famed mines of Golconda and Peru, yet comparatively neglected. When will some sleepless statesman, some *Clinton* arise in the West, to point out to the people, those vast resources of industry, of comfort, of happiness, wealth and power!" *Remarks made on a Tour to Prairie du Chien . . .* (Columbus, Ohio, 1831), 16.

[87] *Missouri Republican,* September 4, 1822; L. C. Beck, *Gazatteer of Illi-*

A rapidly growing population participated in these good times. On the eve of the war with Great Britain the town contained just over 1,000 inhabitants, but by 1818 this number climbed to 3,500.[88] Though the pace slackened during the depression, the figure passed 5,000 in 1828, and two years later the city claimed over 6,000 residents.[89] In this great increase the French character of the community gave way before the American newcomers. Paxton could find only 155 families of the "original and other French" in 1821.[90]

The two central elements in St. Louis's economy — fur and lead — expanded quickly in the late twenties, and their agents did business over the whole expanse of wilderness stretching from the Mississippi to the Pacific Ocean. The removal of government factories in the Indian country paved the way for increasing activity in the peltry trade. Two new companies, the Rocky Mountain and American, captured the bulk of the commerce, replacing the Missouri Fur Company, which failed at the end of the decade. This industry was the city's largest employer as well as its biggest exporter, and its prosperity ramified throughout the whole community.

The lead industry grew even more rapidly. As the great outfitting center, St. Louis provided the mining areas with men, capital, and merchandise. In addition, the city afforded transportation and storage for the ore on its way to market. The expansion of lead activity during the twenties, especially in Illinois and Wisconsin, was remarkable. Fever River fields, for example, increased production from 383,000 pounds to 6,824,389 within two years, and then doubled that figure in the next twelve months. The number of licenses granted to work this federal property told the same story, jumping from five in 1825 to thirty-one three years later. In 1826 over 450 miners, using five furnaces, worked the Fever River region alone, and they could not "smelt as fast as they dig." Thomas Hart Benton,

---

nois and Missouri, *Containing a General View of Each State* (Albany, 1823), 327; *Missouri Republican*, July 6, 1830.

[88] Paxton, *St. Louis Directory.*

[89] *Missouri Republican*, November 4, 1828, October 5, 1830. Population figures for St. Louis, no matter how official, are unsatisfactory because a large number of its residents spent most of their time in the mountains or mines.

[90] Paxton, *St. Louis Directory.*

reflecting St. Louis's deep interest in the industry, tried to facilitate this exploitation by asking the government to turn the mines over to private parties.[91]

St. Louis was essentially a commercial city, but its leaders constantly tried to lure money into manufacturing. Though a depot for a rich hinterland on both sides of the river, the town did not have adequate milling equipment, and as late as 1826 it imported over six thousand barrels of flour from Ohio and Kentucky. Not only did the erection of a steam mill seem urgent, but many thought the proximity of coal and iron suggested that "we can manufacture steam engines and sugar mills, as well as the people of Pittsburgh." [92] Local workingmen argued that St. Louis ought to produce both steamboats and textiles,[93] while the newspapers constantly complained of having to import supplies from Ohio when they could be profitably made at home.[94] Despite these opportunities the city's industry grew only slowly, and most surplus capital sought the lucrative and traditional mercantile channels.

About 1830 the second era of urban history in the West came to a close. Having reorganized their economies after the postwar collapse, the cities reached a new level of prosperity. Populations more than doubled, commerce grew, and new industries flourished. If the pace was too fast for Lexington, other towns like Cleveland and Detroit demonstrated promising vitality. Though the chastening experience of the depression was not quickly forgotten, the old confidence and optimism returned. The period after 1815, however, not only saw the material growth of the new country, but also witnessed the rapid maturing of its social and intellectual institutions. Not content merely with the goods of life, Western townspeople turned increasingly to the cultivation of the good life.

[91] *Missouri Republican*, June 2, 1829; September 14, 1826; *Kentucky Reporter*, June 23, 1823.

[92] *Missouri Gazette*, June 14, 1817; *Missouri Republican*, August 29, 1825, June 1, 1826; August 25, 1825.

[93] *Proceedings of the Friends of the American System at a Meeting of the Mechanics and Workingmen. Held at St. Louis, February 19, 1831* (St. Louis, 1831), 15.

[94] For example, see *Missouri Republican*, October 5, 1830.

Chapter 7

The Changing Social Structure

The irregular development of the postwar years put new strains on the social structures of the young Western towns. Larger populations and the expansion of commerce and industry created new groups and interests, thus adding to the complexity and sophistication of city life. Already stratified after a generation of growth, these communities found lines sharpened, class divisions deepened, and the sense of neighborliness and intimacy weakened. The fragmentation caused by the increasing specialization of urban economies and the greater size of the towns meant that the easy familiarity of small-town life more and more gave way to the impersonality of city living.

To oldtimers, the changing social configuration bred a deep nostalgia and raised the image of happier, simpler days. "We cannot help looking back, with sorrowful heart, on that time of unaffected content and gaity," a Pennsylvanian lamented, "when the unambitious people . . . in the village of 'Fort Pitt' in the yet unchartered town of Pittsburgh, were ignorant and careless of all the invidious distinctions, which distract and divide the inhabitants of overgrown cities." As the early years receded they were invested with Arcadian plainness. "Then all was peaceful heartfelt felicity, undisturbed by the rankling thorns of envy; and equality, without the intervention of demogagues, was a tie that united all ranks and conditions in our community." [1] Town life in the West had never been so idyllic as that, but the vision was itself a measure of the swiftness and extent of urban change.

Everywhere growth and expansion intensified earlier stratification. "We have our castes of society, graduated and divided with as

---

[1] Jones, *Pittsburgh in 1826*, 43.

much regard to rank and dignity as the most scrupulous Hindoos maintain, in defence of their religious prejudices," the *Pittsburgh Directory* admitted in 1826. Moreover, social distances were great. "Between the . . . classes . . . there are lines of demarcation drawn, wide, distinct, and not to be violated with impunity," observed the same source. Even within groups refinements arose. "You will frequently be amused," a traveler noticed, "by seeing a lady, a wife of a dry-goods storekeeper, look contemptuously at the mention of another's name, whose husband pursues precisely the same occupation, but on a less extensive scale, and observe that 'She only belongs to the third circle of society.' " [2]

Though the order in the urban hierarchy remained the same in the postwar decades, the distribution of power and influence shifted markedly. The merchants, who had presided over town affairs unchallenged for a quarter of century, saw their supremacy contested by the strengthening of other groups, especially the wage-earning and professional classes. The old leaders maintained their predominance only by yielding along many fronts to the newcomers. In addition, the tightening of social lines led all elements to assert their claims more forcefully and articulately. The breakdown of the sense of community attendant upon urban growth not only deepened the divisions between groups but also intensified the need for association within the group.

The merchants especially felt these tensions, for new elements seemed to threaten their primacy and jeopardize their control. The postwar depression shook both their prosperity and confidence, and in the 1820's they increasingly banded together for common purposes. James Hall later noticed that they, like the "masses," be-

[2] Jones, *Pittsburgh in 1826*, 43; Ferrall, *A Ramble*, 230–31. Mrs. Trollope, who would have preferred more class consciousness in Americans, noted that social lines were carefully, if tortuously, drawn. At a party in Cincinnati, she discovered that a certain young lady was missing. On inquiring, she was told, "You do not yet understand our aristocracy, . . . the family of Miss C. are mechanics." When Mrs. Trollope observed that the young lady's brother owned a large shop, her interpreter replied "He is a mechanic; he assists in making the articles he sells; the others call themselves merchants." Trollope, *Domestic Manners*, 155.

came more and more class-conscious, being "imbued with the opinion that wealth and poverty, commerce and labor, education and want of education, constitute hostile interests." The awareness of these divisions allowed for a clearer definition of the urban elite. "The business community," the same author declared, embraced "all those who are engaged in the great occupations of buying and selling, exchanging, importing and exporting merchandise, and including the banker, the broker and underwriter." [3] In Pittsburgh and Lexington, manufacturers were added to this group. Held together by common activity and similar views, these men increasingly acted in concert.

Though coffee houses had earlier served as casual clubs for the towns' traders, many now desired more formal organization. In 1829 Cincinnati's mercantile leaders formed a Chamber of Commerce "to promote and facilitate the commerce of the city — to examine and adjust such matters in dispute amongst merchants and others as shall be submitted to them — and to establish and render uniform the commercial usages of the city." Two years earlier St. Louis businessmen had created an exchange to further the "spirit of comity and liberal intercourse among the merchants." And in Louisville the City Exchange Building set aside a hall "for the use of our merchants" which soon became the focus of trading activity in that town.[4]

Though day-to-day competitors, Western businessmen increasingly recognized their common interests and cooperated on many economic issues. Thus they often acted to regularize mercantile customs and practice. In some cities leading merchants made agreements to set up "a uniform system . . . in relation to the rate of STORAGE and FARES on merchandise." [5] In others, tavern owners fixed prices for room, board, and services to protect themselves against charges of extortion, and to push price-cutters to the wall. They directed their most concerted effort, however, against the system

[3] Hall, *The West*, 1–3.
[4] *Cincinnati Gazette*, December 29, 1829; *Missouri Republican*, July 12, 1827; *Louisville Public Advertiser*, March 18, 1829.
[5] *Liberty Hall* (Cincinnati), May 16, 1823.

of auction selling which began during the war and spread rapidly in the following years. Most of the auctioneers were local citizens, but shopowners and retailers felt that their extensive activities threatened normal enterprise. Throughout the twenties the business community tried constantly (but without success) to get state legislatures to stop the encroachment.

This growing economic cooperation among businessmen in the marketplace was solidified by many other contacts, for they were not only the cities' most prosperous group but also socially the most prominent. Their wives belonged to the same clubs, their children went to the same schools, and they participated in the same amusements and recreations. Nearly all the developments of the twenties — the depression, the rise of new classes, and mounting urban populations — heightened this sense of separateness. Though new families entered the circle and older ones fell out, the circle itself became tighter and more distinct.

Indeed, the exclusiveness was physical as well as social, for the homes of the well-to-do pre-empted the choice spots while other people moved to less desirable areas. "All the rich people lived on Main Street," John Darby recalled as he reminisced about early St. Louis. Frances Trollope's bazaar failed in Cincinnati because she built in the wrong end of town. In Pittsburgh, the movement was toward Penn Street, which boasted "most of the fashionable residences" and was "quiet, airy and clean in comparison with other parts." [6] Each community developed its preferred sections, and by 1830 social lines could be plotted on a map of the city.[7]

Within these confines the West's elite established a strenuous

[6] J. F. Darby, *Personal Recollections of Many Prominent People I have Known, and of Events — Especially Those Relating to the History of St. Louis — during the First Half of the Present Century* (St. Louis, 1880), 10; E. W. Blythe to J. C. Green, July 22, 1824, MS, Carnegie Library (Pittsburgh).

[7] The lines were also drawn at the other end of the economic scale. In 1825 William Merrill of Cincinnati wrote in his diary of going "into the S. E. part of the city" which he called "the abodes of poverty." Later he referred to the same area as "that refuse part of the city." Diary, August 24, 1825, August 11, 1827 (MS, Historical and Philosophical Society of Ohio, Cincinnati).

routine — dinner parties, dances, the theatre, and social clubs through the winter, and extended stays at the fashionable resorts and watering places in the summer. Under the aegis of the women the social calendar was always full. A week in the lives of the William Henry Harrisons of Cincinnati was typical. "Our town has been very gay for some time past," the future president's wife wrote to a friend; "there is to be dancing Assembly's [*sic*] once every two weeks and Cotillion parties. Mrs. Duval my next door neighbor is to have a large party on Monday evening . . . Mrs. Macalister is to give a dance on Wednesday next . . . Mrs. Kilgour gave a large party a few days since — every person talked on nothing else scarcely for a week." Every urban community had a similar group. Even in Pittsburgh, where the merchants and manufacturers had a reputation for a narrow dedication to business, there was "a dashing, fashionable set, much like the same class elsewhere." [8]

By the twenties the high society of Western towns reminded some of comparable circles across the mountains. "The refinements of society, both of a social and moral kind, exist in a degree that would justify comparison with the larger and older cities of the East," one traveler asserted. A visiting artist, commissioned to sketch Louisville's wealthy belles, thought society there equal to any he had seen in other sections of the country. James Atherton, residing in the same place in 1831, was even more impressed: "I have passed the week here pleasantly. I have had an opportunity to see all the beauty and fashion of the place. The fashions are carried to more ridiculous extremes [*sic*] than in Atlantic cities. The ladies dress more extravagantly and give the most splendid balls. They are passionately fond of music and dancing." [9] In Cincinnati Mrs. Benson announced in 1826 that she was going to "show the folks what Philadelphia style is," but after her entertainment "a great

---

[8] Mrs. W. H. Harrison to Mrs. J. Findlay, January 1, 1826, MS, Torrence Collection; Mrs. E. Blythe to J. C. Green, July 22, 1824, MS, Carnegie Library.

[9] Quoted in D. Smalley, ed., Trollope, *Domestic Manners*, xx; J. W. Jarvis to R. Etting, November 11, 1820, MS, Gratz Papers, Wilson Collection; J. H. Atherton to M. A. Atherton, October 25, 1831, MS, University of Kentucky Library.

many returned from it most awfully disappointed as they saw nothing more than we have at all our parties." [10]

The first generation of wealthy families not only established the social ritual of the cities, but also handed down an elite tradition to their children. Indeed, the young set moved in an even more insulated circle than their parents. Without a public school system, contacts among urban youths were more classbound than they had been earlier or would be later. The "best families" sent their sons and daughters to selected local institutions, or, in many instances, to Eastern academies and colleges. Those who could afford higher education generally went across the mountains, and it was not until the 1820's that Transylvania in Lexington broadened the opportunities for Western youths.

The most sheltered group in transmontane cities were the daughters of the rich, whom Mrs. Trollope called a "privileged class." Carefully guarded by socially sensitive mothers, screened from the world outside from birth, and educated in fashionable schools, they lived well removed from the rest of urban society. Leisure and frivolity increasingly occupied their time. Timothy Flint, himself a representative of the mercantile community, complained of their total uselessness, asserting that they never put "their own lily hands to domestic drudgery" and that they had no higher interests than dressing smartly, reading romances, and playing the piano. "We traverse the streets of our own city, and the wires of the piano are thummed in our ears from every considerable house," and inside sits "the fair, erect on her music stool, laced and pinioned . . . *dinging* . . . at the wires, as though she could in some way hammer out of them music, amusement and a husband." [11]

Nor did this relaxed life end with marriage. Matrimony merely

[10] Mrs. W. H. Harrison to Mrs. J. Findlay, January 1, 1826, MS, Torrence Collection. In 1829 Cincinnati's leading women formed a "Cincinnati Convention of Fashion and Good Society" to formalize the social ritual. *Saturday Evening Chronicle*, November 14, 1829.

[11] Trollope, *Domestic Manners*, 45; *The Western Monthly Review*, III (1835), 403.

set off new social rounds, with domestics handling the household chores. An index of the growth of the upper class was the mounting complaints about the servant situation. The wealthy found it difficult to get good cooks and maids, some of whom worked only a little while and then married, while others moved into better paying jobs at the first opportunity.[12] Increasingly, Negroes and mulattoes monopolized this occupation, but even they proved unreliable, and the problem persisted throughout the decade.

Though sharing the same background, the sons of the well-to-do were more energetic and worldly than their sisters. Enjoying unusual educational opportunities and graduating from college in increasing numbers, this group provided Western cities with a new generation of business and professional leaders. From their fathers they learned to work hard, and their schooling gave them a training and polish which set them apart from other youths. Many moved into family enterprises, others practiced law or medicine, and a few drove their families to distraction by failing in every activity they touched. Their social life revolved around clubs and societies. These were quasi-academic in purpose, but their main function was to maintain class ties. In Pittsburgh the bright young men of means formed the Quintilian Society; in Lexington, the Whig and Union Philosophical societies; while in Cincinnati Philomatians and Erophebics competed for the city's rising leaders.[13]

By 1830 the business community represented a well-defined unit. Bound together by economic interest, fortified by constant social contacts, and set apart by wealth and education, the mercantile class presided over urban affairs. Beneath it were several other groups with varying degrees of prestige and esteem, who became increasingly aware of their status. Though the personnel of each level continually changed, the lines between them grew constantly more distinct. To put it another way, there was a double development in urban societies: one was the movement of many individuals

---

[12] *Liberty Hall* (Cincinnati), June 13, 1822.

[13] A. B. Butler to S. Bolles, October 12, 1820, Samuel Bolles Letters, Wilson Collection (University of Kentucky Library).

up or down the social ladder, the other was the widening of the distance between rungs.

The professional classes were one of the great beneficiaries of postwar urban expansion. As the cities grew, the need for specialized skills multiplied, and in the twenties doctors, lawyers, ministers, teachers, and editors flocked to Western communities. Indeed, the demand was so great that the new country could no longer depend on an irregular flow of talent from the East and undertook to develop its own sources. Fortunately, the facilities required to meet this problem were close at hand. Some of the younger generation, having no inclination for a business career, were looking around for other avenues of advancement, and Transylvania University, under the aggressive leadership of Horace Holley, established schools of law and medicine offering training previously available only at great cost across the mountains. In addition, religious denominations surveyed Western towns to find appropriate spots for seminaries, while urban colleges provided an increasing number of teachers for expanding school systems.

In every city professional groups showed substantial growth. In 1807 Pittsburgh had only four physicians, but twenty years later there were sixteen and by 1830 more than a score. While no figures are available for an earlier date, the thirty-six attorneys in the Iron City in 1826 represented a comparable increase in lawyers. In St. Louis the number of doctors more than doubled in the decade following 1810, and the legal fraternity showed a similar expansion. Louisville's notorious health problem made that place attractive to the medical profession, especially after the epidemic of 1822, which brought to town not only general practitioners but doctors interested in research as well. In fact, so many physicians settled at the Falls that a run of good health in the mid-twenties created serious unemployment.[14] Lexington, the home of the West's

[14] Jones, *Pittsburgh in 1826*, 97; Paxton, *St. Louis Directory*, 1821; *Louisville Public Advertiser*, October 3, 1827; Trollope, *Domestic Manners*, 89.

leading medical and law schools, boasted one of the most distinguished professional classes in the nation, and proportionately the largest. Everywhere the teaching ranks swelled, especially in municipalities that established public school systems.

Journalists also found a market for their talent in Western cities, where new papers constantly sprang up. Every town supported at least two weeklies, and by 1830 Cincinnati had seven in addition to two dailies. Indeed, the reading public grew so rapidly that some publishers directed their journals to the tastes and interests of particular groups. The *True Blue and Castigator* tried to cater to Cincinnati's lower classes with sensational — and often irresponsible — reporting, while the *Cincinnati Chronicle and Literary Gazette* was "much read by the Exquisites" and "long heads" because of its detailed critiques of cultural life.[15] Among the editors were men of accomplishments; some, like Amos Kendall, Duff Green, Charles Hammond, and Moses Dawson, achieved a distinction and influence that spread well beyond their own locality.

The increase of these groups allowed some professions to organize their membership more formally than had seemed necessary when each town had but a handful of practitioners. The doctors, whose societies dated back to the beginning of the century, tightened their associations and widened the scope of their activity. They not only tried to keep out the untrained and quacks, but also sought to raise the standards of their colleagues and enhance their economic position. In Lexington and Cincinnati, local physicians published their own journals, while in other cities medical societies heard members read scientific papers.

Though the law and, to some degree, journalism remained too competitive for cooperation, other groups tried to get together on common concerns. Teachers increasingly recognized the need for association to keep up with the many innovations in the educational field. For instance, in Pittsburgh they called a county convention in 1830 "for the purpose of reciprocal conference as to the best plans to be pursued in imparting instruction, exciting dormant talents, securing punctual attendance . . . and the introduction of

[15] *Cincinnati Chronicle and Literary Gazette*, June 5, 1830.

any new methods." [16] Ministers, already organized along denominational lines, banded together frequently to promote Sabbath School Associations, Bible Tract societies, charitable organizations, and a host of other semi-religious projects.

As the professional classes grew, they became more independent of the business community. To be sure, the old connections were still there. Lawyers continued to seek clients among the wealthy, private-school teachers catered to the children of the well-to-do, and doctors and ministers relied heavily on the elite for support. But the relationship had altered; the dependence of earlier days disappeared. Even in 1816 some professional men openly challenged commercial values and "the sordid rage for accumulating wealth." [17] Others, especially lawyers, became spokesmen for different groups, and liberal editors led the attack on conservative supremacy in the cities. Though not the wealthiest section of Western society, these people enjoyed esteem and influence that greatly exceeded their economic status. In the twenties their numbers and prestige increased as they provided articulate and energetic leadership for almost every division of urban life.

The broadening contacts of the professions were symptomatic of the enlargement of other sections of urban society, especially the wage-earning class, whose numerical growth outstripped that of all other groups. Though the flow of working people into frontier cities slackened during the depression, it never stopped, and in the late twenties it reached flood tide again. Indeed, except during a few years in Pittsburgh and Lexington, the labor supply seldom met the demand. In many instances businessmen issued blanket invitations to migrants, pointing out local openings and promising good wages. "There is, perhaps, no place in the United States where Mechanics of every description are in greater demand than they have been during the summer and continue to be in St. Louis," the

[16] *Pittsburgh Gazette*, November 16, 1830.
[17] *Liberty Hall* (Cincinnati), December 23, 1816.

editor of the *Missouri Republican* noted in 1827, while discussing the "high price" of labor.[18] Opportunities like these drew large numbers of wage-earners to transmontane cities, swelling the ranks of a class which became increasingly aware of its status and strength.

One measure of this growing consciousness was the spread of trade unions. In the first decades of the century, organization had been sporadic and touched only a few crafts. In the twenties, however, the movement developed rapidly, affecting new occupations and influencing political as well as economic affairs. Underneath this upsurge lay not only a desire for better wages and hours, but also new awareness of labor's social position. As the decade wore on, the "workies" sharpened their attacks on the elite and asserted their own claims to importance. In St. Louis the mechanics avowed that the "entire fabric" of the community "rests" on "the labouring classes." In Cincinnati an uneasy editor noticed these stirrings. "Quite a new era seems to be dawning upon this class of society. . . . The members of the various mechanical professions are manifesting a disposition to unite and act in concert." [19]

Though Louisville and St. Louis saw some spread of unionism, it proved most successful in cities outside the slave area. In both Pittsburgh and Cincinnati it witnessed great expansion. By 1819 the Mechanical Association in the Queen City embraced thirty-two trades, including all the important crafts as well as more specialized occupations such as sieve workers, glass blowers, and stone cutters. On the Fourth of July of that year over 800 delegates marched in the Independence Day parade.[20] Pittsburgh's workingmen had a longer history of association, and even during the dark days of the depression the major crafts kept together. In the late twenties they were strong enough to carry on a wide campaign for fewer hours. In both places, however, strikes were few, since the general prosperity encouraged employers to grant demands without stoppages.

[18] *Missouri Republican*, October 4, 1827.

[19] *Proceedings of the Friends of the American System at a Meeting of the Mechanics and Workingmen: Held at St. Louis, February 19, 1831; Cincinnati Chronicle and Literary Gazette*, October 23, 1830.

[20] *Liberty Hall* (Cincinnati), July 9, 1819.

Labor's major drive in this period was for a shortened work week. The carpenters led the fight against the "sunrise to sunset system" asserting that "it reduces man nearly on a level with the slave, . . . deprives him of an opportunity of cultivating his mind, and not only makes his life a burden to him, but injures his health through excess of labour, and must ultimately shorten his days." The demands of the workingmen of Pittsburgh afford a good description of the daily routine of this class. In 1826 they bargained for a work day that would run between sun-up and 6 P.M. in the summer and until sun-down in the winter with an hour off for breakfast and lunch, "as is the custom in most eastern cities of America, and the immemorial practice of European tradesmen." [21] The objective disclosed the realities. Wage-earners toiled long hours — longer, indeed, than in seaboard cities — and by 1830 no great advance had been made in lightening their burden.

Some progress was made, however, in establishing facilities for the job-seeker. While towns were small, no employment agencies were necessary, for opportunities quickly became common knowledge. But in the twenties clearing houses were formed in the larger places to aid laborers seeking openings and assist merchants and manufacturers in locating help. In 1827 James E. Cimmins inaugurated an "Intelligence Shop" in Pittsburgh, commenting that "in other cities, such offices have been found very serviceable." Its purpose was to post jobs as they became available and to guide strangers who sought employment. The Cincinnati General Agency and Intelligence Office had an even broader scope, handling information on houses, rents and land sales, and even operating a lost-and-found service. [22]

The constant labor shortage in Western towns brought an increasing number of women and children into shops and factories. Responsible opinion regretted this, and leading citizens were reluctant to discuss it. Indeed, all references to it were couched in highly

[21] *Liberty Hall* (Cincinnati), August 9, 1825; *Pittsburgh Statesman*, June 24, 1826; *Pittsburgh Mercury*, January 3, 1827.

[22] *Pittsburgh Mercury*, July 3, August 7, 1827; *Liberty Hall* (Cincinnati), January 26, 1827.

defensive language designed to show that working conditions in transmontane cities were much better than in Eastern communities. Pittsburgh's Phoenix Cotton Factory employed over seventy women. But when the *Gazette* announced this figure, it reassured its readers (and the outside world) that "manufactures are not injurious to the morals" of these workers. In fact, it continued, "the order, regularity and innocence of the hands of the Phoenix Factory would be creditable to any academic institution." In less industrialized Cincinnati the problem was not so acute, but the editor of *Liberty Hall* often complained of the "very inadequate price paid, in cities like ours, for female labor." [23] In other places early directories reveal that a growing number of women found employment, usually in the needle trades or as shopkeepers.

More troublesome to wage-earners than competition from women, however, was the question of adequate housing. This was no new problem, because population in these young cities generally outran available shelter. The depression loosened the situation somewhat in Lexington and Pittsburgh, but prosperity brought shortages again. Though construction figures seemed impressive to contemporaries, they did not begin to meet the surging demand. In a single year Cincinnati erected 480 dwellings,[24] and Louisville between 150 and 215, while St. Louis did more in 1824 than in "three or four years past." At best this effort merely kept abreast of obvious requirements. By the late twenties every town except Lexington faced a housing crisis. Not only was there a lack of new homes, but age had already deteriorated old ones.[25]

Wage-earners could have afforded better housing if it had been available, but their other great requirement, education, was beyond the means of most. The need was twofold: instruction for children

[23] *Liberty Hall* (Cincinnati), May 4, 1829.

[24] Cincinnati, Minutes, February 11, 1829. *Liberty Hall* put the figure at 416, but it made no official count; April 6, 1830. The housing figures for Cincinnati in the late twenties were impressive: 185 in 1826, 308 in 1827, 496 in 1828. *Saturday Evening Chronicle* (Cincinnati), February 14, 1829. One editor thought this a better record than Boston's. *Ibid.*, March 7, 1829.

[25] *Louisville Public Advertiser*, October 3, 1827; *Missouri Republican*, July 4, 1825; Jones, *Pittsburgh in 1826*, 39.

and some kind of training for young men and adults. In the twenties progress took place along both these lines. In most cities free public schooling took care of all children for at least a few years, while the establishment of mechanics' institutes and apprentices' libraries extended opportunities to adults. A few benevolent citizens usually started and supported the libraries, but the workingmen organized their own institutes. Dedicated to "the promotion of the useful Arts and Sciences, the improvement of its members in practical knowledge, and the advancement of public education," these organizations became the focus of working-class efforts for self-development.[26] By 1830 Western wage-earners had begun to break down one of the barriers that most clearly separated them from the more fortunate classes.

The most dramatic evidence of the growing influence of the working people, however, was their increased political activity. "There are various indications at the present moment," wrote a Cincinnati editor, "that the laboring classes of the community are beginning to think for themselves, and to reflect seriously on their own rights." Initially, mechanics' associations merely endorsed candidates of local parties by publishing a list of names "to be supported by the *mechanics* at the ensuing election." In the process some urban figures like James W. Gazlay in Cincinnati and Walter Forward in Pittsburgh became known as labor politicians, while others made overt appeals for working class votes. This was limited participation, but it was effective enough to bring complaints from older groups who felt their leadership jeopardized.[27]

The mounting political activity underlined the growth and importance of the wage-earning class in Western towns. In Cincinnati "Anodyne" began a letter to an editor by proudly announcing, "Sir, I am one of those 'common men.'" Then, turning his fire on the Queen City's ruling families, he asserted that party leaders

[26] *Pittsburgh Gazette*, June 15, 1830. See also *Liberty Hall* (Cincinnati), October 24, November 19, 1828.

[27] *Liberty Hall* (Cincinnati), August 13, 1822; September 11, 1822; for example, see *Pittsburgh Gazette*, August 3, 1830; *Liberty Hall* (Cincinnati), September 11, 1822; September 21, 1822.

chose only the wealthy for office while turning down wage-earners. " 'No,' you still say; 'no *my candidate* rolls in the first circles, and sets his arms akimbo; belongs to various coffee house clubs, smokes Spanish segars, and if he gets drunk, does it like a gentleman, upon good old Madeira of two dollars the bottle, or cogniac [*sic*] brandy at four dollars the gallon.' " The ordinary man had no such credentials. " 'Your candidate gets swipy on whisky, and if he has the advantage of mine by the articles of honesty, mine more than overbalances the account by the *genteel company* he keeps.' " [28]

Though trade unions still generally worked inside established parties in 1830, the demand grew up for more independent action. In Pittsburgh they established a Workingmen's Party, which organized throughout the region. Several meetings were held, leaders pounded out a program, and members listened to speeches, one "by particular request, by an operative mechanic, on the rights and interests of the Workingmen." Taking their platform from similar groups in New York and Philadelphia, they modified certain planks for local purposes and underlined their support of internal improvements.[29] The objectives were broad, including free education, abolition of imprisonment for debt, and a host of other reforms which attracted support outside laboring ranks. Since the movement was still young, however, this agitation was more important as a symbol of the wage-earners' awareness of status than as a political phenomenon.

While the professional and wage-earning classes grew in numbers and influence, another group lost ground. The transients — boatmen, wagoners, migrant laborers, and drifters — suffered a proportional decline, occupying increasingly a peripheral position in most cities. As town life became more settled, their importance dimin-

[28] *Saturday Evening Chronicle* (Cincinnati), March 24, 1827.

[29] *Pittsburgh Gazette*, August 3, 1830; November 19, 1830; *Missouri Republican*, December 28, 1830.

ished, even though expanding trade and immigration added somewhat to their ranks. Rough, untutored, unstable, and without meaningful ties to any community, they remained a jangling element.
By 1830, however, they were no longer a formidable force, and
local authorities viewed them as a police and health problem rather
than as a serious threat to the community.

St. Louis was the single exception. It continued to suffer from
what one editor called "the rudeness of coarse, vulgar wagoners,
steamboat sailors and draymen." But leaders there recognized the
uniqueness of the situation. "We are for the most part a congregation of strangers," the city's mayor candidly admitted in 1823. Later
a committee, tangling with many of the problems arising from this
fact, went to the root of the matter. "In advancing to the north west
frontier St. Louis is the most considerable town; and hence it becomes the rendezvous of all who seek their fortune in that direction." In addition, the Mississippi metropolis had a peculiar problem. "The army of the United States is the most fruitful source of
the evil," the committee declared. "Jefferson Barracks, the largest
military post of the union, is within ten miles, and all the forts on
the upper Missouri and Mississippi are in direct connection with
St. Louis. The soldiers discharged from the garrisons are thrown
upon society, without regular employment or industrious habits." [30]
These factors gave St. Louis society a looseness and roughness which
contrasted markedly with the growing maturity of towns farther
east, and created difficulties which other cities knew only in a lesser
degree.

In the late twenties, however, the canal boom in the West brought
a new group of transients to Pittsburgh, Cincinnati, and Louisville.
The construction of new waterways required large contingents of
workers, and neighboring towns could provide only a small portion.
Hence the new country was flooded with vagabond laborers who
lived haphazardly and moved from job to job, staying in cities only
when building was nearby. But at Louisville the Portland Canal
attracted large numbers of the unskilled who resided for several

[30] *Missouri Republican*, April 20, 1825; St. Louis, Minutes, April 14, 1823;
December 15, 1829.

years. In 1827 nearly ten per cent of the population found employment on the project.[31] Though some settled down quickly, others remained floaters — working by day, drifting by night — a constant irritant to local officials.

The irregular life of the transient population centered upon a few blocks in each city. Usually located near the waterfront and business districts, these spots contained rooming houses, cheap hotels, grogshops, and tippling houses. Sealed off from the rest of town — especially after dark — these areas developed habits and patterns of their own. Employment of these people was generally seasonal, often taking them out of the city. Some toiled on the canals, in lead mines, or in the mountains, while boatmen and wagoners spent most of their time on the water or road. Urbanites usually saw these transients between jobs and concluded that they were always idle and shiftless. "Our city is at present infested with a set of men who have no visible means of making a living," a St. Louisan complained in 1824, "and whose only occupation is gambling and swindling." [32] Local authorities could not completely control them, and were happy to see their activities increasingly concentrated in a few blocks, permitting a more tranquil and safer existence for the rest of the community.

Though confined to narrow physical limits, this group was not completely detached from local interests. In fact each city provided exactly what these men wanted — tippling houses, taverns, grogshops, and entertainment centers. In 1819 a Pittsburgher protested the growth of these in the Iron City, and he especially singled out a local variation called " 'the Idalian Bowers,' " which, "from their great increase in numbers — their locality, and the notorious manner in which their inmates celebrated their orgies, have become a very serious inconvenience." A Grand Jury in the same year declared "an abominable nuisance . . . the women of pleasure, that of late swarm in our city." The same presentment noted that over thirty dram shops were operating without licenses and were the "direct

[31] *Louisville Public Advertiser*, October 31, 1827.
[32] *Missouri Gazette*, January 7, 1824.

or remote cause of nine-tenths of the indictments" filed in municipal court.[33]

Every river city witnessed the same kind of development. In 1820
conditions proved so bad in Cincinnati that a grand jury was called
to investigate. It found the lower Market Street area laced with
disorderly houses. One it called "a nuisance to the neighborhood
. . . where every species of rioting, revelling and debauchery are
publicly and shamelessly practiced"; in another a converted weigh
shack became "a resort for the idle and intemperate." In the same
year a Louisville grand jury discovered a similar situation. Referring
to a few downtown blocks as the "nurseries of vice and immorality"
and the "sinks of society," it protested against "the great and unusual
increase of tippling houses and houses of ill fame." The problem
persisted, however, and four years later a town meeting established
a committee of thirty prominent citizens, including many doctors
and ministers, to "suppress" those engaged in "gambling, drunken-
ness, and other practices subversive to the peace, comfort and good
order of society." [34] No effective action followed, and as work began
on the canal, complaints against this class mounted.

❧

Contemporaries, confronted with civic problems created by transients, could not see the relative decline of that urban element. There
was no doubt, however, about the growth of another class both
numerically and proportionally, for Negroes were readily identified.
Nor was their increase confined to Southern towns. Pittsburgh and
Cincinnati attracted more than their share; indeed in 1828 ten per
cent of the population of the Ohio city was colored. In slave areas
blacks made up the largest single group in the community, constituting never less than a quarter of the total and in Lexington
better than a third. But whether they lived in North or South,

---

[33] *Pittsburgh Gazette*, July 30, 1819; *Pittsburgh Statesman*, October 12,
1819.

[34] *Louisville Public Advertiser*, April 26, 1820; December 22, 1824.

whether free or in bonds, they constituted a menial class. Cut off from the rest of society, denied ordinary opportunities, Negroes still occupied the lowest rung on the social ladder.

The census provides a convenient index of their increase. In 1820 Louisville's colored population numbered 1,123, and a decade later it rose to 2,630; Lexington's figures in the same period were 1,764 and 2,267. This rise was proportionally greater than that of the whites in the Blue Grass capital, where the white population remained static. St. Louis's statistics are not very satisfactory, being available only for the county; nevertheless, the story is the same. In 1820 1,950 Negroes lived in this larger unit, and ten years later the count jumped to 3,016. A local census in 1830 showed 1,455 inside the corporation boundaries.[35] In these Southern cities the vast majority of blacks were slaves, less than ten per cent being "free persons of color."

Pittsburgh's Negro population was never very large, but in growth it kept pace with the whites. From 185 in 1810 it rose to 285 in 1820 and to 453 in the next decade. In Cincinnati, however, the record was more spectacular. From 433 in 1820 the number leaped to 2,259 in 1828, when the blacks constituted a tenth of the total.[36] Located just a river's width from slave territory, the Ohio metropolis became the great depot for freedmen and a sanctuary for runaways.

Negro life in Southern cities did not markedly change in the postwar years. The newcomers took their places alongside other slaves in factories, shops, hotels, construction work and domestic service. Ownership continued more widely diffused than on the countryside, and the blacks still lived either in the master's house or, more generally, in shacks facing rear alleys. No "Little Africas" grew up, since the colored people were spread quite evenly across the town. In

[35] United States Census, 1820, 33; United States Census, 1830, 114–15; United States Census, 1820, 33; United States Census, 1830, 112–13; United States Census, 1820, 40; United States Census, 1830, 150–51; *Missouri Republican*, October 5, 1830.

[36] United States Census, 1810, 44; United States Census, 1820, 15; United States Census, 1830, 68–69; United States Census, 1820, 35; for a detailed treatment of Negro growth in Cincinnati, see R. C. Wade, "The Negro in Cincinnati, 1800–1830," 43–57.

Louisville, for example, the assessment books of 1834 reveal that each of the five wards, except the fifth, was about half Negro. Further-more, only twelve taxpayers had more than ten slaves apiece, the largest holder being a merchant with fifty-four.[37] Housing was still wretched, living standards were low, and hope for improvement or freedom slight.

If the growth in black population did not basically alter employ-ment or living patterns, it did increase the pressure on slave institu-tions. The whole thrust of urbanism was, as has been noted, to weaken the ties between master and bondsman. Negroes could not be isolated from their neighbors, few city owners could profitably utilize all their hands, and constant contact with townsmen, both freedmen and whites, corroded the traditional discipline of the sys-tem. Moreover, the existence of free territory a few miles away made slaveholders apprehensive. To meet these threats, local authorities throughout the twenties tightened their restraints on all colored people.

Their first concern was the hiring-out labor system. This arrange-ment met a genuine urban need, for it allowed owners who could not keep all their slaves busy to lend some to short-handed employers, the slave-holder being paid for their use. This exchange, however, was hard to control, and soon many Negroes acted as free agents, finding their own jobs, making their own bargains, and paying part of their wages to their master. These men were more free laborers than slaves, and their existence seemed to endanger the whole struc-ture of Southern urban society.

The case of Louisville is illustrative. Townspeople there con-tinually complained of blacks hiring themselves out. In 1820 a grand jury warned of the "pernicious effects" resulting from "the privileges allowed by masters to their slaves of permission to hire their time, to the serious injury of society, and contrary to the laws of this state." In the same year one observer counted 150 Negroes engaged in this practice and estimated that Kentucky could collect $5000 an-nually in fines if it enforced its own regulations. A half decade later

---

[37] City of Louisville, Assessment Book, 1834.

another resident emphasized the danger. "Those who hire their own time, not only act without restraint themselves, but their example induces others to believe that they can take the same liberties . . . that they can work or play as they please." In 1827 twenty-nine prominent people gave public notice that "from the first day of January next, they will rigidly, and without respect to persons" prosecute both slaves and masters involved in the system, which "is much complained of, and generally admitted." [38]

Urban conditions, then, severely tested slave institutions, but Western cities beneath the Ohio encountered additional difficulties. Freed Negroes gravitating toward the towns became troublesome for local authorities. One official in Louisville called them "an unprofitable and dangerous part of the population," and many ordinances linked them with hired-out slaves as a threat to racial order. [39] Not less irritating were runaways, many of whom used Louisville as a springboard to freedom. Newspapers continually complained that Ohio and Indiana knowingly harbored fugitives, and the many advertisements for fleeing slaves were a constant reminder of the problem. [40] Despite all this, however, no large movement for emancipation developed in these cities, the residents preferring slavery with all its handicaps to any proffered alternative. [41]

For Negroes who fled the South and settled in Northern cities, life was still difficult. They had to take employment where they could find it. Few had any skill that could demand preference, and trade unions generally denied them membership. They were "disciplined to laborious occupations," Daniel Drake observed in Cincinnati, where he found them "prone to the performance of light and menial drudgery." Some became porters, vendors, shoeblacks, and messen-

[38] *Louisville Public Advertiser*, April 26, 1820; June 24, 1820; December 28, 1825; November 10, 1827.
[39] *Louisville Public Advertiser*, February 14, 1829; Louisville, City Journal, January 23, 1829.
[40] For example, see *Louisville Public Advertiser*, April 1, 5, and 8, 1820, and for a typical group of advertisements for runaways, April 2, 1825.
[41] Even the colonization idea met with little support before 1830. See for example, *Louisville Public Advertiser*, October 25, February 9, 1822.

gers, and women often hired out as domestics.[42] Mostly, however, blacks worked on the construction of roads and canals, or as laboring hands in the expanding commerce and manufacturing of the cities.

Not much is known of colored life in these towns, but enough evidence remains in Cincinnati to establish its outlines. In the twenties most of the Queen City's Negroes lived in the first and fourth wards — known as "Little Africa" — where they were cut off, though not segregated, from the white population. Some were well-housed, especially before the postdepression influx. Their increase, however, strained available facilities. More and more they were crowded into wooden shacks and shanties along Columbia Street and Western Row. By 1827 frame tenements ten or twelve feet high covered the entire district, creating health and fire hazards. In one instance two families converted a blacksmith's shop into a combined dwelling and grocery store where at least a dozen people lived.[43] A fire whipped through this area in 1830, graphically portraying the congestion and warning the town of the consequences of continued neglect.

As the colored community grew, it developed its own institutions. Schools and churches provided the rudiments of learning to the younger generation, while informal agencies joined religious organizations to aid adults in finding useful work and recreation. In these areas, however, a pattern of segregation emerged. Whites often lent support to Negro enterprises, but they carefully sealed off the blacks from participation in nearly all the town's activities. Since the churches restricted their membership, the colored people established two of their own, the African Methodist and Methodist Episcopal.

Schools followed the same exclusive practices. In 1815 the Cincinnati Lancaster Seminary made the segregation policy official by erecting a separate Negro institution.[44] Fourteen years later, when

[42] Drake, *Statistical View*, 72; *Liberty Hall* (Cincinnati), July 9, 1829.

[43] *Cincinnati Advertiser*, August 18, 1830; Cincinnati Tax List, 1818. *Cincinnati Centinel*, quoted in the *Western Star* (Lebanon, Ohio), August 29, 1829; Cincinnati, Minutes, August 22, 1827.

[44] Drake, *Statistical View*, 157.

the city established a common-school system, it made special provision for colored children. By the twenties the social life of the Ohio metropolis sanctioned the increasing separation of the colored community. In other words, at just the time when the black population expanded most rapidly, its contacts with other Cincinnatians lessened markedly.

The whites watched with anxiety the mounting numbers of Negroes in the city. The editor of *Liberty Hall* warned in 1825 that "the rapid increase of our black population, to say nothing of slavery, is of itself a great evil." The formation of the Cincinnati Colonization Society in 1826 with 120 members, including many prominent citizens, reflected the growing uneasiness of some residents. Two years later the city council appointed a committee to look into a petition asking the local government "to take measures to prevent the increase of negro population within the city." This concern derived in part from the discussion of the general question of slavery, but its intensity stemmed from the emergence of a significant colored community in the Queen City. By 1829 one out of every ten residents was Negro. Some feared that "we shall be overwhelmed by an emigration at once wretched in its character and destructive in its consequences." [45] This fear easily slipped into hostility, and that hostility soon spilled over into violence.

The "riot" of 1829 came at the end of a decade of increasing restiveness. The issue was drawn in July of that year when the Trustees of the Township, acting as overseers of the poor, announced that after thirty days they would enforce the Ohio "black laws" of 1804–7, which had lain dormant for better than two decades. A ward election in the spring had centered around this proposal, and the new officials felt compelled to move. [46] All Negroes were directed to register, present their certificates of freedom, and enroll the name of a bondsman or leave the city.

[45] *Liberty Hall* (Cincinnati), June 28, 1825; Cincinnati Colonization Society, *Proceedings* (Cincinnati, 1833), 3; Cincinnati, Minutes, November 19, 1828; *Daily Gazette* (Cincinnati), July 24, 1829.

[46] *Daily Gazette* (Cincinnati), July 4, 1829; *Cincinnati Advertiser*, March 27, 1829.

Debate on this question, which had been submerged for many years, immediately came to the surface. The enemies of the Negro were outspoken. "Our constitution was framed and adopted by white people, and for their own benefit," "Wilberforce" stated bluntly, "and they of course had a right to say on what terms they would admit black emigrants." The editor of the *Chronicle* was even more direct, saying that the time had come to stop talking and get down to business. "There is but one way — we must remove that population from our territory, while the power is still in our hands." [47]

Others, however, doubted both the wisdom and legality of the move. "Negroes and mulattoes are men, and have, at least, some of the rights of men under the laws. The proposition to drive fifteen hundred to two thousand from their homes, is one that ought not to be made or attempted" without full deliberation. "Blackstone" was even more disturbed. "We are, by straining the construction of the constitution, paving the way for the destruction of our own liberties," he observed. "It is just as constitutional to proscribe a man for the size of his head, as for the color of his skin." [48] The town was deeply divided. Indeed, no local issue in Cincinnati had ever received the extended public debate that surrounded the demand to evict the city's colored residents.

While the argument raged, the Negroes tried to put off the deadline for another month. Leading colored citizens called a meeting which drew up a petition to the state legislature asking for the repeal of "those obnoxious black laws." Signatures of many prominent Cincinnatians, including such people as Nicholas Longworth and Wykoff Piatt, gave the document broad support. But the blacks themselves were split over tactics. The powerful Methodist Episcopal Church dissociated itself from the petition, declaring that "all we ask is a continuation of the smiles of the white people as we have hitherto enjoyed them." Meanwhile, Israel Lewis and Thomas Cressup went to Canada to find a place for resettlement.

[47] *Daily Gazette* (Cincinnati), July 24, 1829; *Cincinnati Chronicle and Literary Gazette*, July 4, 1829.

[48] *Daily Gazette* (Cincinnati), July 4 and 27, 1829.

"If the act is enforced, we, the poor sons of Aethiopia, must take shelter where we can find it. . . . If we cannot find it in America, where we were born and spent all our days, we must beg it elsewhere." [49]

The drive against the colored population continued, however, with support coming from many sections of society. The transients, always ready for a frolic, joined the bigots. Some unskilled workers, fearing Negro competition on the job, also came into the movement. But most important was the support of the Cincinnati Colonization Society. Founded in 1826, this branch of the national association quickly attracted public attention and recruited its leadership among the city's most influential people. Though its membership totaled only 120 in 1829, its list of officers read like the social register. "Now is the time for the Colonization Societies 'to be up and doing,'" wrote one of them in the midst of the crisis.[50]

With this support the tension grew. The exact order of events is hard to establish. The first ultimatum was given about June first, and extensions placed the deadline at the beginning of September. But raids into the colored section took place during the interim, reaching a climax on the weekend of August 22, when "some two or three hundred of the lowest canaille" descended on the blacks, bent on terror and pillage. By Saturday evening the Negroes, despairing of official protection, armed to defend themselves. Fighting broke out around midnight, and in the scuffle Eli Herrick, one of the raiders, was killed and two others were injured. The police rounded up ten blacks and seven whites. After a hearing the Mayor released all the Negroes, declaring they had acted in self-defense, and at the same time fined the others a total of $700.[51]

These raids on the colored community sharpened the issue and

[49] J. Malvin, *Autobiography of John Malvin* (Cleveland, 1879), 11; 13; *Daily Gazette* (Cincinnati), July 4, 1829; *Cincinnati Advertiser*, March 27, 1829.

[50] *Western Star* (Lebanon, Ohio), August 29, 1829; quoted from a Cincinnati newspaper in the *Hamilton Intelligencer* (Hamilton, Ohio), July 21, 1829.

[51] The best description of the weekend is in the *Western Star* (Lebanon, Ohio), August 19, 1829.

threw into bold relief the grim tendency of events. Public sympathy, for a long time mixed and confused, went out to the Negroes, leading many whites to review the situation and re-examine their position. Before this could take place, however, over half the blacks fled the city. Lewis and Cressup had located some land near York in Canada, later called Wilberforce, where many of the refugees settled. The land "beats all for beauty and fertility," they boasted. "Our rights here as freemen, will be respected. We shall be as free as the atmosphere we breathe." [52] The Quakers donated some money to facilitate the migration, and other large contributions came from New York and Pennsylvania. But most of the funds were raised among the Negroes of the Queen City.

By winter the crisis had passed. Though there is no way of knowing exactly how many colored people left Cincinnati, the number was certainly no less than 1,100 and probably more. Among these displaced persons were many of the most industrious, stable, and prosperous members of the Negro community. They had the financial resources and social energy needed for movement, while the less successful and weaker stayed behind. Some leaders remained in the city, but the cream had been skimmed off. In September the editor of the *Gazette*, who had earlier supported the enforcement of the "black laws," appraised the entire episode and spoke for a chastened town:

It has driven away the sober, honest, industrious, and useful portion of the colored population. The vagrant is unaffected by it. The effect is to lessen much of the moral restraint, which the presence of respectable persons of their own colour, imposed on the idle and indolent, as well as the profligate. It has exposed employers of coloured persons to suits by common informers, where no good or public motive was perceptible. It has reduced honest individuals to want and beggary, in the midst of plenty and employment; because employers were afraid to employ them. It has subjected men of color who own property to great sacrifices. It has furnished an occasion for the oppressor and common informer to exhibit themselves, and commence their depredations on the weak and

[52] *Daily Gazette* (Cincinnati), July 30, 1829.

defenceless, under cover of law. It has demonstrated the humiliating fact, that cruelty and injustice, the rank oppression of a devoted people, may be consummated in the midst of us, without exciting either sympathy, or operative indignation.[53]

The attempt to enforce the "black laws" was the critical point in the early history of Cincinnati's Negroes. Success would not only have radically reduced the number of blacks, but would have removed the Queen City as the central link in the life line which brought so many slaves and freedmen to Northern safety. The riots of the next decade, though more spectacular, never carried this same implication. By 1830 Negroes had earned the right to live in Cincinnati; the next struggles were over the right to a better life.

In the postwar decades, then, urban development in the West produced highly stratified societies comparable in kind if not in degree with those of older cities in the East. The first generation of settlers, bringing ideas of social distinction with them, created the nucleus of each group, and their children maintained and deepened the cleavages. The notion of equality, though perhaps powerful in the countryside, did not prevail in the towns. In fact, by 1830 classes were becoming increasingly aware of their separateness and status. Rhetoric emphasized distance, and institutions formalized the differences. In addition, the greater size of communities and the growing anonymity of city living intensified the need for meaningful association on many levels.

This stratification, however, did not necessarily bring dangerous tensions, for in most cities the relations between groups remained amicable. Indeed, except for the problem of the Negro in the North, urban society was more settled and tranquil than in earlier years. Though population growth still came largely from immigration, each town found every year a larger number of its residents eager to stay and drive roots into the community. Every index of urban

---

[53] *Daily Gazette* (Cincinnati), September 17, 1829.

maturity seemed to rise: life and property were safer, economic opportunities greater, and the material things of life were abundant. But no barometer was more encouraging than the cultural one, for travelers and local citizens alike agreed that in this regard Western cities provided a surprisingly rich and varied offering.

Chapter 8

The Better Life

While the West's economy expanded hesitantly and irregularly in the postwar decades, its cultural and intellectual life enjoyed a more uniform growth. The comforts and opportunities of the East increasingly reached settlers in the new country. Not content to remain satellites, however, transmontane leaders consciously aimed at equality with the older sections of the Union. "As the day is fast approaching when we shall be able to repay our eastern brethren in domestic produce and manufactures for the foreign luxuries with which they may supply us," wrote a Pittsburgh editor in 1820, "so we hope in the commerce of literature, there will be reciprocity, and that on every occasion we will be able to return them a *quid pro quo.*" Though this target was too high for immediate achievement, it did not seem unattainable. In fact, visitors were continually impressed with the advance already made. "The progress of civilization and improvement, is wonderful," a Philadelphian observed in St. Louis in 1821, adding that in that city "both the scholar and the courtier" could "move in a circle suiting their choice and taste." [1]

Almost every aspect of cultural life showed the general enrichment. Education flourished on all levels, with each city adding new facilities and some taking the first steps in establishing free public instruction. Churches multiplied, new sects organized, and Sunday schools brought religious training to children of all classes. The theater gained prestige, offering Western audiences a fare comparable to that of many Eastern towns, while museums and libraries afforded opportunities to the culturally ambitious. Merchants corralled fine goods from Europe and the Orient, and shops displayed

[1] *Pittsburgh Gazette*, February 1, 1820; Paxton, *St. Louis Directory* (unfolioed).

a wide assortment of fashions from the seaboard. The urge for polish and refinement left few corners of society untouched. Even barbering played a part. Edward F. Pratt, a Philadelphia barber who believed that culture and sophistication ought to follow "the sceptre of empire," moved across the mountains to Pittsburgh with the announcement that "the blessings of our art should be diffused through the west, and that improvements in shaving and hairdressing, should go hand in hand with the progress of high steam and bank paper."[2]

In the cultural development of the West the cities performed a strategic role. As centers of economic activity, they attracted the ambitious and the talented, and soon became reservoirs of social and intellectual wealth. A St. Louis editor, noticing this function, commented in 1820 that "cities have arisen in the very wilderness, . . . and form in their respective states the *foci* of art and science, of wealth and information." Cincinnati's "Dion" made a similar observation. The countryside, already bound to urban communities by trade, readily admitted its dependence. The *Pittsburgh Gazette* merely stated the obvious when it commented in 1819 that "at this moment" the surrounding region "looks up to Pittsburgh not only as the medium through which to receive the comforts and luxuries of foreign commodities, but also as a channel from which it can most naturally expect a supply of intellectual wealth."[3] Thus while urban merchants staked out markets in the rural hinterland, civic leaders established a cultural dominance in the same area.

Every city had a much greater influence in the surrounding area than its population warranted, while two — Lexington and Cincinnati — had a reputation and distinction throughout the entire West. In each case cultural leadership followed commercial power. Lexington, the largest and richest trans-Allegheny town in the prewar decades, also surpassed its neighbors in other attainments. The depression, however, brought a realignment of urban strength, and by 1830 this economic shift had manifested itself in the emergence of Cincinnati as the region's social and intellectual center.

[2] *Pittsburgh Directory*, 1819.

[3] *Missouri Gazette*, December 20, 1820; *Pittsburgh Gazette*, April 30, 1819.

But the correlation was never quite precise. Lexington, dying hard, refused, for more than a decade after losing its mercantile primacy, to relinquish its commanding cultural position.

In fact, in the twenties Lexington was the most exciting place in the West. Already the region's self-proclaimed Athens, the Blue Grass metropolis tried to offset its commercial and industrial decline with cultural expansion. Admitting that the center of economic power had moved elsewhere, its leaders declared that nonetheless Lexington was the transmontane "capital of Science and Letters."[4] Nor was this a vain boast. During the twenties the town became the resort of the most talented men of all kinds in the new country. Educators, scientists, painters, lawyers, architects, musicians, and their patrons all flocked there. Its university attained national eminence, attracting much of its faculty from the East and students from better than a dozen states. Like a Renaissance city of Italy, Lexington provided the creative atmosphere for a unique flowering which for a decade astonished travelers and stimulated the best minds of the West.

The nerve center of this intellectual awakening was Transylvania University. Though a college in name as early as 1798, it remained a grammar school in fact for twenty years. Religious differences among the state-appointed trustees prevented the development of any program and, indeed, for a time thwarted the election of a president. The Presbyterians, though constituting only a small fraction of the population, held a slim majority on the governing council and considered Transylvania a kind of educational arm of their church. In 1817 a broad coalition of other sects, Republican politicians, and Lexington civic leaders, rising up against this domination, persuaded the legislature to appoint a new set of trustees and induced Horace Holley to accept the presidency.[5] Within a few years the school was transformed into a first-rate university with a distinguished faculty and a student body comprising many of the West's bright young men.

[4] *Kentucky Reporter*, February 21, 1827.
[5] For an excellent treatment of the "revolution at Transylvania," see Sonne, *Liberal Kentucky*, 135–60.

The new regime immediately established standards of admission, introduced the four-class system, and divided the academic year into two semesters. The physical plant was remodeled and enlarged; on-campus lodging and a refectory, operated on a nonprofit basis, reduced student costs; and state and local sources raised $14,000 for the purchase of books. In addition, Transylvania widened its curriculum, offering degrees in law and medicine. The rise in enrollment reflected the West's approval of the school's rejuvenation. From fewer than 80 students of all kinds in 1817 the number increased to 235 in 1820 and 282 in 1821, and ranged between 387 and 418 during the next five years.[6] By the middle of the decade the university compared in size and repute with the great colleges of the East.[7]

The driving force behind this remarkable development was Horace Holley, a Unitarian minister from Boston and the central figure in Lexington's renaissance.[8] Though not an accomplished scholar, he had a ranging and fearless mind which played over a great many fields and questions. Temperamentally, he was decisive, preferring to take a problem by storm rather than patiently laying siege to it. This eclat and directness gave color and dash to his administration and, indeed, to the whole epoch. For ten years Holley laid his mark on the life of the town, and when he moved on, "he left behind him," a contemporary observed, "a vacancy that has not since been filled, and a sense of loneliness that has not been removed."[9]

Before removing to Kentucky, he had been a highly successful

[6] These figures include preparatory, law, and medical students as well as undergraduates. *Kentucky Reporter*, February 3, 1823; Sonne, *Liberal Kentucky*, 173n, 174n.

[7] For Transylvania's reputation, see Sonne, *Liberal Kentucky*, 175, 175n.

[8] C. Caldwell, *A Discourse on the Genius and Character of the Rev. Horace Holley, Late President of Transylvania, with an Appendix, Containing Copious Notes Biographical and Illustrative* (Boston, 1828), 109. The frontispiece is an engraving from Gilbert Stuart's portrait of Holley. See also E. A. Jonas, *Matthew Harris Jouett, Kentucky Portrait Painter, 1787–1827* (Louisville, 1938), 55, for a later portrait by Matthew Jouett.

[9] Caldwell, *Holley*, 253.

clergyman at Boston's South End Church, a member of the city's School Committee, and an Overseer of Harvard University. His great fame, however, rested upon his oratory, which won him national renown. The road of advancement in the East lay open before him when he decided to accept the challenge of Transylvania. "It is a great opening," he wrote to his reluctant wife. "This whole Western country is to feed my seminary, which will send out lawyers, physicians, clergymen, statesmen, poets, orators, and *savans*, who will make the nation feel them." [10]

President Holley brought to Lexington not only remarkable oratorical skill and demonstrated administrative talent, but also a broad urbanity which soon affected the whole community. He patronized the theater, attended dances, and even took in an occasional horse race, displaying a worldliness and tolerance which sharply contrasted with his predecessors at Transylvania. His home became the center of lively and polished entertainment, the rendezvous for artists, intellectuals, and their friends. A traveler who had moved in these circles compared Lexington with Philadelphia and Boston. "There *'the learned, the gay, the witty and the grave'* can find congenial spirits." [11]

The whole West responded to Holley's leadership, and soon students came to Transylvania from all over the region. The provenience of the graduating class of the medical school in 1826 demonstrates the extent of the University's reputation and influence. Sixty-seven degrees were granted in that year; 28 of the recipients came from Kentucky, 10 from Tennessee, 5 each from Virginia, South Carolina, and Alabama, 3 from Ohio, 2 each from Mississippi, Illinois, and Louisiana, and 1 each from North Carolina and Georgia. During the twenties the college trained many of the West's most distinguished people. In politics alone it turned out at least seventeen congressmen, three governors, six United States senators, and the President of the Confederacy. In the same decade the school produced scores of lawyers, clergymen, and physicians, who did

[10] Caldwell, *Holley*, 162.
[11] *Kentucky Reporter*, December 31, 1819.

much to raise professional standards in the new country.[12] Few universities have left such a deep mark on a generation; in its heyday Transylvania fully deserved its title of the "Harvard of the West."

The students absorbed much of the sophistication, geniality, and earnestness of their president. Extracurricular activity revolved around two organizations, the Whig and Union philosophical societies. Each was large enough to own a library of nearly 750 volumes, and they sponsored debates, public lectures, and occasional plays and benefits. Members plunged into the excited politics of Kentucky, taking sides in elections and constantly arguing state and national issues.[13]

University life in the city, however, was not all business, and many students learned much that was not included in the formal curriculum. Blue Grass leaders might call their town the "Athens of the West," but to the young people it was also something of a Paris. "Lexington is a fine place for amusements, to get into frolicks, visit the girls and all such things," a Cincinnati student wrote to a friend at home, "but it is a d — d poor place to study law." Robert Gaines, another Ohioan, admitted in similar vein that "this town has been to me . . . one unvaried scene of frolick." Diversions were many, and not the least disturbing was Cupid. "I anticipate a dreadful struggle between the little fellow, and those 'dark and barbarous' volumes," he acknowledged, "but I hope to bring him to the ground by one blow from the black letter of my Lord Coke." George Wilson, son of Cincinnati's most prominent minister, summed up Lexington's reputation: "People may say what they will about Cincinnati but there is no place in the world like Kentucky for real enjoyment. . . . There is nothing here to call off the attention of a young man but downright disapation [*sic*]." [14]

[12] *Kentucky Reporter*, March 13, 1826; R. and J. Peter, *Transylvania University; Its Origins, Rise, Decline, and Fall* (Louisville, 1896), 125n.

[13] *Kentucky Reporter*, May 13, 1829; for student political discussion, see E. L. Drake to R. T. Lytle, February 8, 1824, MS, William Lytle Collection.

[14] E. L. Drake to R. T. Lytle, February 18, 1824; R. M. Gaines to R. T. Lytle, January 4, 1823; G. M. Wilson to R. T. Lytle, July 23, 1823; MSS, William Lytle Collection (Historical and Philosophical Society of Ohio, Cincinnati).

The luster of Lexington's renaissance came in large part from Transylvania's faculty. Competent when not brilliant, it represented the most distinguished group of educated men the West had ever seen in a single city, much less in one institution. The medical department achieved a special distinction. Its seven professors, all trained in the East and most holding degrees from the University of Pennsylvania, enjoyed wide reputations before going to Kentucky.[15] Charles Caldwell, the dean of the division and Dr. Benjamin Rush's favorite pupil, accepted a position at Transylvania after turning down requests from New York, Philadelphia, and Baltimore to organize new medical schools there. An accomplished, if somewhat superficial, lecturer, he stood next to Holley in prestige and esteem. In 1821 he toured Europe, buying books for the library with $10,000 given him by the state legislature.

Some of Caldwell's colleagues were at least his professional peers. Charles Wilkins Short was one. A graduate of Transylvania in 1810 and later a student of Caspar Wistar at Pennsylvania, he joined the faculty in 1825. Retiring in manner and frequently absent from town on botanical field trips, he left the public skyrockets to others, preferring to spend his time collecting plants and arranging his herbarium. He wrote sparingly, most of his work appearing in *The Transylvania Journal of Medicine and Associated Sciences*, which he edited. Though a beloved teacher, his fame is due, as Asa Gray observed, to the "excellence of his personal collections, and to the generous profusion with which he distributed them far and wide among his fellow laborers in this and other lands." In addition to Caldwell and Short, Transylvania's medical school also numbered on its staff Samuel Brown, Daniel Drake, John Esten Cooke, William H. Richardson, and Benjamin Winslow Dudley. Dudley made important advances in surgery, insisting on hot water and cleanliness during operations; he removed 225 gall stones with only three fatalities.[16] Throughout the twenties, students could find in Lexing-

---

[15] R. and J. Peter, *The History of the Medical Department of Transylvania University* (Louisville, 1905).

[16] A. Gray, "Dr. Charles Wilkins Short," *The American Journal of Sciences and Arts*, new series, XXXVI (1863), 131; Peter, *Medical Department*,

ton training and facilities equal in most respects to those found in the older medical schools in the East.

No other university, however, had anyone like Constantine Samuel Rafinesque, the restless, furtive, and erratic Turkish-born botanist who joined Transylvania in 1819. Of all the figures in this wilderness renaissance he most looked the part. A small, bent man, he had a sensitive face with a high forehead and dark, darting eyes. His lank, unkempt black hair added a wild touch, and when he got excited, even his friends doubted his stability. "A most eccentric person," a student later recalled, "his extreme absent-mindedness contributing to his foreign ways to make him peculiar." Believing the world filled with enemies, suspicious of even those who helped him, he lived a haunted and fear-ridden life. Rafinesque had no doubt of his own greatness, however, conceding that he was "like Bacon and Galileo, somewhat ahead of my age and my neighbors." [17] But for all his oddness, or perhaps because of it, he fascinated students and townspeople alike.

It was hard for contemporaries to judge this curious figure. Untrained and undisciplined, he often seemed a charlatan. Yet his prodigious work, wide reading, and speculative boldness demanded serious attention. In retrospect it is easy to see that whatever else he may have been, he was part genius. It is not necessary to accept Donald Culross Peattie's estimate — that "amongst all the naturalists who have ever worked on the American continent, Rafinesque is the only one who might clearly be called a titan" — to appreciate his many contributions.[18] With characteristic audacity he rejected the artificial Linnean system of classification and attempted to set up a more natural one. The list of new genera and species now credited to Rafinesque is enormous, putting him among the ranks of the most

25. See also W. C. Bullock, "Dr. Benjamin Winslow Dudley," *Annals of Medical History*, VII (1935), 201–13.

[17] Quoted in D. C. Peattie, *Green Laurels* (New York, 1936), 265; quoted in E. D. Merrill, *Index Rafinesquianus, The Plant Names Published by C. S. Rafinesque with Reductions, and a Consideration of his Methods, Objectives and Attainments* (Jamaica Plain, Mass., 1949), 49.

[18] Peattie, *Green Laurels*, 263.

productive botanists.[19] His early papers on Mediterranean fishes and his *Ichthyologia Ohiensis* alone would assure him a permanent place in the history of American zoology. The seven years he spent at Transylvania were his most fruitful. Besides writing over two hundred articles, he traveled extensively and made many of his best discoveries during this period.

Transylvania's president and faculty were the center of Lexington's great cultural display in the twenties, but around them moved other figures — artists, architects, musicians, and poets — who gave added glitter to the movement. Of these one of the most important was the portraitist, Matthew Harris Jouett. A Kentuckian by birth, a student of Gilbert Stuart in Boston, he was the West's foremost painter. A gentleman himself, he created a valuable gallery of the commonwealth's "best people" and most active citizens. He worked prodigiously, producing more than five hundred canvases in the decade between 1817 and 1827. Admirers have hurt Jouett with absurd claims, calling him "the Kentucky Reubens," but his talents were considerable and he deserves much better than he has received — extravagant praise or near-neglect.

Music and the theater also profited from the general cultural enthusiasm. Though the city could claim no distinguished players of its own, it "liberally and generously rewarded *exotics*" from the outside. For a few months, for example, Anthony Philip Heinrich conducted in the town, and on November 12, 1817, Lexingtonians heard the first performance of a Beethoven symphony in the United States.[20] The Blue Grass metropolis also rolled out the carpet for Samuel Drake's traveling company, which brought professional standards to the Western stage. So completely did the cosmopolitan spirit engulf the city that the drama encountered little opposition from religious groups.

[19] Controversy still surrounds Rafinesque's reputation as a scientist. E. D. Merrill has judiciously sifted the evidence and many claims in his introduction to *Index Rafinesquianus*.

[20] *Kentucky Reporter*, February 17, 1823; W. T. Upton, *Anthony Philip Heinrich, A Nineteenth Century Composer in America* (New York, 1938), ix.

Lexington did not have to depend on the outside for an architect equal to its renaissance, for in Gideon Shyrock it produced a singularly creative figure. The son of a builder, and himself a student of William Strickland of Philadelphia, he became one of the most skillful exponents of the Greek Revival in America. His first big work was the state capitol at Frankfort. Though only twenty-three, he won the job in competition. This performance brought him immediate fame and led a modern critic to assert that it "was almost a decade ahead of its time even when judged by sophisticated eastern standards." [21] Shyrock's triumph gave a great impetus to Revival architecture throughout the West, and Greek details crept into private houses as well as public buildings. In Lexington the new movement reached its climax, symbolically enough, at Transylvania in 1833, when Shyrock invested Morrison College with the quiet dignity of classical design.

The world of letters fared less well. No literary figure emerged from the enthusiasm of the decade, and the town was better known for its appreciation of good literature than for creating it. *The North American Literary and Political Register* suffered a quick and richly deserved death in 1826 after only a few issues. More a newspaper than the voice of the *avant-garde*, it printed works of local poets and novelists. William Gibbs Hunt's *The Western Review and Miscellaneous Magazine* achieved higher standards, and between 1819 and 1821 it published the writing of many of Lexington's leading intellectuals. Contributions included verse by President Holley, a variety of Rafinesque's articles, a few addresses by Caldwell, and the poetry of George Beck, a classical scholar of better than average gifts. The *Review* reached the city's many reading rooms and the magazine tables of the sophisticated, contributing a link between the university and the townspeople.

Though Lexington's enlightenment derived from a group of highly talented men, its vigor spread throughout the city. Residents

---

[21] T. Hamlin, *Greek Revival Architecture in America: Being an Account of Important Trends in American Architecture and American Life prior to the War between the States* (New York, 1944), 244.

gloried in the town's reputation, and they turned commencements into "Literary Festivals" attracting people from all over the West. And the cultural urge fused with many activities; even courting felt its elevating hand. A group of young men and women founded a fortnightly society which met under the supervision of a married couple and listened to compositions on literary and scientific topics. No one seemed beyond improvement. "Typographus," for example, scrutinizing a copy of the *Kentucky Reporter*, found 314 typographical mistakes, 114 "false punctuations, exclusively of the dashes," and 146 instances of "bad orthography." [22]

Despite the great popularity of Holley and Transylvania and the broad support of the town, education had its enemies in this Athens. The Presbyterians, who never accepted the new regime, from the very outset carried on a campaign against it on the ground that the university had fallen into irreligious and immoral hands.[23] The tactics of the attack, however, were less commendable than its motives. While powerful spokesmen harried Holley on a philosophic plane, the less scrupulous intrigued effectively on a lower level, using gossip, rumor, and insinuation in an effort to drive out the new group.[24] "What is the character of Mr. Holley in a practical point of view, and as an example to youth," asked a detractor. Charging him with being a "warm advocate" of "the Theater, Ball room, the Card table," he asserted that Holley was "both by precept and example . . . well qualified to lead youth in the way of the destroyer." Unrelentingly the Presbyterians stalked the administration, questioning its decency, criticizing the private

[22] *Kentucky Reporter*, July 15, 1822, July 18, 1825; March 23, 1825; May 19, 1823.

[23] The Presbyterians were the first to attack Transylvania. "Justicia" wrote to the *Kentucky Reporter* in 1824: "You ask, 'why was this attack made on Transylvania University, by a few Presbyterian clergy only who reside in and about Lexington?' I answer briefly 'because they know best what is going on.'" *Kentucky Reporter*, March 8, 1824.

[24] For the sordid side of the attack, see Charles Caldwell, *Autobiography* (Philadelphia, 1855), 218ff; Peter, *Transylvania*, 145; Sonne, *Liberal Kentucky*, 210.

tastes of the president, and frequently casting doubt on the financial accounting of university officials.[25]

An attack by a single religious organization could never by itself have brought down Transylvania. Outside forces joined the assault, however, and by 1826 succeeded in persuading the state legislature to cut off financial aid to the institution. The hostility came from many sources. Louisville, disturbed by Lexington's attitude on other issues, sought to strike its rival in this most vulnerable spot. Countryfolk increasingly viewed the college as the resort of the rich and of dandies. Most fatal of all, the question became mixed up in the relief politics of the state, arraying the Jacksonians against Holley. With the handwriting plainly on the wall, the president stepped down. As he did so he made a final report on his stewardship. Noting that in nine years Transylvania had given 644 degrees compared with only 22 in the previous nineteen years, he asked the public to judge. "We are satisfied with the contrast. Are they?" [26]

Holley's defeat brought Lexington's golden age to an end. Some tried to carry on, but most of the leading figures scattered. The heart had gone out of the movement. Transylvania's prestige remained so high in the East, however, that the trustees induced Reverend Alva Woods to leave the presidency of Brown University to pick up the reins. The new regime at once turned its back on the free atmosphere of the Holley days, declaring that "intellectual excellence, however desireable, is purchased too dearly when obtained at the expense of moral worth." Henceforth the school's "first anxiety . . . will be directed to the *character* and *conduct* of the pupils." But student enrollment dropped and the legislature continued its freeze on funds. Newspapers began to speak of the "falling condition" and "depression" of the university. On May 9, 1829, the final blow fell. The "College proper" caught fire, and in "two brief hours the edifice which was the pride of the state and

[25] Quoted in Sonne, *Liberal Kentucky*, 205; 208.

[26] For Louisville opinion, see for example, *Louisville Public Advertiser*, October 15, 1825, September 17, October 3, 1827; for the rural argument, see "A Farmer of Jefferson" in the *Kentucky Reporter*, February 16, 1824; Sonne, *Liberal Kentucky*, 249ff; Caldwell, *Autobiography*, 210–11.

the town, was reduced to a heap of ruins." [27] Lexington was no longer Athens, and the scepter of cultural leadership, so uniquely held for a generation on the Blue Grass, moved across the river to Cincinnati.

๏

The Queen City, already the commercial hub of the West, stood ready to assert its cultural supremacy as the Kentucky town faded. And its credentials were impressive. The editor of the *Saturday Evening Chronicle* proudly listed them in 1827:

Need we name our two museums, both respectable — one the pride of the city; the Medical College of Ohio, preeminent in local advantages; our schools and Academies, both numerous and respectable; the Academy of fine arts, yet in its incipient stage, but establishing on a firm basis; the circulating library, increasing in books and readers; the Western Medical and Physical Journal, a work of much promise with already 400 subscribers; and lastly the Western Quarterly Review.

A few years later, James Hall, seeking a place congenial to his genius, settled in Cincinnati. The river metropolis stood "first in art, knowledge and civilization," he asserted. "It requires no prophet's eye to see in the Miami-capitol of Ohio, the future seat of literature and learning; the Athens of Western America." [28] No other town had such formidable claims to leadership, but everywhere development was encouraging.

Nothing better illustrated Western advance than the expansion of urban educational facilities. On every level opportunities widened. Not only did grammar schools multiply and colleges and nurseries make their appearance, but most cities either adopted or prepared to adopt free public schooling. Though private institutions took on increasing numbers, they could not cope with the flood of children

[27] *Kentucky Reporter*, July 23, 1828; January 5, 1828; May 13, 1829.
[28] *Saturday Evening Chronicle* (Cincinnati), May 12, 1827; *Illinois Monthly Magazine*, II (1832), 468.

which accompanied the great growth of population. "There are probably 20 or 30 common schools now in Pittsburgh," wrote one resident as early as 1816, "yet no person of observation who walks the streets during the study hours would imagine that scarcely one-fourth of the children of suitable age . . . attended school anywhere." [29] During the twenties the demand for a publicly supported system became irresistible. Within a few years every city except Lexington and St. Louis provided some kind of municipally financed free instruction for its young people.

The pattern of educational development in the new country was generally the same, but local situations varied substantially. Cincinnati, for example, had probably the best facilities, ranging from the lowest grades to the colleges, while St. Louis, though the scene of much ambitious planning, fell behind other towns. Pittsburgh and Louisville each excelled in some category — mechanics enjoyed the greatest opportunities in the Iron City and the Kentucky port was the first to adopt a comprehensive public system — but in both places there were serious gaps in the school structure. The unchallenged superiority of Lexington on the university plane gave that city a richly deserved national reputation; yet its lower levels were never adequate.

Cincinnati's educational edifice was the firmest and had the best balance. Its base was a network of small private schools, located in every neighborhood and offering rudimentary instruction of many kinds. Many were of uncertain quality and all charged tuition. The forty-seven in 1829 had a total enrollment of more than 1,600. In addition Lancastrian Seminary, founded in 1814, taught basic skills at a lower cost through the monitorial system. Furthermore, in 1822 the Kidd Foundation made $1,000 a year available for needy students. The Seminary, perhaps feeling the pinch of hard times, later merged with the newly established Cincinnati College. This institution traveled a rocky road throughout the twenties, being continually beset with internal problems and financial shakiness. But residents nursed high hopes for it. The editor of *Liberty*

[29] *Pittsburgh Commonwealth*, April 17, 1816.

Hall thought it "the pride and boast of the town," while another observer happily announced that it gave *"eclat* to our town." [30]

These promising beginnings, however, failed to meet the problem. The school population continued to expand faster than facilities. Low-income families could not afford even the cheapest instruction, and teachers were both scarce and underpaid. Thoughtful people turned increasingly to the possibility of a public system. Newspapers whipped up enthusiasm for the idea, and their columns demonstrate that they evoked a wide popular response. Throughout the twenties Cincinnatians lobbied at the state capitol for a broad plan to cover all Ohio communities. Finally, despairing of getting all their neighbors to adopt a tax-supported, free program, the city succeeded in 1829 in getting an amendment to its charter which gave the local government the power to establish its own system.

The enactment put the city almost a decade ahead of Ohio generally and prepared the ground for educational advances throughout the region. In fact, during the whole struggle for tax-supported, free schooling, Cincinnati was the driving force.[31] Nearly every important movement in the state started in the Queen City, received its major impetus from the local press, and was carried in the

[30] *Cincinnati Directory of 1829*, 183; *Liberty Hall* (Cincinnati), March 27, 1882; November 4, 1816, August 4, 1817.

[31] The whole history of the development of Ohio's public schools has been obscured for a long time by an interesting but not wholly relevant controversy over whether New Englanders were responsible for establishing the state system. Edward A. Miller argued that the impetus came from Yankees, while William McAlpine demonstrated that this contention could not stand analysis. More fundamental was the urban stimulus which spread out from Cincinnati and, to a lesser degree, Columbus. McAlpine hit upon this fact in his provocative article, noting that "The great movements of education in Ohio prior to 1845, started usually from Cincinnati and received able support from the papers, pulpit and teachers of the deaf and dumb and blind at Columbus." Again, "If any section of the state was the educational missionary, it was Cincinnati." But he was so busy destroying the old notion that he did not construct a new and better one. E. A. Miller, "The History of Educational Legislation in Ohio from 1803 to 1850," Ohio Archaeological and Historical Society, *Publications*, XXVII (1918), 1–142, and W. McAlpine, "The Origins of Public Education in Ohio," Ohio Archaeological and Historical Society, *Publications*, XXXVIII (1929), 409–47.

legislature through the efforts of Hamilton County representatives. Among the most influential names in the agitation of the twenties were Benjamin Piatt, Nathan Guilford, and William Henry Harrison, all of whom held key committee posts at Columbus. It is also significant that the first superintendent of common schools in Ohio was Cincinnati's Samuel Lewis. Nor is this urban leadership surprising. The cities, as the great population centers, felt the educational pressure first and most acutely. In addition, they alone had the wealth needed to launch ambitious programs for large numbers of children.

Under the new legislation the Council divided each of the town's five wards into two districts where two-story brick schoolhouses were built on city property. The tax rate was established at two mills on the dollar, which covered teachers' salaries, fuel, and equipment. Though authorities had some initial difficulty, the first report of the Trustees and Visitors of the Common Schools showed great progress. More than two thousand children registered, and the daily attendance averaged over 1,500. The payroll listed twenty-two instructors with a combined pay of $6,578. With justifiable pride the officials concluded that "the system embraces success, economy and efficiency." [32]

While the Queen City laid the groundwork for public education, private efforts extended opportunities for both the very young and the more advanced. Two "infant schools" met a growing need for nursery care, and Cincinnati College and the Medical College of Ohio gave sporadic training at the higher level. Neither of these, however, built very solidly, and they never approached the distinction of Transylvania. The medical school had high ambitions, hoping to be "a powerful rival of the Kentucky school, and ultimately to go beyond it." But internal problems and financial instability dogged its progress at every step. The struggle to establish these institutions was important in itself, however, for it conveys the educational enthusiasm which infected the river metropolis and

[32] Cincinnati, Minutes, February 10, 1830.

led one resident to predict that "ere the lapse of many years, our city will be as celebrated for its Literature as for its Commercial superiority." [33]

If Cincinnati's educational foundation was the strongest in the West, St. Louis's was the weakest. Throughout the postwar years residents and visitors alike complained of the meager facilities. In 1818 the editor of the *Missouri Gazette* admitted that "the want of schools has long been lamented by the thinking part of the population," and six years later another newspaper declared that this shortage "deters many" who otherwise would come to the Mississippi town. In 1828 an old settler admitted that it "cannot, I think, be questioned" that "the means of instruction are lacking in St. Louis." More than that, "the city which ought to offer the young population of the surrounding country, the means of instruction, is herself destitute." Local authorities concurred in this judgment, the Mayor himself asserting in 1823 that "a free school is more needed here than in any town of the same magnitude in the Union." [34]

This failure did not stem from indifference, for the twenties witnessed many attempts to better conditions, including an effort to organize a common-school system. In fact, as early as 1817 the territorial legislature established a board of trustees in St. Louis "for the regulation of the schools in the town" and enabled these officials to "erect or procure suitable buildings, and provide the necessary apparatus for instruction, and transact such other business as they shall find necessary and proper." The law involved no grant of taxing power, but it was assumed that the revenue would come from public lands within the city whose sale for educational purposes Congress had authorized in 1812. In the following decade, however, it proved difficult to recover the property. Local authorities, failing to oust the occupants, memorialized the national government in 1829 to remove the "intruders" and allow the disposal.

[33] *Cincinnati Daily Gazette*, March 22, 1830; *Liberty Hall* (Cincinnati), January 14, 1823; November 7, 1821.

[34] *Missouri Gazette*, January 23, 1818; *Missouri Republican*, March 1, 1824; October 7, 1828; St. Louis, Minutes, April 14, 1823.

Despite these efforts and the growing popular demand for public schools, nothing was accomplished by 1830.[35]

The gaps in the public-school structure were partially filled by religious instruction. St. Louis's large Catholic population provided a broad and expanding base for a college of that faith. In 1819 Father Francois Neil and three other priests opened St. Louis Academy, which, the president asserted, was the first step in the founding of a university. For the next six years the academy had a staff of nine teachers and between sixty and seventy students, including the sons of Thomas Hart Benton, William Clark, and Governor Alexander McNair.[36]

In 1828, after the Academy had been closed for three years, Bishop Rosati fulfilled his predecessor's promise by launching St. Louis College. The new institution was on the west side of town, its situation being "elevated, healthy, and at some distance from the more thickly inhabited parts of the city, which will considerably favor the application of the pupils, and remove any occasions of dissipation." Residents of all faiths welcomed the new school, and the college authorities promised "no undue influence" would be exercised on the students "in matters of religion." Tuition was free, but the applicant had to be of "good moral character." [37]

St. Louis, then, founded a college before its primary schools were well established. But there were other distortions in the structure as well. In 1830 a group of women formed an Infant School Society whose object was "a gratuitous education of children under six years of age." Two years earlier Elijah P. Lovejoy's school had introduced instruction "in the manner of the High Schools in our Atlantic cities, which have become so deservedly celebrated." To some all this looked more luxurious than sensible. "It is beginning at the wrong end," "Philopaidias" protested. "It is an attempt to

[35] *Laws of the State of Missouri*, I, 521; St. Louis, Minutes, December 4, 1829.

[36] *Missouri Gazette*, September 15, 1819; Rothensteiner, *St. Louis Archdiocese*, 276.

[37] *Missouri Republican*, September 2, 1828; October 27, 1829; October 7, 1829.

polish the marble, ere it is rough hewn." [38] Only a comprehensive public plan would assure to all children an opportunity to acquire the rudimentary tools of reading and writing, much less any solid love of learning. Another generation of leaders would make St. Louis an educational laboratory for the whole nation, but that happy day could not be foreseen in 1830.

Louisville, though the only Western town with no interest in a college, was among the first to adopt free public schooling. Indeed, the Falls City started its municipal system a few months ahead of Cincinnati. Local residents took great pride in this leadership, as did the *Louisville Public Advertiser*, which announced in 1829 that "for the first time on this side of the Ohio, there is established . . . a school at public expense; which is open to the children of all our [white] citizens, free from any charge, but that of public taxes." Another spokesman expressed his enthusiasm with a flattering analogy. "It is gratifying to us that Louisville has the honor of taking the lead in the West as New York did in the East." [39] The exultation, however, reflected the difficulty of achievement, for success followed a decade of heated discussion and agitation.

As early as 1821 the newspapers advocated the establishment of common schools, and five years later the city council petitioned the legislature for authority to set up its own system. In 1828 local officials adopted a resolution to move ahead on the program, declaring that "the genius of intelligence are distributed indifferently among the rich and the poor" and opportunities must be open to all. Though earlier plans called for five district schools, the state of the treasury allowed only one for the whole town and that to be operated on the monitorial principle. Negro children were excluded, but all white youths between six and sixteen were welcomed on a tuition-free basis. In the next year 257 students were admitted and daily attendance averaged over 180.[40]

[38] *Missouri Republican*, February 23, 1830; March 4, 1828; February 23, 1830.

[39] *Louisville Public Advertiser*, December 26, 1829; June 10, 1829.

[40] *Louisville Public Advertiser*, October 6, 1821; Louisville, *Trustees Book*,

Probably no city felt the need for better schools more deeply than Pittsburgh. As the foremost manufacturing entrepôt of the valley as well as the great funnel for migrants moving into the interior, it found itself constantly flooded with youths needing care and instruction. "The great mass of our population," an editor asserted, "consists of people, who are apt to be careless of the minds and morals of their children, and the constant influx of strangers . . . must always have a tendency to unsettle." Civic leaders early recognized this problem, and in 1818 the Pittsburgh Union Society opened a school for needy students, declaring that "among the children of this city are hundreds who may forever be lost and undone for want of early instruction." Despite continual discussion of alternatives, education remained in the hands of over two score private schools of varying degrees of competence.[41]

Meanwhile higher and lower education fared better. A college, the Western University of Pennsylvania, incorporated in 1819, offered intermittent instruction through the next ten years. Though not comparable to other transmontane institutions of the kind, its faculty comprised some of the best-educated men in the community and provided a center for intellectual life. At the other end of the scale the Pittsburgh Infant School took care of children under six years old.[42] These opportunities rounded out the educational system. No doubt conditions would have been better if the depression had not hung on so long in the Iron City, but even the lash of hard times could not completely still the vigorous impulse for improvement.

A valuable auxiliary to the educational offerings of Western towns were Sunday schools, which provided religious instruction to young people. Every community had many of these. In fact, by 1820 Cincinnati possessed six, attended by more than 600 students and utilizing nearly 100 teachers. Two years earlier the Pittsburgh Sabbath School Association reported more than 500 pupils attending its

October 20, 1826; Louisville, *City Journal*, April 25, 1828; April 24, 1829; November 20, 1829.

[41] *Pittsburgh Gazette*, December 29, 1818; March 31, 1818; Anderson, *Pittsburgh*, 12.

[42] Anderson, *Pittsburgh*, 14; *Pittsburgh Gazette*, July 20, 23, 1830.

five branches, including forty Negroes. Though these enterprises were sponsored by Protestant groups, they flourished even in such Catholic areas as St. Louis, where the regional organization served "several thousand children" in and around the Mississippi metropolis.[43] The instruction was on a very simple level, with Bible reading and recitation the staple exercises. Yet the schools welcomed rich and poor alike, and no doubt many Westerners first discovered the world of books in the neighborhood church or in a makeshift Sunday classroom above the local marketplace.

Like education, the press also flourished in the postwar years; and as with education, too, its prosperity mirrored the general cultural growth of the urban West. Not only were there more newspapers in each city, but their quality and frequency increased. There were some soft spots such as Pittsburgh and Lexington, but these reflected depressed economic conditions locally, and with the return of better times the Iron City joined the journalistic upswing. Established papers shifted to semiweeklies and often to dailies, new enterprises sprang up, and literary and scientific journals made their appearance. The *Missouri Republican,* noting the plans for several new sheets in St. Louis, summed up the tendency well when it observed that "newspapers promise to be 'thick as blackberries in the spring.'"[44]

This profusion was a rough gauge of urban development. Cincinnati, the fastest growing city, also had the most papers — seven weeklies, two dailies, a literary monthly, a medical journal, and even a magazine for teenagers.[45] The expansion of Louisville and

[43] *Liberty Hall* (Cincinnati), September 30, 1820; *Pittsburgh Mercury,* April 24, 1818; *Missouri Republican,* May 3, 1827.

[44] *Missouri Republican,* February 17, 1829.

[45] The youth magazine was called the *Olio* and ran weekly for more than a year. The prospectus stated that it was "chiefly intended for the younger class of the community, who are just on the verge of manhood." *Olio* (Cincinnati), May 26, 1821.

St. Louis found similar journalistic expression in new publications. On the other hand, the flagging fortunes of Lexington and Pittsburgh had the opposite effect. The *Lexington Reporter* attempted to keep abreast of other towns in 1827 by coming out twice a week, but a year later it had to revert to its old practice because of the high cost of printing and insufficient support.[46]

The *Pittsburgh Statesman* expatiated on this connection between urban growth and the development of journalism. In explaining his decision to publish on a semiweekly basis the editor wrote: "Our city, with its environs, contains at least fourteen thousand. In industry, enterprise and intelligence, it is no vain boasting to insist, that we are second to none of our sister cities." Yet there were no dailies in the metropolis. "The question . . . has been frequently asked, both at home and abroad — and with much well founded surprise, why weekly papers *only* issue from our presses?" Moreover, comparison with a neighboring rival was hardly flattering to the Iron City. "In Cincinnati . . . which in solid wealth and population, does not surpass our own, there are two daily papers, three or four semiweekly papers, together with a number of weekly papers, magazines, &c., &c. all of which are freely and fully encouraged and supported." The editor then concluded with an appeal for support of his new enterprise. "Shall Pittsburgh, by her backwardness, in this particular, give plausibility to the belief, which her enemies are anxious to propagate, that she is destitute of public spirit and pride — of literary taste and intelligence?" [47]

The increased size of urban centers also led to a different emphasis in the treatment of news. The old reliance on verbal accounts of local happenings was no longer adequate. Though gossip could still handle neighborhood affairs, towns had become too big, too complex, and too impersonal for word-of-mouth coverage. Increasingly the press recorded city events, commented on municipal problems, and printed the views of their own residents. Of course, na-

---

[46] *Kentucky Reporter*, January 5, 1828.

[47] *Pittsburgh Statesman*, November 4, 1826. Nor was this merely a local view; the *Erie Gazette* bluntly stated, "We think the city of Pittsburgh should support a daily paper." Quoted in *Pittsburgh Statesman*, December 2, 1826.

tional and international items still predominated, but columns devoted to local matters multiplied. In some places, in fact, newspapers became forums for lively debates over municipal issues, problems of urban expansion, and even the future shape of the city.

Meantime, another kind of journal made its appearance, handling broad literary or scientific questions and publishing either monthly or quarterly. Though Lexington's John Bradford printed a few copies of *The Medley, or Monthly Miscellany* as early as 1803, the West had no serious periodical until 1819, when William Gibbs Hunt in the same city brought out *The Western Review and Miscellaneous Magazine, a Monthly Publication Devoted to Literature and Science.* It lasted only two years, perishing for want of enough subscribers. In 1827 Timothy Flint launched *The Western Monthly Review* in Cincinnati, hoping to make it the arbiter of literary taste in the entire area. "The proper object" of such a journal, he said, "is to foster literature" by including both established names and regional authors. Most of the numbers contained synopses and critiques of current writing and an immense amount of original material by the editor. Within three years, however, the project folded. Pittsburgh's experiment in the same field proved even less happy, the *Hesperus and Western Miscellany* giving up the fight after only a few months.[48]

Many people thought these efforts were premature, but almost immediately James Hall announced the first issue of the *Illinois Monthly Magazine*. After publishing first in Vandalia and then St. Louis, Hall brought the enterprise to Cincinnati, where, under the title of *The Western Monthly Magazine*, it enjoyed unusual success. Starting with fewer than 500 hundred subscribers, its sales reached three thousand by 1833, "a support greater than had been given to any western periodical, and which few of those of eastern cities have attained." [49]

While literary leaders struggled to raise the reading tastes of Westerners, specialized periodicals tried to stimulate activity in

[48] Quoted in Rusk, *Literature on the Middle Western Frontier*, I, 169; Anderson, *Pittsburgh*, 38.

[49] *The Western Monthly Magazine*, I (1833), 428.

other fields. Religious journals appeared fitfully, none lasting more than a few years and even the best having trouble in meeting expenses. Medical publications fared better, and a few made real contributions to the profession. John D. Godman edited the first of these, *These Western Quarterly Reporter of Medical, Surgical and Natural Science*, which became the organ of Cincinnati's young doctors, but which discontinued after only a few issues.[50] Within a few years, however, the Queen City had a more successful venture, *The Western Medical and Physical Journal*, which flourished for over a dozen years under the guidance of Daniel Drake. In 1828 John Esten Cooke and Charles W. Short founded *The Transylvania Journal of Medicine and the Associated Sciences*, whose life span proved equally long. The presence of these magazines — both general and technical — reflected not only the rise of professional groups in trans-Allegheny cities, but also a sophisticated reading public of significant size.

The growth of libraries kept pace with the development of journalism. Even before the war most cities had witnessed promising beginnings. Lexington, the most progressive, had a subscription company, an apprentices' society, and Transylvania University, boasting collections which together totaled over four thousand volumes. Pittsburgh's Permanent Library had two thousand books by 1816, and Cincinnati's contained about half that number in the same year. Neither St. Louis nor Louisville had succeeded in putting even a reading room on a solid basis, though many attempts had been made in both towns. Meanwhile private resources increased, and bookshops and general merchandisers offered a wide variety of titles to the occasional buyer. Indeed, Paxton declared, Bishop Dubourg's own collection in St. Louis, which numbered 8,000, to be "without doubt, the most complete, scientific and literary repertory of the western country, if not of the Western world." The estimate was probably too liberal, but individual libraries generally were much larger than is often assumed. In a single year, for example, 22,465 books were sold in Pittsburgh.[51]

[50] *Liberty Hall* (Cincinnati), March 9, 1822.

[51] Lexington Library, *A Catalogue of Books*; Huntley Dupre, *Rafinesque*

The postwar depression, however, threatened libraries because subscribers fell behind in their dues. In Cincinnati, for instance, where membership dropped to a mere handful, "Cleon," a director, gave up in despair after pleading continuously for financial support. He finally suggested that all the books be taken "en masse, to the Commons in front of our city and committed to the flames, and while dancing around the smoke of the last vestige of literary taste," the residents could "proclaim to the world, that in a city containing ten thousand inhabitants, renowned for their industry, enterprise and public spirit," there were not a few dozen to give two dollars a year to keep the doors open. But the emergency soon passed. Within four years the officers announced that the debt had been almost wiped out and the collection contained 3,500 volumes.[52]

Meanwhile some leading citizens established an Apprentices' Library "for improving the minds of the laboring class of our youth." Begun in 1821, it soon had thirteen hundred books, over two hundred of which went out each Saturday. But, like its parent organization, the new enterprise had its financial difficulties. One editor, noting that the partisans of Greek independence had no trouble in collecting money in Cincinnati, urged that residents pay more attention to this fledgling institution. "While we are assisting the Greeks to regain their liberties, let not our own youth, who are destined to the more essential occupations of industry and the mechanical arts, become Turks in stupidity and ignorance." Three years later Pittsburgh opened the same kind of library, to lure mechanics away from "their gross and ruinous amusements." [53]

The planting of colleges in Western cities was a powerful stimulus to the growth of libraries. Not only did the faculty need a working collection, but student groups and clubs organized their own. Medical schools counted their technical volumes as a precious part of

---

in Lexington, 1819–1829 (Lexington, 1945), 19; Anderson, *Pittsburgh*, 30; *Liberty Hall* (Cincinnati), April 1, 1816; Paxton, *St. Louis Directory* (unfolioed); Jones, *Pittsburgh in 1826*, 87.

[52] *Daily Gazette* (Cincinnati), September 20, 1820; June 29, 1824.

[53] *Liberty Hall* (Cincinnati), June 4, 1824; November 28, 1821; June 4, 1824; *Pittsburgh Gazette*, June 18, 1824.

their facilities, and at Transylvania the law division brought together specialized material for teaching purposes. It is significant that the only trans-Allegheny town of any size without adequate library resources was Louisville, which also lacked a college of any kind. By 1830, however, few urbanites could contend that there were not enough books for either general or professional use. Some might complain that they were not readily available to everybody, but widening educational opportunities and apprentices' libraries were rapidly remedying that situation.

$$\mathcal{A}$$

The theater shared the general cultural prosperity of the postwar West. The success, however, was neither uniform nor easily won. The depression checked the promising development of the century's first two decades, and the theater still had to contend with religious and moral objections. The latter hostility, however, declined markedly as the drama season became regularized and the appearance of traveling players ceased to be a novelty. But the opposition did not completely end. In 1820, for instance, "some malicious wretch" broke into the theater in St. Louis and slashed the curtains and scenery. In Cincinnati Joshua Wilson carried on his guerilla warfare against the stage, albeit with dwindling support and diminished enthusiasm. Though only the "fastidious in morals" objected, managers were careful not to rouse any latent animosity. They constantly gave benefits for various groups, raised money for local projects, and emphasized the positive morality of the drama. The motto on the proscenium of the Pavilion Theater in Cincinnati bore the mark of an early public relations genius: "The means, pleasure — the *end*, virtue." [54]

There can be no doubt that the second generation of Western urbanites was more receptive to the drama than the first. The press

[54] *St. Louis Enquirer*, March 29, 1820 — see also Rusk, *Literature of the Middle Western Frontier*, I, 435; *Liberty Hall* (Cincinnati), February 17, 1817, May 11, June 25, 1819; *Missouri Observer*, July 25, 1827; Rusk, *Literature of the Middle Western Frontier*, I, 434.

almost universally supported it, and local officials were generally friendly. Though every city placed a tax on the theater, and the wording of ordinances indicated a suspicion of the stage, the relations between managers and municipal authorities were usually cordial. In fact, the city records reveal that town officials gave the theater as much aid as the law would allow, favoring it over all other forms of amusements embraced by the same ordinance. In the early days of the drama Cincinnati charged as much as $10 for a nightly permit; but by 1830 it had scaled down the price to $3. Lexington reduced its fee to $2 by 1823, while in Louisville troupes could play without charge if they gave one benefit performance a season. Even this requirement was eliminated in 1828, and playhouses paid only normal property taxes. St. Louis showed a similar tenderness. In 1828 the city council urged the abolition of the tax altogether, "in as much as it has been represented to this Board" that licenses were not required "in any other city than St. Louis." [55] The last statement was exaggerated, but it did show the Western tendency to encourage the theater as a cultural asset rather than to scrutinize it as a dubious recreation.

Actually apathy proved a greater danger than hostility. If the drama had a complaint, it was nonsupport rather than cruelty. Friends of the stage constantly grumbled about it. "This place is not only sufficiently large in point of population, but it is more than sufficient in wealth, to support a theater," the *Missouri Observer* declared in 1827, yet attendance was low. The same held true in other places. Deploring the "wretched support" of the 1827 season, Cincinnati's *Liberty Hall* observed that "last winter and spring the Players absolutely starved" and "it appears, from the Lexington Public Advertiser of October 11, that they are in a fair way of starving there." [56]

Despite these troubles, patrons increased in most cities throughout

[55] Cincinnati, Minutes, April 14, 1830; Lexington, Trustees Book, October 2, 1823; Louisville, Trustees Book, April 2, 1823; March 14, 1828; St. Louis, Minutes, December 20, 1820, June 29, 1827, August 7, 1828.

[56] *Missouri Observer*, July 25, 1827; *Liberty Hall* (Cincinnati), October 24, 1828.

the twenties. In fact, the prize seemed great enough to attract competing troupes into the area, each hoping to monopolize the Western circuit. William Turner, who had brought the first professional company in 1811, enjoyed a short supremacy, appearing in Lexington, Louisville, Cincinnati, and, while the legislature was in session, Frankfort. Four years later, however, Samuel Drake moved into the scene, buying up a string of Kentucky theaters and even threatening Turner in Ohio. Within a short time he eliminated his rival completely and for nearly a decade dominated the whole area. In 1827 a new power entered. James Caldwell, a successful manager in New Orleans, brought players to St. Louis, an undertaking which ultimately won him control of nearly every theater in the West. Meanwhile, Noah Ludlow started to perform in the very heart of Drake's empire, Cincinnati and Louisville.[57]

This increasing activity by professionals pushed the amateurs off the boards. Local groups still performed for various benefits and to fill gaps in the regular season, but traveling companies took over most of the time. Few of these players won anything more than regional recognition, and all lived precariously on irregular incomes and the hospitality of patrons on the circuit. Only the Drake family enjoyed a reputation beyond the mountains, and only one of them, Mrs. Alexander Drake, became a national star on the Western stage exclusively. To be sure, Edwin Forrest made his first appearances in this area, but his closest associations and finest days were in the East.

Yet the West did not lack top performers. The "star" system, recently established in Atlantic cities, was taken up by the leading companies, and soon playgoers in Cincinnati and Louisville jammed the theaters for such headliners as Thomas Abthorpe Cooper, Junius Brutus Booth, Madame Celeste, and Clara Fisher. In 1829 Forrest returned as a celebrated name to the same boards he had walked obscurely but a half dozen years before. And the urbanites appreciated his quality. When Booth played *Richard III* in Cincinnati,

[57] The best discussions of the Western theater in this period are Rusk, *Literature of the Middle Western Frontier*, I, 352–439, and W. G. B. Carson, *The Theater on the Frontier* (Chicago, 1932), 1–134.

he drew "the most overflowing house ever known" there, and as many people had to be turned away as were admitted.[58]

Moreover, the theater was popular culture, not yet having become the property of the sophisticated and well-to-do. Admission prices were moderate, programs were designed for a broad appeal, and classes mingled freely at the performances. For some people, indeed, the playhouse was too democratic, smacking of rowdyness, the blurring of social distinctions, and the cultivation of low instincts. "The object of the theater is to reform and not to countenance barefaced profligacy and unblushing prostitution," "A Traveling Amateur" protested after seeing a Louisville production. Worried about the "coarse language of these *celestial tenants*" on the cheap benches, he suggested that the gallery and boxes be separated and each section have its own entrance. "Men came into the lower tier of boxes without coats," Mrs. Trollope remembered with some horror from Cincinnati, "and I have seen shirt sleeves tucked up to the shoulder; the spitting was incessant, and the mixed smell of onions and whisky was enough to make one feel even the Drakes' acting dearly bought by the obligation of encuring its accompaniment." [59] Nevertheless, the theater was undoubtedly an effective mixing bowl, and its popular character made it, along with education and the newspapers, an important carrier of refinement and taste.

While Western urbanites could boast of their schools, newspapers, libraries, and, in some places, their theater, they could not be so proud of their support of the fine arts. Outside of Lexington, music, painting, and sculpturing at best struggled for attention and at worst had none. Though Hiram Powers was beginning a promising career in Cincinnati in the twenties, only his frivolous work brought him any notice. Audubon for a brief time lent his considerable

---

[58] *Daily Gazette* (Cincinnati), December 15, 16, 1828.
[59] *Louisville Public Advertiser*, May 6, 1829; Trollope, *Domestic Manners* (Smalley, ed.), 133.

genius to a museum in the same city, but without acclaim. Pittsburghers probably enjoyed more good music than any other Westerners, but even there patronage was capricious. Towns like Louisville and St. Louis demonstrated even less enthusiasm for the creative arts. When the Academy of Fine Arts gave up the ghost in Cincinnati after a six weeks' exhibition, a disgusted resident observed that only 150 people had attended the show, while "hundreds and hundreds of persons, night after night, for months past, have visited the circus to witness the feats of a clown riding at full speed with his head on the saddle and his heels in the air." [60]

It was never a case of total deprivation, however. Cincinnati, for example, had a lively cultural elite. Frederick Eckstein, a German painter and sculptor, founded an academy for interested or promising artists. He was joined in this field in 1828 by Auguste Hervieu, who opened a school for drawing, and whose canvas "The Landing of Lafayette in Cincinnati" was well received both locally and in the East. Though Hiram Powers was yet quite young, a few recognized him "as a young man of exceptional talent and promise." [61] In addition, the Queen City had a large number of physicians, lawyers, journalists, and teachers who could be counted among the patrons of the arts. Yet they were not numerous enough to sustain a serious museum, a coterie of painters, or more than an occasional concert. Narrow enthusiasm was no substitute for broad support.

No one knew this problem better than the censorious English visitor, Frances Trollope, who spent two painful and expensive years trying to infuse her kind of refinement and culture into Cincinnati. To this end she erected an extraordinary bazaar in 1829, which Timothy Flint later described as "a queer, unique crescented Turkish Babel, so odd, that no one has seen it since, without wonder and a good humored laugh." Built at a cost of better than $25,000, it rose four stories and eighty-five feet above the river, a fantastic mixture of Moorish, classical, and Turkish design. Inside were an Exchange Coffee House, an "elegant Saloon" where ice and other refreshments lent "their allurements to the fascination of

[60] *Daily Chronicle* (Cincinnati), December 20, 1828.
[61] Trollope, *Domestic Manners* (Smalley, ed.), xxix.

architectural novelty," a bar room, a picture gallery, a large ballroom, a circular structure for "Panoramic Exhibitions," and a shop which handled fancy imported items.[62] Mrs. Trollope's failure was on a scale that matched the edifice. The sheriff seized all her goods to satisfy angry creditors, an ambitious Musical Fantasia flopped, and even a mildly successful showing of Hervieu's depiction of Lafayette failed to shore up the enterprise.

More attuned to popular taste was the Western Museum. Founded in 1820 by Daniel Drake for scientific purposes, it became "one of the proudest ornaments" of the city. It was soon evident, however, that natural history and archaeology had a very slim appeal, and the stockholders, tired of chronic deficits, handed the whole project over to Joseph Dorfeuille, who had been its curator for almost three years. Though a naturalist of some attainments, the new director took to featuring oddities, freaks, and wax models to meet the competition of a neighboring commercial museum. His real masterpiece was a frightening display of scenes from Dante's "Divine Comedy," called the "Infernal Regions." The idea was probably Mrs. Trollope's and the artistic work that of Powers and Hervieu. Very little was left to the imagination. The life-size figures, uttering "unearthly sounds, horrid groans, and terrible shrieks," were arranged against a realistic backdrop of hell. This exhibit touched a popular chord, the curious visiting it in such numbers that a traveler mistook the throng and the excitement for a religious revival.[63] Nor was Cincinnati unique. Every city had a counterpart of the Western Museum, where science and natural history mingled with two-headed pigs, eight-footed lambs, assortments of wax figures, and patriotic paintings.

Music showed the same hesitant development as the other arts. Relying almost completely on local talent, activity in this area consisted of church singing, amateur dabbling, and theatrical accompaniment. In most cities informal groups put on a few concerts

[62] Quoted in Trollope, *Domestic Manners* (Smalley, ed.), xiv; xxxv.

[63] *Liberty Hall* (Cincinnati), June 29, 1822; quoted in Trollope, *Domestic Manners* (Smalley, ed.), xxxiii; *Cincinnati Saturday Evening Chronicle*, May 9, 1829.

annually, and traveling performers occasionally worked through the West, but the fare seldom proved satisfying. Pittsburgh's offerings were better than those elsewhere, thanks largely to William Evans. Coming there in 1811, he quickly became the town's leader and teacher in this field. He formed the Pittsburgh Music Society in 1818, a similar one across the river in Allegheny the next year, and a professional military band in 1820. All these organizations, as well as the revived Apollonian Society, provided the residents with the fullest schedule in the entire valley.[64] No other place proved so fortunate, and, except as a religious adjunct, music did not play an important part in the lives of city-dwellers.

Part of the story of the social and cultural advance of the postwar years appears in the success of urban churches. Everywhere old congregations grew, new sects organized, and activity increased. Nothing, however, testified more eloquently to the prosperous state of religion than the large, substantial, and occasionally elegant buildings. Paxton's directory of St. Louis in 1821 told the story simply. "The inhabitants have seen a fine brick cathedral rise, at the same spot where stood formerly an old log cabin, then sufficient, but which now would scarcely be able to contain the tenth part of the Catholic congregation." The new edifice was the city's pride. It "can boast of having no rival in the United States," the *Directory* declared, "for the magnificence, the value and elegance of her sacred vases, ornaments and paintings; and indeed few churches in Europe possess anything superior to it." The editor, a former Philadelphian, could hardly restrain himself. "It is a truly delightful sight to an American taste, to find in one of the remotest towns of the Union a church decorated with the *original* [*sic*] paintings of Rubens, Raphael, Guido, Paul Veronze [*sic*] and a number of others by the first modern masters of the Italian, French and Flemish

[64] The best account of Pittsburgh musical development is E. G. Baynhem, "The Early Development of Music in Pittsburgh," unpublished doctoral dissertation (University of Pittsburgh, 1944), 36ff.

schools." [65] Though no other city could rival this effort, all witnessed the rise of new religious buildings of pretension and permanence.

A steady rise of church membership matched the new construction in postwar years. Though exact figures are not available, Pittsburgh's experience is illustrative. The famous First Presbyterian Church continued to attract adherents, and under the energetic leadership of the Reverend Francis Herron it not only paid off a considerable debt but enlarged its facilities without contracting new obligations. Moreover, Presbyterianism proved strong enough to support two congregations; the Second Church quickly established itself in another part of the town. The Baptists, who had met in private homes in their earliest days, built a wooden chapel in 1820 and continued to thrive in the next decade. Pittsburgh's Methodists also increased rapidly, totalling nearly six hundred in the twenties. Meanwhile Trinity Episcopal Church challenged the First Presbyterian in social prestige, though its membership grew more slowly.[66] Other cities enjoyed a similar development, but the relative strength of the various denominations differed widely.

No group prospered more in the twenties than the Roman Catholics. Though always powerful in St. Louis, they had only slender roots in other Western areas. The great expansion of urban population, however, coupled with the demand for canal workers, led to a significant flow of Catholics into trans-Allegheny towns. In 1826 Cincinnati Catholics dedicated an imposing new cathedral, which could accommodate a thousand communicants and contained "an elegant organ" from Germany and some paintings by "one of the first Roman masters." Three years later work began on St. Paul's Cathedral in Pittsburgh, which, when finished in 1834, was the largest church in the United States. Louisvillians, though less

[65] Paxton, *St. Louis Directory* (unfolioed).

[66] W. W. McKinney, "Early Pittsburgh Presbyterianism . . . 1758–1839," unpublished doctoral dissertation (University of Pittsburgh, 1938), 142; 168–69; O. O. Page, "Sketch of the 'Old Round Church,' 1805–1825; the Original Edifice of Trinity Church, Pittsburgh," *Pennsylvania Magazine of History and Biography*, XIX (1895), 358.

ambitious, erected a brick chapel in 1819, and the parishioners increased rapidly in the twenties.[67]

St. Louis remained the focus of Western Catholicism. Its supremacy there, however, was not without challenge as new settlers swarmed in from the East. As early as 1818 the local priest noted the threat. "The French part of the population will soon be absorbed by the American and English, among whom only a small portion are Catholic," Father de Andreis wrote; "the greater part are Protestant of various denominations." More ominous still was the large number of "infidels, who call themselves nullifidians, that is to say, without any religion whatsoever." Within three years the Baptists had a brick church and the Episcopalians a wooden one, and the Methodists and Presbyterians met in rooms provided by the city. These sects continued to grow throughout the decade, their activity branching out into charity work and education. Yet St. Louis continued fundamentally Catholic, partially realizing the hope of its first bishop that it would become "the center of all religious and literary instruction" of "the extensive country" around the city.[68]

Part of the religious harvest of these years consisted in the establishment of new denominations. The Unitarians and Universalists made their first appearance in the twenties, and even the Swedenborgians discovered enough adherents to formalize their activity in Cincinnati. The Jews, too, organized in the Queen City, founding their first congregation in the West in 1824. Within a few years more than a score worshiped in private homes, but no synagogue arose until the next decade.[69] In addition, itinerant preachers and unorthodox thinkers had a wide hearing, stimulating discussion and often garnering converts.

While churches multiplied and membership steadily expanded

---

[67] *Cincinnati Advertiser*, December 6, 1826; Anderson, *Pittsburgh*, 24; McMurtrie, *Sketches of Louisville*, 140.

[68] Rothensteiner, *St. Louis Archdiocese*, 268; 259; Paxton, *St. Louis Directory* (unfolioed).

[69] D. Philipson, *Oldest Jewish Congregation in the West* (Cincinnati, 1894), 13ff.

in the postwar years, the growth did not satisfy the more zealous, who could see only evil and corruption everywhere. "St. Louis is no more fit for a Christian than hell is for a powderhouse," declared one traveling preacher. In Cincinnati "Union Prayer" meetings sprang up to combat the "prevalence of *profane swearing, sabbath breaking* and other immoralities, together with the low and languishing state of vital godliness." The Presbyterian Synod of Kentucky lodged similar charges against the residents of Lexington and Louisville, listing the vices and calling these towns centers of infidelism.[70]

To such minds the cities harbored many obstacles to salvation. Besides the obvious temptations of idleness and vice — gambling, drinking, and worse — there were the subtle and more dangerous attractions and activities which, though legitimate in themselves, drained off attention and energy from religious affairs. Joshua Wilson, Cincinnati's leading minister, was an astute though unhappy witness to this attrition. His diary sketches a futile struggle against worldly competition. "Spent the evening at home with a group of friends, including Doc Drake, Rev. Osborne, Maj Ruffner — topic was commerce. I would be glad to hear more about the way to heaven than the way to become wealthy." Later a funeral visit drove home the same truth. "When I went into the room to see the corpse, there were Genl Findlay, Genl Harrison, Col Davis and some others disputing about a bill of rights. But why should I be surprised? He that is of the earth speaketh of the things of the earth." [71]

Yet the bewitchment of the city did not prove fatal to all youth interested in religious careers, for enough sought ministerial training to justify the establishment of seminaries, both Catholic and Protestant. Despite some suspicion of urban life, the various faiths chose to build their schools in cities. For their part, the towns were anxious to attract the new institutions. When the Presbyterians de-

---

[70] *St. Louis Enquirer*, February 19, 1820; *Liberty Hall* (Cincinnati), October 23, 1822; *Kentucky Reporter*, November 3, 1823.

[71] Joshua L. Wilson, Diary (MS, Durrett Collection, University of Chicago Library), August 14, 1821; July 6, 1824.

cided to open the Western Theological Seminary, both Cincinnati and Pittsburgh offered sites and inducements. To be sure, their motives were not uncomplicated by commercial considerations. In fact, "A Citizen," writing in *Liberty Hall*, coldly calculated that 100 to 150 students would need enough food and clothing to keep many local merchants happy.[72] But, basically, thoughtful people in each place envisioned their city as a religious center, and looked forward to the day when its institutions would furnish the whole surrounding area with priests and preachers. In the decades that followed their hopes found realization.

Though there were some relatively untouched spots on the cultural canvas of trans-Allegheny cities, the total picture seemed promising. At least most indices showed substantial progress in the postwar years. Yet statistics of multiplying newspapers, more and better schools, increased library resources, thriving churches, and a prospering theater do not convey the meaning of these improvements for individual town dwellers. Evidence of a personal sort is scanty. Luckily, however, the diary of a young Cincinnatian, William Merrill, later the founder of a successful pharmaceutical house, reflects day-by-day activity in the Ohio metropolis. The document not only details a fascinating story of the frail beginnings of a great firm, but uniquely mirrors the social and cultural life of the community. Though matter-of-fact in tone and sketchy in places, it imparts something of the flavor of affairs and the variety of opportunities which the city offered.

Merrill first came to Cincinnati during the war to visit an uncle. He liked the new town, but decided to go back East for schooling, ultimately graduating from Hamilton College in Clinton, New York. In 1823 he returned to the Queen City with the intention of entering the ministry. Quickly, however, he got drawn into the vortex of the town's business life, initially as a small manufacturer of lead and porcelain and then as a retailer of drugs. As he did so

[72] *Liberty Hall* (Cincinnati), November 8, 1825.

his enthusiasm for a religious career waned. "Today," he wrote in his diary in 1824, "the thoughts of speculations in which I am engaging constantly rush in my mind and scarcely allow me to think of ought that pertains to my laying up treasures in heaven." As his mercantile ventures developed he gave up all thought of entering the ministry. "I am not ready to be crucified with Jesus," he observed.[73]

While getting his economic footing, Merrill availed himself of the many educational opportunities around him. After beginning lead manufacturing, he attended the "chemical lectures" of Elijah Slack at the medical school and rummaged through the circulating library for scientific books. William Henry Harrison, who took a liking to the youthful entrepreneur, gave him his own borrowing card. Merrill read widely; his diary mentions volumes ranging from encyclopedias to Oriental stories and current novels. His taste for the latter made him feel guilty and uncomfortable, and indulgence usually brought remorse. At one point he wrote, "In the evening read the first chapter of a Chinese tale — not a very good preparation of the mind for the Holy Sabbath." Less than two weeks later he sighed again, "I took up a novel, 'The Recluse of Norway' and . . . had my thoughts so entirely occupied with it that I quite forgot the better object of attending the prayer meeting."[74]

These laments were the residue of an earlier determination to enter the ministry. Indeed, a tone of self-flagellation runs throughout the diary. It was hardly justified, however, because Merrill was an active and faithful layman. When not working on Sunday, he went to church three times, once for services, again to teach Sabbath School, and finally to hear a lecture on some religious topic. In 1824 he began instructing in the African Sunday School, where he had charge of "a few little boys who are just commencing their alphabet." A year later he helped organize in the run-down section of town another class of children who were "all very indigent and mostly so

[73] Merrill, Diary (Historical and Philosophical Society of Ohio, Cincinnati), May 25, 1824; November 4, 1824; April 10, 1825; July 4, 1828.
[74] Merrill, Diary, November 18, 1823, February 14, 1824; April 3, 1824; April 14, 1824.

poorly clothed that the parents would not send them before the next Sabbath." [75] Broad in his sympathies, he attended meetings of many denominations, including Catholic and Swedenborgian, and belonged to several societies devoted to theological discussion.

Merrill's religious feelings were genuine and deep, but they did not keep him from worldly enjoyments. In 1823 he made his first visit to the theater to see *The Point of Honor* and a farce called *Miss in Her Teens.* "I have been accustomed to consider playhouses, the nurseries of unhallowed pleasures," he confessed. "But . . . I think visiting them occasionally is not in itself a vice. I was much amused with the performance but have not in the least changed my opinion of the stage." Generally, music created no spiritual problems, and Merrill took in concerts whenever he could. If a performance came on Sunday, however, it raised the old issue. "In the evening of the 16th," he wrote in 1824, "I attended a concert of the Apollonian Society: was much fatigued and heartily sorry that I had not preferred the house of God." [76]

Despite such misgivings, the budding businessman seems to have missed few opportunities for improvement or relaxation. Shortly after getting settled, Merrill paid three dollars for a season ticket to the Western Museum and continued to patronize it for many years. He listened to Captain John Cleves Symmes argue one month that the earth was hollow and then heard him conclusively refuted the next. He joined the curious to watch Dorfeuille administer laughing gas to "11 or a dozen gentlemen," and the next night, either as a scientific experiment or a lark, took some himself.[77] Whenever the circus or animal shows stopped in Cincinnati, Merrill tried to attend, though after entering the drug business he found little time for this kind of amusement. But, no matter how pressing his affairs, he spent two or three evenings a week at meetings, lectures, or informal discussions and seldom missed church services.

[75] Merrill, Diary, August 8, 1824; April 24, 1825.
[76] Merrill, Diary, June 4, 1823; April 17, 1824.
[77] Merrill, Diary, October 4, 1824; February 21, March 12, 1824; February 14, 16, 1824.

There is no reason to think Merrill's experience unique. True, his college education set him apart from most of his age, giving him tastes not shared by the bulk of Cincinnatians. Yet his interests, being broad, extended to the popular as well as the more refined. Hence his account is something more than a Baedeker of the activities of a member of the elite. It is also an intimate description of the increasingly rich and varied society in the urban West. Though lacking the high polish of Atlantic metropolises, these young cities nevertheless offered many possibilities for a full and good life, and whatever facilities were not available to the postwar generation would doubtless be provided by the next.

Chapter 9

Toward Urban Maturity

The remarkable growth of Western urban life did not come without pain. Burgeoning populations and expanding economies strained municipal institutions, intensifying old issues and creating new ones. City governments, faced with crises along many fronts, broadened their scope, increased their competence, and stepped up their activities. William Carr Lane, many times mayor of St. Louis and the West's best student of urban affairs, put the problem in its proper perspective. "A few years since this place was the encamping ground of the solitary Indian trader," he observed in 1825, "soon it became the depot and residence of many traders, under the organization of a village, and now you see it rearing its crest in the attitude of an inspiring city." This development was important for public officials, for "the Regulations adopted in the first stage, did not suit the second, and those of the second, are in their turn out of date. Vicissitudes in commerce, and different states of society require corresponding changes in municipal policy." [1] In the postwar decades, transmontane leaders attempted to provide their rapidly growing cities with an appropriate legislative and administrative framework.

In the process every town found its charter inadequate to some degree. Though the period down to 1815 had witnessed a substantial expansion of the competence of local governments, all of them discovered that additional grants were needed. Many revisions were minor, bestowing narrow authority here or widening jurisdiction there. More important, however, each metropolis sought a change in its fundamental status, petitioning for incorporation as a city. The resultant charters generally established greater home rule, and especially broadened the enforcement power of local officials. More-

[1] St. Louis, Minutes, April 28, 1825.

over, they often conveyed increased fiscal responsibility, loosening debt restrictions and providing for greater revenue. A few enlarged the physical boundaries of the town, and, in the case of Pittsburgh, a two-house council replaced a single legislature.

The pressure for incorporation proved most intense in the larger cities. The first move came from Lexington in 1815. Ironically, however, the issue was not carried to the Kentucky legislature because the town immediately fell on hard times, and the economic crisis pushed all other considerations aside. The petition was not renewed for a quarter of a century, and the place first ready for the status of a city was the last to achieve it. In retrospect 1815 marked the high noon of Lexington's fortunes. The years that followed were ones of waning light, and even the gaudy sunset of its cultural renaissance could not conceal its essential decline.

Increased population was usually enough to warrant incorporation, but the greatest inducement was the need for a more efficient police and court system. "The curtailing of the business of the court of quarter sessions by the mayor's court, was the principal object of incorporation," a Pittsburgh editor declared frankly in 1818, two years after the Iron City received its new charter. Similarly, a "Memorial of the Citizens of Cincinnati to the Ohio Legislature" in 1817 asserted that "from the experience of two years it has been fully demonstrated that the charter . . . is insufficient to answer the ends of its enactment, the establishment of a well regulated police within the town —." The same consideration drove Louisville and St. Louis to seek revision and ultimately city incorporation.[2]

The states reluctantly yielded wider jurisdiction, though they more readily gave up police power and court competence than fiscal control. They continued to insist on strict tax limitations. When Pennsylvania elevated Pittsburgh to a city, it gave its western metropolis the same revenue privileges as Philadelphia, but other legislatures had no such yardstick to draw on. Hence their concessions tended to be less generous and more specific. In 1816 the Trustees of Louisville,

---

[2] *Pittsburgh Gazette*, December 8, 1818; December 30, 1817, MS, Torrence Collection; *Louisville Public Advertiser*, November 22, 1823, October 9, 1824; St. Louis, Minutes, January 14, 1829.

declaring that their income was "intirely [*sic*] insufficient to answer the purposes of the town," petitioned Kentucky to triple its allowance. Later it succeeded in pushing the lid up a little higher, to permit a forty-cent levy on every $100 of personal property, as well as a $1.50 poll tax on all free adult males, "excepting paupers." Cincinnati's charter put its ceiling at one fifth of one per cent, while St. Louis could not exceed state rates.[3] In addition, every municipality could charge license fees on a great variety of businesses, vehicles, and amusements.

Revenue from all these sources, however, barely met expenses. Cities needing major public improvements had to look elsewhere for funds. Yet borrowing was also under state control. Occasionally the restrictions were reasonable, as in the case of Louisville, whose limit was $25,000 a year. But more often the figure was much smaller. For example, Cincinnati, the fastest growing city in the West, was legally confined to $5,000 annually, though it soon devised means of circumventing the regulation.[4] Designed to curb extravagance and induce fiscal responsibility, these restraints proved to be straitjackets on enterprising administrations trying to solve urgent problems.

In addition to fixing maximum tax rates and limiting indebtedness, the states also engaged in some punitive legislation. They often established salary scales for city employees, specifying which jobs carried remuneration and how much. Missouri stipulated that St. Louis could not pay its officials more than a total of $2,000 each year, though it was public knowledge that the normal figure was slightly higher. Mayor Lane referred to this as "tacit censure" and condemned the state for acting simply "for the purpose of manifesting *power*." "Let us guard," he continued, "against the seductive influence of the 'little brief authority.' " Throughout the twenties Cin-

[3] *By-Laws and Ordinances of the City of Pittsburgh and the Acts of Assembly Relating Thereto* (Pittsburgh, 1828), 13; Louisville, Trustees Book, September 17, 1816; *Collection of the Acts of Virginia and Kentucky*, I, 55–56; *Laws of the State of Missouri*, I, 206.

[4] *Collection of the Acts of Virginia and Kentucky*, I, 53; *Acts . . . Passed at the First Session of the Twenty-fifth General Assembly of the State of Ohio* (Columbus, 1827), XXV, 45.

cinnati sought charter changes, only to be constantly frustrated. The Queen City "has been the sport of the Legislature for the past four or five years," complained the *Daily Gazette*, charging that the assembly had continually "modified and mangled" good amendments.[5] Despite the reluctance of the states, most towns managed to accumulate power, and by 1830 enjoyed considerably more home rule than two decades earlier.

While municipalities sought changes in their legal structure, they also altered their practices. Added jurisdiction and greater responsibility required more employees, and each city developed a small bureaucracy. Most elected officials served without pay, or nearly so, but the day-to-day work of the government depended on a growing staff of full- and part-time workers. Salaries, once a negligible portion of the budget, now constituted a major item, in some instances reaching twenty per cent of all expenditures. Increased payrolls reflected the expansion of city functions. Some new posts represented fresh duties, others indicated that older ones had become so demanding that remuneration was necessary. The major burden of the government's increased activity, however, fell on the mayor, who increasingly became the focus of power and the most important figure in municipal affairs.

City councils shared the increased responsibilities embodied in the new charters. They, too, adjusted their procedures to meet widened obligations. To give continuous attention to persistent problems, they introduced standing committees. Pittsburgh, for instance, had nine of them, covering finance, water, streets, paving, claims and accounts, appeals from assessments, wooden buildings, canals, and wharves and public landings.[6] Many cities appointed Boards of Health composed of physicians and trustees who examined a great variety of conditions. In addition, the number of special committees grew, and the range of their investigations broadened. Haphazard practices were tightened up. Budgets were published before final adoption, and every few years the city issued a compilation of the latest

[5] St. Louis, Minutes, April 28, 1825; *Daily Gazette* (Cincinnati), October 12, 1829.

[6] Pittsburgh, Ordinances and Minutes, January 12, 1828.

ordinances. The public, recognizing these new services, usually supported campaigns to pay their officials.

The benefits of the new charters and more vigorous officers were not immediately apparent, however, for the postwar depression created a fiscal emergency in Western cities which forced them to retrench and postpone any attacks on urban problems. The collapse could hardly have come at a more inopportune time, for local governments were faced with a series of crises. Police and fire protection, the paving of streets, health and sanitation, all needed immediate attention and financial support. Yet municipalities had trouble simply meeting current expenses, and some fell heavily into debt. Until the mid-twenties this tight budgetary situation dominated the thinking and activities of transmontane civic leaders.

Though hard times handicapped every government for a few years, Pittsburgh and Lexington were virtually crippled for a decade. The Iron City's diminished revenue indicates the gravity of its plight. In 1814 the town's expenditure reached $14,681. This figure dropped to $13,095 in 1817 and to $12,160 two years later. As the crisis deepened, retrenchment continued. By 1820 the budget was down to $10,000, and more than half of it went for "debts and deficiencies." But worse was yet to come; in the following months the bottom dropped out. The city allocated only $5,500 for all items in 1822 and only $6,000 in each of the next two years. Before the tide turned, Pittsburgh's indebtedness amounted to $20,000, and the government was nearly paralyzed. Moreover, the damage went beyond mere economies. A visitor in 1824 noted that the "proper public spirit" had dried up, and "the unfortunate change in the business of this place has discouraged most of the inhabitants." [7]

Elsewhere fiscal shakiness caused postponement of necessary improvements or reduction of essential services. Louisville for this

[7] *Pittsburgh Mercury*, March 28, 1815; *Pittsburgh Gazette*, April 15, 1817; February 16, 1819; February 1, 1820; January 25, 1822; January 23, 1824; January 7, 1825; *Cincinnati Literary Gazette*, February 28, 1824.

reason abandoned a project to build hay scales. Lexington, whose income was sliced in half by 1821, sharply reduced its police facilities, though it beat back a movement to eliminate them altogether.[8] Pittsburgh lost two market houses and its watch, and was unable to cope with mounting relief requests. These curtailments represented a twofold setback; not only did cities fail to meet old problems, but they could not begin to handle the new ones stemming from increased populations.

By the middle of the decade, however, the fiscal condition of most Western towns had improved. The younger ones, having greater resilience, bounced back quickly, but Pittsburgh and Lexington recuperated very slowly. The Blue Grass capital, stunned by a decade of defeat, maintained a cautious policy, and as late as 1829 it reduced police salaries, announcing "that economy was the leading object in view." By this time Pittsburgh, once again enjoying prosperity, was working on a budget that exceeded $50,000 annually, and felt strong enough to borrow over $100,000 for major improvements.[9] These expenditures were eight times those of the early twenties, and the indebtedness was now a gauge of confidence rather than insolvency.

Cincinnati rebounded more quicky. By 1825 it loosened its retrenchment policy and began limited expansion of services and expenditures. Budgets which had shrunk to about $10,000 at the depth of the depression moved upward after 1825. By 1830 the city was spending over $40,000 a year and debating a proposition to stabilize its position with a $100,000 loan from Eastern bankers.[10] Moreover, it pushed ahead on such long-delayed projects as a water system, a new market house, and gas lights.

The experiences of Louisville and St. Louis resembled Cincinnati's. The Falls City pulled out of the slump in the mid-twenties and by 1828 operated out of a $40,000 budget. A year later, a special

[8] Louisville, Trustees Book, December 29, 1822; Lexington, Trustees Book, February 1, 1821.

[9] Lexington, Trustees Book, March 5, 1829; *Pittsburgh Mercury*, January 1, 1828; *Pittsburgh Gazette*, December 31, 1830.

[10] *Cincinnati Advertiser*, January 30, 1830.

committee gave the green light to the trustees. "The finances of the city," it reported, "are favorable to a vigorous prosecution of the system of improvements by the extending of the graduation and paving of the streets, filling & draining of the ponds" and other programs.[11] St. Louis had not suffered as much as other towns, but its rate of development lagged with hard times. By 1825, however, the old pace was renewed, and the government moved to meet mounting problems. As in other Western cities, the arrival of better days prepared the way for an assault on pressing urban issues.

ஆ

By the time prosperity returned to transmontane towns, crises had developed along many fronts. Old ills had worsened and new ones appeared. Each place had its special emergency. Louisville, for instance, the victim of almost yearly epidemics, faced a serious health situation. Lexington, suffering economically in its inland confinement, desperately needed a road or canal link with the Ohio. Streets in every city deteriorated, and in St. Louis they became a civic disgrace. Cincinnati and Pittsburgh were both too large to live much longer without an adequate and convenient supply of water. In addition to particular difficulties, all had to deal with the whole range of normal urban problems — problems greatly complicated by mushrooming populations and fluctuating financial resources.

The situation clearly called for something more than temporary solutions and haphazard methods. Yet these cities, young and inexperienced, had few established precedents to draw upon. The very urgency of the crisis, however, seemed to breed responsibility. Thoughtful citizens, worried about the consequences of further delay, proceeded to give continuous attention to the multiplying ills. As a result local governments increasingly turned to long-range programs, seeking to avoid mere patchwork remedies. Many, recognizing the interdependence of various issues, began city-wide planning on a modest scale. In fact, the central development of the

[11] *Louisville Public Advertiser*, December 1, 1827; Louisville, City Journal, February 27, 1829.

twenties was the emergence of this type of urban statesmanship. All places were not equally fortunate, and in some the fruits were not immediately evident, but everywhere municipal affairs received closer scrutiny, administrations showed greater vision, and much genuine progress followed.

No one better illustrated the new tendency than St. Louis's energetic and reflective mayor, William Carr Lane. Elected five consecutive times to the highest office, he was the town's most popular and powerful figure. Carr Lane (as his constituents knew him) was not only a genial, warmhearted politician, but also the shrewdest observer of urban problems in the West. Throughout the twenties, he began each year's business with a state-of-the-city address which outlined the needs of the corporation and presented a legislative program. Couched in broad, almost philosophic terms, these messages constituted model municipal papers. Analysis of them reveals the growing responsibility felt by many urban leaders and throws a shaft of light on the problems of young cities in their second generation of development.

Lane was peculiarly suited for the task of urban leadership. Born in Fayette County, Pennsylvania, in 1789, he spent most of his life in the West. After studying at both Jefferson and Dickinson Colleges, he became an apprentice to doctors in Louisville and Shelbyville, Kentucky, concluding his medical training in Philadelphia at the University of Pennsylvania. An army surgeon during the war, Lane moved to St. Louis in 1815, where he immediately threw himself into local affairs. By this time he had lived in many cities, both in the East and the West, and had seen how they handled urban problems. "Experience is the best guide, in all human affairs," he told the council in 1825. "The record of other towns is a source from whence we may expect to derive useful hints. . . . 'Like circumstances produce like effects' over all the world, it is therefore incumbent upon us to examine carefully what other communities similarly situated have done . . . , & what were the results." [12] Before embarking on major programs, Lane sought information from

[12] St. Louis, Minutes, April 28, 1825.

municipal officers elsewhere, often writing to Boston, New York, Philadelphia, Baltimore, or New Orleans for help.

Lane took a broad view of municipal functions, believing that only a strong, energetic administration could come to grips with the city's many pressing problems. He constantly counseled his colleagues to use every bit of power that they could squeeze from the charter. Admitting that the boundary of municipal law was undefined, he asserted that "all cities and corporations . . . exercise more or less authority, not directly granted by their charters" because "they find it necessary to do so to effect objects expressly authorized." However, Lane recognized restraints on this doctrine. "To come up to the true limit of the charter, & not to transcend it is the grand difficulty." He realized also that much local government concerns trivial matters which "are in themselves contemptible," but he urged officials to treat them seriously, "as if you were legislating on High Treason," for "A right of person or property, even the most trifling, is dear to him who is in soul a Freeman." [13]

Most of Lane's state-of-the-city addresses concentrated on immediate, specific issues. Yet he always kept his vision large, arguing against "hasty legislation" and advocating a planned approach. Observing in 1823 that the treasury was virtually empty, he cautioned the government to take on programs "of the first necessity only; but let whatever is undertaken, be according to some general plan; so that when the different parts are ultimately united, they will form a perfect whole, without any additional expense or material alteration." During his many terms he continually urged uniformity and system, trying to regularize procedures on routine jobs and put the city's housekeeping on a businesslike basis. Interested in beauty as well as utility, he also fought the constant attrition of St. Louis's foliage, becoming a champion of shade trees and parks.[14]

Despite these progressive views on urban affairs, Carr Lane was basically conservative. He was a Federalist in youth and a Whig in later life. He feared an unbalanced budget and carefully avoided

[13] St. Louis, Minutes, May 3, 1824; April 28, 1824.

[14] St. Louis, Minutes, April 28, 1825; April 24, 1823.

the many desirable but not absolutely essential projects which drained the treasury. Yet he did not hesitate to borrow for necessary improvements, especially if they had a long-range usefulness. Carefully setting these apart from current demands, he said "there are certain objects requiring expenditures, wherein those that are to come, are as much benefitted, as are the people for the time being; for such disbursements, posterity may be taxed with perfect propriety; a market house, town house, public offices, and works to supply the town with water, are, I conceive, objects of this kind." A year later he added to the list "Aquiducts [*sic*] or public fountains, public edifices and wharves, nay our pavements, which will last some twenty or thirty years." [15] Lane's theory was bolder than his practice, but his recommendations broke the ground for succeeding administrations.

What most distinguished the approach of St. Louis's mayor from the earlier generation of urban leaders was its perspective. The first residents were pioneers; they remembered the town as a wilderness outpost or a crude village. Their thinking was conditioned by the youth and newness of the settlement. Those a few decades later found an established city, and thought in terms of permanence and expansion. Even this comparatively short time seemed to invest the town with stability, continuity, and even history. "The fortunes of inhabitants may fluctuate; you and I may sink into oblivion, and even our families may become extinct," Lane told his fellow St. Louisans, "but the progressive rise of our city is morally certain, the causes of its prosperity are inscribed upon the very face of the earth, and are as permanent as the foundations of the soil, and the sources of the Mississippi." Likewise, the editor of Cincinnati's *Saturday Evening Chronicle* counseled city officials that they "not only look at the present condition of things, but at which may exist twenty or fifty years hence. Unless this be done, we are neither true to ourselves nor faithful to posterity." [16] This was a new point of view, but nearly all those who came to promi-

[15] St. Louis, Minutes, April 14, 1823; May 3, 1824.
[16] St. Louis, Minutes, April 14, 1823; *Saturday Evening Chronicle* (Cincinnati), March 14, 1829.

nent municipal positions in the twenties shared it. They tended to look more to the long run, to plan with a grander vision and take greater pride in their local attachments.

Though no other city had so articulate a spokesman for the new outlook as St. Louis, all acted under its general influence. One result was the reduction of mercantile influence in local governments. Officials did not become overtly hostile to businessmen, but they did begin to consult other interests in making important urban decisions. This inclination was strengthened by the antipathy to merchants produced by the depression and the increase of other classes during the twenties. Traders, bankers, and manufacturers still sat on local councils and continued to dominate social life, but decisions on municipal affairs no longer clearly bore their imprint. In fact, the business community complained of high taxes, protested against extravagance in administration, and resisted their city's growing indebtedness. In a sense these laments were a tribute to the new statesmanship, for at its best it transcended the demands of any one segment and acted on behalf of the entire community.

Though the influence of commercial elements declined in the postwar period, the market lost none of its importance as an urban institution. In fact, the growing population made its management and conduct a matter of vital interest. Most cities, finding existing facilities inadequate, embarked upon extensive building programs. Local officials carefully guarded against fraud and struggled to preserve competitive conditions. Occasionally governments even resorted to price fixing to protect consumers from exorbitant charges. None of these activities, however, required additional authority from the state, since municipalities had exercised these powers since their earliest years. But the number of ordinances on this problem demonstrates that it continued to be a fundamental concern.

By 1815 every town had at least one market house. Those with more found it difficult to keep them going through the depression, and Pittsburgh and Lexington abandoned some. But better fiscal conditions made expansion possible again. Nothing better illustrated the strategic position of the exchange in city affairs than the new buildings. Much larger and more elaborate than their predecessors, they included municipal office space, rooms for circulating libraries, and places for groups and civic organizations to meet, thus making the market even more than ever the heart of urban life. These structures were expensive, the Cincinnati project of 1829 costing more than $30,000. Hence private groups, often partners in similar earlier enterprises, had to abandon the field to public bodies which alone had the necessary revenues.

While extending these facilities, local officials also tightened their regulations. Especially difficult was the preservation of competition. Overseeing trade practices had long been a central function of town authorities, but multiplying markets and swelling populations greatly complicated the task. Forestalling, monopolizing, and rigging increased, causing shortages and high prices. Twenty Pittsburghers described the scope of the problem in their memorial to the city council: "The injury complained of . . . is wholly occasioned by Butchers, and a lot of mongrel merchants who attend regularly the ferrys and market space in the evenings preceding market days and then and there monopolize pork beef flower [*sic*] meal cheese honey butter eggs potatoes and in short every commodity for table use." The next day they sold at an advance of thirty to fifty per cent. Convinced that the municipality could act, the signers urged "your interference in some way to lessen the intolerable evil." [17]

The cities responded by increasing fines on forestallers, rigidly enforcing trading hours, and restricting the activity of retailers in the market. St. Louis, for instance, prohibited any "grocer, huxter or any other dealer in provisions" from buying more than six pounds of butter, six dozen eggs, or fifty pounds of bacon or hams before ten o'clock. In addition, local officials kept control over vendors through the rental of stalls, revoking the privileges of those who violated regulations. The resort to price fixing was unusual and generally did not extend beyond tavern rates and bread. St. Louis's Mayor Lane best expressed the object of this restrictive legislation

[17] Pittsburgh, City Council Papers, February 9, 1818.

when he said that "the whole secret of improving a market consists in producing fair competition; & that is done simply by bringing all the vendors and purchasers together." [18] For this purpose, municipalities laid down the ground rules, tried to prevent interference in the free exchange of goods, and gave some protection to consumers against unreasonable prices.

❧

A more urgent problem than the regulation of the market was the care and improvement of streets. No other question occasioned so much legislation or cost so much money. Municipal councils often devoted whole meetings to grading and paving, while budgets usually allocated over a quarter of all expenditures to those projects. In 1828, for example, Cincinnati marked $14,221 out of $38,800 for surfacing and cleaning, and two years later Louisville put aside $17,031 out of $46,245 for the same purpose. Even when Pittsburgh had to use a large portion of its income to retire its debt, over twenty percent of all revenue went into streets.[19] In postwar years, creating adequate transit facilities constituted the major activity of most transmontane towns.

By 1815 many places had made some headway with this problem, having paved the market area, the main thoroughfares, and a few streets leading to the wharves. But everywhere a big job remained. Typical was the complaint of a Kentucky resident in 1822 that "there is not a worse mud-hole within 20 miles of Louisville, than our much admired MAIN STREET." He estimated that the "unwary traveller" would need four policemen to "circumnavigate that 'Slough of Despond.'" An even uglier situation confronted Pittsburghers, whose sidewalks and avenues became cluttered with pools and filth. "In some places they are already assuming a greenish hue," the editor of the *Gazette* warned grimly in 1819.[20] The de-

[18] St. Louis, Ordinances, May 31, 1822; St. Louis, Minutes, May 3, 1824.

[19] Cincinnati, Minutes, March 24, 1828; Louisville, City Journal, February 25, 1830; *Pittsburgh Gazette*, January 29, 1830.

[20] *Louisville Public Advertiser*, March 13, 1822; *Pittsburgh Gazette*, July 23, 1819.

pression made an attack on these conditions difficult, and by the mid-twenties some communities faced real emergencies.

Indeed, in St. Louis the emergency took on crisis proportions. Thoroughfares, neglected during the city's early years, deteriorated badly in the postwar period. As early as 1816 one editor declared that "several streets are rendered impassable by the want of a common footway or drains to carry of [*sic*] the rain water. Nuisances are to be met with in every shape from one end to the other." Seven years later, "Jonathan," annoyed by the delay of officials on this question, satirically gave "Hints for the Mayor and Aldermen": "*By all means prevent the paving of Main Street.* That street is the only navigable water-course *through* the city for craft of the larger size, though there are several which will answer well for *scows* and *dung-outs.*" He cautioned against any action, saying that surfacing would "transform it into terra firma, to the great and manifest detriment of all men settled along its banks and living by its navigation." [21]

The situation soon became intolerable. Lane devoted the bulk of his annual message to it in 1824, and criticism increased. "So much has been said and written, in vain, about the condition of our streets, that I despair of ever seeing them better," wrote "A Citizen." "And why? The *ostensible* reason is, that it is expensive." Yet, he observed, residents "spend in a single night, at a public hall, or at the theatre, enough to make the necessary improvements in Main Street." The nub of the problem was the refusal of property owners to pay the cost of paving. Claiming that the responsibility belonged to the city, they would not support a building campaign. The Mayor shared their view in part, asserting that though footwalks ought to be done by proprietors, "the horse or carriage part . . . , being in its character altogether a highway, whereon no person has any privilege beyond another should be paved . . . and kept in repair, by the whole community." [22]

The discussion was a prelude to action. Allowing owners tax

---

[21] *Missouri Gazette,* July 13, 1816; *Missouri Republican,* April 9, 1823.

[22] *Missouri Republican,* January 29, 1823; St. Louis, Minutes, May 4, 1824.

relief to the extent of their paving expenses, the city mapped a program of improvement. In the years following 1827 this question dominated the meetings of the city council, accounting for most of the ordinances and a good share of the budget.[23] By 1830 the major streets had been surfaced, cleaning procedures established, and during the hot season busy corners sprinkled to settle the dust. The issue almost disappeared from the newspapers, though officials continued to be chided about nuisances, obstructions, and broken pavement.

Other municipalities had less trouble in surfacing their streets, but keeping them clean caused no less difficulty. Initially the basic responsibility rested with individual residents, who cared for the strip in front of their property. With the increase of traffic and population, however, this system broke down. But municipalities hesitated to take over because of the expense involved. Hogs and dogs were less reluctant, and for years they formed the first line of defense against filth. "In truth the pigs are constantly seen doing Herculean service in this way through every quarter of the city," Mrs. Trollope observed in Cincinnati; "and though it is not very agreeable to live surrounded by herds of these unsavory animals, it is well that they are so numerous, . . . for without them the streets would soon be chocked up with all sorts of substances in every stage of decomposition." [24] Yet this expedient proved to be more dangerous than economical. One editor, sensing trouble, warned that "the swarms of hungry hogs . . . are ready to swallow our young children and half grown young men and women" as soon as the "usual supply of garbage" declined. This was not idle sarcasm, for a month later one child was mangled and another attacked. As a result, local authorities began to clamp down on the strays, and responsible citizens started to look around for a better solution.[25]

[23] St. Louis, Minutes, May 9, 1828.

[24] Trollope, *Domestic Manners*, 39. Some cities tried to control the animals, Mayor Lane suggesting that they be allowed to roam "only from the first day of May until the 1st day of Dec. in every year." St. Louis, Minutes, May 5, 1828.

[25] *Cincinnati Advertiser*, June 4, 1823; July 30, 1823.

Ordinances tightened the enforcement provisions against recalcitrant owners, and city officials were given broad powers to pick up roaming animals. Moreover, many places gave health boards authority to remove nuisances which might foster disease. All these measures helped, but the problem did not yield to partial remedies. Local governments soon discovered that nothing less than regular attention by paid employees would do the job. Some hired full-time street cleaners, or appointed commissioners who organized their own crews. In any case, the community took up the responsibility and allocated increasingly large sums to the task. Improvement was slow but noticeable.

Progress, however, was constantly impeded by clumsy drainage systems. Early sewers ran down either the middle or the sides of the streets, relying upon rainfall and gravity to carry off the refuse. Poorly constructed, clogged when not dry, they complicated the problem. Newspapers were filled with complaints against the "filthiness of the gutters and sewers," the "greenish hue" of the accumulations, and the "noxious exhalations," which not only obstructed passage but also created health hazards.[26]

In the East, municipalities had begun to install subsurface systems, but smaller and younger places did not have the revenue. Cincinnati alone in the West considered such a radical and expensive project. In 1827 the council instructed the Board of Health to contact authorities in New York, Philadelphia, Baltimore, and Boston to see "how far the sinking of common sewers is approved of in those Cities." Four months later the committee submitted a favorable opinion from the four mayors along with detailed sketches of the various systems.[27] Nothing was done immediately, but continuing drainage difficulties made this remedy indispensable to the next generation.

The demand for smoother, cleaner streets stemmed in part from commercial necessity. Booming trading towns required a rapid flow of goods both into the city and through it. Merchandise had to pass between wharves and warehouses, from countryside to market,

---

[26] *Pittsburgh Gazette*, June 4, July 23, 1819.
[27] Cincinnati, Minutes, October 6, 1827; February 20, 1828.

and from shops to homes. Cities tried to reduce congestion by formalizing driving practices, keeping pedestrians on the sidewalks, and badgering builders and retailers who cluttered the passageways. Moreover, in the late twenties municipalities cut alleys through downtown blocks to absorb some commercial vehicles, and at the same time widened many of the most traveled streets. By 1830 traffic moved more freely than before, but the amount of legislation on the topic indicated continued concern.

ꝏ̃

For river towns, landing facilities were as important as good markets and streets. Though the handling of this problem had been one of the conspicuous successes of early municipal efforts, the great postwar trade expansion required substantial changes. Cities not only had to accommodate a larger number of craft, but the increased use of steamboats necessitated overhauling old installations. Local authorities responded by building new wharves, paving the water front, regulating loadings, and keeping goods and passengers moving across the docks. All the river entrepôts felt the urgency of improvement, for, as St. Louis's mayor observed, "commerce is the vital principle of the town." [28]

No municipality, however, built rapidly enough to handle the mounting traffic. Ordinances throughout the twenties reflect the increased crowding and the struggle of officials to keep ships moving and docks cleared. Vessels could not loiter in port, certain space was reserved for special cargoes, and building and repair yards were moved away from the landing. Wharfage fees supported a harbormaster and provided funds for maintenance and improvement. Nevertheless conditions were far from ideal, and complaints continued to roll in. Unclaimed merchandise cluttered the pavement, stagnant water and driftwood made loading difficult, and in the case of St. Louis, a sandbar obstructed the approach to the city.

Increasing commerce placed a new importance on the crossriver connections of Western towns. Carr Lane expressed it best when he

[28] St. Louis, Minutes, May 4, 1824.

reminded his colleagues of "the identity of interest between the citizens of our town & those of Illinois to a great extent around," and urged them to render "the means of mutual intercourse as easy & prompt as possible." [29] Control of ferries was clearly a municipal function, but since private operators were plentiful, cities confined their activity to regulating competitors. Annual licenses kept pilots under surveillance, and detailed rates protected travelers and merchants from exorbitant charges. Growing trade required additional service, and most places had at least two or three lines constantly at work. In addition, steam ferries quickened the journey and permitted larger cargoes. By 1830 the rivers had ceased to be barriers for the nearby countryside, and had become instead broad highways to urban markets and shops.

While buttressing their economic institutions, Western cities also strengthened the protection of life and property. The first generation of civic leaders had failed to establish adequate defenses against fire, and only Louisville and Lexington put police on the streets with any degree of regularity. Pittsburgh organized patrols in 1816, but the depression brought a quick end to that effort.[30] Though St. Louis provided for an emergency force, it had no round-the-clock coverage. Cincinnati proved even more lax. Not until 1818 did the council pass the first legislation, and five more years elapsed without any effective implementation.

Cities below the Ohio led the West in the development of police protection. Fear of Negro unrest made them establish regular patrols for the control of slaves and free blacks as well as for the safety of life and property. Indeed, so great was the anxiety in Lexington that even during the prolonged agony of the depression the town did not dare take its watch off the streets. Likewise, while other towns retrenched in the early twenties, Louisville organized its first salaried force. In supporting this move, the editor of the *Pub-*

[29] St. Louis, Minutes, April 28, 1825.
[30] *Pittsburgh Gazette*, August 30, 1816, March 14, 1817.

lic Advertiser emphasized the need to restrain Negroes, and urged the new officers to break up illegal assemblies and prevent slaves from walking about at night without permits.[31]

In the postwar years both Kentucky towns developed elaborate police departments. Men on the beat were more than adequately equipped, Louisville providing them with "a staff, . . . a pike and hook on one end, a dark lathern [*sic*], a rattle and trumpet, a small ladder and flambeau, a pair of scissors and a tin pot with a spout for the purpose of filling lamps . . . with oil." Conspicuously armed and publicly appointed, they became the symbols of law enforcement. For undercover work Lexington hired "two confidential persons" and Louisville used a "secret patrol." In addition, the former established mobile forces which put horsemen on the streets in case of emergency.[32] A captain of the watch directed the operation, and a division of the city into police precincts sharpened responsibility on the block level.

The performance of Kentucky police, however, was more impressive on paper than in fact. Official documents reveal a continuing effort to raise standards and maintain discipline and morale. In one instance Lexington authorities admonished the captain of the watch for not breaking up a riot; a few years later they fired the whole force. In 1827 a petition attacked the chief "for sleeping in the watch house 6 to 8 hours in the night," and certain others who "sometimes intoxicate themselves with ardent spirits to the manifest injury of the public interest." Louisville had the same trouble, once discharging almost every member of the patrol and advertising for "vigelant [*sic*] and temperate men." A few years later the trustees had to warn the guard not to "frequent the theatre, circus or any exhibition during watch hours," and dismiss Peter Schwartz for the "improper treatment of an unprotected female." [33]

---

[31] *Louisville Public Advertiser*, February 5, 1820.

[32] Louisville, Trustees Book, December 31, 1821; Lexington, Trustees Book, December 20, 1819; Louisville, Trustees Book, December 31, 1821; Lexington, Trustees Book, December 20, 1819.

[33] Lexington, Trustees Book, March 28, 1820, September 1, 1825; Louisville, Trustees Book, November 7, 1822; April 3, 1829; December 31, 1829.

The record of other cities was still less impressive. After Pittsburgh dissolved its patrol for economy's sake in 1817, law enforcement reverted to the constable, and little was done in the twenties to better the situation. Meanwhile, public order disintegrated. In 1823, one anxious resident wrote that "we have in the midst of us, a population of the most abandoned kind, whose conduct is a reflection both on our police and our laws." Almost defenseless, the people watched the depredations mount. A network of gangs grew up, sometimes operating on a city-wide scale, and always proceeding "with impunity." Only occasionally did the law strike back. In 1829 the police sprang a trap on a group of thugs who had been systematically plundering half the town.[34] Yet this success was unique, and nothing substantial was accomplished until 1831 when Pittsburgh established a full-time, paid watch.

Cincinnati's experience was similar. A growing metropolis, bulging with new wealth and population, it attracted the scheming and the lawless. Scarcely a year passed without a wave of thefts. Indeed, the Queen City acquired an unhappy reputation for its crime rate. "I have long heard it famed as a place of iniquity," a Cincinnati assemblyman admitted; "corruption seems to have dug her deepest den there." Even officials were not safe, and a series of ordinances increased the fines for those who molested policemen. In 1823 the council declared that a voluntary watch was "insufficient," but it hesitated to assume the expense of a regular force.[35] Only slowly did the city come to understand that nothing less than a permanent, salaried force could provide adequate protection for the booming community.

Though Cincinnati was badly policed, it was a good deal safer than St. Louis. In 1821 a resident there observed that the town's only night watch were prowlers who stole everything in sight and, worst still, terrorized women and children. Not only were gambling and assault common, but even kidnapping thrived. In 1823 gangs

---

[34] *Pittsburgh Gazette*, November 28, 1823; Pittsburgh, City Council Papers, January 17, 1824; *Pittsburgh Gazette*, October 30, 1829.

[35] *Liberty Hall* (Cincinnati), January 26, 1822; Cincinnati, Minutes, October 8, 1823.

wandered through the city, frightening citizens and finally producing a cry for better protection. Actually ordinances gave officials the power to establish adequate forces, but the money was never available. Pressure continued to build up, however, and in 1828 the mayor put a "limited night patrol" high on his list of recommendations.[36] Yet in 1830 St. Louis had no regular police, and the Mississippi metropolis challenged Cincinnati's primacy in violence and lawlessness.

Inadequate street lighting complicated the protection of life and property. Though an increasing number of private oil lamps brightened downtown areas and some residential districts, and both Lexington and Cincinnati had erected a few public ones, no extensive municipal systems developed. In 1821 Louisville required land owners to put up posts and lamps "not exceeding four to each square" and ordered the watch to attend them. However, early experiences had not been encouraging. The equipment required care at nightfall and daybreak, fuel costs were high, and vandals damaged the installations. Cincinnati authorities were so harassed that they finally retired theirs to the market-house basement, and other cities restricted their activity to regulating private lighting.[37]

Yet growing populations and rising crime rates made dark and unsafe streets intolerable, and local officials began to consider proposals for gas lighting. In 1817 and again in 1826 Lexington established committees to look into the possibility. Louisville authorities admitted that it "would be very desireable [*sic*], and would add materially to the comfort of the place," but declared that the estimates of $94 per lamp made adoption impractical. However, Pittsburgh and Cincinnati prepared to embark on ambitious projects. In 1827 the Queen City's councilmen approved a resolution stating that "the interest as well as the safety of the City will be advanced from the introduction of Gas lights into general use." Furthermore

[36] *Missouri Gazette*, August 15, 1821; *Missouri Gazette*, January 7, 1824; St. Louis, Ordinances, January 1, 1818, February 9, 1826; St. Louis, Minutes, May 5, 1828.
[37] Louisville, Trustees Book, December 31, 1821; Cincinnati, Minutes, June 7, 1819; January 29, 1823.

they called for the erection of "the same number of Public lamps as in the City of Philadelphia." During the same year Pittsburgh examined a variety of proposals and received bids from two companies which were prepared to begin construction.[38]

But both towns hesitated to launch an undertaking of such magnitude without exploring different methods. A Pittsburgh committee, after inquiries in Philadelphia, Baltimore, and New York, suggested that the city build its own system. Asserting that public ownership would be "very profitable," their report declared that "there was no reason for subjecting the inhabitants to the discretion of a joint stock company in a matter of so much and so rapidly increasing consequences." This suspicion of private enterprise as well as the broad theory of municipal power were characteristic of urban thinking in this period. The franchise ultimately went to a local firm, the Pittsburgh Gas Company, but not until the city had driven a hard bargain and had stripped from the contract a clause which would have given the company a monopoly. In the same year, 1829, Cincinnati granted Warner Hatch and Company exclusive gas-lighting privileges, attaching to the agreement however, the corporation's right to purchase the entire operation after five years.[39] Work did not begin in either place until 1830, and effective illumination was still some time away, but these forward steps placed Pittsburgh and Cincinnati among a half dozen of the country's metropolises which led in adopting or planning to adopt the new system.

Fire protection in the urban West was almost as inadequate as police protection. The prewar record had not been reassuring, and as cities grew the problem grew. Housing shortages resulted in

---

[38] Lexington, Trustees Book, October 15, 1817; January 7, 1826; Louisville, City Journal, March 27, 1829; Cincinnati, Minutes, September 5, 1827; Pittsburgh, City Council Papers, April 30, May 10, 1827.

[39] Pittsburgh, City Council Papers, May 14, 1827; Pittsburgh, Ordinances, February 23, 1829; Cincinnati, Ordinances, September 9, 1829. The privileges were later extended to 35 years. See ordinance of October 21, 1829.

hasty construction, while crowding reduced empty spaces and encouraged contiguous building. Water supplies were limited, especially in areas removed from the rivers, and primitive equipment made control of flames difficult even if aid arrived immediately. Indeed, the physical expansion of cities was so great that municipalities had to reappraise their whole attitude toward this question. What was insufficient for a town of five thousand was obviously inadequate for a place four times that size.

Everyone admitted that the defenses were weak. "I will venture to say that there is not a town or city in the United States," a Cincinnatian asserted in 1819, "so entirely unprovided with the means of extinguishing fires, whose situation is so much exposed." Four years later seventy-eight residents of Pittsburgh advised their council that conditions were so bad that they were forming an emergency committee "for the express purpose of *carefully guarding* and *protecting* the property of their fellow citizens from the unsparing elements of fire." Nor was this anxiety unjustified, since the best engine in town was over thirty years old. Louisville was in even worse shape. After a $20,000 blaze in 1827 an editor admitted that "we are alike destitute of fire hooks and scaling ladders, and two of the three engines, were out of repair." In St. Louis a major disaster found the city completely unprepared — "buckets broken and without handles, and not half enough of these: the engines unfit for service: everyone gaping at the fire instead of forming a line to convey water." [40]

Local authorities, painfully aware of these shortcomings and haunted by the fear of a general conflagration, strove for improvement. Increasingly they whittled down the independence of volunteer companies, assuming an ever wider responsibility for fire protection. Municipalities began to screen applicants, passed ordinances to establish discipline during emergencies, and supervised company finances. Moreover, councils took over almost the entire burden of furnishing the apparatus and keeping it in repair. In 1829 Cin-

[40] *Liberty Hall* (Cincinnati), December 10, 1819; Pittsburgh, City Council Papers, November 28, 1823; September 12, 1826; *Louisville Public Advertiser*, March 10, 1827; *Missouri Republican*, November 21, 1825.

cinnati, going even further, paid its firemen a modest salary, symbolizing the growing competence of government in this field.[41]

In addition to establishing closer control over the volunteers, cities took precautionary measures to reduce hazards. They extended the list of prohibited activities, insisted that inflammable material be taken out of the corporation limits or carefully sealed, and regulated industrial practices to minimize risks. More important than these, however, were the housing ordinances. Alarmed at the increasing number of fires in downtown areas, municipalities tried to protect their crowded centers by forbidding the erection of wooden buildings there.[42] The legislation applied only to future construction, but its vigorous enforcement reflected the determination of authorities to curb the danger.[43]

Despite these precautions, property damage increased. Not only did small fires become more frequent, but each place witnessed spectacular blazes which sometimes wiped out whole blocks and occasionally threatened the entire city. In 1827 a fire got out of control in Louisville, jeopardizing the northern part of town and inflicting a loss of more than $200,000. Four years earlier, the corner of Market and Liberty Streets in Pittsburgh went up in flames, causing three deaths and destroying more than $100,000 in property. At the end of the decade Cincinnati suffered the worst disaster of the period. Though there was only one injury, the fire raged for a good part of the night, cutting a path through the heart of the business district and consuming thirty-three buildings.[44] But no town knew better than Lexington the destructive power of this element. In 1828 it tearfully watched Transylvania University go up in smoke, and with it the pride and hopes of the citizenry.

[41] Cincinnati, Minutes, May 20, 1829.

[42] Pittsburgh had the first of these; see *Pittsburgh Statesman*, September 16, 1826. The agitation for it began much earlier, however. See, for example, *Pittsburgh Gazette*, November 21, 1823.

[43] The minute books of both Pittsburgh's and Cincinnati's councils demonstrate that authorities strictly enforced the law, turning down all kinds of hardship pleas. See, for example, Cincinnati, Minutes, May 23, 1827.

[44] *Louisville Public Advertiser*, March 10, 1827; *Pittsburgh Gazette*, November 21, 1823; *National Republican* (Cincinnati), December 14, 1829.

Each new disaster deepened the anxiety of Western urbanites. Nothing agitated the newspapers more, and local officials, sensitive to public fears, struggled constantly to shore up their defenses. Cities bought the latest model engines in the East and experimented with new equipment. Additional men were put on the job. Organization became more elaborate, and the fire captains assumed greater authority during emergencies. But the effort was not enough. The danger grew faster than the protection. In 1830 civic leaders, though proud of past progress, knew that their cities were more vulnerable than ever.

The West's poor fire-control record in part reflected inadequate water systems. So long as towns remained small, rivers and springs were sufficient, but as building moved inland shortages became critical. Even before 1815 some people saw the need for comprehensive service through reservoirs and pipes, but the cost seemed prohibitive. The denser cities, however, worried by growing property damage, could no longer postpone action.[45] And the timing was right, for construction costs were well below the prewar level. In the twenties Cincinnati and Pittsburgh installed city-wide systems, St. Louis prepared to build, and agitation began in Louisville. Only Lexington lagged, its sluggish economy making even discussion somewhat Utopian.

In 1817 the Queen City's council granted the Cincinnati Manufacturing Company a 99-year monopoly on providing the town with water. For the privilege, the concern paid $100 annually and promised to have service up to "James Ferguson's kitchen in the second Ward" within two years. The deadline was later extended to 1820, but before that time families on the "bottom" had ample amounts for household needs. By the middle of the decade 26,349 feet of wooden pipe carried water from a 200,000-gallon reservoir to 254 industrial and home users. A steam engine lifted the supply from the Ohio, while gravity carried it around the city. The whole con-

[45] Pittsburgh, City Council Papers, May 25, 1822.

struction cost about $40,000; in 1824 the operation showed a profit of more than $1,600, and two years later it netted $2,900.[46]

Despite these promising beginnings the company ran into financial difficulties and could not undertake a needed expansion. This crisis touched off a lively debate over the ownership of the system. A government committee, after surveying the whole problem, concluded: "We believe the city ought to own it — and that it is a work of so public a character that its management should be directed more to the public Interest than to individual emolument." Support for the idea came from unofficial sources, too. "Voter" wrote to the *Advertiser* that "the possession of these [works] ought to be in the hands of the city," while others emphasized the shortcomings of the company.[47]

Meanwhile the defenders of private ownership entered the arena. Most of the argument centered on the cost of purchase, which seemed too high for the debt-ridden government. Some of those who believed in municipal management were convinced that the city could not afford to buy, at least until its financial position improved. However, the fiery Moses Dawson, Jacksonian editor of the *Advertiser*, based his objections on principle. Declaring that he would oppose the proposal even if the price were much less than $30,000, he warned that public "ownership would be a sink of corruption. The patronage of the council would be so much augmented that it would lead to endless contests for places and appointments." But Dawson was no advocate of laissez-faire. He suggested that the corporation lend the company the money for expansion and recommended a small annual subsidy.[48] The proponents of private management ultimately staved off the attack, but distrust of the company remained, and several times before 1830 the government had to take action against it for failure to fulfill the contract.

[46] Cincinnati, Ordinances, March 31, 1817; November 27, 1818; Cincinnati, Minutes, February 18, 1824; *Cincinnati Advertiser*, April 11, 1826. There was 670 feet of iron piping, but the bulk of the construction was wooden.

[47] Cincinnati, Minutes, February 18, 1824; *Cincinnati Advertiser*, February 28, 1824.

[48] *Cincinnati Advertiser*, March 2, 1824; February 28, 1824.

In Pittsburgh the discussion brought a different result, with the council deciding on public ownership. The government made the first move in 1821 when, in response to a petition of sixty-one prominent residents, it took over the pumps remaining in private hands. Four years later, a town meeting urged local officials to begin construction of city-wide installations, declaring that the people "will cheerfully defray any taxes necessary for the accomplishment of the object." Within a few months an ordinance provided enabling legislation. Rather than raising the money immediately, however, the bill authorized borrowing, asserting that the project was "a permanent improvement" and the cost ought to be shared by a whole generation of users.[49]

Work began in 1827 under George Evans, a well-known engineer, who drew an annual salary of $1,000. On a much grander scale than Cincinnati's, the plan provided "for raising a larger supply . . . than may be required for many years to come, the Committee believing it to be the finest economy to make such arrangements as would enable the City to increase that supply at a moderate expense." The system took water from the Allegheny and pumped it into a million-gallon reservoir at a rate of 600,000 gallons a day. Two twelve-inch pipes carried the water along Market and Front Streets "to the most central and populous part" of the town. Though original estimates put the cost at $40,000, the ultimate bill was much higher. Paying partly out of current revenue, but mostly by borrowing, local authorities placed a high priority on the completion of the job. "It would perhaps be proper to suspend other public improvements" counseled a citizen's committee in 1825, and three years later the council itself said that finishing the work was "paramount to all other" activity.[50]

After all kinds of difficulties, including defective pipes, a serious leak in the reservoir, and charges that iron manufacturers were fleecing the city, water began to move. The council appointed a

[49] Pittsburgh, City Council Papers, March 3, 1821; *Pittsburgh Statesman*, December 31, 1825; Pittsburgh, Ordinances, February 16, 1826.

[50] Pittsburgh, City Council Papers, January 8, 1827; *Pittsburgh Statesman*, December 31, 1825; Pittsburgh, City Council Papers, February 4, 1828.

committee to supervise the entire operation, giving it broad power to distribute the water, expand facilities, and hire needed help. Regulations prohibited excessive use and fined anyone responsible for "an unusual flow or unnecessary waste." By 1830 a total of 40,495 feet of pipe had been laid, and residents in the neighboring Northern Liberties petitioned for inclusion in the system.[51] The completion of the water works was a major accomplishment, and it gave Pittsburghers, only recently free from the grip of hard times, a well-deserved civic lift.

The only other Western town to move into this field was St. Louis. As early as 1821 there was a general awareness that mounting fire hazards required a better water supply. Two years later Mayor Lane began advocating a city-wide system, a suggestion he repeated annually for five years. In 1829 the council offered $50 for the best plan, only to discover that no one had the "necessary information." A committee then made inquiries in Philadelphia and New Orleans "on the subject of conveying water and the best means of conveying it." Within a few months local authorities signed a contract with Wilson and Company.[52] By 1830 work had begun on installations, but no water moved through the pipes until the next decade.

ꝗ

Growing populations also presented increased health hazards. Overcrowding, shortages of good water, poor sanitation, and inadequate medical facilities produced frequent epidemics and kept the incidence of sickness high. In Louisville this problem became the central issue of the twenties, while other cities faced recurrent crises. Almost every year the hot weather brought trouble, and no summer passed without grim "news" of rampant smallpox or yellow

---

[51] Pittsburgh, City Council Papers, January 21, 1829; *Pittsburgh Mercury*, January 1, 1828; Pittsburgh Ordinances, February 23, 1829; Pittsburgh, Minutes, December 27, 1830; September 27, 1830.

[52] *Missouri Gazette*, February 7, 1821; St. Louis, Minutes, April 14, 1821; May 4, 1829; June 9, 1829; September 15, 1829.

fever. Actually the situation was seldom as bad as the rumors. A few cases were easily transformed into a dangerous siege. But the exaggeration was itself significant, because it reflected the fears of urbanites, most of whom were haunted by disasters in Eastern cities, especially Philadelphia's yellow fever epidemic in 1793.

To meet this problem municipalities assumed broad powers. "The security of the public health is of primary importance," a Cincinnati committee declared, "and should ever employ the zeal, the foresight of those to whom Providence has given the direction of public affairs." Indeed, this responsibility transcended all others. When the Ohio metropolis adopted an ordinance requiring all slaughtering to take place outside of the town's crowded center, officials asserted that while they hesitated to obstruct "any individual or class of their fellow citizens, in carrying out of their business and occupations," they nonetheless felt that "in the present instance they have a paramount duty to perform. The public health calls for the intervention of the power of the council; and we do believe that every other consideration vanishes when put in competition with it." [53]

Fortified with this theory of wide responsibility, local governments strove to improve conditions and head off major crises. They moved especially against contagious diseases, which constituted the most consistent and dangerous peril. By the twenties resistance to vaccination had subsided, and many cities required it against smallpox and chicken pox. Municipalities provided free treatment for the poor, and in some places paid most of the bill for other residents. In addition, river towns tried to protect themselves against the introduction of disease from the outside by searching vessels for afflicted passengers or contaminated goods.

As long as the contagious cases were few, officials left the matter in the hands of individual physicians. Hence in 1817 during a smallpox siege a Pittsburgh committee declared that the doctors were doing well enough so as "not to require any interference on the part of the council." [54] If the menace increased, however, the city

[53] Cincinnati, Minutes, April 26, 1826; October 15, 1823.
[54] Pittsburgh, City Council Papers, May 12, 1817.

stepped in, quarantining the patients or removing them from the town altogether.[55] In severe emergencies, some went even further. During an epidemic in 1817, Louisville authorities took over John Gwathmey's textile factory for hospital purposes, ordering the managers to "suspend all further work therein, and the sales and manufactures of cotton until further directions of the board." [56]

In addition to these emergency measures, communities tried to meet the problem on a long-range basis. The establishment of a board of health was the most common remedy. Louisville, concerned over the gravity of its own situation, led the way in the spring of 1822, St. Louis followed suit a few months later, and Cincinnati created its commission in 1826. Equipped with broad powers, the new bodies were charged with securing the city "from the evils, distresses, and calamities of contagious, malignant, and infectious diseases." The committees varied in composition, but they usually included laymen as well as physicians and local officials. For a time Cincinnati paid its members, though generally they served without salary.[57] Despite this attention, however, the problem persisted, and soon boards were dealing with questions well beyond their original jurisdiction.[58]

The mounting volume of illness compelled larger communities to build hospitals. Since local funds were insufficient, municipal

[55] In addition, Cincinnati assessed fines from $100 to $300 on those knowingly bringing contagious diseases into the city. Cincinnati, Ordinances, May 12, 1826.

[56] Louisville, Trustees Book, July 5, 1817. The occupation lasted over three months; *ibid.*, October 10, 1817.

[57] Louisville, Trustees Book, May 14, 1822; St. Louis, Ordinances, September 12, 1822; Cincinnati, Ordinances, April 26, 1826; Cincinnati, Ordinances, May 12, 1826.

[58] Not all boards, however, faithfully fulfilled their responsibilities. In 1829 *The Western Journal of the Medical and Physical Sciences* complained that "more than twelve months ago, the City Council of Cincinnati instituted a Board of Health; and delegated to it a variety of advisory and other powers. . . . It is believed . . . that the said conservators of the public health, have but seldom been together." The editors suggested that henceforth the board be composed *"entirely* of medical gentlemen." *The Western Journal of the Medical and Physical Sciences*, II (1829), 221.

authorities turned to the states for assistance. The cities felt justified in this request for two reasons. In the first place, though they had done much themselves, the job was simply too large for their limited resources. Furthermore, they urged that the problem was not simply a local one, since a large influx of people from the outside constantly aggravated the situation. "We generally have on our hands a greater number of sick, than of right belong to us," St. Louis's mayor told his councilmen. "The traveller who sickens in the wilds around us, exerts all his might to reach this point, in the hope of finding more comforts here than where he may chance to become ill." Hence municipalities felt, as Lane put it, that "the county ought to contribute, the state itself ought to extend its arm." [59]

The logic and the need seemed persuasive, and many states assisted cities in hospital construction. Sometimes legislatures taxed auction sales for that purpose; in other instances they authorized lotteries to raise the money. Private contributions, often including land and buildings, and municipal funds provided additional support. By the twenties only Pittsburgh lacked such medical facilities, and even there the movement was only a few years away from success. The new institutions were crude but promising. In Cincinnati and Lexington they benefited from use by local medical schools, and everywhere physicians welcomed the opportunity to furnish better care. Financial difficulties, however, reduced the effectiveness of the hospitals, and frequent reports revealed that conditions were often unsatisfactory. Nevertheless their establishment made possible a level of medical treatment in urban communities which was not available in the countryside.

Despite many precautions and improved facilities, Western cities continued to live under a mantle of anxiety. Later, the epidemic of 1832 proved these fears to be justified, but even before then town dwellers had learned the hard way the full scope of the danger. And none knew it better than the people of Louisville. Completely surrounded by stagnant ponds and always crowded with river travelers, the Falls City suffered more than any other place. In 1817 smallpox

[59] St. Louis, Minutes, April 14, 1823.

struck the community, causing a civic emergency which lasted three months. The next years were calmer, but 1822 brought a real catastrophe. In mid-June cases of "bilious fever" began to increase. On August 3 the *Public Advertiser* made the grim admission that the city was "sorely afflicted." Within a month over 120 fatalities had been registered inside the corporation and a score more in neighboring Shippingport. A cool September had a "happy effect" on the epidemic, and the worst was then over, though mild attacks continued.[60]

The epidemic's damage to the town and its reputation provoked a demand for the draining of the stagnant water on the city's edge. For two decades there had been sporadic attacks on the problem, but they were shortlived and only temporarily successful at best. This time officials, determined to wipe out the menace, gave the project the highest priority. Other expenses were trimmed or postponed while work on the swamps got under way. The legislature authorized a lottery to raise $60,000, the Louisville Theater played a benefit for the "Pond Fund," and the council appropriated generously. Later a Town Engineer was appointed and instructed to "fix on some general plan" to give coordination to the effort. For six years this activity was "the settled policy" of the government and its major enterprise.[61]

Despite this official enthusiasm, interest often lagged. As early as 1823, an editor, fearing a tragic encore to the preceding year, complained that "no sooner are we completely over the effects of a 'spell of sickness,' than avarice seems to resume her sway, and each man begins to look out for himself." Yet the city persisted, building sewers and drains and filling in ponds. By the end of the decade conditions were much improved (as "the limited incomes of our physicians generally attest," an editor observed), and the urgency surrounding the question declined. Of course, Louisville was still

[60] *Louisville Public Advertiser*, August 3, 1822; September 4, 1822; September 7, 1822.

[61] *Louisville Public Advertiser*, January 15, May 21, 1823; Louisville, Trustees Book, March 21, 1823; July 1, 1826; Louisville, City Journal, February 27, 1829.

exposed to diseases brought in by visitors, but it had done much to reduce its own hazards. And the *Public Advertiser* could take justifiable pride in announcing that the "Graveyard of the West" had fewer deaths in 1829 than any other city in the Valley.[62]

Less spectacular campaigns were carried on elsewhere. Communities became increasingly conscious of the need for cleanliness and sanitation. The number and competence of doctors rose, especially after the opening of the Transylvania and Cincinnati medical colleges. Drug houses sprang up to serve hospitals, physicians, and patients. This concentration of professional skills and equipment made the cities the West's health centers, and many contemporaries thought the towns, despite the problems occasioned by population growth, had less sickness than the hinterland. In 1819 the *Pittsburgh Gazette* expressed a common feeling when, while reporting an outbreak of dysentery in the neighboring area, it asserted that "this fact confirms a position, which is the fruit of many years of observation, viz., that Pittsburgh is more healthy than the country." [63] Generalizations on this question are difficult to make, but the evidence indicates that both medical conditions and care were better in the cities than on farm and frontier.

By 1830 urban communities had come to grips with most of their pressing problems. The power of local governments had been significantly widened either by charter changes or by usage, and a group of new leaders brought a broader view to city affairs. Indeed, even a hint of municipal planning emerged from the constant effort of authorities to solve urgent questions. Though financial resources remained slender, the return of economic prosperity in the mid-twenties furnished a sturdy base for expanding revenues. The larger towns felt able to embark on such ambitious projects as city-wide water and gas lighting systems. All improved the pro-

[62] *Louisville Public Advertiser*, May 21, 1823; October 3, 1827; September 12, 1829.
[63] *Pittsburgh Gazette*, September 7, 1819.

tection of life and property, bettered the conditions of their streets and harbors, and made strides in the promotion of health and medical care. Yet many problems remained, and the large number of migrants moving into the Valley every year underlined the need for continuous activity. However, city dwellers who had watched their towns double many times over in a few decades could be excused if they saw opportunity rather than danger in these swelling populations.

Chapter 10

The Urban Dimension of Western Life

By 1830 the rise of the cities was one of the dominant facts of Western life. Visitors continued to be startled by it, though a growing volume of travel literature emphasized this urban development. "Notwithstanding all that I have heard about the improvement and growth of Cincinnati," John Sharkey wrote in 1829, "the sight of it filled one with astonishment — I could not have imagined . . . anything like it . . . either as to the extent or the style and magnificence of its buildings." This was a common response. At about the same time James Hall declared that "strangers, with scarce an exception, are struck upon walking through Cincinnati, with the apparent age and finish of the place; with the taste shown in the construction of private houses; with the appearance of wealth, cultivation, and polish." [1]

Nor was the Ohio metropolis unique. "This is one of the examples to be met with in the western country," another visitor observed in 1832, "of towns springing into importance within the memory of comparatively young men — A log home is still standing which is shown as the first habitation built by the backwoodsmen, who squatted in the forest where now stands a handsome and flourishing city." Speaking of the entire valley, Morgan Neville remarked that "the stranger views here with wonder, the rapidity with which cities sprang up in the forests; and with which barbarism retreats before the approach of art and civilization." [2]

[1] J. Sharkey, "Travel Diary, July 16–29 [1829] of Voyage Down the Ohio River from Point Pleasant Virginia to the Mouth of the Ohio" (Photostatic copy, Filson Club, Louisville, Kentucky), unfolioed; *Illinois Monthly Magazine*, II (1832), 467.

[2] S. A. O'Ferral, *A Ramble of Six Thousand Miles through the United States of America* (London, 1832), 66; Neville, "The Last of the Boatmen," 108.

Indeed, this urban growth was so extensive that old municipal boundaries could no longer contain the new settlers, and many spilled over into the suburbs. For instance, Allegheny, Bayardstown, Birmingham, Lawrenceville, Kensington, Hayti, and East Liberty added nearly 10,000 to Pittsburgh's population, bringing the total up to 22,000. The same was true of Cincinnati, where 2,000 people lived in Eastern and Northern Liberties. In Louisville, Preston's and Campbell's "enlargements" and Shippingport and Portland swelled the city's total to 13,000. St. Louis and Lexington had proportionally as many suburbanites.

Oddly enough, this centrifugal movement was strongest in Pittsburgh, where geographic factors made expansion most difficult. The rivers seemed to preclude municipal enlargement on the north, south, and west, while steep heights to the east suggested another natural limit. James Hall once remarked that Grant's Hill sharply divided town and country. "The city lay beneath . . . ," he wrote, "enveloped in smoke — the clang of hammers resounded from numerous manufactories — . . . churches, courts, hotels and markets and all the 'pomp and circumstance' of busy life, were presented in one panoramic view." Yet on the other side of the summit "were all the silent soft attractions of rural living." [3] Thus confined, Pittsburgh's expansion took place on the narrow flats along the Allegheny and Monongahela. Some of the building was residential, but commerce and industry claimed most of it, creating factory suburbs which were miniatures of the Iron City itself.

Along the northeastern boundary stretched the Northern Liberties, which had been laid out "as a continuation of Pittsburgh" and boasted the impressive Phoenix cotton factory and the Juniata Iron Works. South of the city, along the Monongahela, lay Kensington, heavily industrialized, with "two steam rolling mills, a wire manufactory, an air foundry, a steam grist mill, a steam engine for turning and grinding brass and iron, and a brewery." [4] Across the river rose Birmingham and Sidneyville, which quickly became the producers of the famous "Pittsburgh glass." There were other

[3] James Hall, *Letters from the West* (London, 1828), 22–23.
[4] Jones, *Pittsburgh in 1826*, 8; 9.

suburbs, too, but none so important as Allegheny, a town which grew so rapidly that many wondered if it would not some day compete with the Iron City itself.

By 1830 many of these surrounding communities had been granted privileges of self-government, but in every other important respect they remained tied to the metropolis. In fact, in commenting on Allegheny, the *Gazette* declared that the bridge over the river was "only a covered street, and the village part of our city." Perhaps Jones expressed the position of the suburbs best when he wrote that "they contribute to, and are supplied from the great *center*, with which their strength and prosperity are intimately connected."[5] And, despite the great discrepancy in power, relationships between the parent city and its offspring remained good, often being marked by mutual help rather than jealousy.

The growth of suburbs around Pittsburgh, though more extensive than elsewhere, was typical. Louisville and Cincinnati expanded rapidly, and, like the Iron City, brought cross-river settlements into their orbit. In fact, the Kentucky villages opposite Cincinnati arose as extensions of the metropolis. A traveler noticed that the streets of Covington were "laid out as to appear as a continuation of those of Cincinnati." Another visitor included Newport in the same observation. "The streets of these towns," wrote Woods, "are laid out to correspond with those of Cincinnati, so that from the upper part of the city you see the streets of Newport and Coverly [Covington], without perceiving the river between them, and thus the whole appears but one town."[6] Jeffersonville and New Albany, Indiana, were not bound so closely to Louisville, but by 1830 their chance for independent growth had lessened, and they increasingly became economic appendages of the Falls City.

And already urban centers encountered the familiar problems suburbs create. As early as 1813 the Lexington assessor reported difficulty in collecting taxes in the outlots because residents there

---

[5] *Pittsburgh Gazette*, November 19, 1830; Jones, *Pittsburgh in 1826*, 8.

[6] George Ogden, *Letters from the West* (New Bedford, 1823), 21; John Woods, *Two Years' Residence in the Settlement on the English Prairie, in the Illinois Country, United States* (London, 1822), 101.

"alleged no benefit resulted to them from either the Watch, Lamps, fire buckets or fire companies." In other places people on the periphery seemed to be enjoying advantages without paying for them. In 1823, for example, Cincinnati officials complained that those living on the town's edge did not contribute "their quantum of taxes." Six years later the St. Louis council petitioned the state legislature to enlarge the corporation, because so many settlers just beyond the borders had "all the benifits [*sic*] of a City residence without any of its burdens." Furthermore, the memorial prophesied that "altho the evil is now in its infancy it promises to increase greatly in a few years and produce much evil." In Louisville the same worries initiated a movement to annex Shippingport and Portland, with the hope of paring down expenses and spreading the financial responsibility more equitably.[7] Though every city boasted of its growing suburban brood, it also learned that parenthood is a source of problems as well as pride.

The rise of the suburbs was an index of the increasing pace of the West's urbanization. Another measure of this process was the growing specialization of activity. The cities offered continually widening opportunities, which attracted mechanics, merchants, and professional men from the East as well as enterprising youths from the countryside. The urban economy rested on occupational diversity, and the larger the town the greater the need for skilled people. Hence those who hoped to develop special talent settled in the cities. "I have from serious reflection become convinced that a town will suit your profession better than the country," a Kentuckian wrote to an aspiring lawyer; "your time will not be divided between law and farming but your exertions and attention [can be spent] in becom[ing] one among the first in your calling."[8] This ad-

[7] Lexington, Trustees Book, June 3, 1813; Cincinnati, Minutes, June 25, 1823; *Louisville Public Advertiser*, October 10, 1829.

[8] L. Grayson to J. C. Breckenridge, January 7, 1814, MS, Breckenridge Papers (Library of Congress).

vantage was evident from the very beginning, and it is not surprising that early documents disclose extensive specialization in transmontane towns.

As early as 1802 Cramer's *Almanac* counted forty-six different classes of master tradesmen in Pittsburgh in addition to merchants, tavernkeepers, manufacturers, physicians, and attorneys. Four years later Lexington revealed even greater diversity, the directory cataloguing over fifty occupations, which ran all the way from nail makers to portrait painters. Of course, cities as they grew could support larger numbers within each occupation. For instance, a Cincinnati manufacturing census in 1810 numbered 46 shoemakers, 52 blacksmiths, 25 coopers, 22 saddlers, and 21 hatters. By 1822 the Queen City's mechanics had thirty-two different organizations based on separate crafts.[9] The division of labor extended even to the mercantile community, where the general store gradually gave way to a variety of retailers concentrating in certain commodities. At the end of the period, Western towns presented an employment complex comparable to that of older and larger places in the East.

Another and perhaps even more significant mark of increasing urbanization was the growing tendency of residents to work outside their homes. While settlements were still villages, most shopkeepers, tradesmen, and professional people lived and labored in the same place, using the front or first floor of the building for their calling and the rear or second floor for lodging. As towns grew, this practice broke down. Large numbers now sought employment in factories, mercantile firms, or construction projects. Rising rents forced many to move their families out of the shop into residential districts. Of all indices of urbanization probably none is more important than the separation of work from home. Unfortunately, information on this development is not extensive; but it is quite conclusive.

The *Directory of 1815* reveals that in Pittsburgh this phenomenon appeared very early. Iron and glass factories absorbed the largest

<hr/>

[9] C. R. Staples, *The History of Pioneer Lexington, 1779–1806* (Lexington, Kentucky, 1939), 253–259; *Liberty Hall* (Cincinnati), January 1, 1811; June 29, 1822.

segment of the population, and even the skilled trades began to divorce the place of work from living quarters. Housing statistics in a directory four years later confirm this tendency. Of the city's 1,873 buildings, 1,140 served as dwellings, while the rest were mills, warehouses, taverns, factories, stores, and shops.[10] This meant that nearly half the construction was non-residential, being used exclusively for commercial or industrial purposes.

Other Western towns experienced the same development, though at a slower pace, since none was as heavily industrialized. In 1815 Daniel Drake estimated that Cincinnati contained 1,100 buildings "exclusive of kitchens, smoke houses and stables." About 660 were used as dwellings, while "public buildings, shops, warehouses and offices" made up the rest. Four years later the same totals (this time counted more carefully) jumped to 1,890 and 1,003. The Queen City differed from its upriver rival, however, in that most of its business construction was in warehouses, grocery stores, and commercial edifices, rather than factories, shops, and mills. Employment figures in the same year provide an even better illustration of the separation of work from residence. Excluding manufacturers and retailers, 234 shops hired 1,238 men, demonstrating that in the category of skilled trades and services most urbanites earned their living away from home.[11]

This detachment of work from residence was an important index of the spread of urban institutions. It emphasized the growing specialization of economic functions; it modified housing patterns by dividing towns between residential and commercial buildings; and, indeed, by taking the breadwinner out of his dwelling, it altered the habits of family life. The arrangement contrasted sharply with rural practice, where the farmer's entire existence revolved around the connection between his land and hearth, where he performed nearly every task within sight of his house, and where father and son, mother and daughter constituted a tight economic unit.

Increasing impersonalization was another result of urban growth.

[10] *Directory of 1819*, 48. Many of the dwellings were occupied by two or more families, since 2,360 families resided in 1,140 buildings.

[11] Drake, *Statistical View*, 134; *Directory of 1819*, 48–51.

As populations expanded, the easy familiarity of village and small town diminished. "A next door neighbor is, with them, frequently unknown," a visitor to Pittsburgh observed in 1818, "and months and years pass, without their exchanging with each other the ordinary compliments of friendship and goodwill. As in the case with many of the cities of Europe, a simple partition renders unknown, for a great length of time, those who live under the same roof." [12]

The development of neighborhoods restored some of the old friendliness and intimacy, but the appearance of these subdivisions also underlined the breakdown of the sense of close community characteristic of smaller places. No one any longer knew everyone else, and despite physical proximity people counted most of their fellow residents as strangers. To some the loss of familiarity was lamentable. "Do we enjoy the real, unfashionable contentment with which our rural predecessors were blessed?" asked the Pittsburgh directory in 1826. "Where are our pleasant social tea-drinkings; our sturdy blind-man's bluff; our evening chit-chat, in which both sexes participated, without thought of visiting cards, warning calls, or preconcerted 'accidentals'? Where are the strawberry hustings; the unclassed balls; the charming promenades, of which all partook with light hearts?" [13]

The appearance of city directories reflected this growing impersonality. These lists of residents by street and occupation became handy guides for individual reference and for business purposes. They also signaled the end of the day when such information was common property. Of course, the largest towns needed them first. Lexington published a directory as early as 1806, Pittsburgh followed in 1815, Cincinnati in 1819, and St. Louis two years later. Louisville alone was tardy, not producing one until 1832. Compiled by editors, civic leaders, or, as in the case of Paxton in St. Louis, experienced census men, they lacked official authority and varied in comprehensiveness and value. Yet the directories met a

[12] Estwick Evans, *A Pedestrious Tour, of Four Thousand Miles, Through the Western State and Territories During the Winter and Spring of 1818* (Concord, N. H., 1819), 252–53.

[13] Jones, *Pittsburgh in 1826*, 44.

real demand, and they were redone or brought up to date frequently. Cincinnati issued four and Pittsburgh three before 1831, and when Louisville's first finally appeared, the publisher asserted that new editions ought to be brought out annually "as in other cities of equal and greater population and business." [14]

Another mark of the widening inroads of urbanism was the disappearance of grass and foliage. As a result of continuous construction, yards and lots were reduced, grassy areas pared down, and trees destroyed. Despite sporadic protests, the attrition was relentless. Paved landings and warehouses despoiled waterfronts, contiguous building filled empty spaces in business districts, and constant subdividing diminished natural groves in residential sections. During the twenties residents in the larger cities mobilized to save what was left, and even sparked campaigns for restoration. Though urban foliage found no greater single champion than St. Louis's William Carr Lane, Cincinnati organized the most lively city-wide movement. In 1830 its spokesman offered a comprehensive program which included a fashionable boulevard on Fourth Street, a "highly attractive retreat" around Deer Creek, and shade trees along most thoroughfares. Farsighted conservationists warned that delay would be costly. "Some future generation," an editor predicted, "like our contemporaries of New York will destroy blocks of buildings, and expend millions of money to obtain what may now be had with ease and economy." [15]

The destruction of rural features not only separated the metropolis from the countryside, but also distinguished the larger towns from the smaller. James Hall, making this distinction in the *Illinois Monthly Magazine*, wrote that "in the term *town*, we include only such large towns, as have brick houses, paved streets, market houses, mayors, merchants, manufactories and people of fashion." Lesser places he called villages, where "the forest trees are still growing in the streets, the birds warble out side windows, and the

[14] R. W. Otis, *The Louisville Directory for the Year 1832* (Louisville, 1832), iv.

[15] *Cincinnati Chronicle and Literary Gazette*, July 24, 1830; *Saturday Evening Chronicle* (Cincinnati), October 27, 1827.

solitude of the country is all around . . . , all of which are *capital* things, though they may not be very city-like." [16]

As rural compounds disappeared, residents sought relief from urban life in resorts in the hinterland. The well-to-do traveled many miles to escape. Indeed, the distance was significant, for any retreat near town was too accessible to be exclusive. For example, outside Louisville some sulphur and mineral springs offered a choice spot for those fleeing "the disagreeable atmosphere of the cities," and McMurtrie observed that its only objectionable feature was "its proximity to Louisville, it being so near, it requires neither equipage nor the expenses of a journey to arrive there, things absolutely required to render every place of the kind perfectly *a la mode*." [17] Cincinnati's elite congregated at Kentucky's Big Bone Lick, where they spent summer months in play and relaxation. "Horace," himself a devotee of the famed watering place, lavished a long ode on its beauty and, in some passages, its therapy.

> Tis pleasant, after having long
>   Endured the city's smoke and noise,
> To quit awhile the busy throng
>   For humbler scenes and purer joys.
>
> . . . .
>
> Adieu to dust, and smoke and noxious air;
>   To dandies, flirts, and flirters of the city;
> To merchants overborne with anxious care,
>   And debts they ne'er can pay — the more's the pity. [18]

When extended vacations were not possible, the social set found its recreation in nearby rural settings. As early as 1811, Cincinnatians sponsored fox hunts through Mill Creek's wooded countryside. During the next decade, however, the town spread out over this area and forced sportsmen to take weekend trips before they could find game and seclusion. The Independent Hunting Company made annual excursions to Chestnut Knobs, Indiana, "fully and properly equipt with dogs, guns and camp equipage for a systematic *hunt*."

[16] *Illinois Monthly Magazine*, II (1832), 474.
[17] McMurtrie, *Sketches of Louisville*, 170.
[18] "Horace," *Odes of Horace in Cincinnati* (Cincinnati, 1822), 40, 44.

This development was ironic. Less than a generation before, every settler owned fire arms, yet now by the twenties shooting had become a novelty. "They enjoyed their new mode of life with great zest," the club's secretary reported, and they "returned to the city with their venison, all in good health and much invigorated by their rural exercise." [19]

Most urbanites could not afford the luxury of vacations or hunts and had to be content with more modest resorts. In St. Louis they frequented the Mound Gardens, just beyond the city line, which afforded "a delightful and pleasant retreat from the noise, heat and dust of a busy town." Louisvillians crossed the river to neighboring springs or strolled along the Kentucky side of the river. A number of commercial gardens presented some relief to Cincinnati's residents by offering artificial groves that were "sufficiently detached from the bustle and confines of business" to be "tranquil" and "refreshing." [20]

From Pittsburgh, however, there was no easy escape. "No public garden within the city, or its environs," Jones protested, "affords a retreat from the drudgery of business, the heat of the sun, or the smoke of the chimies [*sic*]." Even weekends seemed oppressive. "Sunday is a fearfully long and wearisome day for most of us. Those who do not choose to attend one of our numerous churches, who cannot afford to take a canter on horseback, or pay for a seat in a hack, as far as the Arsenal, Gillespie's or Noodle Doosey, in the pleasant time of the year must be content to promenade the streets, saunter to the bank of the Monongahela to view the steamboats; stroll across one of the bridges, or climb the hills that look down so invitingly upon us." [21] By 1830 urban expansion had almost obliterated the reminders of rural days, and as it did so it emphasized the growing cleavage between town and country.

[19] *Liberty Hall* (Cincinnati), February 20, 1811; *Saturday Evening Chronicle* (Cincinnati), December 13, 1828; *Liberty Hall*, November 22, 1825.

[20] Paxton, *St. Louis Directory; Liberty Hall* (Cincinnati), June 5, 1815.

[21] Jones, *Pittsburgh in 1826*, 46.

Urban growth in the West, even in its most expansive periods, was not completely haphazard. From the earliest days, residents and civic leaders had a vision of the kind of city they wanted to build. This image was drawn from the great metropolises of the East — New York, Boston, Baltimore, and especially Philadelphia — whose ways, development, and culture young settlements hoped to emulate. Though Western towns arose on virtually unsettled land, indeed, in some cases on the very edge of the frontier, and though their situation freed them from old restraints and traditions, their deepest urge was to be like the great cities across the mountains. In short, the challenge of the West, far from producing a bold and fresh response from urbanites, led to a concerted effort to bring established institutions and ways to the new country.

This emulation characterized nearly every aspect of development — from the width of streets to the fashions of people who strolled along them. In fact, the imitation was so obvious that travelers constantly commented on it. "Rambled through and round the city of Lexington," William Faux recorded; "the outline is large and resembling Philadelphia, particularly in the form and construction of the market." "The town is built on the model of Philadelphia," Henry B. Fearon observed in Cincinnati, "and should it ever become as large, . . . its whole appearance will be more pleasing." Flint noted the New Orleans influence on St. Louis's architecture, while John Cotton remarked that Pittsburgh's streets "are mostly laid out like those of Philadelphia." Smaller towns also followed Eastern leads, and John Palmer, visiting Zanesville, Ohio, pointed out that the plat was drawn up "after the manner of Philadelphia." [22]

Similarly, Western urbanites patterned their institutions and man-

[22] Faux, "Memorable Days in America," in Thwaites, ed., *Western Travels*, XI, 188; H. B. Fearon, *A Narrative of a Journey of Five Thousand Miles Through the Eastern and Western States of America* (London, 1818), 229; Flint, *Recollections*, 110; J. Cotton, "From Rhode Island to Ohio in 1815 — Journal of a Trip Through New York, Philadelphia, Harrisburg, and Pittsburgh to the Pioneer Towns of the State of Ohio," *Journal of American History*, XVI (1922), 46; J. Palmer, *Journal of Travels in the United States of America* (London, 1817), 70.

ners on Atlantic models. For instance, in the establishment of a Mechanics' Institute in Cincinnati, one of the most powerful arguments used was that "various cities of Europe and America" had found such education "beneficial to the interests of the community." The same contention aided the campaign for the St. Louis Philanthropic School, whose advocates asserted that "the plan is now practised upon in Philadelphia, New York and Boston, with great success." Likewise, Dr. Edward H. Stall publicized the opening of his vaccine shop by asserting that "establishments of this kind exist in our eastern cities, and have been found of great public utility." [23]

Anything that conformed to practices in Eastern metropolises appealed to Western townspeople. Thus *Liberty Hall* supported an apprentices' library by declaring that "the experiment has been tried in New York and Albany, and we believe that the most sanguine expectations of the patrons of those institutions, are thus verified." Clothing styles had to have a similar stamp of approval. Pittsburgh's Isaac Roberts ran a typical advertisement in 1810 declaring that his products were "in the latest fashions" and that he had "opened a correspondence with one of the best taylors in Philadelphia, whom he can depend on for the fashions being regularly sent him." [24]

But the most conspicuous area of emulation was urban improvement. Whenever new problems confronted young settlements, their first reaction was to find out how older and larger places had responded to the same question. Believing with Mayor Lane that "experience is the best guide," local officials enquired about municipal practices elsewhere, hoping for *"similar success* with *similar means."* [25] The borrowing, however, was selective, not slavish. Investigation usually revealed a wide variety of possibilities, from which Western cities could choose the most appropriate technique. Nevertheless, the indebtedness was enormous, running all the way

[23] *Liberty Hall* (Cincinnati), November 19, 1828; *Missouri Republican*, December 21, 1826; *Pittsburgh Gazette*, February 2, 1810.

[24] *Liberty Hall* (Cincinnati), January 31, 1821; *Pittsburgh Gazette*, February 2, 1810.

[25] St. Louis, Minutes, April 28, 1825; Pittsburgh, City Council Papers, n.d.

from the general shape of local government to such details as school slates and models of street lamps.

The whole structure of municipal law was determined in consultation with Eastern experience. "We have been informed by the president of the common council . . . ," a Pittsburgh editor stated in 1819, "that in the formation of our code, recourse was had to that of Edinburgh, and many other cities in Europe as well as this country." Five years later, when charter revision became an issue, officials wrote to New York, Philadelphia, and Baltimore for copies of their constitutions and ordinances. The same was true in St. Louis, where the local administration instructed one of its members who made a trip to Philadelphia "to purchase while there a copy of the laws of that city for the use of this board." Mayor Lane, however, illustrated the selectivity of this process when he protested against the unnecessary detail and verbiage in municipal regulations. "I believe we have borrowed, or rather inherited the deformity from the British, & why we do not lay it aside, when so many better examples are before us, is to me wonderful." [26]

Yet virtually no major project was launched without a close study of established urban practices. St. Louis's council instructed its water works committee to "procure from the cities of Philadelphia and New Orleans such information as can be obtained on the subject of conveying water and the best manner of clearing it." When Cincinnati discussed introducing underground sewers, an official group was designated to "ascertain from the city authorities of New York, Philadelphia, Baltimore and Boston, how far the sinking of common sewers is approved in those cities." Pittsburgh undertook gas lighting only after exhaustive research and "very full enquiries at New York and Baltimore." Moreover, the Iron City's fundamental housing ordinance, prohibiting the construction of wooden buildings in the center of town, was "in substance, and nearly in words" taken from a Philadelphia statute of 1796.[27]

[26] *Pittsburgh Gazette*, July 23, 1819; Pittsburgh Minutes, January 17, 1824; St. Louis, Minutes, June 26, 1828; April 28, 1825.

[27] St. Louis, Minutes, June 12, 1829; Cincinnati, Minutes, October 6, 1827; Pittsburgh, City Council Papers, May 10, 1827; *By-Laws and Ordinances of*

Nothing illustrates this process better, however, than the creation of Louisville's school system in 1829. The council sent the new principal, Mann Butler, "to the eastern cities, to examine the most respectable of their *monitorial* establishments." Local residents were proud that theirs was the first city in the new country to adopt public education. Yet it must be noted that this pioneering did not consist in striking out boldly along new paths, but rather in closely copying the achievements of older communities. "It is gratifying to us," an editor remarked, "that Louisville has the honor of taking the lead in the west, as New York did in the East, in the adoption of the monitorial system, which has been so thoroughly tried, and is now so highly approved, in London, Edinburgh, and in our sister states in the East." Butler visited Baltimore, Philadelphia, New York, and Boston, taking detailed notes at each place and submitting them both to the trustees and, through the newspaper, to the people. Obviously satisfied with his findings, he declared that the trip "will save our city funds from . . . expensive errors and fruitless experiments." [28]

A year later the first report of the school committee demonstrated the extent of Louisville's indebtedness. The building was "mainly after the plan of the High School of New York, united with the Public School Rooms of Philadelphia." But the construction material, at least, was indigenous, being "a cement which has been copiously obtained from the beds of the Louisville and Portland Canal." The faculty, however, except for Butler, was imported, one from Columbia, another from Yale, and a third from London. Likewise the curriculum, including reading assignments, derived from "the High School of New York and some of the Boston establishments." The borrowing even reached down to small items such as slates and cards which Butler brought from Philadelphia.[29] Public education thus came to Louisville in answer

the City of Pittsburgh, and the Acts of Assembly Relating Thereto (Pittsburgh, 1828), 252.

[28] *Louisville Public Advertiser*, June 10, 1829; August 12, 1829.

[29] *An Account of the Louisville City School, Together With the Ordinances of the City Council, and the Regulations of the Board of Trustees*

to urgent local demand, but shaped in content and development by Eastern experience.

Though Western towns drew upon the experience of all the major Atlantic cities, the special source of municipal wisdom was Philadelphia. Many Western urbanites had lived or visited there; it provided the new country with most of its professional and cultural leadership. It was the model metropolis. "She is the great seat of American affluence, of individual riches, and distinguished philanthropy," a Pittsburgh editorial declared in 1818. "From her then we have everything to look for." [30] Newspapers often referred to it as "our mother city." But no matter what the precise wording, trans-Allegheny towndwellers expressed their admiration in many ways.

The most flattering, of course, was imitation. From street plans to cultural activity, from the shape of market houses to the habits of people, the Philadelphia influence prevailed. Robert Peterson and John Filson, who had a hand in the founding of Louisville, Lexington, and Cincinnati, borrowed the basic grid pattern of the original plats from the Pennsylvania metropolis. Market location and design came from the same source, as did techniques for fire fighting and police protection. Western towns also followed Philadelphia's leadership in street lighting, water works, and landings. Even the naming of suburbs — Pittsburgh's Kensington and Cincinnati's Liberties — came from the mother city. The result was a physical likeness which struck many travelers, and which Philadelphians themselves recognized. Gideon Burton, for example, remembered his first impression of Cincinnati: "How beautiful this city is," he remarked, "how much like Philadelphia." [31]

Moreover, the Quaker City spirit went beyond streets, buildings, and improvements, reaching into a wide range of human activity. Businessmen, yearly visitors in the East, brought marketing techniques and promotion from there; young labor movements took their

---

for the Government of the Institution (Louisville, 1830), 5ff; *Louisville Public Advertiser*, August 12, 1829.

[30] *Pittsburgh Gazette*, October 27, 1818.

[31] G. Burton, *Reminiscences of Gideon Burton* (Cincinnati, 1895).

platforms from trade union programs in the mother city; employment agencies were "conducted principally on the Philadelphia plan." [32] The same metropolis trained most of the physicians in the West, and a large share of the teachers and ministers. Caspar Wistar's famed Sunday evening gatherings of the intelligentsia provided the idea for Daniel Drake's select meetings of Cincinnati's social and cultural elite. Moreover, Philadelphia furnished the model of the perfect civic leader, for the highest praise that Western towndwellers could bestow upon a fellow citizen was to refer to him as their own "Benjamin Franklin." In short, Philadelphia represented the highest stage of urban development, and progress was measured against this ideal.

But no matter which city provided the model, transmontane towndwellers readily admitted their dependence on the East. Indeed, some thought the process had gone too far. The editor of Cincinnati's *Liberty Hall*, for example, urged his readers to forget what happened across the mountains, and turn "every morning to the west, instead of *worshiping* toward the east — and we shall be right." Others believed that the new country was picking up bad habits along with the good. A visitor to Pittsburgh in 1824, unhappy about its development, explained that its failures were "probably . . . occasioned in a great measure by an idea that it was destined to become one of the greatest cities in the world, and that therefore, it became proper to imitate other great cities as much as possible; — to imitate the evils and defects of other cities, was however, all that was in their power." More specifically, another observer blamed mounting municipal debts on this same tendency. "Because other cities have incurred heavy debts, it is thought wise and proper that Cincinnati should follow the example; and so anxious do they appear . . . in this respect [that] they seem to have lost sight of every other principal object." [33]

Complaints were futile, however, because emulation had deep roots in the experience and background of Western urbanites. Many

[32] *Pittsburgh Mercury*, August 7, 1827.

[33] *Liberty Hall* (Cincinnati), September 4, 1851; *Cincinnati Literary Gazette*, February 28, 1824; *Cincinnati Advertiser*, January 2, 1830.

had been born in Eastern metropolises and many others had visited them. Exact figures are lacking, but the evidence suggests that an extraordinary number of towndwellers in the new country came from other urban communities, and that the large migrations from rural areas did not come until later. These newcomers brought with them some knowledge of city ways which they could draw upon to meet problems in their adopted homes.

This development is most easily traced by looking at the background of some of the West's important urban figures. Cincinnati's Daniel Drake, for instance, though born on the frontier, spent some of his early years in Philadelphia, studying medicine. On returning across the mountains, he entered public affairs and consciously tried to shape the Queen City's future along Philadelphian lines. Indeed, his *Statistical View*, which did so much to establish the reputation of both Drake and Cincinnati, used Mease's *Picture of Philadelphia* as a model.[34] Moreover, in later years Drake taught in Lexington and Louisville, leaving his mark on these communities as well as on the Ohio emporium.

William Carr Lane had similar origins. Born in Western Pennsylvania and later a resident of several places in the Ohio Valley, he went to Philadelphia for medical training. During his five terms as Mayor of St. Louis he often referred to Quaker City practices and urged their adoption. In a different but not less significant fashion, Horace Holley tried to bring the culture and sophistication of Boston to Lexington. And Transylvania's reputation as the "Harvard of the West" not only reflected the preeminence of the university in the new country, but also revealed the exalted objectives of its administrators. No one, however, had a more varied urban background than the printer and editor Joseph Charless, who came to the United States in 1796 and jumped from city to city until he landed in St. Louis in 1808. By that time he had lived in New York and Philadelphia and edited newspapers in Lexington and Louisville. In prescribing for St. Louis, as he did for a quarter century, he drew upon a rich store of urban knowledge.

The same pattern emerges wherever origins can be traced. For

[34] Drake, *Statistical View*, vl.

example, Cincinnati had eleven presidents of its governing council between 1802 and 1819; of these seven had either been born in a large city or lived in one for some time. Only James Findlay seems to have been without any previous urban contact, though his activities were so wide and varied that he must have visited Philadelphia or New Orleans. The evidence on the other three officials is too scanty for judgment.[35] An analysis of the recorders of the council during the same period produces similar results. Unfortunately, directories which dealt with the background of residents in Western cities listed only the state or — in the case of foreign immigrants — the country of origin. Yet it is not hazardous to assert that most of the people in policy-making positions in these towns knew a great deal about other cities from first-hand experience.

The urban origin of Western towndwellers was significant, for it meant that the new cities would be built in the image of older ones. There was little need to experiment, because tried ways and methods were well known and seemed appropriate. Indeed, the newcomers, their lives disrupted by movement, were anxious to recreate as much as possible of the familiar landscape they had left. Hence it is not surprising that Western towns bore a physical likeness to Eastern ones. Even social institutions were shaped by the same impulse. Whatever provided continuity was cherished. Churches, above all, furnished ties, and they multiplied rapidly. Class distinctions and the sense of status, so meaningful in older communities, also came with the migrants. The urge to imitate, then, sprang from deep needs, giving the urban pioneers both a lifeline to the past and a vision of a grand future.[36]

[35] The council presidents were: David Ziegler, 1802–3; Joseph Prince, 1803–4; James Findlay, 1805–6, John S. Gano and Martin Baum, 1807, Daniel Symnes, 1808–9, James Findlay, 1810–11, Martin Baum, 1812, William Stanley, 1813, Samuel W. Davies, 1814, William Correy (Mayor), 1815–9. Greve, *Cincinnati*, 438. Background material comes largely from Greve, supplemented by a variety of sources, including newspapers.

[36] This process was such a natural one that it was repeated very early on a smaller scale in the Ohio Valley itself. In 1815 promoters announced the

Part of Philadelphia's appeal to towndwellers was its leadership among the nation's cities, for nearly every young metropolis in the valley coveted a similar primacy in the West. Indeed, one of the most striking characteristics of this period was the development of an urban imperialism which saw rising young giants seek to spread their power and influence over the entire new country. The drive for supremacy, furthermore, was quite conscious, infusing an extraordinary dynamic into city growth, but also breeding bitter rivalries among the claimants. In the ensuing struggles, the economically strongest survived and flourished, while the less successful fell behind. Smaller places were trampled in the process, some being swallowed up by ambitious neighbors, others being overwhelmed before they could attain a challenging position. The contest, however, produced no final victor. In fact, the lead changed three times, and though Cincinnati commanded the field in 1830, Pittsburgh, Louisville, and St. Louis were still in the running.

The rivalries developed very early. Lexington jumped off to a quick start, but by 1810 Pittsburgh, enjoying a commercial and manufacturing boom, forged ahead. The postwar depression undermined its leadership, however, and Cincinnati moved forward to take its place. The fierce competition led to widespread speculation about the outcome. Most of the prophecy was wishful, stemming from the hopes of boosters and involving doubtful calculations. In 1816, for instance, a Pittsburgher summed up many of the elements of this competition in a chart (with ratings presumably on a scale of excellence from one to ten) designed to illustrate the inevitability of the Iron City's supremacy: [37]

	Pittsburgh	Lexington	Cincinnati
Situation for inland trade and navigation	9	2	6
Adaptness for manufactures . . .	9	3	5

establishment of New Cincinnati farther down the river. *Liberty Hall* commented that "it seems that we too are destined to have a baby-suckling to hang upon our skirts, and vex us with its squeals for nourishment." *Liberty Hall* (Cincinnati), October 2, 1815.

[37] *Pittsburgh Mercury*, February 3, 1816.

Fertility of surrounding soil . . .	2	7	4
Salubrity	9	7	5
Pleasantness and beauty	.3	1	.6
Elegance of scite [*sic*] and environs	1	.3	.6
	30.3	20.3	21.2

Not only did the author work out the estimates in scientific detail, but he also predicted that the totals represented the population (in thousands) which each would reach in 1830.

Before a city could hope to enter the urban sweepstake for the largest prize, it had to eliminate whatever rivals arose in its own area. In many instances the odds in these battles were so uneven that smaller places gave in quickly. In others, a decision came only after a bitter and prolonged struggle. Edwardsville, Illinois, fell easily before St. Louis, but Wheeling's submission to Pittsburgh followed a decade of acrimony. Sometimes defeat meant the end of independence for a town. Louisville, for example, ultimately annexed Shippingport and Portland, while Pittsburgh reached across the river to take in Allegheny. In other cases, the penalty for failure was the lessening of power and prestige. Steubenville and Wheeling, unable to sustain their position against Pittsburgh in the Upper Ohio, had to settle for a much reduced pace of development. The same fate befell Ste. Genevieve, an early challenger of St. Louis's domination of the Mississippi and Missouri. Occasionally a victor reduced its competitor to a mere economic appendage. This is what happened to Jeffersonville and New Albany, Indiana, after Louisville captured the trade of the Falls.

Though struggles for regional primacy characterized the urban growth of the entire West, the most celebrated was Piitsburgh's duel with Wheeling. Both were situated on the Ohio and both hoped to capture its flourishing commerce. Wheeling's great advantage lay in its down-river position, where it outflanked the shoals and rapids which dominated the approach to Pittsburgh. During the late summer, low water made navigation difficult and at times impossible, inducing some merchants to use the Virginia town as a transshipment point to the East. This fact alone made

Wheeling a competitor, for in no other department could it match
the Iron City. Pittsburgh's detractors saw this situation as early as
1793, when the Army considered establishing a post at Wheeling.
Isaac Craig complained that "this new arrangement, . . . has Originated in the Brain of the Gentlemen in Washington who envy
Pittsburgh, and . . . have represented to General Knox, that Navigation is practicable from Wheeling in the dry season." [38] The
same consideration made Wheeling a stop in the mail route to the
West and the Ohio River terminus of the National Road.

Despite these advantages, Wheeling's population barely reached
1,000 by 1815, while Pittsburgh had become the new country's
leading metropolis. A serious rivalry seemed almost ridiculous. But
the postwar depression, felling the Iron City, gave its smaller neighbor the hope of rising on the ruins. This prospect brightened in 1816,
when, after many abortive attempts to change the terminus, the
National Road was completed to Wheeling. Optimism about the
town's future abounded throughout the valley. A Steubenville editor
caught the spirit in verse:

> Wheeling has secured her roads,
> Come waggoners, come and bring your loads.
> Emigrants, come hither, and build a town,
> And make Wheeling a place of renown.

By 1822, 5,000 wagons were arriving annually in the booming settlement. "Wheeling is a thriving place," a traveler observed; "it
bids fair to rival Pittsburgh in the trade of the Western country." [39]

The Iron City, troubled by a stagnant economy and worried about
its future, warily watched the progress of this upstart. Actually,
Wheeling's challenge was only a small part of Pittsburgh's total
problem, but its very ludicrousness made the situation all the more
intolerable. "A miserable Virginia country town, which can never

[38] I. Craig to J. O'Hara, June 15, 1793, MS, Isaac Craig Papers, Carnegie
Library of Pittsburgh.

[39] C. B. Smith, "The Terminus of the Cumberland Road on the Ohio
River" (M.A. Thesis, University of Pittsburgh, 1951), 69; *Western Herald*
(Steubenville), April 12, 1816; Smith, "Cumberland Road," 71; Woods,
Illinois Country, 75.

be more than two hundred yards wide, having the mere advantage of a free turnpike road and a warehouse or two, to become rivals of this *Emporium* of the West!" exclaimed the incredulous editor of the *Statesman*. As Wheeling continued to prosper, Pittsburgh accused its competitor of unfair practices, particularly of circulating the rumor that ships could not go up the river to "the Point." "They have taken to lying," the *Statesman* snapped. "We cannot believe this report," the *Gazette* asserted with more charity; "the citizens with whom we are acquainted in that place, are too honorable to countenance such childish, hurtless falsehood," especially since "everybody acquainted with the river knows that the water is as good if not better above than for 100 miles below." [40]

Civic leaders in Wheeling, feeling their oats and certain that the National Road provided a secure base for unlimited growth, continually goaded the stricken giant. "Strange that a 'miserable Virginia Country Town,' a 'mere village,' should have attracted so much attention at the 'emporium of the West,'" the *Northwestern Gazette* observed. Moreover, it asserted that the difficulty of navigation on the Upper Ohio was not mere rumor. "During the drier part of the season the greater part of the Western Merchants order their goods to Wheeling and *not* to Pittsburgh. This fact is a stubborn and decisive one. It speaks volumes. It is a demonstration." A patronizing condescension expressed an increasing confidence. "Pittsburgh may, if she will, be a large and respectable manufacturing town. She may also retain a portion of the carrying trade," the same source graciously conceded. There seemed no limit to Wheeling's assurance. Travelers reported that its residents were "actually doing nothing but walking about on stilts, and stroking their chins with utmost self-complacency. Every man who is so fortunate as to own about 60 feet front and 120 feet back, considers himself . . . snug." [41]

The next few years demonstrated, however, that history was only teasing. Wheeling's hopes for greatness were soon dashed. The

[40] *Pittsburgh Statesman*, June 2, 1821; *Pittsburgh Gazette*, May 4, 1821.
[41] *Northwestern Gazette* (Wheeling), June 16, 1821; *Pittsburgh Gazette*, December 18, 1818.

National Road proved disappointing as a freight carrier, and Pittsburgh recovered from its depression, once again becoming the urban focus of the Upper Ohio. Though the Virginia town could boast over 5,000 inhabitants in 1830, its rate of growth lagged and its future prospects dimmed. To some shrewd observers the outcome was not unexpected. A Steubenville editor, consoling his readers in 1816 after their efforts to get the National Road had failed, asserted that cities could not be reared on mere highway traffic. "Rely on agriculture and manufactures," he counseled, "and you will do well without the mail or the turnpike bubble — it is not the sound of the coachman's horn that will make a town flourish." [42]

Though Pittsburgh beat back Wheeling's challenge, it could not maintain its Western leadership. Cincinnati, less affected by the postwar collapse, surged by the Iron City and established its primacy throughout the new country. It was not content, however, to win its supremacy by another's injury. Rather it developed its own positive program to widen its commercial opportunities and spread its influence. In fact, the city was so alive with ideas that one visitor referred to it as "that hot bed of projects," and another observed "great plans on foot; whenever two or three meet at a corner nothing is heard but schemes." In broad terms the object of Cincinnati's statesmanship was threefold: to tap the growing trade on the Great Lakes by water links to the Ohio, to facilitate traffic on the river by a canal around the Falls, and to reach into the hinterland with improved roads. Later another canal — this time down the Licking "into the heart of Kentucky" — a bridge across the Ohio, and a railway to Lexington were added. [43] Success would have made the entire valley dependent upon this urban center, and given the Ohio metropolis command of the strategic routes of trade and travel.

This ambitious program caused great concern in Pittsburgh. "We honestly confess," the *Gazette* admitted, that "a canal from the lakes either into the Ohio or the Great Miami . . . adds an-

[42] Smith, "Cumberland Road," 69; *Western Herald* (Steubenville), September 20, 1816.

[43] *Pittsburgh Gazette*, January 22, 1819; February 5, 1819; *Liberty Hall* (Cincinnati), January 21, 1823; November 25, 1825.

other item to the amount of our present uneasiness." By tipping the commerce of the valley northward, Cincinnati would substantially reduce the Iron City's importance as the central station between East and West. "Without this trade," the *Statesman* warned, "what can Philadelphia and Pittsburgh become but deserted villages, compared with their great rivals?"[44] Pennsylvania responded to this threat by improving the turnpike between its urban centers and ultimately constructing an elaborate canal across the mountains. In addition, Pittsburgh proposed to head off Cincinnati by building a water route to Lake Erie or tying into the Ohio system below Cleveland.

The challenge to Cincinnati's supremacy, however, came not only from a resurgent Pittsburgh, but also from a booming downriver neighbor, Louisville. As early as 1819 a visitor noted this two-front war. "I discovered two ruling passions in Cincinnati; enmity against Pittsburgh and jealousy of Louisville." In one regard the Falls City was the more serious rival, because as a commercial center it competed directly with the Ohio emporium. In fact, guerilla warfare between the two towns for advantage in the rural market began early in the century.[45] But the great object of contention was the control and traffic on the river — the West's central commercial artery.

In this contest Louisville held one key advantage. Its strategic position at the Falls gave it command of both parts of the Ohio. All passengers and goods had to pass through the town, except during the few months of high water when even large vessels could move safely over the rapids. It was a clumsy system, and from the earliest days many people envisaged a canal around the chutes. Nothing came of these plans until the coming of the steamboat immensely expanded traffic and made the interruption seem intolerable. Though nearly every shipper favored a canal, it was not until Cincinnati, anxious both to loosen river commerce and weaken a

[44] *Pittsburgh Gazette*, January 22, 1819; *Pittsburgh Statesman*, November 26, 1818.

[45] *Pittsburgh Gazette*, February 5, 1819; *Louisville Public Advertiser*, June 21, 1820.

rival city, put its weight behind the improvement that any real activity developed.

Cincinnati had a deep stake in this project. A canal would not only aid the town generally but also advance the interests of some powerful groups. The mercantile community was anxious to get freer trade, and many residents had large investments in companies which hoped to dig on either the Kentucky or Indiana side of the Falls.[46] Others owned real estate in the area. William Lytle, for example, had large holdings around Portland of an estimated value of between $100,000 and $500,000.[47] Moreover, ordinary Cincinnatians had come to the conclusion that a canal would serve a broad public purpose. Hence in 1817 a town meeting was called to discuss the issue. An editor provided the backdrop: "No question was ever agitated here that involved more important consequences to this town." And from the beginning Louisville was cast as the villain of the piece. *Liberty Hall* referred to it as "a little town" trying to make "all the upper country tributary to it, by compelling us to deposit our goods in its warehouses and pay extravagant prices for transportation around or over the Falls." [48]

Since the Falls City could frustrate any project on Kentucky soil, Cincinnati's first move was to build on the opposite side. The Indiana legislature incorporated the Jeffersonville Ohio Canal Company in 1817, empowering it to sell 20,000 shares of stock at $50 apiece, and authorizing a lottery for $100,000 more. From the outset it was clear that the scheme stemmed from the Queen City. Not only did that town provide more than half the concern's directors, but also the campaign for funds emphasized its role. "The public may be assured that the wealth, influence, enterprise and talents of Cincinnati are at the head of this measure," *Liberty Hall* declared in

[46] For example, see the account of the Ohio Canal Company in *Liberty Hall* (Cincinnati), March 24, 1817.

[47] The William Lytle Collection in the Historical and Philosophical Society of Ohio library includes a series of letters which explain his stake in the canal. He owned most of the land in the Portland area through which the canal ultimately passed. For a statement of its value, see D. McClellan to W. Lytle, October 21, 1817, Lytle Collection.

[48] *Liberty Hall* (Cincinnati), December 29, 1817; March 26, 1817.

1818. Moreover, advocates underlined the stake of the Ohio metropolis, warning residents that if they did not support the drive they "deserved to be hewers of wood and drawers of water" for Louisville. In May 1819 a prominent Cincinnatian gave the ceremonial address as digging began on the Indiana side.[49]

Louisville hesitated to support any canal. The city had flourished on the transportation break, and many inhabitants felt that facilitating travel over the rapids would destroy the very *raison d'être* of the place. That view was probably extreme, but in the short run no one could deny that certain interests were jeopardized. "It must be admitted that the business of a portion of our population would be affected," the *Public Advertiser* confessed. "The storage and forwarding business would probably be diminished — and there might be less use for hacks and drays."[50] Tavern and hotel owners shared this anxiety, while the pilots who guided the ships through the chutes faced almost certain unemployment.

Unwilling to sacrifice these interests and uneasy about the town's future, Louisville leaders tried to deflect the mounting enthusiasm for a canal. Their first strategy was to suggest a small cut around the Falls which would accomodate keelboats and lesser craft. This expedient found few supporters, and Louisville next tried to reduce the pressure by paving the road to Portland and Shippingport, thus, facilitating the transshipment process.[51] But this, too, was inadequate, and within a few years the clamor for a canal became irresistible.

Yet the city still hoped to salvage something out of defeat, to find some compensation for the loss of its strategic position. In 1824 a local editor laid down the conditions. "It is true that we could feel but little interest in opening a canal merely for the purpose of navigation," he conceded. "A canal to be useful . . . should be constructed to give us ample water power, for various and extensive

---

[49] *Liberty Hall* (Cincinnati), June 5, 1818; February 25, 1818; May 20, 1818; May 6, 1818; May 14, 1819.

[50] *Louisville Public Advertiser*, February 7, 1824.

[51] *Liberty Hall* (Cincinnati), March 18, 1816; *Louisville Public Advertiser*, October 16, 1819.

manufacturing establishments; and a sufficient number of dry docks for the building and . . . repair of nearly all the steamboats employed on western waters, should be constructed as necessary appendages." If the project included these items, he declared, then "the citizens of Louisville will be found among its most zealous advocates." [52]

The Falls City could afford to take its pound of flesh, because building on the Indiana side was much less feasible than the Kentucky route. The engineering problems were immensely more complicated, and the cost was nearly three times as great. In 1819 an official committee, comprised of delegates from Virginia, Pennsylvania, Ohio, and Kentucky, estimated the expense of the northern plan at $1,100,000 and the southern one at $350,000.[53] Hence few people acquainted with the situation took seriously the Jeffersonville Ohio Canal Company's enterprise. Yet the disadvantages of the Indiana route were not insurmountable, and Louisvillians realized that in the long run the Falls would be skirted on one side or the other. If they dragged their feet too much, their opponents would press for action regardless of the cost or difficulty. This possibility ultimately brought the Kentucky emporium to its knees.[54]

While Louisville reluctantly yielded at the Falls, Cincinnati pursued the rest of its expansion program. By 1822 the Miami Canal to Dayton was open, and work had begun on the state system which ultimately connected the Great Lakes with the Ohio River. Though the Queen City could claim less success in the Kentucky area, its economic supremacy in the West was not questioned. The new country's largest urban center, it had corralled the bulk of the region's mounting commerce and become the nexus of trade lines that reached from the Atlantic Ocean to the Gulf of Mexico.

Cincinnati's economic primacy, however, did not yet carry with it cultural leadership. This honor still belonged to Lexington, whose polish and sophistication were the envy of every transmontane town. "Cincinnati may be the Tyre, but Lexington is unquestion-

---

[52] *Louisville Public Advertiser*, January 21, 1824.
[53] *Louisville Public Advertiser*, November 17, 1819.
[54] *Louisville Public Advertiser*, February 7, 1824.

ably the Athens of the West," *Liberty Hall* conceded in 1820. This admission reflected a sense of inadequacy which constantly shadowed the Queen City and compromised its claim to total supremacy. One resident suggested an ambitious lecture program to overcome the deficiency and "convince those persons at a distance who pronounce us as a *Commercial* people alone, that we have here, both the *Tyre* and the *Athens* of the West." Another observer, though not armed with a remedy, made the same point. "It may be well for us," he counseled, "when we can catch a moment from the grovelling pursuits of commercial operations, to cull and admire the varied sweets of those literary and scientific effusions, which have stamped Lexington as the headquarters of *Science and Letters* in the Western country." [55]

The establishment and success of Transylvania University aggravated this inferiority complex. Not only did it lend prestige to another place, but it also lured local youths to its classrooms. The *Western Spy* admitted that it was "particularly mortifying to see the College of a neighboring state attract both Students and Professors" from the Ohio metropolis. In the early twenties Cincinnati countered with a medical school which it hoped would become a "powerful rival" and "ultimately go beyond" the Kentucky institution.[56] But it was not until financial difficulties and fire brought down Transylvania that the Queen City could claim cultural parity with its Blue Grass rival.

Lexington's position also bred jealousy in Louisville. Though the larger and more prosperous of the two by 1825, the Falls City had to concede that intellectual primacy rested with its Kentucky neighbor. This admission was not easy to make, because the two towns had been bitter foes for many years. They contended for political leadership in the state; earlier, in fact, each had hoped to become its capital. Moreover, their economic interests often collided, with Lexington depending upon manufacturing and protection and Louis-

[55] *Liberty Hall* (Cincinnati), May 27, 1820; December 17, 1819; May 27, 1820.

[56] *Western Spy* (Cincinnati), October 13, 1817; *Liberty Hall* (Cincinnati), January 14, 1823.

ville emphasizing commerce and wanting freer trade. Neither yielded readily to the other on any issue. Yet the cultural leadership of the Blue Grass town was too obvious to be denied, and, from the Falls City viewpoint, it was certainly too important to be permanently surrendered.

There was, however, something of a family quarrel about this rivalry. Despite their differences, both professed love for mother Kentucky, and occasionally one deferred to the other out of filial pride. In 1820, for example, Louisville's *Public Advertiser* supported state aid to Translyvania, explaining that "distinguished institutions of learning in our own state, where education from its cheapness, shall be within the reach of the poor, is the *pivot* on which the grandeur of the state depends." In addition, the Falls City stood to gain by its success. "Louisville cannot be jealous of Lexington," the same newspaper declared; "her future interest is measurably blended with that of Transylvania University; for as that flourishes Lexington will become a more extensive and important customer to her in a commercial point of view." Likewise, when Lexington tried to get money for a hospital, its old foe offered support, but for perhaps less elevated reasons. If the Blue Grass got such an institution, "one of the same kind at this place cannot, consistently, be refused," the editor observed.[57]

And nothing forced the two to discover common interests more quickly than the appearance of a hostile outsider. When Cincinnati planned a medical school to compete with Transylvania, Louisville stood behind the testimony of the university, whose spokesman urged the state to give additional money to the institution. Otherwise, he warned, "in the struggle that must ensue, we of Transylvania will be compelled to enter the lists naked and defenceless, our opponents of Cincinnati being . . . armed. The issue of such a conflict cannot be doubted. We shall certainly be vanquished and your young men will . . . repair to the eastern schools for medical education, or Kentucky must become tributary

[57] *Louisville Public Advertiser*, September 20, 1820; September 27, 1820; December 20, 1820.

to the state of Ohio." [58] Lexington reciprocated when the Queen City threatened a canal on the Indiana side of the river.

Kind words were few, however, and mutual aid sporadic. Usually the two communities did little to conceal their animosity. In fact, Louisville had no sooner supported Transylvania's expansion than it began again its vicious barrage on the school and its town. The attack stemmed from a mixture of political, economic, and urban motives, but it centered on the university because it was at once the symbol of Lexington's importance and its most vulnerable spot. The city's economy never recovered from the postwar depression and only its cultural renaissance kept stores and shops open. If the college failed, all failed. This was understood in the Falls City. Indeed, the *Public Advertiser* noted that the "ablest and best citizens" of the Blue Grass metropolis had tried to give a "new impetus" to the place by the encouragement of its "literary establishments." [59] Knowingly, then, Louisville struck at Lexington where it would hurt most.

Nor was there anything gentle about the tactics. In 1816, during the first debate over state assistance to Transylvania, John Rowan from the Falls City argued that the institution ought to be moved elsewhere to keep it from "improper influence" and the "many means of corrupting the morals of youth," which existed in the town. Four years later the criticism had become more barbed. "If you wish to jeopardize every amiable trait in the private character of your son, send him to Lexington," the *Public Advertiser* contended, linking the college to radical politics. "If you wish him to become a Robespierre or a Murat, send him to Lexington to learn the rudiments of Jacobinism and disorganization." By 1829 a Louisville editor was warning parents that at the university their children would be "surrounded by political desperadoes" and that "the very atmosphere of the place has been calculated to pollute the morals and principles of the youth attending it." [60]

---

[58] *Louisville Public Advertiser*, November 27, 1820.

[59] *Louisville Public Advertiser*, August 23, 1820.

[60] *Kentucky Reporter*, February 14, 1816; *Louisville Public Advertiser*, September 9, 1820; October 13, 1829.

Lexington, though an old veteran of urban rivalries, had not anticipated this bitterness. "We thought of all our institutions, it was the pride and boast of the town; and the least calculated to excite the envy, and stir up the opposition of any individual or section of the country." But the assault threatened the city's very life, and it fought back. The defense was generally constructive, detailing the achievements of Transylvania and extolling its influence on students and the new country. Graduates wrote testimonials and local citizens publicized the healthfulness and "literary atmosphere" of the community, while officials dispelled rumors about the snobbery of the college.[61]

The case was good, but Lexington strategists bungled in several respects. In 1829 not a single Jacksonian was appointed to the Board of Trustees, and not enough was done to quiet the uneasiness of either the farmers or the highly religious.[62] As a result, when Transylvania needed support most, it was almost friendless. By 1830 the campaign instituted by Louisville had destroyed Kentucky's brightest ornament and pulled the most substantial prop from Lexington's economy.

Even before Transylvania's demise Lexington felt itself slipping economically, and it tried to steady itself by better connections with the trade of the Ohio River. Canals and roads proved either impractical or inadequate, and in 1829 civic leaders planned a railroad. The act of incorporation in the next year left the northern terminus undecided, with the understanding that it would be either Louisville or Cincinnati. The uncertainty set off a curious kind of competition between those two cities. Neither could foresee the impact that a railroad might have on its own importance, yet they equally feared that it would give their rival a substantial advantage.

Louisville was especially wary. This looked like the canal issue in another form, and many people thought it wise to wait for the results of the first project. Moreover, some of the same local interests

---

[61] *Kentucky Reporter*, March 7, 1827; March 10, 1823, February 21, 1827, September 8, 1828.

[62] For these problems see, for example, *Louisville Public Advertiser*, October 29, 1829.

seemed to be threatened. The hack and dray owners protested that their $125,000 business would be jeopardized. And since the railroad would pass through the city and continue on to Portland, others feared the growth of a "rival town" on the Western end of the Falls. The city council, walking gingerly because of this opposition, appointed a committee to look into the question, and called a public hearing to sound out local opinion. The meeting attracted over three hundred people, and after a lively debate, it voted to keep the tracks out of Louisville.[63]

Very quickly, however, civic leaders realized that any alternative terminus was more perilous to the Falls City than the possible dislocations occasioned by accepting the railroad. Thus "S" wrote that if "we are to have a rival town, the nearer to us the less dangerous," and a "Gentleman in Lexington" warned that its "great rival, Cincinnati" was "straining every nerve" to induce the company to build in that direction. By December 1830 the tide had turned, and the council invited the Lexington and Ohio Railroad to come to Louisville.[64]

Cincinnati, despite its official policy, had many qualms about a railroad from Lexington. "Why should the citizens of Cincinnati be so anxious to create a rival town across the river?" asked the editor of the *Advertiser*. Yet the same logic which drove Louisville to change its mind sustained the Queen City's original decision. On December 7, 1830, a public meeting declared that the project "would conduce to the prosperity of this city, in an eminent degree," and a committee of prominent civic leaders invited the company's directors to come to Cincinnati to discuss details.[65] These events, coupled with Louisville's acceptance, brought great rejoicing to Lexington, for it now looked as though the railroad would bring it a share of the Ohio's commerce and arrest at last the economic

[63] *Louisville Public Advertiser*, December 8, 1830; November 2, 1830; Louisville, City Journal, October 20, 1830; October 29, 1830; *Louisville Public Advertiser*, November 4, 1830.

[64] *Louisville Public Advertiser*, November 3, 1830; November 5, 1830; Louisville, City Journal, December 3, 1830.

[65] *Cincinnati Advertiser*, December 11, 1830; *Liberty Hall* (Cincinnati), December 10, 1830.

decay which had brought the "Athens of the West" to the very brink of disaster.

The struggle for primacy and power — and occasionally survival — was one of the most persistent and striking characteristics of the early urban history of the West. Like imperial states, cities carved out extensive dependencies, extended their influence over the economic and political life of the hinterland, and fought with contending places over strategic trade routes. Nor was the contest limited to the young giants, for smaller towns joined the scramble. Cleveland and Sandusky, for example, clashed over the location of the northern terminus of the Ohio canal, the stakes being nothing less than the burgeoning commerce between the river and the lakes. And their instinct to fight was sound, for the outcome shaped the future of both.

Like most imperialisms, the struggle among Western cities left a record of damage and achievement. It trampled new villages, smothered promising towns, and even brought down established metropolises. Conflicting ambitions infused increasing bitterness into the intercourse of rivals, and made suspicion, jealousy, and vindictiveness a normal part of urban relationships. Yet competition also brought rapid expansion. The fear of failure was a dynamic force, pushing civic leaders into improvements long before they thought them necessary. The constant search for new markets furnished an invaluable stimulus to commercial and industrial enterprise. And, at its best, urban imperialism bred a strong pride in community accomplishment. As one resident put it, "there exists in our city a spirit . . . which may render any man proud of being called a Cincinnatian." [66]

The struggle for supremacy among the young cities dramatized the growth of urbanism in the West. By 1830 the towns had created a society whose ways and habits contrasted sharply with those of the countryside. Not only was its physical environment distinct,

[66] *Liberty Hall* (Cincinnati), January 9, 1829.

but its interests, activities, and pace of life differed greatly. In 1811 a farmer near Lexington expressed the conflict as contemporaries saw it in a dialogue between "Rusticus" and "Urbanus." The latter referred to the "rude, gross appearance" of his neighbor, adding, "how strong you smell of your ploughed ground and corn fields. How dismal, how gloomy your green woods. What a miserable clash your whistling woodland birds are continually making." "Rusticus" replied with the rural image of the town dweller. "What a fine smooth complexion you have Urbanus: you look like a weed that has grown up in the shade. Can you walk your streets without inhaling the noxious fumes with which your town is pregnant? . . . Can you engage in calm contemplation, when hammers are ringing in every direction — when there is as great a *rattling* as in a storm when the hail descends on our housetops?" [67]

This rural-urban division was increasingly reflected in political life. Though the rhetoric of the period often obscured them, differences existed from the very beginning. Suspicion of the towns led states to avoid economic and cultural centers when locating their capitals. Nearly all these cities sought the prize, but none proved successful. The *Missouri Gazette* candidly stated the issue in 1820. "It has been said that St. Louis is obnoxious to our legislature — that its growth and influence . . . are looked on with a jealous eye, and its pretentions ought to be discouraged." [68] The same clash occurred elsewhere. Kentucky leaders virtually invented Frankfort to keep the capital away from Louisville or Lexington. In the same manner, Ohio created Columbus rather than choose Cincinnati, Steubenville, or Zanesville, all of which eagerly wished it and by size and influence had substantial claims.[69]

As the West developed, the conflict became more apparent, though it was still expressed cautiously. Political leaders hesitated to attack

---

[67] *Kentucky Reporter*, July 2, 1811.

[68] *Missouri Gazette*, December 6, 1820.

[69] The most common argument against choosing major cities as capitals was that they were not situated in the middle of the state. This contention was largely a mask for jealousy. It is interesting to note in this regard that Lexington is located more centrally in Kentucky than Frankfort.

rural areas, but they increasingly spoke of an urban interest in a manner intended to emphasize the difference between town and farms. For example, a Cincinnatian, writing in a local campaign, asserted that "the voters of the city should have a special regard for the necessities of the city itself." Making the same point, a Queen City editor declared, "we acknowledge that the interests of the township and city are identified; yet, we must be permitted to say, that in Cincinnati we have separate interests." [70] "Nothing are dearer to us than the interests of the city," a handbill announced in 1827, as it urged "Pittsburgh and Pittsburgh's friends" to back John Brown, who had always "supported Pittsburgh in the Legislature." [71]

State and national elections tended to bring this issue to the surface because often rural and urban candidates faced each other in a test of strength. When this happened, municipal newspapers quickly took sides. "The person elected," the *Public Advertiser* observed in 1820, "should not only be capable but warmly attached to the interests of the western country, and particularly to the town of Louisville." "The growing influence of the city of Pittsburgh," the *Gazette* declared in support of a fellow townsman, "requires that we should be ably represented at Harrisburg." Sometimes the campaign got so bitter on this issue that the losing side hated to face the consequences of defeat. "The election has terminated," a Falls City editor once noted fearfully, "and . . . we are to be represented by a gentleman who resides in an adjoining county, to whom we shall be compelled to confide our most important interests. This is what we term serving the town of Louisville & the county of Jefferson, 'with a vengeance.' " [72]

The countryside also recognized the separate interests of the

[70] *Cincinnati Daily Gazette,* October 12, 1829; *Cincinnati Advertiser,* September 16, 1829.

[71] The handbill was for the election of 1827 and was signed by "A Citizen of Pittsburgh," Denny-O'Hara Papers (see above, p. 45, n. 16).

[72] *Louisville Public Advertiser,* August 2, 1820; *Pittsburgh Gazette,* July 29, 1817; *Louisville Public Advertiser,* August 23, 1820; for an extended treatment of the split between Pittsburgh and its neighbors, see J. A. Kehl, *Ill Feelings in the Era of Good Feelings, Western Pennsylvania Political Battles, 1815–25* (Pittsburgh, 1956), 39–47.

cities and tried to reduce their importance in state affairs. The most common technique was to gerrymander the assembly districts to the detriment of urban centers. Legislation for this purpose was almost continuous and usually not very well disguised. About one re-apportionment bill in Kentucky in 1828 the *Louisville Public Advertiser* could truthfully comment that its sole object was "to curtail the weight and influence of both town [Louisville] and county [Jefferson] in the councils of the state." [73] By 1830 the traditional imbalance had grown up in western commonwealths, with agrarian elements being more fully represented than urban ones. Despite these obstacles, however, the political power of the cities increased rapidly.

Of course, farm dwellers easily outnumbered urbanites, but the latter wielded disproportionate power. The case of Jefferson and Oldham counties in Kentucky was illustrative. In the mid-twenties the combined vote reached 3,200, Louisville residents casting roughly a quarter of the number. Yet the state senator and both representatives came from the city. In 1829 when a third assemblyman was added, the rural interests pleaded with Louisville leaders to name someone from the surrounding area. "It may seem strange," wrote one observer, "that it would be necessary thus to ask for the liberality of 800 voters, in favor of 2,400. . . . Nevertheless, the concentrated energies of 800 do entirely outweigh the scattered influence of the 2,400 — that all past experience teaches." [74] The situation was the same elsewhere. At one time all of Missouri's representatives in Washington — two senators and one congressman — and its governor came from St. Louis.

The cities' political influence rested on their ability to produce leadership. As economic and intellectual centers, they attracted the talented and ambitious in all fields. Politics was no exception. Nearly all the great spokesmen of the West had important urban connections, and their activity often reflected the demands of their town constitutents. Henry Clay was one of Lexington's most prominent lawyers when he went to the United States Senate in 1806.

[73] *Louisville Public Advertiser*, January 16, 1828.
[74] *Louisville Public Advertiser*, July 28, 1829.

Thomas Hart Benton held local offices in St. Louis before moving on to the national scene, and William Henry Harrison had strong ties with Cincinnati through most of his long public life.

In each instance, their stake in the cities was economic as well as political. Clay and Benton built flourishing law practices and participated in mercantile and manufacturing ventures in their adopted towns. Harrison's associates included many of Cincinnati's leading businessmen, and he held stock in many local concerns, notably the Miami Exporting Company, the Bank of Cincinnati, the Miami Sheep Company, and William Green & Company's foundry.[75] In addition, all owned real estate. Of course, not all their investments proved profitable (Harrison's were particularly unsuccessful), but they represented a deep commitment to the welfare and future of the communities.

Moreover, all these men were alive to the interests of their city. Benton's attack on government factories in the Indian territory culminated a long and intense campaign by St. Louis merchants to break federal trade control on the Missouri. Clay's enthusiasm for an ample tariff on hemp derived as much from the pressure of Lexington's manufacturers as from that of the growers on the Blue Grass. And when the West's Athens tried to adjust to the trade revolution on the Ohio occasioned by the steamboat, Clay went to Frankfort as a spokesman for the town to urge turnpikes to both Louisville and Cincinnati. In fact, Clay was so closely tied to Lexington that he never became very popular in Louisville, whose interests so often collided with those of its Kentucky neighbor. Similarly, Harrison's legislative services to the Queen City were many, among which the most prominent were his role in the establishment of the common schools and the Commercial Hospital. Nor were these cases isolated; the entire careers of these men revealed the importance of their urban connections.

In some ways it is ironic that Harrison, Clay, and Benton have been viewed as simply Western leaders, or, occasionally, as frontier heroes. For each had deep urban roots, each had a substantial economic stake in a young city, and each found important political

[75] *Liberty Hall* (Cincinnati), October 8, 1819.

allies in the expanding business class of his community. Even if, as in the case of Clay and Harrison, they lived outside of the formal boundaries of the town, they, like commuters of a later time, found the urban milieu essential, and carried on much of their private affairs and public careers in the city. That is not to say that they were hostile to the claims of the countryside, or that they were unable to speak for a broader constituency. Rather it is to assert that some of their closest ties were to the towns, that they understood best the problems of their own locales, and, indeed, thought of themselves as caretakers of home interests as well as spokesmen of the West. Perhaps nothing illustrates better the rising influence of the cities in the new country than the fact that they provided the area with its most powerful leadership.

By 1830, then, the West had produced two types of society — one rural and one urban. Each developed its own institutions, habits, and living patterns. The countryside claimed much the larger population and often gave to transmontane affairs an agrarian flavor. But broadcloth was catching up with buckskin. The census of 1830 revealed the disproportionate rate of city growth. While the state of Ohio had four times as many inhabitants as it counted in 1810, Cincinnati's increase was twelvefold. The story was the same elsewhere. Louisville's figure showed a growth of 650 per cent compared with Kentucky's 50; and Pittsburgh tripled in size while Pennsylvania did not quite double its population. By 1830 the rise of these cities had driven a broad wedge of urbanism into Western life.

Though town and country developed along different paths, clashes were still infrequent. The West was large enough to contain both movements comfortably. Indeed, each supported the other. The rural regions supplied the cities with raw materials for their mills and packinghouses, and offered an expanding market for their shops and factories. In turn, urban centers serviced the surrounding areas by providing both the necessities and comforts of life as well as new opportunity for ambitious farm youths. Yet the cities represented the more aggressive and dynamic force. By spreading their economic power over the entire section, by bringing the fruits of civilization across the mountains, and by insinuating their ways into the countryside, they speeded up the transformation of the West from a gloomy wilderness to a richly diversified region. Any historical view which omits this dimension of Western life tells but part of the story.

Bibliographical Note

The sources for this book are scattered throughout the Ohio Valley. More than two years were spent in city halls, court houses, libraries, and historical societies working through municipal records, newspaper files, and manuscript collections. The original bibliography of this volume ran to more than fifty pages, and then it included only the more useful items. It is available for use or loan in the Widener Archives at Harvard University. For the general reader it is hoped that the notes for each chapter will be an adequate guide to the sources.

. . . .

The official records of cities are to be found in city halls, court houses, and, occasionally, historical societies or public libraries. Most towns still have somewhere the manuscript books of their city councils, which include the minutes of the meetings as well as municipal ordinances. In some instances there are also additional papers comprising committee reports, grand jury presentments, and tax lists. Court houses have preserved real estate records covering transfer and sale of land and property and, often, drawings and plats of buildings. Material concerning the steady and tangled relationships between municipal and state governments can often be found in state capitols. Nineteenth century urban historians correctly made these public documents the basis for their work, but more recent authors have overlooked them. As the chapter notes indicate, I have returned to the earlier and, I think, sounder practice.

Another invaluable record of a city's life is to be found in its newspapers. Among the first signs of settled and civilized life, they provide the historian with a continuous account of urban affairs. Each city had at least one weekly before 1810, and within another decade semi-weeklies and dailies began to appear. In the 1820's, for example, Cincinnati supported seven weeklies, two dailies, a literary monthly, a medical journal, and even a magazine for teen-agers. As the newspapers multiplied and expanded, they included more and more town news, printed official notices, published letters from citizens, and carried extensive local advertising. Fortunately, most of these papers are still in good condition and are available either in the original or on film. In this study I have worked through the files of thirty-three different journals published in the major Western cities and neighboring small towns.

Monthly periodicals and quarterlies also furnish important information on the cultural and intellectual activities of a community. There were a few of these in transmontane metropolises before 1830. More useful are city directories. Issued sporadically in every town, they contain lists of adult residents, their addresses, and sometimes their occupations and place of origin. Moreover, the editor usually included a brief history of the city by way of introduction, and appended lists of public officials, board members of banks and important corporations, ministers of churches, and officers of fraternal organizations. In the larger places the frequent appearance of these directories provides detailed and generally accurate information that is not available elsewhere.

Travelers' observations constitute another important source for the early history of transmontane cities. Urban centers were the primary beneficiaries of the immense interest in the new country that characterized the first portion of the nineteenth century. Europeans and Americans from the East coast flocked across the mountains to visit, trade, or simply tour. Many later published accounts of their trips, including reflections on what they saw and heard. Over one hundred of these have been of help to this volume. They must be used with caution, however. While a town was still small, a traveler could see most of it himself in a short stay, and his information was therefore especially valuable. But by 1815 Western metropolises had grown large enough to force visitors to rely more and more on others in making their appraisals. Hence what an author said about a place may be what he learned from a few residents, or what he read concerning the city before or after his visit. Fortunately, as travelers became less reliable, other material became more abundant, thus lessening the historian's dependence upon outside sources.

Manuscript sources are almost inexhaustible. City life has so many dimensions that almost every contemporary document has some relevance. A single letter between friends often contains valuable comments on social conditions; a company's account book sometimes reveals economic pressures not so intimately conveyed in larger statistics; the diary of an ordinary citizen can illuminate otherwise hidden aspects of a community's growth. Each of these Western cities has at least one local historical society and public library where this material is gathered. In addition, many individuals have private collections which they are happy to make available for historical investigation.

Secondary works on early Western urban life are, paradoxically, both abundant and scarce. They are scarce in the sense that few comparative studies have yet appeared; abundant in that each town has its own history written many times. The latter efforts have been largely by amateur historians who have brought both affection and insight to the study of their own communities. While these accounts are valuable, they are usually unsystematic and often "dated" by the circumstances of their publication. Professional historians, on the other hand, have generally concentrated on a particular aspect of a single city's development. Their studies, such as John Francis McDermott's articles on early St. Louis libraries or Thomas Senior Berry's work on the Cincinnati market, often achieve special distinction.

Happily, then, throughout this volume I have been able to build on the competence and energy of many who have labored before me.

Index

limitations on taxing power, 76;
finances, 77, 274, 275, 276; wealth
of governing council, 78; public
markets, 80, 280; street maintenance, 83, 84–85, 90, 290; traffic
regulations, 86; police protection,
88, 287, 288; fire protection, 91,
92, 93, 94, 293; water supply, 95,
294; sewage disposal, 98; living
standards, 105, 109, 110, 111; social
stratification, 107–108; doctors in,
116; relieves the poor, 120; Negroes
in, 124–125, 220, 221; tightens
slavery laws, 127; issues city directory, 129, 310; religion, 133, 265;
education, 136, 139; libraries, 139,
141, 142, 254; book stores, 140;
drama, 143–144, 145, 257; music,
147, 259; benefits from War of
1812, 161; suffers depression, 163,
169–170, 177, 182–187; land speculation, 164; has branch of Second
Bank, 166; population, 170, 200;
professional classes in, 210–211;
housing, 215; influence throughout
West, 232–243; periodicals, 253;
health protection, 300; suburbs,
305, 306–307; imitates the East,
314; rivalry with other cities, 322,
330–336
Lexington Reporter, 252
Liberty Hall (Cincinnati), 57, 58, 97,
145, 165, 225, 244–245, 257, 266,
315, 328, 331; established, 130;
blames depression on speculation,
167; urges less dependence upon
the East, 319
Libraries, 6, 139–142, 254–256
Licking River, Kentucky, 22, 23
*Life and Travels of John Robert
Shaw*, 153–155
Liguest, Pierre Laclede. *See* Laclede
Limestone, Kentucky, 49

Lisa, Manuel, 61
Little Miami River (Cincinnati), 22
Liverpool, Cincinnati's trade with, 56
Living Standards: of merchants, 110–
111, 206–210; of wage earners, 116–
120, 214; of Negroes, 124–128, 222;
of professional classes, 210–212
Longworth, Nicholas, 109, 123, 226
Losantiville (Cincinnati), 23
Louisiana, 235; development, 2–6
Louisiana Purchase, 4, 5
Louisville, 2, 19, 22, 42, 72, 73, 75, 82,
90, 101, 148, 152, 173, 183, 184, 185,
187, 190, 251, 318, 320, 337, 340;
founding to *1800*, 13–18; population, 17–18, 64–65, 198, 341; misuse
of waterfront, 29; barge traffic, 41;
commerce and industry *1800–1815*,
64–66; taxing power, 76, 271–272;
finances, 77, 274–275, 276; subject
to mercantile influence, 79, 104;
traffic regulation, 86; police protection, 88, 287, 288; street maintenance, 90, 282, 290; fire prevention,
92, 292, 293; water supply, 95, 294;
drains standing water, 96–97; social
stratification, 108; living standards,
110; doctors in, 118; Negroes in,
124–125, 221; effects of slavery on,
126, 127, 213, 220, 222–223; religion,
133, 263–264, 265; education, 139,
244, 249, 317–318; libraries, 142,
254, 256; benefits from War of *1812*,
161; land speculation, 164; has
branch of Second Bank, 166; avoids
major depression, 172, 188–189; benefits from steamboat traffic, 191;
growth to *1830*, 197–200; organizes
a business club, 205; social life, 207;
doctors in, 210; housing, 215; disturbed by transient workers, 218,
220; attacks Transylvania University, 242; drama, 257, 258, 259; fine

Harvard Historical Monographs

*Out of print